Milton and the Parables of Jesus

Medieval & Renaissance Literary Studies

Originally titled the *Duquesne Studies: Philological Series* (and later renamed the *Language & Literature Series*), the *Medieval & Renaissance Literary Studies Series* has been published by Duquesne University Press since 1960. This publishing endeavor seeks to promote the study of late medieval, Renaissance, and seventeenth century English literature by presenting scholarly and critical monographs, collections of essays, editions, and compilations. The series encourages a broad range of interpretation, including the relationship of literature and its cultural contexts, close textual analysis, and the use of contemporary critical methodologies.

Foster Provost	Albert C. Labriola	Richard J. DuRocher
EDITOR, 1960–1984	EDITOR, 1985–2009	EDITOR, 2010

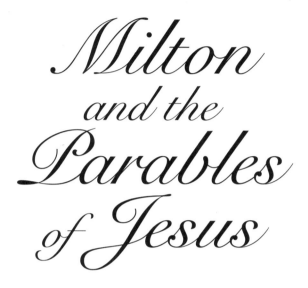

Milton
and the
Parables
of Jesus

Self-Representation and the
Bible in John Milton's Writings

DAVID V. URBAN

The Pennsylvania State University Press
University Park, Pennsylvania

Library of Congress Cataloging-in-Publication Data

Names: Urban, David V., author.
Title: Milton and the parables of Jesus : self-representation and the Bible
in John Milton's writings / David V. Urban.
Other titles: Medieval and Renaissance literary studies.
Description: University Park, Pennsylvania : The Pennsylvania State
University Press, [2018] | Series: Medieval & Renaissance literacy
studies | Includes bibliographical references and index.
Summary: "Examines Milton's identification with characters in Jesus's
parables. Connects Milton's engagement with the parables to his
self-representation throughout his poetry and prose"—Provided
by publisher.
Identifiers: LCCN 2018042985 | ISBN 9780271080994 (cloth : alk. paper)
Subjects: LCSH: Milton, John, 1608–1674—Criticism and interpretation.
| Milton, John, 1608–1674—Religion. | Jesus Christ—Parables—
In literature. | Bible—In literature. | English literature—Early modern,
1500–1700—History and criticism.
Classification: LCC PR3592.B5 U73 2018 | DDC 821/.4—dc23
LC record available at https://lccn.loc.gov/2018042985

The Pennsylvania State University Press is a member
of the Association of University Presses.

It is the policy of The Pennsylvania State University Press to use
acid-free paper. Publications on uncoated stock satisfy the minimum
requirements of American National Standard for Information Sciences—
Permanence of Paper for Printed Library Material, ANSI z39.48–1992.

To Adrienne, Daniel, and Gabriel
Et Ad Patrem

CONTENTS

ACKNOWLEDGMENTS

Unless otherwise noted, citations of John Milton's poetic works are from *John Milton: Complete Poems and Major Prose*, edited by Merritt Y. Hughes (New York: Macmillan, 1957), cited parenthetically in the text by line number (in the case of the longer poetic works, by book and line number). Citations of Milton's prose are from the *Complete Prose Works of John Milton*, edited by Don M. Wolfe et al., 8 vols. (New Haven: Yale University Press, 1953–82), cited parenthetically in the text as *CPW* by volume and page number. To avoid confusion, particularly among nonspecialists, I have in a small number of cases lightly modernized Milton's prose, including by adding an apostrophe plus *s* several times, and changing "then" to "than" in keeping with its contemporary meaning. While I fully acknowledge the outstanding work of John K. Hale and J. Donald Cullington in their 2012 translation of *De Doctrina Christiana* (volumes 7 and 8 of *The Complete Works of John Milton* [Oxford: Oxford University Press, 2012]), I have, for citations of *DDC*, retained the use of volume 6 of *CPW*, translated by John Carey. My most significant use of *DDC* comes in chapter 8, and less so in chapter 10, both of which were published, in earlier versions, before 2012. Having compared, in the specific passages I cite, Carey's translation with Hale and Cullington's translation and their accompanying Latin text, I concluded that there were too few substantive differences to merit substituting their translation for Carey's. Unless otherwise noted, all biblical citations are from the Authorized King James Version.

Various portions of this book have been published previously. Chapter 1 is a revised and expanded version of an essay that appeared in *Milton Studies* 43 (2004): 1–18. A portion of this earlier essay was excerpted and revised, along with a new paragraph, to appear as a chapter in *Milton in France*, edited by Christophe Tournu (New York: Peter Lang, 2008). This paragraph has also been incorporated into chapter 1 of the present volume.

Chapter 4 is a revised version of an essay that appeared in *Milton Studies* 47 (2008): 1–23. Chapter 8 is a revised version of a chapter in *Milton's Legacy*, edited by Kristin A. Pruitt and Charles W. Durham (Selinsgrove, Pa: Susquehanna University Press, 2005), 208–19. Chapter 10 is a revised version of a chapter in *Uncircumscribed Mind: Reading Milton Deeply*, edited by Charles W. Durham and Kristin A. Pruitt (Selinsgrove, Pa: Susquehanna University Press, 2008), 292–306. That chapter expanded a portion of an essay that originally appeared in *Leviathan: A Journal of Melville Studies* 4, nos. 1–2 (2002) and was reprinted in *Melville and Milton: An Edition and Analysis of Melville's Annotations of Milton*, edited by Robin Grey (Pittsburgh: Duquesne University Press, 2004).

My thanks go out to the many people who helped this book come into being during its long and circuitous journey to publication. I am deeply grateful to the many individuals, some of them named below, others unnamed, who encouraged and/or challenged my efforts in Milton scholarship and this book in particular.

In the decades before this project was conceived, my late mother, Yvonne Urban, sparked in me a youthful love for literature that found a special place to bloom in Albert R. Cirillo's undergraduate course on Milton at Northwestern University. The idea to pursue the study of Milton and the parables of Jesus was suggested to me by Michael Lieb—my earliest scholarly influence in Milton and an enduring presence throughout this book—who graciously and skillfully directed my early work on this project. Special thanks go to Professor Lieb and to Stanley Fish, Robin Grey, Donald Marshall, and Leland Ryken for their support, insight, and challenges in the early stages of this book's development.

In the years that followed, various portions of what became this book were developed into several published essays, as noted above. In addition to the individuals named above (with special thanks to the very demanding Robin Grey), others came forward to offer their insights by reading and commenting on earlier versions of those essays, among them John Bryant, Angelica Duran, Charles Durham, Susan Felch, William B. Hunter, Edward Jones, Paul Klemp, Albert C. Labriola, Jameela Lares, Kristin Pruitt, John T. Shawcross, Christophe Tournu, James Vanden Bosch, Hugh Wilson, and various anonymous peer reviewers, along with the numerous individuals who attended my 2008 Newberry Library Milton Seminar and offered insights on the essay that became chapter 2 of this book.

As my scholarly attention turned to other projects, including Milton bibliography and various articles, Miltonic and otherwise, and as family health issues became overwhelming, several individuals encouraged me to soldier on with what became *Milton and the Parables of Jesus*. They include Brian Ingraffia, whose insights proved invaluable in developing this book's introduction; Edward Jones, whose exhortations during long runs at Milton conferences catalyzed my efforts, especially with respect to chapter 2; then director of Duquesne University Press, Susan Wadsworth-Booth, who continued to prod and encourage; and, most remarkably, the general editor of the Medieval and Renaissance Literary Studies series, Rebecca Totaro, who, as I was recovering from various family health challenges and my father's death and was badly lacking confidence, agreed to read my book manuscript chapter by chapter as I wrote and revised month after month. Her persistence, faithfulness, and affirmation enabled me to complete the book. Thanks also to the anonymous manuscript reviewers for Duquesne University Press, who offered valuable suggestions. In the wake of DUP's closure, the Medieval and Renaissance Literary Studies series was acquired by Penn State University Press, and I offer my heartfelt thanks to PSU Press editor-in-chief Kendra Boileau and her colleagues for adopting my project. Finally, I thank Suzanne Wolk for her editorial expertise in the closing stages of manuscript revision.

Special thanks go to Calvin College for granting me a Calvin Research Fellowship and also a sabbatical release—ostensibly for a different project—that enabled me to revise the completed manuscript. Thanks also to the Calvin Center for Christian Scholarship and its director, Susan Felch, for awarding me a small grant for subvention funds.

On a more personal level, my deepest thanks—and perpetual apologies—go to my beloved wife, Adrienne, and to our wonderful sons, Daniel and Gabriel, for their love and admonitions throughout this long journey. This book is my gift to them.

I would also like to thank the many scholars throughout the decades and centuries whose work I have engaged in the course of this book, including its endnotes. It is my sincere hope that those who read it will agree that I engaged their labors fairly.

Some of the scholars whose work has most deeply influenced my own passed from this earth before this book was completed. Two of them—Albert C. Labriola and John T. Shawcross—took a special interest in this project from its inception, and I will never be able to repay their generosity.

My greatest debt to the dead is to my father, William E. Urban, a longtime high school chemistry teacher who, early in his career, also taught *Paradise Lost* to students in his hometown in rural Wisconsin. He revealed his often silent dedication and support when he told me that he had, unprompted, read a very early version of the manuscript three times. I regret that I failed to complete this book before his death, in July 2014, but writing now on Father's Day 2018, I dedicate this book to him.

S. D. G.

Introduction

Milton's Hermeneutic of Parables, Milton's Parabolic Imagination

In "Listening to the Parables of Jesus," Paul Ricoeur writes, "To listen to the Parables of Jesus . . . is to let one's imagination be opened to the new possibilities disclosed by the extravagance of these short dramas. If we look at the Parables as at a word addressed first to our imagination rather than to our will, we shall not be tempted to reduce them to mere didactic devices, to moralizing allegories. We will let their poetic power display itself within us."[1] Although he preceded Ricoeur by three centuries, there is perhaps no writer who followed Ricoeur's admonitions more thoroughly than John Milton. For, as I seek to demonstrate in this book, certain of Jesus's parables—and the characters, or figures, presented in them—captured Milton's imagination, manifesting their poetic power throughout his writings, profoundly influencing his self-conception and self-presentation, inspiring and invigorating his art in verse and prose. As we shall see throughout this study, these parables excited Milton's imagination, and Milton in turn appropriated them in ways that made them his own.

On one level, Milton incorporated these parables in a manner firmly in line with the established mode of Reformed Puritan parable interpretation of his day and in ways that demonstrated the common early modern English Protestant practice of finding a biblical "place" for oneself in certain passages of scripture.[2] At the same time, Milton went beyond such standard practices, incorporating throughout his imaginative writings the larger ideals he found in these parables, all the while maintaining the parables' close relationship to his own conceptions of himself and his self-presentation. Indeed, I will go so far as to say that Milton's conceptions and representations of himself, both explicit and implicit, are largely manifestations of the connections he made between himself and certain parabolic figures. More-over, I suggest throughout this study that the larger ideals Milton found within these parabolic figures become prominent, even dominant, concepts in his early, middle, and late works and are often used to demonstrate the particular kind of thoughtful, godly heroism that emerges as a consistent theme throughout his writings. Ultimately, I hope to show that a study of Milton's relationship to Jesus's parables reveals a new and helpful way to understand both Milton himself and his overall creative achievement, offering a valuable perspective on Milton the man and not a few prominent Miltonic characters who, as many critics have noted, bear a distinct resemblance to their creator.[3]

This introduction situates this book within the larger framework of previous studies of Milton's use of the Bible and specific biblical genres, and it explains Milton's hermeneutic of parables in light of the history of parable interpretation. It recognizes that Milton's more explicit references to parables place him squarely in line with the Reformed and Puritan practice of using the figures of Jesus's parables to reflect larger classes of persons, an interpretive framework also practiced by present-day biblical scholars who take the restrained allegorical approach to parable interpretation, a movement begun in the late twentieth century. This introduction also addresses both how Milton's strong connections with certain characters in Jesus's parables reflect the seventeenth-century English practice of believers' finding biblical passages or "places" to which they related their own spiritual experiences, and how Milton's imaginative use and pervasive awareness of the parables in his longer works anticipate the recent view that the parables are transformational metaphorical narratives that encourage readers "to reshape their vision of reality"[4] and, in the words of Ricoeur, allow the parables' "poetic power [to] display itself within" them.

This book investigates the relationship between Milton's writings and the biblical parables, specifically those parables with which Milton demonstrates a strong degree of self-identification. I hope to situate this study within the larger arena of Milton studies that explore Milton's use of the Bible as an imaginative and structural framework for his own writings. In this respect, I seek to extend the exploration of such themes initiated by James Sims's *The Bible in Milton's Epics* (1962), continued in Kitty Cohen's *The Throne and the Chariot: Studies in Milton's Hebraism* (1975), Sims and Leland Ryken's edited collection of essays *Milton and Scriptural Tradition* (1984), and Mary Ann Radzinowicz's "How Milton Read the Bible" (1989), and seen more recently in Regina Schwartz's "Milton on the Bible" (2001) and Phillip J. Donnelly's *Milton's Scriptural Reasoning* (2009). In investigating Milton's use of a particular genre or portion of biblical literature, I hope to complement such previous studies as Leland Ryken's *The Apocalyptic Vision in "Paradise Lost"* (1970), Timothy O'Keefe's *Milton and the Pauline Tradition* (1982), Youngwon Park's *Milton and Isaiah* (2000), and, more notably, Mary Ann Radzinowicz's *Milton's Epics and the Book of Psalms* (1989).[5] Radzinowicz examines Milton's use of the biblical genre of the Psalms and demonstrates his tendency to portray the Psalms through their New Testament representations; she also reveals Milton's practice, while he incorporates the Psalms into his epics, of using a poetic parallelism that reflects the parallelism of the Psalms themselves.

This study investigates the hermeneutical, stylistic, and imaginative issues that concern Milton in his use of biblical parables, a genre that has received tremendous attention in biblical studies throughout the twentieth and twenty-first centuries but has not been addressed sufficiently by Miltonists. In this sense, I seek to extend Barbara Kiefer Lewalski's discussion in her *"Paradise Lost" and the Rhetoric of Literary Forms*, in which she emphasizes that Milton uses various literary genres "to accomplish his poetic purposes."[6] Significantly, Lewalski's seminal study includes no discussion of parabolic literature, an omission, I believe, that speaks to the appropriateness of the present investigation. More directly, I seek to build on the outstanding efforts of Dayton Haskin, whose *Milton's Burden of Interpretation* provides the most extensive investigation into Milton's identification with the unprofitable servant of the parable of the talents (Matt. 25:14–30). I seek to move beyond Haskin by analyzing in depth how Milton's identification with the unprofitable servant, evident in various works, is mitigated by his identification with the last-called laborers of the parable of the laborers (Matt. 20:1–16); moreover, I also address at length Milton's identification with the ideal of the wise virgin in the parable of the wise and foolish virgins (Matt. 25:1–13) and with the householder of the parable of the householder (Matt. 13:52).

Defining "Parable"

As we enter our discussion of John Milton's use of the biblical parables in his poetry and prose, we would do well to define as closely as possible the term "parable" (Greek *parabolē*) as it is found in the Christian scriptures and, from this definition, seek to place Milton within the history of parable interpretation. Klyne Snodgrass notes that "the Greek word *parabolē* has a much broader meaning in the Gospels than the English word 'parable,'" an assertion also made by Madeleine Boucher.[7] John Sider points out that the common ancient Greek word for "analogy" was *parabolē* (as opposed to *analogia*, the word used for "resemblance"), and that the authors of the synoptic Gospels employ the same terminology.[8] Sider notes that "the function of analogy" is "the most significant common denominator in all the *parabolai*," encompassing types as various as proverb, question, taunt, simile, metaphor, riddle, and others. Snodgrass writes that the semantic range of *parabolē* is derived from the Hebrew word *mashal*, which is generally translated as *parabolē* in the Septuagint, the Jewish Greek translation of the Hebrew scriptures.[9] Sider also affirms that "*parabolē* as a label for particular sayings is reserved in the Gospels exclusively for instances of those various forms that embody analogy." Sider's broad concept of parable as analogy also encompasses the idea of allegory, recognizing that "the *essence* of allegory is elaborated analogy."[10] We should note that Sider's approach differs from what has been the modern "scholarly consensus," which rejects any sort of allegorical interpretation in favor of an approach that contends that each parable is only making a single main point. While this "single main point" approach to parable interpretation has come under critical scrutiny in recent decades, it has accumulated a host of notable adherents.[11] One of the most prominent champions of this earlier consensus, C. H. Dodd, offered the following definition of "parable" in 1935: "At its simplest a parable is a metaphor or simile drawn from nature or common life, arresting the hearer by its vividness or strangeness, and leaving the mind in sufficient doubt about its precise application to tease it into active thought."[12] We should note that Dodd's representative definition hardly resembles the multifaceted manner in which Milton and his contemporaries made use of the parables, including their emphases on personal application. Literary scholars seeking insight into Milton's use of the parables would be better served by the parable theory articulated by scholars such as Sider, Craig Blomberg, Madeleine Boucher, and Leland Ryken. In contrast to those who, like Adolf Jülicher and his followers, insist on a sharp distinction between parable and allegory, these scholars advocate a broader understanding of allegory that recognizes the "exemplary characters" in parables as "examples of a particular category of people."[13] Such a recognition is distinct from the fantastical "allegorizing" that was popular among many commentators until well into the nineteenth century. Furthermore, such a methodology more closely resembles Milton's own use of the parables, and helps to explain his tendency to apply particular parables to certain persons in a variety of different ways—a practice, as we shall see, that was common to many of Milton's contemporaries, especially in their tendency to identify with (or to encourage their audience to identify with) certain characters in the parables.

A Brief History of Parable Interpretation, and Milton's Place in It

A brief examination of the overall history of parable interpretation will aid our investigation of Milton's parabolic hermeneutic and his place in the history of parable interpretation. This examination will also demonstrate why neither the elaborate allegorization commonly practiced from the early church through most of the nineteenth century, nor the total rejection of allegory that pervaded most twentieth-century parable theory, coincides with Milton's own incorporation of the biblical parables in his poetry and prose. Rather, the practice of understanding parable figures as "exemplary characters" is in fact the mode of parable interpretation practiced by Milton and many of his contemporaries; it is thus is a truly helpful interpretive framework through which we may discuss Milton's use of biblical parables. Because the history of parable interpretation is a vast, multifaceted, and much-covered enterprise, the following discussion emphasizes the interpretive movements that are most germane to our understanding of Milton's own use of the parables.[14]

Allegorical Approaches

Throughout most of church history, and most certainly before the Reformation, the dominant mode of interpreting the parables was allegorical. This mode was championed in varying degrees by different church fathers, and their attempts to demonstrate that each detail of a particular parable signifies a larger category often reached dimensions later judged ludicrous by certain Reformation exegetes and by the vast majority of post-nineteenth-century scholarship. Such exegesis is demonstrated by Clement of Alexandria (ca. 150–215) in his exposition of the parable of the prodigal son. Clement's extensive allegorization of this parable can be seen below:

1. The lavish robe the father puts on the prodigal son = the robe of immortality.
2. The ring the father puts on the son's finger = the divine seal that demonstrates consecration and glory.
3. The shoes = imperishable shoes that clothe feet washed by Jesus for the journey to heaven. These heavenly shoes replace the earthly shoes that represent the sin that weighs down the sinful soul.
4. The fatted calf the father kills for his son's feast = Jesus, the Lamb of God (cf. John 1.29).[15]

Another example of such overdone allegorical exegesis is Augustine's interpretation of the parable of the Good Samaritan in *Quaestionum Evangeliorum* 2.19. There, Augustine (354–430) contends the following:

1. The wounded man = Adam.
2. Jerusalem = the heavenly city from which Adam has fallen.
3. Jericho = the moon, representing human mortality.
4. The thieves = the devil and his angels, who rob Adam of his immortality.
5. The priest and Levite = the Old Testament law, which was powerless to save anyone.
6. The Samaritan and his binding of the man's wounds = Christ, who forgives sins.
7. The inn = the church.
8. The innkeeper = the Apostle Paul.
9. The two denarii = the two commandments of love/the promise of this life and the promise of the life to come.[16]

Throughout church history there were various calls to modify or do away with the allegorical approach to parable interpretation. Thomas Aquinas (1225–1274) was the most prominent pre-Reformation proponent of such change. Although Aquinas never advocated elimination of the allegorical approach, he did champion a greater focus on literal interpretation of the scriptures to balance out the metaphorical emphasis of his time. According to Aquinas, "nothing necessary to faith is contained under the spiritual sense which is not elsewhere put forward by the Scripture in its literal sense" (*Summa Theologica* 1.1.10 ad. 1). During the Reformation, Martin Luther (1483–1546) excoriated allegorizing interpreters, calling them "spiritual jugglers," linking them with perceived heresies in the Roman Catholic Church, and calling for the scriptures to be interpreted according to their "plain sense" or "literal sense." John Calvin (1509–1564), whose analysis of Jesus's parables is discussed throughout this study, also castigated allegorical interpreters, calling them unchristian "meddlers" whose allegorizations were "too futile to deserve an answer."[17] Despite such efforts, however, allegorizing interpretation was common in varying degrees until the end of the nineteenth century, a phenomenon seen throughout Archbishop Richard Chenevix Trench's (1807–1886) *Notes on the Parables of Our Lord*, the most prominent nineteenth-century British work on the subject.[18] Ironically, Trench's book warns against allegorical excesses even as it indulges in them regularly.

Despite allegorical interpretation's remarkable endurance, two main problems with this approach were being recognized. One was the wide range of ideas concerning what particular details represented. A second problem involved the anachronistic interpretations that were often set forth, interpretations that would have been impossible in light of a parable's original audience. An obvious example is Augustine's aforementioned equating of the innkeeper with the Apostle Paul.

Challenges to Allegory: Parables as Extended Similes with Single Main Lessons

The scholar whose writings proved devastating to allegorical interpretation of the parables was the German liberal Adolf Jülicher (1857–1938). Jülicher's seminal two-volume study *Die Gleichnisreden Jesu* (1888–89) contended that each parable was a concise representation of first-century Palestine and was markedly different from the sort of artificial constructs that characterized allegories.[19] Unlike allegories, which could be made sense of only through elaborate decoding, the parables had simple, one-point messages. Jülicher's contrast between parable and allegory was based on the Aristotelian distinction between metaphor and simile. While both metaphors and similes compare two things, similes are more self-explanatory because they use words such as *like* or *as* to make the comparison explicit. Jülicher wrote that the parables were simply extended similes (something clearly demonstrated in the words "the kingdom of God is like . . .") and thus distinct from allegory. Rather, they brought forth a clear single lesson for Jesus's audience. Jülicher, like many subsequent scholars, emphasized the need to understand Jesus's parables in their original form, unembellished by Jesus's followers, within the context of Jesus's historical *Sitz im Leben*. In doing so, Jülicher asserted that any allegorical explanation in the biblical text (such as what Matthew 13 records of Jesus's explaining the meaning of the parable of the sower) was not part of the authentic teaching of Jesus but the later addition of the early church.

Jülicher's claim regarding the historical inauthenticity of Jesus's allegorical explanations of certain parables was given credence by Jülicher's contemporary William Wrede (1859–1906).[20] Wrede argued that the early church imposed the idea of the "messianic secret" upon Jesus's original teachings. According to Wrede, Jesus never actually claimed to be more than a man, but his followers, who came to believe after his death that he was the messiah and the Son of God, presented a Jesus who revealed more important secret teachings to his disciples, teachings he withheld from the masses in his public instruction. These private teachings included allegorical interpretations of his parables, as seen prominently in Mark 4 and Matthew 13.

Important scholarship on the parables throughout most of the twentieth century followed Jülicher's and Wrede's model. The two most influential parable studies of that century were C. H. Dodd's *The Parables of the Kingdom* (1935) and Joachim Jeremias's *The Parables of Jesus* (1947). Both of these books emphasize the need to understand Jesus's original message by stripping away details added by the Gospel writers, and both studies attempted to recover the parables' original form by removing allegorical elements added by the evangelists. Dodd and Jeremias also follow Jülicher in asserting that each parable makes one single main point—although their teachings concerning what each particular parable's main point is varies considerably, and, like Jülicher, they occasionally employ allegorical interpretation even as they decry it.[21] Given this dominant mode of parable interpretation, it is hardly surprising that parable scholarship of this sort has had little influence on the scholarship of literature in general. Certainly, it is not helpful in our analysis of Milton's use of the biblical parables. While Milton's multifaceted use of the parables resists the intricate allegorization of some of the patristic writers, his appropriation of the imagery and characters of the parables reveals a methodology in conflict with the "single-meaning" approach.

The influence of the Jülicher-Dodd-Jeremias tradition remained dominant until roughly 1970.[22] The 1960s and following years saw the rise of various interpretive approaches to the parables, and although the *Sitz im Leben Jesu* emphasis of the Jülicher-Dodd-Jeremias tradition has remained highly influential in many of the schools of thought that have emerged in recent decades, that tradition's assumptions have been challenged as well, particularly its position that each parable teaches only one main point. Various recent treatments of the parables include existentialist, artistic, and early literary approaches, studies that emphasize the Palestinian culture in which Jesus's parables were spoken, ideologically driven studies, reader-response-based studies that argue that parables are polyvalent,[23] and studies advocating restrained allegorical interpretations of the parables. Both of the final two approaches challenge the single-main-point tenet advocated by Jülicher and his followers, but it is the restrained allegorical approach that is particularly applicable to our study of Milton's use of the parables.

The Restrained Allegorical Approach to Parables

Work that follows the restrained allegorical approach to the parables, often conducted by scholars with considerable literary training in their own right, can be incorporated profitably into our discussion of Milton's writings in ways that earlier parable scholarship cannot. An early contributor to this approach, Madeline Boucher, provides in *The Mysterious Parable* (1977) a thorough dismantling of Jülicher's single-main-point principle. Arguing that allegory is simply "an extended metaphor in narratory form," Boucher states that allegory is not actually a literary genre but rather a "device of meaning" that can be found within various literary genres, including parables. Arguing that parables are themselves often extended metaphors, and that "any parable which has both a literal and a metaphorical meaning is an allegory," Boucher convincingly refutes Jülicher's distinction between parable and allegory.[24] In a series of articles and later in a book-length study, John Sider follows Boucher's rejection of Jülicher's categorization of parables, agreeing with her assessment of allegory and parable and describing parables as "proportional analogies."[25] In an influential study, Craig Blomberg explains that "proportional analogies . . . *can be expressed by means of a series of equations of the form* 'A *is to* B *as a is to* b *with respect to* x.'" In this formula, the "exemplary characters" of the parables serve as "examples of a particular category of people."[26] Leland Ryken, a Bible-as-literature and Milton scholar, articulates this phenomenon by noting that the anonymous characters in the parables "become universal character types."[27] Blomberg's restrained allegorical approach to interpreting the parables employs a guiding principle that "would enable commentators to affirm more than just one point per parable without moving to the opposite extreme and endorsing an unlimited number of points."[28] Blomberg also notes that the restrained allegorical approach protects against the potentially unrestrained uncertainty of reader-response approaches, offering "an attractive middle ground between the Procrustean bed of Jülicher's one main point and the sea of relativism of some kinds of poststructuralist polyvalence."[29] Blomberg's interpretive principle is as follows: "Each parable makes one main point per main character—usually two or three in each case—and these main characters are the most likely elements within the parable to stand for something other than themselves, thus giving the parable its allegorical nature."[30] Blomberg's "one main point per main character" principle has been criticized as too simplistic by other scholars who nonetheless stand in basic agreement with the modified allegorical approach he asserts,[31] but clearly the restrained allegorical approach has become a significant alternative approach to the increasingly discredited "single main point" approach.[32]

Parables as Metaphorical Narratives

One other recent movement in parable interpretation, I would cautiously suggest, is applicable to our understanding of Milton's use of the parables, particularly his more imaginative use of them. This is a trend that views parables as "metaphorical narratives" and that emphasizes, in the words of Stephen I. Wright, that the parables are "stories that *as a whole* invite hearers into a world in order to reshape their vision of reality."[33] I connect this interpretive movement to Milton cautiously because scholars advocating this emphasis tend to shy away from applying parable characters to specific referents, something Milton clearly did when he applied various parable characters to himself. I also advocate caution here because certain scholars—most notably John Dominic Crossan—advocate such an indeterminate approach to the parables' meanings as to border on hermeneutical nihilism. For Crossan, parables are "devoid of content and referent" and "are unable to disclose" any genuine "understanding" regarding "the person of Jesus, the world, the Kingdom of God, or the hearer";[34] moreover, the "entirely negative function of metaphor and parable ultimately render[s] language itself a failure and contradiction."[35] In Crossan's words, metaphorical language, including that of the parables, has "a *void of meaning* at its core,"[36] and, given what Crossan believes to be the absence of the "security" of a transcendent grounding that would limit legitimate metaphorical interpretation, an interpretive "*regressus ad infinitum*" must be allowed for.[37]

But regardless of this interpretive school's association with Crossan, its emphasis upon the parables' transformative nature fits very well with Milton's practice of allowing his identification with certain parable characters to transform his view and representation of himself in his many writings. Among the scholarship associated with this approach, the writings of Paul Ricoeur are particularly applicable to Milton because of Ricoeur's emphasis on reader application and his related affirmation that parables have multiple (but not unlimited) references, and also because of his resistance to Jülicher's "single main point" principle despite his rejection of allegorizing.[38] Unlike Crossan, Ricoeur believes that parables "have both sense and reference,"[39] with their "*ultimate reference*," in Ricoeur's words, being "human experience, conceived as the experience of the whole man and of all men."[40] According to Ricoeur, parables can "refigure human action," and they contain a "world of the text" that "its interpreters may inhabit, a world that can move them to new understanding,"[41] one that calls us, says Ricoeur, to "let [the parables'] poetic power display itself within us."[42] Such a life reconfiguration, such an inhabitation of the parabolic text's world, such a display of the parables' poetic power, is evident throughout John Milton's engagement with Jesus's parables.

The Restrained Allegorical Approach Among Reformed and Puritan Commentators

Milton's own connection to certain figures in Jesus's parables reflects that he, like many sixteenth- and seventeenth-century Reformed and Puritan commentators, interpreted the parables in a way that paralleled the restrained allegorical approach. Certainly this approach to parable interpretation provides scholars with an effective tool for better understanding Milton's connection with specific characters in Jesus's parables. Ryken notes that parable characters serve as "archetypes" that connect with the feelings and circumstances in the lives of any given audience member.[43] As we shall see throughout this study, Ryken's observations apply to Milton in numerous ways. The restrained allegorical approach also helps readers understand literary and spiritual dimensions of Milton's imagination that the "single main point" principle cannot. As Mary Ford has noted, the "single main point" principle demonstrates both "a literary ignorance" and a "secularism" that shows a "distinct distaste for God as active in history and in individual human lives."[44] Milton's belief in the God-breathed scripture and its powerful influence upon the individual believer's life can hardly be denied, and his dynamic relationship with specific parable characters strongly exemplifies this belief.

Milton's contemporaries' methods of interpreting parables vary considerably. On one hand, the excessive allegorization of the patristic period still had prominent adherents in Milton's day. One such adherent was the Reverend Nehemiah Rogers (1593–1660), whose *The True Convert, or An Exposition upon the XV Chapter of St. Luke's Gospel* (1632) contains extended expositions of the parables of the lost sheep, the lost groat (coin), and the prodigal son. In this nine-hundred-page work, Rogers unfolds the following elaborate scheme in his interpretation of the parable of the lost groat (Luke 15:8–10):

1. The woman = the pastors and governors of the church, with Christ being the chief. (Rogers also provides a lengthy explanation of why the figure of a woman would be used to represent Christ.)
2. The ten pieces of silver = mankind in general.
3. The one lost coin = the elect, yet uncalled.
4. The candle = the Gospel, called a light.
5. Lighting the candle = preaching the Gospel.
6. The house = the church, God's Israel.
7. The broom = ecclesiastical discipline/the censures of the church.
8. The sweeping of the house = the execution of the above discipline/censures upon offenders for their reclaiming.
9. The friends and neighbors = angels.

Rogers's allegorical method, we can see, is no less elaborate than the earlier cited examples of Clement and Augustine. Several decades later, the Baptist minister Benjamin Keach (1640–1704), in *An Exposition of the Parables*, criticized Rogers for his excessive allegorization of the parable of the lost coin.[45] Despite such criticism, Keach himself offers an interpretation of the parable of the Good Samaritan that is reminiscent of Augustine:

1. Man on his way to Jericho = fallen man/first Adam.
2. Jerusalem = unfallen paradise.
3. Priest = law/priesthood of Aaron.
4. Levite = legal sacrifices.
5. Samaritan = Jesus.
6. Oil = Holy Spirit.
7. The Samaritan's beast = doctrine of free grace.
8. Inn = church of Christ.
9. Host of inn = minister of church.[46]

While this sort of extended allegorization was clearly alive and well in Milton's time, there is also good evidence that many of Milton's contemporaries actually employed the same restrained allegorical method that has been articulated in recent decades by scholars such as Blomberg, Sider, and Ryken. Although the standard Reformed and Puritan hermeneutic strongly disapproved of allegorizing the scriptures, insisting instead that proper Bible interpretation should reveal a scripture passage's plain meaning,[47] the Puritans nonetheless recognized the presence of allegorical passages in the Bible. As Barbara Lewalski notes, early modern Calvinists often regarded Jesus's parables "as a fictional form related to allegory."[48] The Scotch Presbyterian James Durham (1622–1658) asserted that "there is a great difference betwixt an Allegorick Exposition of Scripture, and an Exposition of Allegorick Scripture," citing Jesus's parables as a kind of allegory and stating that "in Divinitie" there is no "difference between Similitudes, or Parables, and Allegories."[49] Similarly, Westminster assemblyman William Bridge (1600–1670) contended that "sometimes the Scripture is to be understood Literally, sometimes Figuratively, and Metaphorically."[50] For such writers, the plain sense of scripture coincides properly with a restrained exegesis of plainly metaphorical passages. As John Ball (1585–1640) observed, a given passage has "but one proper and natural sense, though sometimes things are so expressed, as that the things themselves do signify other matters, according to the Lord's ordinance."[51]

The restrained allegorical approach to the parables is evident in any number of Reformed and Puritan commentaries and sermons. In the following chapters, I discuss in more detail various Reformed and Puritan examples of this approach, but a brief sketch will suffice here. John Calvin, who spoke out against the excesses of allegory, himself used this modified allegorical method, and in his commentaries he relates parabolic figures either to God or to certain classes of people. This can be seen throughout his *Harmony of the Gospels*. One clear example of such exegesis occurs in his discussion of the parable of the prodigal son, where Calvin equates the father with God, the prodigal son with sinners who eventually repent, and the elder son with the self-righteous scribes and "those who want maliciously to restrict God's grace."[52] Matthew Poole (1624–1679) makes almost identical connections in his commentary on this parable.[53] We should note that neither Calvin nor Poole attempts to make any metaphorical connections concerning any of the lesser characters in the parable or any of the animals or inanimate objects. Their analogical, and hence (restrained) allegorical methodology, however, is evident, and it is significant that Calvin actually berates the allegorizers even as he, in the same paragraph, uses allegory himself. His criticism, however, does not make Calvin a methodological hypocrite; rather, the fact that he conducts an allegorical interpretation even as he criticizes allegorization is an implicit demonstration that a different—and presumably more legitimate—sort of allegorical interpretation is taking place. Although neither Calvin nor Poole articulates a clear methodology of parable interpretation, they are in fact using the very sort of restrained allegorical approach championed by Blomberg, Ryken, and Sider in the late twentieth century.

Similarly, in the parable of the ten virgins (Matt. 25:1–13), Calvin holds that the wise virgins represent "the faithful," while the foolish ones represent those persons "who have made poor provision" and will "be excluded from entry into heaven."[54] In his series of sermons *The Parable of the Ten Virgins*, the Puritan pastor Thomas Shepard (1605–1649) notes early on that the ten virgins as a whole represent "the visible church."[55] Shepard goes on to classify the five wise virgins as authentic children of God, while the five foolish virgins represent "gospel hypocrites" who appear as part of the visible church but lack true faith in Christ.[56] Similarly, Andrew Bromhall (1608–

1662), in his sermon "How Is Hypocrisy Discoverable and Curable?," equates the foolish virgins with "all formal Christians that are not regenerated by the Spirit nor put into Christ by faith."[57] Neither Calvin nor Shepard nor Bromhall indulges in lengthy speculation concerning the other details of the parable, but each writer notes a clear correlation between the major characters of the parable and the larger classes of persons they represent.

When we look at various sixteenth- and seventeenth-century exegetes' interpretations of the parable of the talents (Matt. 25:14–30), the parable with which Milton interacts most notably, we see the phenomenon of proportional analogy displayed again. The different servants of the parable represent different classes of persons, although there is no uniform agreement concerning what classes of persons are involved. Calvin equates the different servants with those persons in the visible church: the faithful servants are equated with faithful believers; the wicked, unprofitable servant is equated with persons who do not make good use of the gifts with which God has entrusted them. Like Calvin, the Irish archbishop James Ussher (1581–1656) in 1640 likened the parable's servants to church members, telling his audience that, at the time of judgment, "thou must give an account of all that thou hast received," for God will ask, "I gave thee learning, how didst thou use it? I gave thee other gifts of mind, how didst thou imploy them?"[58] Calvin's view is echoed in John Bunyan's (1628–1688) *The Pilgrim's Progress* (1678), when the faithful pilgrims Christian and Hopeful are greeted in the Celestial City with the commendation the faithful servants in the parable receive: "Enter ye into the joy of your Lord."[59] Richard Sibbes (1577–1635), in *The Bruised Reed* (1630), equates the unprofitable servant with those in the church who are "determined to be damned" by persisting "in having hard thoughts of Christ, that they may have some show of reason to fetch contentment from other things"; Poole in his commentary holds that the servants represent people in general.[60] The latter-day Puritan Matthew Henry (1662–1714), in his commentary on Matthew, expresses the view that the servants represent Christians, adding, "It is probable that *ministers* are especially intended here, who are more immediately attending on him, and sent by him."[61] Furthermore, Milton's contemporary the eminent English Puritan preacher John Owen (1616–1683), in his 1678 sermon "Ministerial Endowments the Work of the Spirit" (which he preached at a younger minister's ordination), holds even more strongly to the notion that the servants represent ministers, asserting that Christ "hath appointed servants to take care of the administration of the affairs of his house and kingdom: and for this end he gives them talents that they may trade with."[62]

Other examples of Puritan exegetes' taking a restrained allegorical approach to the parables can be seen in discussions of the parable of the pearl of great price (Matt. 13:45–46). Sibbes, in his sermon "The Rich Pearl," flatly states that by the pearl "is meant *Jesus Christ*" and the "Merchant *is every Christian*."[63] Similarly, early in his massive *The Christian Man's Calling*, George Swinnock (1627–1673) writes that "the godly man is the wise merchant, trading for goodly pearls, that sells all to buy the field where the pearl of great price is."[64] Not surprisingly, Sibbes's and Swinnock's exegeses of this parable and its figures strongly resemble Calvin's.[65]

Milton's Use of the Parables

Milton's own use of the biblical parables generally reflects this Reformed and Puritan practice of using the characters of the parables to reflect larger classes of persons. Although this is not the only manner in which Milton uses the parables, it is his most explicit practice. While later chapters discuss this practice in more detail, we may outline a few such tendencies here.

In Sonnet 9, the "Lady" to whom the poem is addressed is called a "Virgin wise and pure" (line 14) who fills her "odorous Lamp with deeds of light" (10) as she awaits "the Bridegroom" (12). Here, Milton's "Lady" is shown as being a member of the class of persons that the "wise virgins" in the parable of the ten virgins signify.

In Sonnet 19, Milton's autobiographical speaker explicitly compares himself to the unprofitable servant in the parable of the talents, specifically presenting himself as a member of the class of persons that the unprofitable servant signifies.

Conversely, in *Paradise Lost*, God says to the loyal angel Abdiel, "Servant of God, well done, well hast thou fought / The better fight" (6.29–30). Here, Milton's God addresses Milton's self-referential Abdiel in the manner in which the master in the parable of the talents addresses each of his "good and faithful" servants. The figure of Abdiel is thus classified here as among those individuals whom those servants represent. We may also note here Milton's combination of the parabolic language of the Gospels with that of Saint Paul, as God's words here echo Paul's claim "I have fought the good fight" (2 Tim. 4:7).

In *Paradise Lost*, 6.854–58, we see that the Son

> meant
> Not to destroy, but root them out of Heav'n:
> The overthrown he rais'd, and as a Herd
> Of Goats or timorous flock together throng'd
> Drove them before him Thunder-struck.

The damned demons, likened to a herd of goats being sent to hell, reflect the image of the "accursed" goats in the parable of the sheep and the goats (Matt. 25:31–46). Here, Milton displays these demons as being among the class of persons represented by the goats. He also employs the parable of the tares (Matt. 13:24–30, 36–43), suggesting that the demons are among "the children of the wicked one" (13:38), represented by the tares that are uprooted and burned at the end of the world.

We see a similar approach to the parables in Milton's prose. In *Animadversions*, Milton draws on the imagery of the parable of the tares while criticizing the priorities of Bishop Joseph Hall. Hall busies himself with writing attacks against the pope "while the whole Diocesse be sown with tares, and none to resist the enemy" (*CPW*, 1:731). Here, Milton asserts that the corrupting forces within Hall's diocese are also to be classified with "the children of the wicked one," who are represented by the tares.

Another notable use of the parables in Milton's prose occurs on the frontispiece of his tract *The Doctrine and Discipline of Divorce*. There, Milton placed what is presumably his own translation of Matthew 13:52, the parable of the householder: "Every Scribe instructed to the Kingdome of Heav'n, is like the Maister of a house which bringeth out of his treasury things new and old." This passage follows several subtitles, such as the claim that the work will restore the proper understanding of divorce to "the good of both sexes, from the bondage of canon law, and other mistakes, to the true meaning of Scripture in the Law and Gospel compar'd" (*CPW*, 2.221). Clearly, Milton is placing himself in the role of the parabolic householder, or the scribe to whom the householder or "Maister" is compared. Milton sets himself up as a teacher who falls into the category of a "Scribe instructed to the Kingdome of Heav'n," who thus is able to reveal the genuine truth of the scriptures in spite of the church's past interpretive mistakes.

This brief perusal of Milton's uses of the biblical parables includes several places where he actually a parable figure to himself or to a self-referential speaker or character. Indeed, one of the main purposes of this study is to demonstrate the degree to which Milton does in fact identify personally with a number of parabolic figures, and the following chapters explore his tendency to find an exceptional degree of self-identification in particular parables. Milton's strong connection with specific figures from certain of Jesus's parables puts him squarely in line with the seventeenth-century English Protestant practice, traced back through Martin Luther to Augustine, of individual Christians' finding particular biblical passages, or "places," to which they would relate their own spiritual experiences and development. Dayton Haskin has written at length about this practice, and he has also explored extensively how the parable of the talents was a particularly important, and indeed an "uneasy," place for Milton.[66] I will not seek to duplicate Haskin's thorough efforts here. Rather, my purpose is to investigate how Milton's affinity with several parabolic figures inspired his imaginative efforts throughout his poetry and prose.

Of course, Milton's rather extensive self-referential use of the biblical parables is hardly surprising in light of his tendency to apply the various genres, passages, and characters of the Bible to characters or speakers of his own invention that display autobiographical elements, whether explicitly or implicitly. A very incomplete list of important discussions of Milton's multifaceted use of biblical texts to illumine his poetic inventions includes the following studies. In *The Bible and Milton's Epics*, James H. Sims notes Milton's portrayal of Adam in conjunction with the biblical portrayal of Abraham, Moses, Joshua, and Cain; furthermore, Sims discusses Milton's use of various negative biblical characters—among them Esau, the Babylonian rulers Nebuchadnezzar and Belshazzar, the murderous King Herod, and the traitor Judas Iscariot—to create his portrayal of Satan in *Paradise Lost*.[67] Timothy O'Keefe offers a significant analysis of Milton's depiction of the Pauline theme of "the inverted correspondence between Adam as sinner and Christ as savior" in both *Paradise Lost* and *Paradise Regained* in the figures of Adam and the Son.[68] Mary Ann Radzinowicz notes Milton's imitation of the poetic form of the wisdom song of the Hebrew scriptures in his "self-characterization of the Son" in *Paradise Regained*, and she analyzes in considerable depth Milton's use of the Psalms to develop the character of the Son in the same poem.[69] Barbara Kiefer Lewalski discusses the influence of Job on the character of the Son in *Paradise Regained*, and in another study on *Paradise Regained*, Stella Revard investigates the impact of the Gospel of John, along with the more obvious texts of Matthew and Luke, on Milton's depiction of the Son.[70] Miriam Muskin focuses on Milton's use of the biblical character of David in his portrayal of Samson in *Samson Agonistes*, Radzinowicz discusses how Milton's depiction of Samson incorporates both the biblical Job and the heroes of faith of Hebrews 11, and John Wall Jr. analyzes how Milton modeled some of Samson's speeches after biblical lament Psalms. Regina Schwartz addresses how Milton's controversial hermeneutical perspective on the principle of Christian charity in his divorce tracts manifests itself in the choices made by Adam and Eve in *Paradise Lost*.[71] In the present study, I explore another dimension of an established branch of study concerning Milton and the Bible.

Self-Representation in Milton's Writings

The notion that Milton's poetic characters are self-referential in nature has long been affirmed by various readers. I discuss this matter in greater detail in the ensuing chapters, but for now I will simply state that I concur with a long line of critics who have asserted, to one degree or another, the self-referential characteristics of many of Milton's major poetic inventions. This is not to suggest a naïve equation such as Adam (or Satan, or the Son, or Samson) = Milton himself. I do, however, endorse James Holly Hanford's basic premise that Milton's various characters reflect different aspects of Milton's personality.[72] Hanford's observation is based on his reading of the self-referential relationship between Milton and his characters in *Paradise Lost*, but Hanford's own criticism, the writings of numerous other critics over the centuries, and the present study extend this reading to a number of Milton's other characters. More than a century before Hanford, Samuel Taylor Coleridge (1772–1834) averred, "In the Paradise Lost—indeed in every one of his poems—it is Milton himself whom you see."[73] More recently, Stephen Fallon, whose *Milton's Peculiar Grace* affirms Milton's self-representation throughout his poetry and prose, has affirmed that Milton "insists on being present in his texts."[74] In light of persuasive scholarship by Fallon and others, I do not generally seek to provide strenuous argument concerning such self-referential connections. (The single exception is my discussion of Sonnet 9 in chapter 4, where my argument for Milton's autobiographical relationship to the Lady of that sonnet is necessitated by the newness of my proposition.) Rather, I aim to situate Milton's use of biblical parables within the context of his tendency to identify with certain parable figures, both in places where such self-identification is blatantly obvious and in poetic characters whose self-referential elements have been recognized by sustained critical inquiry. This is not to suggest that all of Milton's uses of the biblical parables are in some way self-referential. But Milton's tendency to apply figures in certain parables—most notably the parables of the talents, of the laborers, of the virgins, and of the householder—to his own experience, and indeed to have these parables help to shape his experience, is the most compelling aspect of his relationship to the biblical parables. Milton's "existential interpretation"[75] of the parables, to use Ricoeur's phrase, is one that recognizes the parables' "capacity to refigure human action" and to shape artistic effort by letting "their poetic power display itself within us."[76]

In the end, I seek to demonstrate that in his use of the parables, Milton is indeed a poet and prose writer who consistently engages in self-representation. To make such a statement is not to suggest that Milton is a kind of supreme egotist, although I recognize that he perhaps ought to have been a little less preoccupied with his own person. Rather, I hope to reveal a portrait of Milton that shows a man whose understanding of the biblical parables, as with the Bible as a whole, is intensely personal in nature; we have in Milton an artist whose study of the Bible is inextricably connected with both his art and his experience.[77]

In this sense, this study extends the discussion of "Renaissance self-fashioning," in that Milton, by means of his identification with figures from certain biblical parables, constructs a "self" in relation to the biblical text and to God himself. Milton's propensity to do so does in fact fall under what Stephen Greenblatt calls one of the "governing conditions common to most instances of self-fashioning": that "self-fashioning . . . involves submission to an absolute power or authority situated at least partially outside the self," such as "God, [or] a sacred book."[78] Indeed, as Leland Ryken has observed in the context of a Puritan literary articulation of self-representation, "Milton naturally turned to the Bible for expressive symbols—indeed, for the very language—by which to express his Puritan vision."[79] Furthermore, as Charles A. Huttar points out, the tendency toward pious self-fashioning (Huttar does not use that phrase) was endemic to Puritan England in the seventeenth century.[80] Huttar cites U. Milo Kaufmann, who notes that the average Puritan "was haunted by the desire to survey his whole life in one glance, to hold his soul in his hands, the better to possess himself."[81] We would also do well to recognize that such an emphasis on self-knowledge was advocated by the Puritans' spiritual forerunner, John Calvin, who, in the opening sentence of the first book of his *Institutes of the Christian Religion*, declares that "nearly all the wisdom we possess . . . consists of two parts: the knowledge of God and of ourselves."[82] This focus on Puritan self-knowledge, combined with our earlier recognition of Reformed preachers' tendencies to relate parabolic figures to certain classes of people, should make Milton's propensity to think of himself in terms of particular parabolic figures all the more understandable. In doing so, Milton shows himself to be not only a product of the British Renaissance but, even more significantly, a product of his Puritan environment.[83] As Ryken notes, "a specific aspect" of the Puritans' "conviction of the centrality of the Bible" was their "knack for reading their own lives in terms of biblical images and characters."[84]

Methodology

Each opening chapter of each part of this study addresses one or more textual examples in which I can most convincingly demonstrate Milton's self-identification with a figure or figures from a particular parable or parables. (Chapter 1 also shows, in Milton's experiences of both tension and resolution between the parable of the talents and the parable of the laborers, how Milton can arrange two biblical "places" with which he identifies to "interpret one another.")[85] Having established a clear textual warrant for Miltonic self-identification, I proceed in the subsequent chapters to demonstrate connections with the general principle of the parable or parables in question throughout certain major works, often expanding my framework considerably beyond Milton's clear allusions to or quotations of the parable(s) under discussion. In each part, I seek to elucidate how Milton's pervasive connections with the figures of the parables in question may be used as an interpretive framework for Milton's portrayals of various self-referential characters in his major works. Indeed, even as Ricoeur holds that the parables can "reconfigure human action,"[86] Milton's identification with these parabolic figures reconfigures both his self-presentation and his art. Another statement of Ricoeur's is particularly germane to Milton's relationships to the specific parables: "To understand oneself before the text is . . . to expose oneself to receive from it a larger self which would be the proposed way of existing that most appropriately responds to the proposed world of the text. . . . [In this sense,] the self is constituted by the issue of the text."[87] Much of this study is dedicated to showing how pertinent issues in the germane parables constitute the self-representation Milton offers through self-referential characters within his major works.

The ten chapters of this book, divided into three parts, demonstrate how Milton's identification with particular parable figures manifests itself, both explicitly and implicitly, in his early, middle, and late works. Part 1 addresses Milton's enduring connections with the unprofitable servant in the parable of the talents and the last-called laborers in the parable of the laborers, connections that sometimes complement and sometimes work against one another, and that cause anguish, tension, and relief and resolution throughout his career. Chapter 1 addresses how Milton's relationships with these parables manifest themselves explicitly in his youthful Sonnet 7 and its accompanying letter "To a Friend"; in *Ad Patrem*, his Latin poem to his father, which thanks his father for his ongoing support and promises his own future poetic achievement; in the sometimes angst-ridden preface to the second book of *The Reason of Church-Government*; and in Sonnet 19, his great reflection, written in middle age, on his life's work, his disappointments, and his blindness. Chapter 2 examines how the ongoing tension in Milton's connections with the aforementioned parable characters manifests itself in his largely self-referential portrayal of Samson in *Samson Agonistes*, a portrayal that eventually offers resolution between the parables in question. Chapter 3 discusses how an idealized relationship between the two parables exists within two of Milton's most idealized self-referential characters: the loyal angel Abdiel, who opposes Satan's rebellion in *Paradise Lost*, and the Son in *Paradise Regained*.

Part 2 explores Milton's ongoing connection with the ideal of the wise virgin, derived from the five wise virgins in the parable of the wise and foolish virgins. Chapter 4 argues that Milton's address to Sonnet 9's "Lady," whom he calls a "Virgin wise and pure," intentionally applies both to Milton's bride-to-be, Mary Powell, and to Milton himself, and establishes the sonnet's Lady as one of Milton's many self-referential characters characterized by zeal and purity. Chapter 5 examines how the ideal of the wise virgin in action is manifested in the Lady of Milton's *A Mask Presented at Ludlow Castle*, a self-referential character who exemplifies Milton's youthful ideal of strength in chastity and whose wisdom is demonstrated in her rhetorical resistance to Comus's attempted seduction. Chapter 6 analyzes the loss of wise virginity in Milton's self-referential characters Eve and Adam in *Paradise Lost*, noting particularly the connection between wrong thinking, self-idolatry/narcissism, and sexual transgression. Chapter 7 examines how the ideal of the wise virgin is lived out perfectly in the Son of *Paradise Regained*, while Samson in *Samson Agonistes* represents one who, having fallen low through sexual foolishness, moves toward recovery of the ideal of the wise virgin through his prudent rejection of Dalia's temptation.

Part 3 reflects on Milton's deep connection with the householder in the parable of the householder, a brief parable in which Jesus states, "every scribe which is instructed unto the kingdom of heaven is like unto a man that is an householder, which bringeth forth out of his treasure things new and old" (Matt. 13:52). Part 3 recognizes throughout that, for Milton, the purity of the wise virgin is a prerequisite for the spiritual insight and inspiration of the householder. Chapter 8 discusses Milton's explicit self-identification with the parable's householder in both *The Doctrine and Discipline of Divorce* and the posthumously discovered *De Doctrina Christiana*. In both works, Milton assumes the role of the inspired householder, who, guided by the Spirit of God, brings forth treasures of theological insight that conflict with the received wisdom of the Christian Church through the ages. Although these treasures are seemingly novel, they are actually old in the sense that Milton insists that his affirmations are nothing new but merely what the Bible itself has always affirmed. Chapter 9 investigates Milton's epic poems to analyze how Milton assumes the role of the inspired householder in composing *Paradise Lost* and *Paradise Regained*, both works that develop canonical biblical narratives in ways that go beyond the scriptural accounts. Commentators are divided over whether Milton believed that he was composing a new scripture or simply reaffirming the overall message of the Bible itself. Chapter 9 also discusses the Son and Mary of *Paradise Regained* to analyze their respective roles as householders. This chapter emphasizes Mary, another of Milton's self-referential characters, and her role as one who ponders both the Hebrew scriptures and the not-yet-codified Christian scriptures, passing on her meditative methodology to Jesus to enable him to recognize himself in the Hebrew scriptures. Chapter 9 also observes that Milton's method of reading the scriptures in *De Doctrina Christiana* reflects Mary's in the brief epic. Finally, chapter 10 examines Samson as a kind of chastened householder, one who, having repented of his lust-driven spiritual self-deception, now submits himself to the written Mosaic law, a posture of obedience that enables him to discern the Spirit's prompting of the "rousing motions" that call him to perform at Dagon's temple and wreak destruction upon the Philistines.

Some may object that my methodology of moving from Milton's explicit self-identification with parabolic figures to his more pervasive implicit manifestation of these figures in his self-referential characters might go beyond the clear warrant of using a scriptural text that can overtly be connected to a given Miltonic text. I am not entirely unsympathetic to such an objection; indeed, I think it right for us to maintain some healthy skepticism toward any approach to literary studies that appears to take undue interpretive liberties by connecting particular scriptural texts to particular literary works.[88] In the end, however, I do not believe that I am going against the spirit of a broader scriptural warrant. Milton is, as many have noted, a poet and prose writer thoroughly concerned with self-representation;[89] furthermore, he is a poet whose artistry is drawn largely from the Bible. In the same way, I argue that both Milton's deeper conceptions of himself and the pervasive frameworks that guided his attitudes and his art are also drawn from the Bible, including prominently the four parabolic figures on which I focus in this study. Just as we recognize his strongly held identification with these figures, I believe that they in turn provide us with a rich interpretive framework through which we may better understand both Milton's major works and Milton himself.[90]

Part 1

The Parable of the Talents and the Parable of the Laborers

We begin our extended examination of Milton's relationship to Jesus's parables by addressing Milton's well-known connection to the parable of the talents (Matt. 25.14–30). Throughout this investigation, we will pay particular attention both to Milton's problematic lifelong identification with the unprofitable servant of the parable of the talents, and to his regular practice of trying to mitigate this identification by laying claim to the grace offered to the last-called laborers in the parable of the laborers (Matt. 20.1–16)—laborers who receive from their employer the same wage as those who work the entire day and parabolic figures with whom Milton identified as relief from his burdensome relationship to the unprofitable servant.

Throughout the various self-representations in his early, middle, and late poetry and prose, Milton's relationship to the parable of the talents varies from tortured to peaceful, largely based on his willingness to view and represent himself as a faithful last-called laborer. Notably, his representations of his midtwenties, seen in Sonnet 7 ("How soon hath time"), its attendant letter "To a Friend" (1632), and his Latin verse epistle *Ad Patrem* (*To My Father*, 1634?), largely succeed in putting off the specter of the unprofitable servant by appealing to a spiritually and artistically profitable future for which he still prepares; and, in the sonnet and the letter, by implicitly and explicitly appealing to his identification with the last-called laborers. Writing in *The Reason of Church-Government* (1642) in his midthirties, however, Milton's identification with the unprofitable servant, unmitigated by any mention of the parable of the laborers, demonstrates a neurotic attitude toward the divine master he fears will judge him for not properly employing his talents to glorify God and defend his church. A decade later, in Sonnet 19 ("When I consider how my light is spent," 1651?), the now blind Milton depicts an acute contest between the two parables and his aforementioned self-identifications, a contest that begins with self-condemnation but ends with an acceptance of grace. A similar contest between the two parables is evident in the development of the self-referential Samson of *Samson Agonistes* (1671), a work whose diction, themes, and final resolution echo those of the sonnet. Conversely, in the idealized self-referential figures of the loyal Abdiel in *Paradise Lost* (1667, 1674) and the Son in *Paradise Regained* (1671), Milton depicts characters whose perfect service before God shows them, simultaneously, to be both the active good and faithful servants in the parable of the talents and the patient last-called laborers in the parable of the laborers.

I

The Talented Mr. Milton
A Parabolic Laborer and His Identity

In *Milton's Burden of Interpretation*, Dayton Haskin notes that while a fair amount of Milton criticism has discussed the poet's fascination with the parable of the talents (Matt. 25:14–30; cf. Luke 19:11–27), surprisingly little has addressed his proclivity "to think of himself as a version" of the "unprofitable servant" of that parable. We recall that, having been entrusted by his master with a talent of money, this servant fearfully buries his talent, unlike his two fellow servants, who busily put their talents to work and double their money. When the master returns, he commends the first two servants as "good and faithful" but chastises the unprofitable servant for his lack of industry, pronounces him "wicked and slothful," and has him "cast . . . into outer darkness." Haskin does much to explain Milton's "uneasy" relationship to the parable and his tendency to identify with the unprofitable servant. Early in his valuable study, Haskin discusses how Martin Luther made the "liberating discovery" that two biblical "places" could "interpret one another."[1] But Haskin does relatively little to analyze Milton's own "liberating" practice of using one biblical passage to interpret the other, specifically in his practice of portraying his connection to the unprofitable servant in light of his comparable self-identification with the last-chosen laborers of the parable of the laborers in the vineyard (Matt. 20:1–16, hereafter referred to as the parable of the laborers).[2] These laborers, unlike the unprofitable servant, receive God's grace and reward in spite of their limited work in their master's vineyard. Very significantly, Milton makes use of this parable in a number of the same works in which his identification with the unprofitable servant in the parable of the talents appears so prominently, including the early Sonnet 7 and its companion letter "To a Friend," and also in Sonnet 19. In these works, Milton employs the parable of the laborers as a mitigating factor, offering the hope of God's favor despite his failures. Although we cannot assert finally that Milton's autobiographical speakers—or Milton himself—ever escape completely the horrible fear of being judged "unprofitable" by God, the parable of the laborers does serve, even if only temporarily, to assuage such spiritual anguish.

Sonnet 7 and a Letter "To a Friend": Vocation and Righteous Delay

It is generally agreed that Milton's Sonnet 7 ("How soon hath time") was written for the occasion of his twenty-fourth birthday, December 8, 1632.[3] A few months later, he included the sonnet in a letter "To a Friend." (The recipient of this poem is unknown, although Milton's former tutor, Thomas Young, is often suggested.)[4] It is helpful to read Sonnet 7 in relation to this letter, and particularly so to acquire a greater understanding of Milton's lifelong identification with both the parable of the talents and the parable of the laborers. The letter was prompted by a conversation from the previous day in which its recipient had, it seems, "admonish[ed]" Milton for not yet having "credible employment" and reminded him "that the howres of the night passe on . . . & that the day wth me is at hand wherin Christ commands all to Labour while there is light." Furthermore, the friend had charged that Milton had "too much love of Learning" and that he had "given up [himself] to dreame away [his] Yeares in the armes of studious retirement like Endymion wth the Moone" (*CPW*, 1:319). We may assume that this well-intentioned friend was concerned that although Milton had earned a master's degree from Cambridge and already had attained the age required for taking holy orders (twenty-four), he was not yet pursuing ordination but instead was engaging in further preparation.

In his letter, which makes no reference to his ambition to become a poet and implies that he eventually will enter the ministry,[5] Milton acknowledges that his life is "as yet obscure, & unserviceable to mankind"; and, given his friend's sincere concern for his welfare, that he considers himself "bound though unask't, to give you account, as oft as occasion is, of this my tardie moving; according to the praecept of my conscience, wch I firmely trust is not w^thout god." What follows is a forthright explanation of his "conscien [tious]" decision to forego immediate employment. About halfway through the letter, the parable of the talents is named explicitly, as Milton asserts his "due & tymely obedience to that command in the gospell set out by the terrible seasing of him that hid the talent" (*CPW*, 1:319–20). He goes on to explain that "this very consideration of that great commandment does not presse forward as soone as may be to underg[o] but keeps off wth a sacred reverence & religious advisement how best to undergoe [,] not taking thought of beeing late so it give advantage to being more fit" (1:320; brack-eted additions in *CPW*). Here, Milton demonstrates an intense awareness of the parable, but he also distances himself from the hapless servant who hid his single talent. A tension within Milton seems evident here, one that betrays his "uneasy" relation to this parable. It is the third, unfaithful servant whom he explicitly mentions, aware that others may well associate him with that "slothful" figure; at the same time, however, he seeks to identify not with that servant but rather with the faithful ones, since he sees extensive preparation as the prerequisite for the faithful service the parable demands.

We may conclude from his letter that Milton's implicit connection between further preparation and true obedience to the parable is closely related to the idea of "conscience." As Margo Swiss explains, "Conscience is itself the essential justification for Milton's procrastination from . . . clerical commitment." Swiss notes that Milton's "scrupulous attention to conscience" reflects the influence of Puritan divines such as William Perkins.[6] Perkins, also a Cambridge graduate, emphasized the need for a man's conscience to be settled fully before accepting a particular calling to God's service. In *How to Live and that Well* (1601), Perkins writes, "Againe, faith is required, whereby every man must beleeve that the calling in which hee is, is the particular calling, in which god will bee served of him. For unlesse the conscience be settled in this, no good worke can be done in any calling."[7] Connecting Perkins's assertion with Milton's statement on conscience, we may speculate that Milton's delay resulted largely from lack of a "settled conscience" about the particular calling of Anglican ministry. Relating Milton's scruples of conscience to his desire to obey the "commandment" of the parable of the talents, we see that Milton hoped to avoid God's judgment of the unprofitable servant by not entering a ministerial vocation prematurely.

To be sure, Milton's lack of certainty about his calling was based essentially on his conviction that, despite his Cambridge education, he was neither intellectually nor spiritually prepared for such a weighty undertaking. Again, his acute sensitivity to the grave spiritual responsibility of the ministry placed him firmly in line with the dominant Puritan attitudes of his day. As Swiss notes, the words of William Whately would have resonated profoundly in the young Milton. In *The New Birth* (1618), Whately exhorts ministers to "study day and night, and by continuall paines, putting forth thy selfe to all laboriousnesse. . . . Consider what a waighty duty, what a great honour it is to bee God's instrument for the regenerating of others."[8] Whately's message contains two major points that parallel closely two of Milton's most important concerns. The first is the need for ministers to apply themselves with ceaseless diligence to pious study, a pattern reflected by Milton both in his Cambridge years and in his periods at Hammersmith and Horton. The second is an admonition to ponder soberly the immense responsibility placed on those who would be shepherds of Christ's flock. Along with such a calling would come a grave reckoning at the end of the minister's life, one in which he would have to give an account of his faithfulness—or lack thereof—before God. The Bible itself is clear that such a reckoning will be even stricter for church leaders, to which this warning from the Epistle of James attests: "My brethren, be not many [of you] masters, knowing that we shall receive the greater condemnation" (3:1).

John Owen's 1678 sermon "Ministerial Endowments the Work of the Spirit"—preached at an ordination service—speaks to the issues of conscience, judgment, and the ministerial call in direct relation to the parable of the talents. In an exposition of the parable pertinent to Milton's own vocational uncertainty, Owen warns against taking orders when one lacks the spiritual gifts requisite to the ministerial vocation: "For men to take upon them to serve Christ as officers in the work of his house, who have received none of these spiritual abilities to work with, is a high presumption, and casts reflection of dishonour on Jesus Christ; as if he called to work, and gave no strength; as though he called to trade, and gave no stock; or required spiritual duties, and gave no spiritual abilities. Christ will say to such on the last day, 'How came ye in hither?'"[9] We may recognize in Owen's warning Milton's own concerns. To be sure, Milton recognized that he was a gifted individual. Were his talents, however, those that would make him a suitable overseer of people's souls? It would be better to wait for certainty than to enter into the ministry presumptuously, only to recognize that he had misunderstood his own talents. Such a situation would be doubly woeful, for he would not only find himself unable to carry out the priestly office but would also be trapped in this office and unable to discharge his true vocation, whatever it might be.

In light of such teaching, Milton's scruples of conscience concerning ordination may be understood all the more clearly. So, for that matter, may his connection with the parable of the talents in the letter "To a Friend." Since Milton believed that a stricter judgment awaited those in church leadership, a conscientious delay was entirely appropriate for one who feared rushing headlong into a judgment like the one that befell the unprofitable servant. Thus, although his "Love of Learning" might appear to some as the kind of "emptie & fantastick chase of shadows and notions" (*CPW*, 1:320) that might characterize the "wicked and slothful servant" (Matt. 25:26), Milton may better be characterized here as one who deems a prolonged period of diligent (albeit ostensibly unproductive) preparatory study a far better—and safer—use of his talents than premature entrance into the high and awesome calling of the priesthood.

Milton's reference in the letter to the parable of the talents is followed immediately by his hopeful connection with the parable of the laborers. Defending his choice to delay employment and endeavor "to be more fit," he offers the following explanation: "for those that were latest lost nothing when the maister of the vinyard came to give each one his hire" (*CPW*, 1:320). By associating himself with the last-hired laborers, Milton seeks to articulate a confidence before the judgment of God that is quite unlike the fearful attitude of the unprofitable servant. As he tries to convince his friend of the rightness of his own deferment from active service, Milton depicts a God who fully understands the young graduate's decisions, a God who is ready to reward Milton equally with those who have begun laboring in the Lord's vineyard earlier than he.

Milton's skillful juxtaposition of the two parables merits further analysis. We may speculate that Milton's friend had mentioned the parable of the talents and admonished young Milton, however gently, "to Labour while there is light" (*CPW*, 1:319) in order to avoid the fate of the unprofitable servant. If Milton's friend was in fact Young, the possibility of such a warning seems all the more likely, for we may assume that his former tutor used various biblical admonitions to exhort his students to diligent labor. Even if this friend did not introduce the subject of the parable, we still may identify the parable as a biblical "place" that resonated strongly not only with Milton but with many other Christians in early modern England.[10] That the parable already had become part of young Milton's consciousness is evident from his allusion to it in Sonnet 7, composed a little while before. Indeed, given his situation in life, the parable of the talents would be a natural scriptural passage for the sensitive young man to ponder. But it is Milton's interplay between the parable of the talents and the parable of the laborers that makes both this letter and Sonnet 7 itself so intriguing with regard to Milton's personality and development, for we can see that Milton uses his identification with the latter parable to mitigate his identification with the former. By employing the parable of the laborers, Milton is able to place himself in relationship to the laborers who, though having worked only the last hour of the workday, have been rewarded by the owner of the vineyard with a full day's wages. By making this connection, he can invert his inclination to associate himself with the "slothful and unprofitable servant" and instead associate himself with the servants who made industrious use of the talents given them.[11]

Shortly after his juxtaposition of these two parables, Milton includes Sonnet 7 in the text of his letter. The letter "To a Friend" aids greatly our understanding of the poem, whose message closely parallels the overall thrust of the larger epistle. We also see in the sonnet Milton's skillful use of the two parables. Its octave reveals the autobiographical speaker's awareness of his coming of age and the meager degree of accomplishment and personal maturity that he can show for his years:

> How soon hath Time, the subtle thief of youth,
>> Stol'n on his wing my three and twentieth year!
>> My hasting days fly on with full career,
>> But my late spring no bud or blossom show'th.
> Perhaps my semblance might deceive the truth,
>> That I to manhood am arriv'd so near,
>> And inward ripeness doth much less appear,
>> That some more timely-happy spirits endu'th.

The octave also mentions the comparative productivity and maturity of any number of Milton's peers, the "more timely-happy spirits" of line 8. These "spirits" often have been identified as poets who had accomplished more than the young Milton had by this age. It seems more appropriate, however, in light of the sonnet's probable connection with the matter of ordination, to identify them as those Cambridge graduates who had already been ordained into the Anglican ministry at the usual age of twenty-four.[12] In any event, the speaker's modest output and humble station in life are magnified by the advanced position of his fellows, a juxtaposition that sets up the sestet's explicit allusion to the parable of the talents. The octave also demonstrates a tone of anxiety and shame that contrasts sharply with the hopeful attitude of the sestet.

The sestet of Sonnet 7 reads as follows:

> Yet be it less or more, or soon or slow,
>> It shall be still in strictest measure ev'n
>
> To that same lot, however mean or high,
>
> Toward which Time leads me, and the will of Heav'n;
>> All is, if I have grace to use it so,
>>
>> As ever in my great task-Master's eye.

This striking expression of resolution mixed with peace may be understood largely in the context of the sestet's combining the parable of the talents and the parable of the laborers. Each accented word of the opening line of the sestet, as Anna Nardo points out, "deliberate[ly] echoes" the "anxious phrases" of the octave.[13] We see that "Yet be it *less* or *more*, or *soon* or *slow*" reflects "much *less* appear," "*more* timely-happy spirits," "how *soon* hath Time," and "my *late* spring" (emphases added). There is a redemptive use of the language of the octave, transforming the pessimistic tone of those phrases into the hopeful paradigm of the parable of the laborers. This transformation becomes complete as the sestet unfolds. Stephen Booth and Jordan Flyer point out "the leveling implications of 'All is . . . As ever'"; they also note that the use of the word "grace" in line 13, in relation to the divine "task-Master," portrays a God "indifferent to distinctions begun early and service begun late." The allusion to the parable of the laborers "both assists in and justifies the assertion that all the distinctions that have previously been the poem's topics do not matter."[14]

At least on the surface, such divine equity in judgment has a profound effect on the young writer. By identifying himself with the late-chosen laborers of the parable, he gains a freedom that allows him to wait and prepare apart from the fear of being judged an unprofitable servant. At the same time, this freedom enables him to employ all the more diligently those gifts entrusted to him. As in the letter, we see in Sonnet 7 that the parable of the laborers is the vehicle that transforms Milton's potentially fearful identification with the parable of the talents into a positive association.

The declaration of line 13—"All is, if I have grace to use it so"—allows for the paradoxical juxtaposition of the theology of "earned rewards" of the parable of the talents and "the metaphysical, supra-logical justice that prevails in the divine economy" of the parable of the laborers. Lines 13 and 14 also display a paradoxical softening of language describing God. On one hand, the title "task-Master" calls to mind Exodus 1:11, which tells of the "taskmasters" set over the Israelites "to afflict them with their burdens." Left by itself, this title evokes, in the context of this poem, a fearful image of the master of the parable of the talents, whose terrifying judgment awaits the unprofitable servant. And yet this "task-Master" is one who, the speaker hopes, gives him "grace" to "use" his talents in a manner proper to both his calling and to the divinely orchestrated time frame in which that calling fully reveals itself. Thus the young Milton may have a more peaceful relationship to the parable, one in which he may view himself as a "good and faithful servant" (Matt. 25:21, 23) because he is permitted, by the grace of his "great task-Master," to labor earnestly in the preparation necessary for his eventual call to active service. In this we may agree with Nardo's paraphrase of the sonnet's final two lines: "All that I do, if I have grace to employ my inward ripeness thus, is done as ever conscious of being in God's sight and having God's guidance." Nardo observes that this ending "reasserts the central concern of sonnet and letter alike: that Milton believes his action and inaction are in obedience to God's will." In his "conscientious" obedience to the will of God in what he does and does not do, young Milton is one whose identification with the two parables has brought about a kind of spiritual tranquility in the face of potentially devastating circumstances.[15]

Despite this apparent tranquility, the optimism that Milton displays in Sonnet 7 is colored with a certain tentativeness. The possession of grace he speaks of is unmistakably conditional: "*if* I have grace to use it so." Milton's tone indicates that he views whatever grace he may be granted as ultimately still dependent on his faithful exercise of his talents. In no way can he take God's reprieve as license for sloth. Such an outlook is consistent with John Calvin's reading of the parable of the laborers. Warning against interpreting the parable to mean that all will have "equality of . . . heavenly glory," Calvin asserts that "we know that slackness is nearly always the fruit of over-confidence. That is why many sit down in the middle of the race as if they had got to the end."[16] Calvin maintains that the parable teaches God's freedom to call whomever he wishes at whatever time he wishes, without obligation to anyone. But he also stresses that "if anyone infers from this [parable] that men were created for activity and that each has his divinely appointed station, so that he shall not sink into laziness, he will not be twisting Christ's words. We may also gather that our whole life is useless and we are justly condemned of laziness until we frame our life to the command and calling of God. From this it follows that they labour in vain who thoughtlessly take up this or that kind of life and do not wait for God's calling." Not surprisingly, Calvin's exegesis of this parable finally echoes his comment on the parable of the talents: that "Christ . . . means that there is no excuse for the slackness of those who both suppress God's gifts and consume their age in idleness." We also may see a distinct similarity between Calvin's words on God's calling and Owen's discussion of that subject and the parable of the talents. In the end, both parables offer the same basic admonition: Listen carefully for the call of God in your life and labor tirelessly in the particular vineyard to which God has directed you.[17]

Thus it is fitting that whatever solace the parable of the laborers offers the young Milton in the letter "To a Friend" and Sonnet 7 is temporary and does not relax the hold that the parable of the talents has upon his consciousness. Indeed, it would be wrong to think that Milton intended it to do so. For Milton at this period of his life, the parable of the laborers softens the severity of the parable of the talents even as it reinforces its message of diligent labor in the light of God's call. The Milton of the early 1630s, with youth yet on his side, can, for a time, seek solace in the notion that he is working faithfully even as he awaits a final clarity of vocation. The parable of the talents, however, remains within his psyche, tamed for a season but present throughout.

Ad Patrem: Promised Repayment for a Debt Owed

Our understanding of Milton's relationship to the parable of the talents during this period can be informed further by an examination of his Latin verse epistle *Ad Patrem* (*To My Father*), probably written in 1634. A close inspection of *Ad Patrem* sheds important light upon not only Milton's relationship with John Milton Sr. but also how that relationship affected his lifelong preoccupation with that parable. Although *Ad Patrem* assumes that Milton's future career will be among the clergy, we can see that the occasion for the poem is a conflict between the writer and his father concerning the subject of poetry.[18] Milton's epistle reveals that his father "despise[s]" poetry (17), that he has "contempt" for it (56) and considers it "futile [*vanas*] and worthless [*puta*]" (57; "idle or unprofitable" in the Flannagan edition);[19] in fact, he appears "to hate" poetry (67). Young John goes on, however, to write that he does not believe his father really hates poetry, for otherwise he would not have provided his son with an expensive education without pressuring him to enter the law or some other more lucrative profession (67–76). Milton thanks his father for his costly gift even as he attempts to convince him that poetry is genuinely compatible with his education and presumed ministerial career. The epistle's tone exhibits a kind of bashful playfulness; Milton is all too aware of his father's previous generosity toward him even as he seems cautiously confident that he will indulge him yet again. At the same time, the young writer displays an earnest ambition. He does not want to be perceived as a freeloader but rather as a wise investment. Although his words are couched in appropriate humility, Milton expresses his clear intention to achieve greatness in his art, a greatness that will serve as a lasting recompense for his father.

The influence of the parable of the talents is evident at various points in *Ad Patrem*, beginning with the lines that describe the elder Milton's attitude toward poetry. The words "idle" and "unprofitable" echo the master's condemnation of the "wicked and slothful" servant, specifically called "unprofitable" in Matthew 25:30. Milton's language also reflects the parable's in the need he feels to repay his father for what he's been given: "I do not know what gifts of mine could more aptly repay yours—though my greatest gifts could never repay yours" (lines 8–10); and "no requital equal to your desert and no deeds equal to your gifts are within my power" (111–12).[20] The writer's acute awareness of his inability to recompense his father, however, is coupled with an implicit desire to repay him through poetic achievement. "However humble my present place in the company of learned men," Milton writes, "I shall sit with the ivy and laurel of a victor" (101–2). Significantly, this declaration of confidence closely precedes the statement in lines 111–12 quoted above; this juxtaposition seems to say, in effect, "Of course I can't ever repay what you've given me, but just you watch—after you see how successful I'll become, you'll consider yourself recompensed indeed." On one level, therefore, Milton seeks to flatter his father by proclaiming that the gift of his education is genuinely matchless, though on another, Milton clearly intends to repay his father with interest.

Two other factors link *Ad Patrem* and the parable. The first is, as John Shawcross argues, an implicit connection between Milton's father and "God the Father." Shawcross observes two such parallels. In the first, Milton asks, "What greater gift could come from a father, or from Jove himself if he had given everything" (95–96)? The notion that his father's gift is, in essence, equivalent to the greatest gift of the supreme God certainly lends credence to an analogy between the letter and the parable. In the second parallel, which concludes the letter, Milton addresses his "juvenile verses" (115) and declares, "perhaps you will preserve these praises and the name of the father / sung again and again, as an example to a future generation" (119–120, Shawcross's translation). Shawcross suggests a connection with God the Father here, because "his manifestation through the Son is [a] constant example to future generations."[21]

The other factor that connects *Ad Patrem* (and John Milton Sr.) to the parable of the talents is the fact the elder Milton was by trade a scrivener whose income largely consisted of lending money "at eight to ten percent interest."[22] We know that he financed his son's education primarily through the interest from such loans, and that he was hardly a pushover when it came to collecting from lackluster borrowers. J. Milton French observes that he went to considerable lengths to recover money owed him, even if his original debtors were deceased.[23] These points are not made to dispute the affectionate relationship that Milton reportedly enjoyed with his father. Nonetheless, it seems highly plausible that his awareness of his father's sternness toward debtors somehow influenced Milton when he wrote in *Ad Patrem* of his inability to "repay" his father's generosity. It seems equally plausible that the scrivener's position as a moneylender significantly informed young Milton's relationship to the parable, specifically to the master, who berated the "wicked and slothful servant" for failing even to "put [his] money to the exchangers" so that his master would have received it back "with usury" (Matt. 25:26–27).

Assuming that *Ad Patrem* was enough to change his father's mind about the value of poetry, Milton still would have to bring forth a body of work to justify John Sr.'s continued investment. The quick production of such poetry would not have been the immediate concern of young Milton, who saw his current situation very much as one of continued rigorous prepara-tion, and who, as his playfully brash prediction in *Ad Patrem* indicates, foresaw literary success in the not-too-distant future. However, in light of the passage of time and Milton's modest early poetic achievement, the burden of such an unfulfilled boast would have grown increasingly heavy. And while Milton's promise that he would "sit with the ivy and laurel of a victor" falls short of being a sacred oath, we still may recognize, in light of the almost divine status he assigns his father in *Ad Patrem*, the severe obligation under which Milton believed the speaker of an oath placed himself. In *De Doctrina Christiana* Milton writes, "An oath which involves a promise must be kept, even if we lose by it, so long as we have not promised something unlawful" (*CPW*, 6:685). Years later, with his promise to his father largely unfulfilled, we see Milton's relationship to the parable of the talents become progressively more uneasy, a discomfort finally mitigated only by a renewed dependence on the parable of the laborers, whose absence is conspicuous in both *Ad Patrem* and *The Reason of Church-Government* of 1642.[24]

The Reason of Church-Government: Milton's Prophetic Burden

We see the parable of the talents appear again in Milton's writing in the preface to the second book of *The Reason of Church-Government* (RCG). Nowhere else is Milton's engagement with this parable so devoid of any mitigating reference to the parable of the laborers. The prime reason for Milton's failure to take solace in the parable of the laborers is that, by this point in his life, his extended time of preparation has officially come to an end, and the time has come for him to begin in earnest his vocation—not that of Anglican priest, as previously had been expected, but that of a Puritan "polemicist-prophet-poet,"[25] one whose messages will be manifested in both poetry and, for the present, polemical prose. Milton embraces this vocation with the greatest seriousness, and now that it officially has begun, he will no longer resort (at least at this time) to the parable of the laborers to explain his delay in beginning his active labor for the Lord. Rather, Milton sees his unequivocal role and duty as making full use, in the immediate present, of the talents he has been lent. We see in RCG a Milton who has come of age on a number of levels. For one thing, this is his first prose tract that is not anonymous, thus inaugurating, in Fallon's words, "a new phase" in "Milton's self-representation."[26] More important for our discussion, by this point he has renounced definitively, once and for all, his previous vocational aspiration to become an Anglican cleric; as this antiprelatical tract proclaims, Milton has become vocally nonconformist in his ecclesiastical convictions. At the same time, we should in no way view his rejection of Anglican orders as an indication that he has abandoned the role of a leader and spokesman for God in his Puritan community. Quite to the contrary, we may see in *RCG* a man who has set aside the priestly cloth only to take up the mantle of an inspired prophet.

As John Spencer Hill observes, we recognize in *RCG* Milton's progressive movement away from the religious and political sentiments of England's mainstream, along with his practice of "mediat[ing] the divine will to a progressively dwindling band of the elect," a practice that "manifested itself in an increasing self-identification with the Old Testament prophets."[27] Such self-identification with the Hebrew prophets may be seen prominently in the preface to the second chapter of *RCG*, where Milton discourses on the "onerous responsibilities of the prophetic office":[28]

> Though they cannot but testify of Truth and the excellence of that heavenly traffick which they bring against what opposition, or danger soever, yet needs must it sit heavily upon their spirits, that being in God's prime intention and their own, selected heralds of peace, and dispensers of treasure inestimable without price to them that have no pence, they finde in the discharge of their commission that they are made the greatest variance and offence, a very sword and fire both in house and City over the whole earth. That is that which the sad Prophet *Jeremiah* laments, *Wo is me my mother, that thou hast born me a man of strife, and contention.* And although divine inspiration must certainly have been sweet to those ancient profets, yet the irksomnesse of that truth which they brought was so unpleasant to them, that every where they call it a burden. (*CPW*, 1:802–3, emphasis in original)

When Milton speaks of the weighty "burden" that God's prophets must bear, he is in fact affirming his "own calling" and justifying "his speaking out against the bishops."[29] Milton sees himself in no uncertain terms as "a prophet called to testify and teach,"[30] one who has been called by God to proclaim God's pure message of truth to England; and the heaviness of this burden is in no small part the result of the inevitable rejection by the majority that Milton, like Jeremiah, must face.[31] Such rejection, however, is ultimately a small price to pay for the assurance that he is on the side of God's truth.

The notion that Milton applies this prophetic "burden" to himself is made all the more clear when we examine it in light of an earlier statement he has made, the first and shorter reference to the parable of the talents to be found in the preface to *RCG*'s second book:

> He who hath obtain'd in more than the scantest measure to know any thing distinctly of God . . . remembring also that God even to a strictnesse[32] requires the improvment of these his entrusted gifts, cannot but sustain a sorer *burden* [emphasis added] of mind, and more pressing than any supportable toil, or waight, which the body can labour under; how and in what manner he shall dispose and employ those summes of knowledge and illumination, which God hath sent him into this world to trade with. (*CPW*, 1:801)

Here again we see Milton displaying an acute self-awareness that the privilege he has been given requires him to use such gifts in a faithful manner. His self-identification with the parable of the talents here manifests itself in a specifically prophetic context, and in a definitively *active* sense as well. His identification with the parable is no longer portrayed in relation to noble work he will accomplish in the future. The ante, we may say, has been upped for—and by—Milton, and the expectation that he must perform in the present is both undeniable and inescapable. In the words of Barbara Lewalski, "his talents" must be put to "immediate use . . . to help overthrow the prelates and thereby advocate reform"; and Ryan Hackenbracht rightly observes that in *RCG* Milton "identifies [polemical] publication as the proper employment of his talents."[33] The pressure of this immediate expectation also causes a change of disposition, revealed in the tone of Milton's writings. Gone is the almost playful manner in which Milton previously discussed his postponed entrance into the vineyard where his talents must eventually be traded. Instead, we see a Milton whose relationship to the parable of the talents is burdensome indeed. This burdensome relationship reveals itself in an almost neurotic attitude that seems inflated in its sense of the import of his task, and strangely oblivious to the fact that his audience is genuinely ignorant of the origin of the personal emotional turmoil that he displays before it.

Milton's anxiety in this section of *RCG* is exacerbated by his explicit connection with Jeremiah,[34] and this self-conscious linking of himself to the Old Testament prophets, and indeed this viewing himself, like Jeremiah, as a mouthpiece for God, merits our asking whether Milton is actually claiming a degree of divine inspiration here that would equate his words with the scriptural utterances of Jeremiah. This matter of Milton's view of his own writing in relation to the written scripture is particularly relevant to Milton's composition of *Paradise Lost*, and indeed various scholars believe that Milton claims that his epic is tantamount to scripture. A number of scholars have connected Milton's prophetic persona in *RCG* to that in *Paradise Lost*, although none of them has gone so far as to assert that Milton believed that his utterances in *RCG* were tantamount to scripture.[35] It seems best to suggest that at this point in Milton's career, the kind of prophetic mantle he assumes suggests that he believes himself to be inspired by the Holy Spirit, but not in a way that makes the kind of superlative claims to inspiration he suggests in his great epic. That the prophetic office he lays claim to in *RCG* seems more general in nature may be seen in the extension of his discussion of the prophetic burden to Sophocles's Tiresias (*CPW*, 1:803), and is further demonstrated by Milton's later comment concerning the divine inspiration of poets: "These abilities, wheresoever they be found, are the inspired guift of God rarely bestow'd, but yet to some (though most abuse) in every Nation: and are of power beside the office of a pulpit, to imbreed and cherish in a great people the seeds of vertu [and various other godly traits]" (1:816). That Milton here suggests that such divine poetic inspiration transcends time, culture, and even religion indicates that he is speaking of a more general spiritual inspiration, one that should not be equated with the special revelation accorded to the biblical scriptures. Milton's words also speak to another phenomenon in his own life—that he has transferred his previous vision for himself as serving in the dual vocation of priest-poet to now serving in the dual vocation of an inspired prophet-poet, one whose "power" is "akin to and perhaps surpassing that of the pulpit."[36] Some seventy-five years earlier, the Second Helvetic Confession had declared, "The preaching of the Word of God is the Word of God."[37] It appears that Milton believes that what he is doing in *RCG* is tantamount to such inspired preaching. But it is curious that Milton's discussion of the inspired poets throughout the ages also lays on them the mantle of the prophetic office; it also speaks volumes that he will see his own poetic calling as increasingly interwoven with the prophetic vocation.[38]

It is within his initial digression concerning the prophetic burden that Milton embarks upon the lengthiest explicit discussion of the parable of the talents in any of his writings, and we must emphasize that his explicit self-identification with that parable here is in the clear context of his self-identification with the prophetic office he has taken upon himself. With a tone of fastidious and even morbid self-examination, Milton ponders the hypothetical scenario of his fate if he, having seen that the church had been "brought under heavy oppression," and given that "God [had] given me ability the while to reason against that man that should be the author of so foul a deed," failed (even if the church were in fact delivered) to make use of "those few talents which God at that present hath lent me" (*CPW*, 1:804). Such a scenario, Milton concludes, would be nothing short of disastrous for him:

> I forsee what stories I should heare within my selfe, all my life after, of discourage and reproach. Timorous and ingratefull, the Church of God is now again at the foot of her insulting enemies: and thou bewailst, what matters it for thee or thy bewailing? when time was, thou couldst not find a syllable of all that thou hadst read, or studied, to utter in her behalfe. Yet ease and leasure was given thee for thy retired thoughts out of sweat of other men. Thou hadst the diligence, the parts, the language of a man, if a vain subject were to be adorn'd or beautifi'd, but when the cause of God and his Church was to be pleaded, for which purpose that tongue was given thee which thou hast, God listen'd if he could heare thy voice among his zealous servants, but thou wert domb as a beast; from hence forward be that which thine own brutish silence hath made thee. Or else I should have heard on the other eare, slothfull, and ever to be set light by, the Church hath now overcom her late distresses after the unwearied labours of many her true servants that stood up in her defence; thou also wouldst take upon thee to share amongst them of their joy: but wherefore thou? (1:804–5)

I quote this passage at length to show the extent to which Milton's conscience and imagination are consumed by this self-appropriated vision of the parable. This fearful outburst is noteworthy on several levels. Milton demonstrates here that the certainty of his prophetic calling is matched by an equal degree of certainty concerning the fearful reckoning that God will inevitably exact from his gifted prophet. Indeed, nowhere is the dreaded responsibility that characterizes Milton's prophetic burden more forcefully stated.[39] And we recognize in these words a Milton whose overwhelming conviction of his divinely given mission has driven him to articulate an inflated sense of self-importance. This sense not only causes Milton great

inner turmoil but also spills over into a kind of bizarre psychic exhibition-
ism that presumes upon the sensibilities of his audience with no apparent
recognition of how inappropriate such a display might be.

We must consider how strangely out of place this outburst seems in the
context of what is supposed to be a rational (note the tract's title's opening
word, *Reason*) discourse concerning proper church government.[40] While
Milton's era did not make a clear distinction between the personal and the
polemical, we may still recognize that such forthright self-disclosure would
have seemed odd indeed to his unsuspecting audience. The oddness of such
a self-conscious ejaculation is intensified in light of the fact that *RCG* was
the first booklet Milton had published under his own name, and that the
privileged education he enjoyed would hardly have been common knowledge to his readership. Certainly, some readers were aware that Milton was
the author of *Of Reformation*, *Of Prelatical Episcopacy*, and *Animadversions*,
along with a handful of published poems, and *A Mask Presented at Ludlow
Castle* but in any case he could not have been considered a celebrity about
whom the public would know such personal information. And yet Milton
seems to assume such knowledge on the part of his audience. He makes
passing mention of his privileged background, but he does so in a vague
manner. He gives his audience no real indication of the privileges he enjoyed.
Some readers would probably have known of Milton's advanced degree
from Cambridge, but it seems unlikely that any but Milton's personal
acquaintances would have known anything of his extended time of study
while in Hammersmith and Horton, which seems to be the funded "ease
and leasure" to which Milton primarily refers in the passage quoted above.

Perhaps this bizarre digression can be explained best by hypothesizing
that Milton has become so consumed with his identification with the parable of the talents that it has become second nature to him—even to the
extent that he assumes that his audience must have some knowledge of his
situation as well, however illogical an assumption. Here too we may see
some telling signs of a narcissistic personality in Milton.[41] We may distinguish *RCG* from the other works we have discussed thus far in that the
letter "To a Friend," Sonnet 7, and *Ad Patrem* were each given to highly
specific and limited audiences: individuals who were personally close to
Milton and would have had intimate knowledge of his educational opportunities and the expectations that would accompany the recipient of such
indulgence. Clearly, *RCG's* audience is far broader, and we have no reason

to believe that these readers would be particularly interested in Milton's personal anxieties, nor would they understand their origin. And yet Milton writes about such matters as if his audience were as familiar with his situation as the readers of the earlier three works.

In any event, in *RCG* more than in any other work, Milton demonstrates a thoroughly negative use of the parable of the talents, a use bereft of the softening effects of the parable of the laborers seen in Sonnet 7 and the letter "To a Friend." Having completed his extended preparation, he does not appeal to that parable to gain another reprieve from God. Rather, the Milton of *RCG* seems wholly dependent on his own efforts to appease his heavenly Father and escape the fate of the unprofitable servant.

Sonnet 19: Bitterness and Grace

Roughly a decade later, however, when Milton in Sonnet 19 ("When I consider how my light is spent") again identifies with the unprofitable servant in his most famous reference to the parable of the talents, he returns to the parable of the laborers.[42] This reintroduction is used at first to expose a weakened, discouraged Milton whose desire to serve God as a prophet-poet ironically manifests itself in bitterness toward God himself; by the end of the poem, however, the parable of the laborers has become a vehicle of grace to teach the self-important, self-condemning Milton that his service to God is under the authority of a sovereign Lord who will accomplish his perfect plan with or without Milton's heroics.

The sonnet's octave is characterized by the autobiographical speaker's discouragement and bitterness, something that his combined use of both parables works to accomplish.[43] When the parable of the talents is referred to explicitly in line 3, we see its connection with all that precedes and follows in the poem. There has been plentiful speculation concerning exactly what the "one Talent which is death to hide, / Lodg'd with me useless" (3–4) really is. Traditional scholarly consensus holds that the "Talent" in question is Milton's poetic gift, and that his "light" that has been "spent" is his eyesight.[44] These conclusions, while not wrong, are too limited. As Haskin points out, Milton's notion of "talent" in the sonnet includes his poetic gift but encompasses a broader gifting.[45] It is better to recognize his poetic gift in conjunction with the prophetic office with which he has been entrusted, even as it is more appropriate to view Milton's vocation as a poet in conjunction with his calling as a prophet.

In the same way, the "light" of Sonnet 19 is certainly on one level Milton's eyesight on one level. However, as with "Talent," Milton moves beyond a limited interpretation of such a potent word. In the context of the poem, "light" encompasses the spiritual enlightenment and direction given to believers, and also the responsibility of the believer to shine forth God's glory and goodness before the world. These aspects of "light" are especially pertinent to Milton's prophetic "office." We may understand his anxiety in relation to his perceived failures as a prophet of God, one whose prophetic energies, for the past decade or more, have been dedicated inordinately to political pamphleteering. Milton's self-doubt here includes his dissatisfaction with his poetic output, but only as his role as a poet is viewed within the larger context of his prophetic office. Indeed, in retrospect we may see the occasion for Sonnet 19 as a turning point in Milton's prophetic career, one in which he seems to eschew the parochialism of his prophetic role within the Puritan political cause in favor of a more universal prophetic office that is conducted more properly through the vehicle of poetry. This vehicle finds its apex in *Paradise Lost*, but it is displayed with immense power in this very sonnet, a sonnet that has touched countless readers in ways that Milton's political prose—the vehicle through which so much of his "light" had already been "spent"—has never done.

Early in the poem, then, we see a discouraged, disconsolate prophet, one whose blindness exacerbates his situation with a stinging and seemingly perpetual irony. We also may note the speaker's sincere desire to labor for God in spite of his disability. Although his "Talent" is "Lodg'd with me useless," he announces that "my Soul [is] more bent / To serve therewith my Maker, and present / My true account" (4–6). His desire to serve, however, is not based on genuine New Covenant faith but is rather a response to his own fear of the unfair, even malicious God he perceives. The sonnet continues: "lest he returning chide; / Doth God exact day-labor, light denied, / I fondly ask" (6–8). That Milton's speaker is thinking wrongly about God here is evidenced by the resolution of the sestet, and Michael Lieb is right to note the absence of Christian sentiment in the octave.[46] Indeed, the speaker demonstrates a misunderstanding of the parable here, even as he misunderstands God himself. In his resolution "to serve," the speaker is not demonstrating "a right will" (contra Roger Slakey), or, for that matter, right reason.[47] He is falling into the same error as the unprofitable servant, whose misperception of his lord as "an hard man" (Matt. 25:24) inspires him to hide his single talent in the ground.[48] Indeed, the speaker's misperception of the parable and God drive him to try to earn God's favor apart from recognizing his grace, and the result of such self-justifying efforts is further frustration and bitterness.[49]

This bitterness is particularly evident when Milton's speaker rejects his once-beloved parable of the laborers. We see that the question "Doth God exact day-labor, light denied" contains a scornful allusion to that parable.[50] It is ironic that this parable, the very text that rescued Milton from his struggles with the parable of the talents in the 1630s, should now reappear in the "fond murmur" of line 7. Clearly, the grace that was received appreciatively by a late-blooming priest in training is less than satisfactory for a blind, middle-aged prophet-poet mired in depression, a man whose lack of hope is no doubt exacerbated by God's choice not to heal his physical disability. (And we may note the significance, irony, and poignancy of the fact that Jesus speaks the parable of the laborers shortly before he heals two blind men who beg him for restored sight [Matt. 20:29–34];[51] Jesus answers their cries for sight, but not Milton's.) Indeed, Milton's spurning of the parable here demonstrates a frightening degree of hubris that transcends even the self-importance Milton displays in *RCG*. I say this because the speaker in essence has transferred his own self-loathing to God himself; that is, because he experiences such disgust toward himself, he portrays God, through the vehicle of the parable of the talents, as effectively rejecting him. What is more, the speaker has turned that perceived divine rejection into an accusation against the character of God. We see here that Milton is in fact "playing God" on two levels, for he simultaneously pronounces God's judgment upon himself even as he pronounces judgment on God.

Milton's rejection of the parable of the laborers manifests itself in his distortion of its message of grace. In the parable, the lord of the vineyard exemplifies God's grace by granting a full day's wage to those laborers he hired only for the final hour of the workday. The speaker's "fond murmur"—which echoes the complaint of the discontented workers in the parable of the laborers, who "murmured against" the lord of the vineyard (Matt. 20:11)—turns this idea on its head. Milton's speaker insinuates that, unlike the generous lord of the parable, God would expect a full day's work from one who lacks the ability to work in the first place. Given the occasion for Milton's poem, we may rightly see in this line the image of a blind man groping helplessly to perform a task that requires sight, or perhaps that of laborers struggling to harvest their crop in the dark of a starless night. At the same time, we can imagine our prophet-poet striving to serve the very God who has withheld blessing from him. In all this, the speaker displays a marked self-righteousness, and to the reader familiar with Milton's earlier affection for the parable of the laborers, this self-righteous striving is particularly noteworthy. Indeed, we can see that Milton has moved even further away from a focus on God's mercy than in *RCG*. There, Milton's public spiritual anxiety strikes us as odd, but it reflects the feelings of a man who, having completed his extensive preparation, earnestly desires to prove himself useful. In Sonnet 19, however, Milton's speaker actually belittles the parable he formerly cherished, rejecting its message of grace. And although Milton's blindness and the obvious sadness expressed in the octave give us genuine sympathy for the speaker, we still may recognize on his part a certain spiritual betrayal against God even as he accuses God of betraying him.

The speaker's words end at this point. Sonnet 19's remarkable turn takes place in the middle of line 8, introducing the character Patience, whose rebuttal of the speaker's murmur makes up the sestet. The speaker's silence is deeply revealing. For what had been the active complaint of an achievement-consumed individual is replaced by his passive reception of Patience's words. We do not get the impression that Milton's speaker willingly steps aside from his posture of active complaint; rather, we see that he has been moved by a higher power—a messenger of the very God he has been accusing. And we sense that there is something at once irresistibly strong and disarmingly gentle about this displacement. To be sure, on one level there is great force behind Patience's words; for the speaker to attempt a rebuttal would be not only foolish but also impossible. And yet, as he hears Patience speak, he recognizes that the God he has distrusted indisputably has in mind the best interests of his cantankerous servant.[52]

Even as Patience's words demonstrate God's compassion toward Milton's speaker, they also reveal a justification of God's character and a clear articulation of the speaker's relationship to him. God's absolute sovereignty is seen throughout Patience's speech, and the need for the speaker to accept this humbly is reinforced by the biblical allusions in the sestet. The words "God doth not need / Either man's work or his own gifts" (8–9) call to mind

Psalm 50, in which God rebukes the Israelites for thinking that he is some-how dependent on their sacrifices. God declares, "I will take no bullock out of thy house, nor he goats out of thy folds. For every beast of the forest is mine, and the cattle upon a thousand hills. . . . If I were hungry, I would not tell thee; for the world is mine, and all the fulness thereof" (50:9–10, 12). In both Sonnet 19 and Psalm 50, those who receive God's rebuke are chastised for thinking that they can act in a way that will somehow enhance God's position. In Psalm 50, those individuals are commanded, "call upon me in the day of trouble: I will deliver thee, and thou shalt glorify me" (15). God does offer them a chance to glorify him, but only through their utter depen-dence upon him. Having been rebuffed in their attempts to add to his glory, they are told in no uncertain terms that they are the needy ones, and that their most acceptable service to God is a humble display of such need.

A second and oft-mentioned allusion appears in Patience's statement "who best / Bear his mild yoke, they serve him best" (10–11). As many have noted, the words "mild yoke" echo Jesus's words in Matthew 11:28–30, where Jesus tells his listeners to take his "easy" yoke upon them.[53] For purposes of our discussion of Sonnet 19, however, we would also do well to quote Mat-thew 11:25–26: "At that time Jesus answered and said, I thank thee, O Father, Lord of heaven and earth, because thou hast hid these things from the wise and prudent, and hast revealed them unto babes. . . . Come unto me, all ye that labour and are heavy laden, and I will give you rest. Take my yoke upon you, and learn of me; for I am meek and lowly in heart: and ye shall find rest unto your souls. For my yoke is easy, and my burden is light." Jesus's opening statement declares that God's wisdom and blessings are not given to those commonly considered wise, but to the humble. This statement is followed by an invitation to the hurting to place themselves in a relationship of total reliance upon Jesus himself. Again, this biblical passage parallels the message of Sonnet 19. Especially if we expand our understanding of "light" to include the spiritual inspiration offered to our author, we see that because of his own pride he finds himself in a state of spiritual deprivation. We see in Jesus's words that the invitation to take up his yoke is also an invitation to learn from him. This dual invitation, however, is predicated upon a faith in him that exhibits complete dependence on him, imitating the humility of the one who describes himself as "meek and lowly in heart" (11:29). For our exhausted prophet-poet, the admonition to "Bear his mild yoke" is ultimately the gateway to restored spiritual light, a light that is superior to that previously expended, for it is purified by the humble obedience of one who better serves a humble master.

These two biblical allusions set the stage for the allusion to the parable of the laborers seen in the concluding line: "They also serve who only stand and wait." These words, Patience's final utterance, reinforce the emphasis on humble dependence on God and the true service rendered by such an attitude. This line recalls the situation of the laborers who have been "standing idle in the marketplace" (Matt. 20:3) for the first eleven hours of the workday, waiting to be hired. Having been hired by the lord of the vineyard at the eleventh hour, they work a single hour and are given a full day's wages, equal to those workers who were hired early in the morning. Noting the connection between the parable and line 14 of the sonnet, E. A. J. Honigmann points out that Milton uses "wait" to mean "stay in expectation";[54] the "idle" workers, by virtue of their willingness to wait to be chosen, demonstrate their total dependence on the call of the vineyard's lord to be made useful. When they are finally called, they are rewarded as much for their patient waiting as for their actual service rendered.

Clearly, this kind of "service" is hardly the sort that Milton the prophet-poet, the busy, experienced veteran of the pamphlet wars, would value for himself or anyone else. Indeed, the early-hired laborers, who scornfully "murmured against" the lord of the vineyard for granting the others an equal wage (Matt. 20:11), have essentially the same attitude as that of the speaker earlier in the poem: an attitude that disdains the grace of God in favor of calling attention to their own strenuous efforts.[55] Like Milton's speaker, these murmuring laborers are silenced. Reminding them of their agreement to work for "a penny" for the day, the lord instructs them, "Take that thine is, and go thy way: I will give unto this last, even as unto thee" (20:14). In a word, these laborers have no right to complain, for they have not been cheated. Ultimately, what they are angry about is the lord's generosity—and the preposterous notion that eleven hours of useless waiting combined with one hour of work should be of equal value in his sight to their twelve hours of hard labor. Yet it is this very same absurd notion that the speaker is forced to accept by the final line of Sonnet 19: God's economy is not that of humankind, not even that of a prophet-poet who has considered all his previous labor service unto God. As with the early-hired laborers, such an idea is offensive to the speaker. It is in the end, however, the very thing that can rescue him, both from his self-hatred and from his anger toward God.

In a thought-provoking recent article, Tobias Gregory has specifically challenged my reading of Sonnet 19, contending that no allusion to the parable of the laborers is present. But to make his argument, Gregory actually misrepresents what I have written, confusing my discussion of *Milton's use* of the parable of the laborers in the sonnet with *my own personal interpretation* of the parable. Gregory writes, "Urban thinks that . . . the point of the parable" is "'When they [the laborers] are finally called, they are rewarded as much for their patient waiting as for their actual service rendered.'"[56] But if one looks at the context of what I have written (see two paragraphs above), it is clear that I am not offering my own interpretation of the parable but rather stating how Milton, in Sonnet 19, creatively makes use of the parable for his own benefit. Milton is performing what Gregory calls "one of Milton's staple autobiographical moves: the impulse to turn disadvantage to advantage."[57] Gregory also notes that the owner of the vineyard, or householder, asks the last-called laborers, "why stand ye here all the day idle?" (Matt. 20:6), adding that the word translated as "idle" in Matt. 20:6 (Greek *argos*) means "lazy, inactive"; and he contends that "to make Urban's reading work, we have to understand 'idle' as implying perseverance. The householder's question . . . does not support such an interpretation. It sounds more like a rebuke."[58] But this is not my reading; it is Milton's—or my reading of Milton's reading, to be precise. And even if the householder's words in 20:6 can be interpreted as a rebuke—which is debatable, both because according to the standard *Greek-English Lexicon of the New Testament*, *argos* in Matthew 20 simply means "unemployed,"[59] and because the laborers in the parable have no employment opportunities until the householder calls them—it would be consistent with Milton's use of the parable (and of parables in general) to turn such a situation to his advantage.

Also intriguing is the argument of Carol Barton, who takes issue with what she calls traditional Milton scholarship's assertion that the sonnet's final line is "an anthem to passive resignation" that exhibits a "namby-pamby 'pity poor me'" attitude. Barton sees Sonnet 19 as "the first major milestone in [Milton's] progress toward reformation of the heroic ethos of classical antiquity," noting that the sonnet represents "the first in a series of penetrating inquiries that lead from the personal ('What can I do now?') to the universal ('What can any Christian man do now?')." Although Barton's dismissal of earlier criticism is rhetorically overstated, and although her rhetoric obfuscates and minimizes the genuine spiritual weariness of the sonnet's speaker, and his absolute need to depend completely on God's grace, her observation that the final line anticipates the speaker's reentry into vigorous action is valuable indeed, and reminds us that obedient resignation before God precedes such action in a number of Milton's later works. As Barton also notes, in *Samson Agonistes*, "'patience' . . . is the corollary—not the antithesis—of the 'invincible might' of the heroic Deliverers who 'with winged expedition / Swift as the lightning glance' (lines 1283–84) execute God's errands";[60] and, as I discuss at length in chapter 10, Samson's own final victory is preceded by his complete submission to the law of God (lines 1386–87). We may also observe that in *Paradise Lost*, Adam's entrance into his new life of active service before God in a fallen world is preceded by his meek resolution to obey and depend on God for all things (12.561–71). Similarly, in *Paradise Regained*, the Son's active resistance to Satan's temptations is preceded by his own obedient following of his Father's mysterious path into the wilderness, a path that offers no specific information concerning the purpose of the Son's journey (1.290–93); he reaffirms his dependence upon his Father in his very first words to the disguised Satan (1.335–36). For Milton's speaker in Sonnet 19, submission to God's will does in fact offer hope for the kind of active service that he longs for, and indeed this submission foreshadows Milton's ultimate fulfillment of his vocation as an epic prophet-poet whose pure submission to God and his word enable him to write the great scriptural epics and drama of his later years.

Such hope, however, in no way diminishes the utter weariness of the sonnet's speaker and his need for complete dependence on God.[61] Any active service must await God's bidding in God's time. In light of the struggles of the octave, and of Milton's life, we may surmise that the resolution of line 14 is hardly easy for Milton's speaker—or Milton himself—to accept. While he must finally be thankful for this resolution, we sense that he accepts it not because it is palatable but because it is a divine decree that he has not the strength to fight; furthermore, we recognize that the demons tormenting the speaker in the octave of Sonnet 19 have not been vanquished permanently; they will return often enough to plague him. Nonetheless, we see here again that the parable of the laborers has given Milton relief from himself and his burdensome relationship to the parable of the talents. Clearly, as the years have elapsed and as his battles, accomplishments, and disappointments have accumulated, it has become increasingly difficult for him to accept the grace of God as exemplified in the parable of the laborers. At the same time, in his blindness, his exhaustion, his despair, he recognizes that he ultimately has no recourse but to receive the very grace that on one level he wishes he didn't need. This acceptance of grace also demonstrates a maturing in Milton's relationship to the parable of the laborers. Whereas in the letter "To a Friend" and Sonnet 7 that parable serves to stave off his self-condemning tendencies while he prepares for active service, in Sonnet 19, written with more life behind him than ahead, the parable does much more than enable him to bide his time. It offers a divine perspective that transcends the autobiographical speaker's self-focused concerns and obsessive self-representation as the unprofitable servant. By turning Milton's attention away from his own limitations and toward God's transcendent power and the wider message of God's word,[62] the parable is a vehicle of grace that offers relief from past failures and divine hope for an uncertain future.

2

Samson's Late Call
Parabolic Tension and Resolution in
Samson Agonistes

The Miltonic tension between the parables of the talents and of the laborers continues to manifest itself throughout *Samson Agonistes*. This subject has received some slight attention, but to my knowledge has received no developed analysis.[1] These two parables are represented in *Samson Agonistes* in a way reminiscent of Sonnet 19. Indeed, I submit that the use of these parables in *Samson Agonistes* is best analyzed in relation to Sonnet 19, which shares with Milton's drama so many similarities in themes and in diction.[2] We may in fact see *Samson* as a kind of extended development of the sonnet, and Sonnet 19 and the parables offer valuable interpretive frameworks with which to analyze the drama, and particularly to argue for a regenerative Samson whose redemptive progress ultimately resolves much of the tension between the two parables.

Before I proceed with this analysis, however, I must outline a few interpretive principles that figure significantly in my discussion of *Samson Agonistes*, Milton's dramatic poem that depicts the blinded, imprisoned Samson's growth in self-understanding, self-control, and humility before God and the written law that anticipates his final act of destruction against the Philistines at Dagon's temple. First, I share the view of the many Miltonists who recognize a strong self-referential connection between the poet and his protagonist, and this recognition significantly strengthens the connection I see between the autobiographical speaker of Sonnet 19 and the Miltonic Samson of *Samson Agonistes*.[3]

Second, I find persuasive Michael Lieb's contention that Samson should be placed in the combative context of the time of Milton's *Defenses* (1651 and

1654, respectively), even as I believe that the final composition of the drama extended beyond the Restoration and that, given its placement after *Paradise Regained* in their 1671 publication in one volume, it should be regarded as Milton's final poem.[4] Such a dating of *Samson* allows us to recognize in Milton's drama the internal and external conflicts of both time periods in Milton's life, even as it acknowledges that Sonnet 19—generally dated between 1651 and 1655—also stands chronologically in the background of *Samson*'s composition.

Third, my confidence in Samson's regenerative progress is strengthened greatly by Lieb's and David Loewenstein's outstanding work demonstrating, through the many similarities between the violence celebrated in *Samson* and that espoused in both Milton's own prose writings and the works of many of Milton's radical Protestant contemporaries, that Milton indeed believed Samson's destruction of the Philistine temple to be God-ordained, however disturbing this notion is to the modern-day reader.[5] Nonetheless, the analysis I offer here is based on a close reading of *Samson* using the two parables in question and Sonnet 19 as my interpretive rubrics. Although my reading gains confidence from the numerous polemical texts that Lieb and Loewenstein have written to justify their often unpopular arguments for Samson's redemptive violence,[6] my own argument relies primarily on how the text of *Samson* itself ultimately seeks to resolve the tension between the parables and fulfill the still-anticipated call to active service with which Sonnet 19 concludes.

Finally, in my close reading of *Samson*, I suggest that in several specific instances the words of the Chorus are used to help propel Samson further down the path of redemptive progress. I am aware that a favorable reading of the Chorus fell out of fashion several decades ago, and I do not claim that its judgment is impeccable, but I do contend that the Chorus—which at times speaks better than it knows—offers Samson a number of valuable insights, and that those insights are all the more recognizable if we consider them in relation to the two parables and the sonnet.[7]

Samson and Manoa

The first appearances of the parable of the talents and the parable of the laborers in *Samson Agonistes* occur in Samson's initial conversation with his father, Manoa. Throughout the play, Manoa displays a kind of naïve optimism that combines genuine hope in God with a failure to fully recognize the enduring consequences of his son's sin.[8] Manoa tells Samson,

> Be penitent and for thy fault contrite,
> But act not in thy own affliction, Son;
> Repent the sin, but if the punishment
> Thou canst avoid, self-preservation bids;
> Or th' execution leave to high disposal,
> And let another hand, not thine, exact
> Thy penal forfeit from thyself; perhaps
> God will relent, and quit thee all his debt;
> Who evermore approves and more accepts
> (Best pleas'd with humble and filial submission)
> Him who imploring mercy sues for life,
> Than who self-rigorous chooses death as due;
> Which argues over-just, and self-displeas'd
> For self-offence, more than for God offended. (502–15)

To be sure, much of Manoa's advice is very good. He is right to encourage Samson to humble himself before God, repent, and seek his grace—this can also be seen, on one level, as the primary message of Sonnet 19. And Manoa's admonition to Samson to refrain from self-destruction and ask God to save his life is certainly sound. More complicated, however, is his statement "perhaps / God will relent, and quit thee all his debt." These words may call to mind the debt owed by the unprofitable servant in the parable of the talents, and Manoa's statement on at least one level seems to challenge that parable.[9] The parable itself makes clear that each of the servants will have to give an account of the talents with which he has been entrusted. And we should note that the unprofitable servant does in fact give back to his master the sum he was given. Strictly speaking, he paid back his "debt" to his lord. And yet he was judged to be "wicked and slothful" and was "cast . . . into outer darkness" (Matt. 25.26, 30). Is it wishful thinking on Manoa's part to think that God will cancel the debt of his faithless son?

Ultimately, I think we need not criticize Manoa for this suggestion. He recognizes the extent of God's grace, and he implores Samson to seek it to the fullest degree. There is, however, a sense in which he underemphasizes the extent to which God, even in the generosity of his grace, will continue to hold Samson accountable for the earthly consequences of his sins.[10]

Manoa hopes that God will grant Samson life, freedom, and (as we see later) even restored eyesight. Indeed, Michael Lieb observes that Manoa "errs . . . in assuming that the full return of [Samson's] strength can be realized without appropriate suffering."[11] To be fair, Manoa's optimism is an appropriate response to Samson's despair. But there is a naïveté in Manoa's outlook, and his perception of God's mildness seems almost as misinformed as his earlier evaluation of Samson, who, Manoa claims, "now no more [can] do [the Philistines] harm" (486).

The echoes of Sonnet 19 and of the two parables can be heard quite loudly as Samson and Manoa's conversation continues. Samson asks,

> by which means,
> Now blind, disheart'n'd, sham'd, dishonor'd, quell'd,
> To what can I be useful, wherein serve
> My Nation, and the work from Heav'n impos'd,
> But to sit idle on the household hearth,
> A burdenous drone. (562–67)

Samson's language here echoes the sonnet in a number of places. His desire to "be useful" is that of the sonnet's speaker, who laments "that one Talent which is death to hide, / Lodg'd with me useless" (3–4)—an echo made all the more clear by Manoa's reference to Samson's strength as "that gift" (577). As in the sonnet, Milton shows in the person of Samson his uneasy relationship with the parable. Samson has been given, "from Heav'n," a "work" to perform. Now, however, the "Talent" or "gift" he has been given to perform this work has been taken away and he has thus been rendered "useless." We know more of Samson's situation, however, than we do of the circumstances of the sonnet's speaker. We can be quite sure that whatever culpability lies with Dalila and the Philistines, Samson himself is to blame for his situation, and he acknowledges this even in his despair. Samson—whom Milton takes pains to depict "as a free moral agent" throughout the drama[12]—is ultimately solely at fault for the wasting of his talent and the accompanying affront to God.[13]

In any event, Samson shares the despair exhibited by the speaker of Sonnet 19. He resists Manoa's wish to bring him home to their country. He says he would rather stay where he is, but this statement is not based on any hope that God will somehow use him in his present location. Instead,

Samson says that he would rather remain active in a state of slavish labor than to rest at home in Israel:

> Here rather let me drudge and earn my bread,
> Till vermin or the draff of servile food
> Consume me, and oft-invocated death
> Hast'n the welcome end of all my pains. (573–76)

Samson's self-destructive tone persists throughout his speech; indeed, we may say that his desire to stay and work in Philistia is a desire to die as quickly as possible, his death hastened by his labor.[14] His desire to remain active is aimed at the most useless of purposes—the expiration of his own life to no one's gain. He expresses his disdain for rest in language that seems to spurn the parable of the laborers. For Samson, "to sit idle" (566—note the diction of Matt. 20:3, 6) is the most despicable of conditions. But his disdain is not based on a proper understanding of rest and sitting still. He is right to spurn a life of self-indulgent rest—such behavior is, after all, what caused his current state of misery. But he does not value the kind of resting and waiting that brings about spiritual healing and allows the one who keeps still to discern God's call upon his life. Far from the sort of "stay[ing] with expectation" with which Honigmann describes the "standing idle" of the not-yet-chosen laborers,[15] Samson cannot recognize the value of standing still before God. Perceiving inaction through the clouded lens of his own sinful life experience, he regards with bitter disdain the notion of rest.

In response to Samson's despair, Manoa continues in his own optimistic rhetoric. In a speech that again echoes the diction of Sonnet 19, he says,

> Wilt thou then serve the *Philistines* with that gift
> Which was expressly giv'n thee to annoy them?
> Better at home lie bedrid, not only idle,
> Inglorious, unemploy'd, with age outworn.
> But God who caus'd a fountain at thy prayer
> From the dry ground to spring, thy thirst to allay
> After the brunt of battle, can as easy
> Cause light again within thy eyes to spring,
> Wherewith to serve him better than thou hast;
> And I persuade me so; why else this strength
> Miraculous yet remaining in those locks?

> His might continues in thee not for naught,
> Nor shall his wondrous gifts be frustrate thus. (577–89)

Manoa should be commended for both his hopeful attitude and his God-focused (as opposed to Samson's self-focused) recognition that God remains willing to use the gifts he has given Samson. As before, however, Manoa's insights are limited by his own ideal scenario. We note with some suspicion that, for Manoa, God's use of Samson's "wondrous gifts," like Samson's ability "to serve him better than thou hast," is contingent upon God's causing "light again within thy eyes to spring." Manoa's limited perspective here may be seen as an optimistic version of the speaker's lament in Sonnet 19 that, because of his "spent" light, he is unable to "serve [his] maker" (1, 4). In both cases, appropriate service to God is contingent upon the light of eyesight, and neither the sonnet's speaker nor Manoa can conceive of a genuinely "useful" exercise of the God-given talents in question apart from eyesight.

Patience Introduced

In any event, Samson is not persuaded by his father's words, and after Manoa's departure he describes himself as hopeless and also prayerless, excepting only his request for "speedy death" (650). At this point, however, another important element is introduced—patience.[16] The Chorus says,

> Many are the sayings of the wise
> In ancient and in modern books enroll'd,
> Extolling Patience as the truest fortitude,
> And to the bearing well of all calamities. (652–55)

Again we hear echoes of Sonnet 19, and they become louder as the Chorus elaborates:

> But with th'afflicted in his pangs thir sound
> Little prevails, or rather seems a tune,
> Harsh, and of dissonant mood from his complaint,
> Unless he feel within
> Some source of consolation from above. (660–64)

In other words, the patience of virtuous human willpower, the kind that even "noble pagans" could champion, is not sufficient for one suffering the extreme hardship Samson now endures. Such an individual must be touched by divine compassion to endure with genuine patience; such is the patience Milton writes of in the proem to book 9 of *Paradise Lost*, when he celebrates "the better fortitude / Of Patience and Heroic Martyrdom" (31–32), over and against the artificial sort of heroism Milton derides in the surrounding verses.

This sort of patience waits hopefully, often amid great suffering, as reflected by its Latin root *patiens*—the present active participle of *patior*, to bear, endure, or suffer—with the hope that God will show forth his grace upon his subject through a renewed call to action. As Judith Anderson notes, for Milton, "patience becomes action, rather than simply giving way to action or being replaced by it."[17] Yet such patience also awaits God's grace on God's own terms—and this is what distinguishes such genuine patience from Manoa's limited understanding of divine grace. Moreover, one who exhibits such Miltonic patience understands that true patience might indeed culminate in martyrdom, as with Milton's most patient hero, the Son in *Paradise Regained*, whose patient resistance of Satan's temptations qualifies him for the ultimate "Heroic Martyrdom," his Passion—also derived from *patiens*—on the cross, by which he later effects the salvation of the world.[18] Despite the attempts of certain scholars to portray the protagonists of Milton's 1671 volume as antithetical to each other,[19] Anderson points out that "doubtless a major reason why *Paradise Regained* and *Samson Agonistes* were published together is that they share a central concern with patience."[20] And the Son's and Samson's patient endurance in preparation for the *patiens* of their heroic martyrdoms[21] suggests that the venerable but often discounted view that Milton's Samson is a type of Christ—more recently affirmed by Russell Hillier in light of various similarities between Hugo Grotius's *Christus Patiens* (1608) and *Samson Agonistes* (and suggested by Milton himself in the preface to *Samson*, where he mentions church father Gregory Nazianian's composition of "a Tragedy, which he entitl'd, *Christ Suffering*")[22]—is legitimate indeed, however unpalatable it may be to post-9/11 sensibilities.

Looking back at Sonnet 19, we can see that genuine patience is what quiets its speaker, who desires to act prematurely to replace his suffering instead of waiting in suffering in preparation for future action in response to God's call. In that poem, patience is not the voice of human reason but the messenger and instrument of God himself. Such God-given patience is what Samson needs, and we shall see that he later embraces it. At this point, however, he is still a prisoner of his own self-loathing. That Samson is making some internal progress, however, becomes evident in his interaction with his estranged Philistine wife, Dalila, soon enough.

Samson, Dalila, and the Rejection of Perverse Rest

Samson's progress while conversing with Dalila may be evaluated in terms of waiting and patience. In this scene, despite the bitterness Samson demonstrates, he consciously chooses to reject a perverted form of rest and move closer to the appropriate ideal of patience. After Dalila explains to an incredulous Samson that she has betrayed him to the Philistines not out of malice but because of her weakness, she invites him to live out the rest of his days with her in sensuous rest, an arrangement she's confident she can procure from the Philistine authorities.[23] She tells Samson,

> though sight be lost,
> Life yet hath many solaces, enjoy'd
> Where other senses want not their delights
> At home in leisure and domestic ease,
> Exempt from many a care and chance to which
> Eyesight exposes daily men abroad. (914–19)

Dalila's offer, obviously, should be very attractive to a blind man engaged in torturous slave labor. But Samson resists this temptation, recognizing that a life of indulgence would place him in an even more debased slavery than that which he now endures. He replies,

> How wouldst thou use me now, blind, and thereby
> Deceivable, in most things as a child
> Helpless, thence easily contemn'd, and scorn'd,
> And last neglected? How wouldst thou insult
> When I must live uxorious to thy will
> In perfect thraldom, how again betray me . . . ? (941–46)

Although these words may display more simple common sense than devotion to God, we should acknowledge that Samson has moved beyond his past slavery to sexual pleasure and the resultant dishonor of such self-seeking inaction. Indeed, we may detect in Samson's employment of the verb "use" (941) an ironic twist on the parable of the talents. Samson does not want Dalila to "use" him as her perversely acquired talent. If he were to give in to her invitation, he would show himself, once again, to be an unprofitable servant, even as *she* hears the words "Well done, good and faithful servant" from Dagon and his priests. To Samson's credit, he recognizes that he can sink lower than he already has. There is a prison worse than his current one, and he tells Dalila, "This Gaol I count the house of Liberty / To thine whose doors my feet shall never enter" (949–50). He also demonstrates some progress in the area of self-control (at least in terms of knowing his limitations) by refusing her request to touch his hand, "lest fierce remembrance wake / My sudden rage to tear thee joint by joint" (952–53). Instead, he tells her, "At distance I forgive thee, go with that" (954). He sends her off "in righteous anger,"[24] but with no bodily contact of any sort. Thus, in this encounter he resists the temptations of sexual license and vindictive violence, both of which he indulged in generously in earlier days. Moreover, in displaying patience and forgiveness, and by accepting blame for his earlier sin with Dalila, Samson places himself in a position where he may be genuinely restored to God.[25]

After Dalila's vitriolic departure, we also witness in Samson a greater resignation to the will of God, an attitude that precedes the disposition of patience he is moving toward. He tells the Chorus,

> So let her go, God sent her to debase me,
> And aggravate my folly who committed
> To such a viper his most sacred trust
> Of secrecy, my safety, and my life. (999–1002)

This statement is curious on a number of levels. In it, Samson simultaneously acknowledges his own culpability for his situation and God's sovereign hand in punishing him. Moreover, his words here betray no bitterness toward God or his judgments, something that already places his progress beyond that of the speaker in the octave of Sonnet 19. We cannot yet see, however, whether Samson has moved toward the kind of hopeful disposition that might open him to God's call upon his life.

Harapha and the Temptation to Premature Action

We begin to see such hope in Samson's next encounter, with the giant Harapha. We also see the tension or "contest" between the two parables, the talents and the laborers, more acutely in this scene. We recognize in Samson not only a renewed willingness to hope that God will use him for his glory but also a strong impulse to use his gift of strength prematurely, before he is genuinely called. Overall, however, his interaction with Harapha, whom recent critics have acknowledged to be a formidable and articulate opponent,[26] demonstrates further progress in Samson's character as he moves toward an attitude of godly patience. From the very start, Harapha antagonizes Samson with insults, and Samson answers the giant's taunts by challenging him to battle, a challenge Harapha is loath to accept. Nothing extraordinary is revealed at the beginning of this exchange, but when the giant claims that Samson's strength was brought about trickery, Samson is quick to defend not himself but God. Harapha says,

> spells
> And black enchantments, some Magician's Art
> Arm'd thee or charm'd thee strong, which thou from Heaven
> Feign'd'st at thy birth was giv'n thee in thy hair. (1132–35)

Samson retorts:

> I know no spells, use no forbidden Arts;
> My trust is in the living God who gave me
> At my Nativity this strength . . .
> . . . .
> For proof hereof, if *Dagon* be thy god,
> Go to his Temple, invocate his aid
> With solemnest devotion, spread before him
> How highly it concerns his glory now
> To frustrate and dissolve these Magic spells,
> Which I to be the power of *Israel's* God
> Avow, and challenge *Dagon* to the test,
> Offering to combat thee his Champion bold,
> With th' utmost of his Godhead seconded:
> Then thou shalt see, or rather to thy sorrow
> Soon feel, whose God is strongest, thine or mine. (1139–41, 1145–55)

Here, Samson articulates something new—a "trust . . . in the living God" in the present. Although his challenge to Harapha may be criticized for being overeager, he clearly issues it with faith in God and for the glory of God. Like the faithful servants of the parable of the talents, he desires to be used by God—what's questionable is his timing. From Samson's current perspective, it is entirely appropriate for him to use his talent "with interest" by defeating his boisterous foe. All the while, however, he is being called to stand and wait. Indeed, he must learn still more before he is called finally to act.

That said, Samson continues to progress. His growing hope in God becomes even more evident after Harapha's next barrage of insults. The giant tells Samson,

> Presume not on thy God, whate'er he be,
> Thee he regards not, owns not, hath cut off
> Quite from his people, and delivered up
> Into thy Enemies' hand. (1156–59)

"This temptation," writes F. Michael Krouse, "is designed to call up the fear [in Samson] that he has been abandoned by his God."[27] It is the temptation of despair. Samson responds, however, in an attitude of humble faith. In reply to Harapha's taunt, he says,

> All these indignities, for such they are
> From thine, these evils I deserve and more,
> Acknowledge them from God inflicted on me
> Justly, yet despair not of his final pardon
> Whose ear is ever open; and his eye
> Gracious to re-admit the suppliant. (1168–73)

This statement again demonstrates Samson's growth. Not only does he continue to acknowledge God's justice in his continuing afflictions but he also demonstrates a genuinely mature hope in God—a hope that demands nothing of God but simply acknowledges his gratuitous mercy. Indeed, Samson here "balances contrition with faith in God's ultimate forgiveness."[28] In this, not only has Samson moved past the purposeless despair he articulates earlier in the drama but he has also now surpassed Manoa's naïve optimism. Unlike Manoa, Samson now speaks of God's mercy on God's terms, unmixed with inappropriate expectations of restored eyesight, and certainly without any notion that restored eyesight is the prerequisite for service to God. Rather, he recognizes that trust in God is the true prerequisite for service. Finally, whatever we may say about his premature challenge to Harapha, we see in the words above Samson's willingness to "stand

and wait" for something significant indeed: God's forgiveness. The hope in God he now demonstrates ultimately puts him in a position where he can again be used by his Lord in powerful ways.[29] He is almost there. He needs now to allow patience to perfect its work in him.

After a few more bitter exchanges, Harapha leaves without physical altercation. In speaking to the Chorus, Samson appears to suffer a relapse of sorts when he says,

> But come what will, my deadliest foe will prove
> My speediest friend, by death to rid me hence,
> The worst that he can give, to me the best.

And yet the despondency of these lines is mitigated by the prophetic nature of those that follow:

> Yet so it may fall out, because thir end
> Is hate, not help to me, it may with mine
> Draw thir own ruin who attempt the deed. (1262–67)

Although on one level Samson continues to despair of his life, his prophetic utterance may well suggest his restored position in God's sight. William O. Harris observes that Samson's "attitude toward death has undergone change. No longer invoking it, praying for it, he patiently awaits it and, in that calmer mood, comes so near an understanding as to foreshadow unknowingly the triumphal catastrophe."[30] Furthermore, the Chorus does not rebuke him but celebrates how wonderful it is for righteous but oppressed persons

> When God into the hands of thir deliverer
> Puts invincible might
> To quell the mighty of the Earth, th' oppressor. (1270–72)

Patience, the Philistine Officer, and Samson's Departure

Having celebrated Samson thus, however, the Chorus adds a caveat to its enthusiastic proclamation, a caveat that ultimately sets the scene for Samson not only to demonstrate the message of the parable of the laborers but also, having done so, to use his talent to the greatest extent. Here is the Chorus:

But patience is more oft the exercise
Of Saints, the trial of thir fortitude,
Making them each his own Deliverer,
And Victor over all
That tyranny or fortune can inflict.
Either of these [i.e., to be a delivering hero or a patient saint] is in thy lot,
Samson, with might endu'd
Above the Sons of men; but sight bereav'd
May chance to number thee with those
Whom Patience finally must crown.
This Idol's day hath been to thee no day of rest,
    Laboring thy mind
More than the working day thy hands. (1287–99)

These words, spoken just before the arrival of the Philistine Officer who summons Samson to the great feast, are among the most significant of the entire drama. On the one hand, the Chorus does not discount the possibility that Samson may act again as the great deliverer of the Israelite nation. On the other hand, it makes the profound (if perhaps obvious) observation that Samson, in his blindness and his inability to wage war as he once could, may very well be called to the role of the patient saint. Indeed, its words may be seen as a subtle exhortation: in his condition, Samson had better be the sort of patient, wise believer the Chorus speaks of. For Samson to attempt to engage in the heroic battle exploits of the past would be foolish, even absurd. Whatever strength has been restored, the role of the traditional warrior hero is simply not an option for him. In this sense, his gift/talent of strength truly does seem useless, or at least comparatively so. And yet, the Chorus implies, Samson's blindness may turn out to be a gift in its own right—because it enables him to receive the divine gift of patience.[31] We cannot seriously believe in Samson's becoming a man who can receive patience, who can patiently "stand and wait" for God's greatest call upon his life, apart from his loss of eyesight. But when the Chorus speaks these lines, we recognize that the once impetuous hero has become, against all expectations, a patient man, and the Chorus's words do more than encourage Samson or plant an edifying suggestion in his mind; they effectively confirm the character trait that has been developing in him throughout the drama. Moreover, by the drama's end, we understand that the Chorus has spoken more truly than it knows. Indeed, Samson is ultimately able to transcend the either/or scenario the Chorus outlines, for God's Spirit empowers him to carry out his final heroic act precisely *because* he submits himself to the work of a patient and obedient saint. And having become a patient man, one who is willing to "stand and wait" amid suffering, he has become eligible to be used by God—and to use his great talent—in a mightier way than ever before. As Lieb notes, Samson, having largely fulfilled "the passive (in the sense of *patiens*) implications of the concept of *agonistes*," has in fact through patience "perfected strength through weakness" and will soon demonstrate *agonistes* actively; he need only wait for his master's call to active labor.[32] Nevertheless, Samson remains in need of the Chorus's additional insight and wisdom, which aid him greatly in the scenes that follow.

Samson's new gift of patience is demonstrated, albeit imperfectly, in his interaction with the Philistine Officer who bids him, by the order of "our Lords" (1310), to come and perform at Dagon's feast. Although their exchange is marked by disagreement and conflict, it is also comparatively civil. The Officer, we may note, is a relatively gentle man. He performs his duty as a messenger for his superiors, and his words implicitly separate his person from their commands. He is, as Irene Samuel notes, "rather kindlier than his office requires."[33] For his part, Samson is neither threatening nor rude to the Officer. His thrice-given refusal is motivated primarily by his desire to obey the Hebrew law, which, according to Samson, "forbids at thir Religious Rites / My presence" (1320–21). While Samson's fastidious interpretation of the law at this moment is ultimately overturned at the Spirit's prompting, his conscientious submission to God and his written word indicates Samson's noteworthy spiritual progress away from his libertine past, and it demonstrates that he has developed into a man who may now rightly discern the Spirit's leading.[34] Furthermore, although the Officer refers to Samson's attitude of refusal as "stoutness" ("pride, arrogance," "obstinancy"),[35] Samson has made no offensive remarks to him; neither has he made disparaging comments about the lords in question—he merely criticizes this particular command. To be sure, the Officer is not pleased with their interaction. But neither is Samson's response vitriolic enough to bring about his speedy execution. Rather, while the Officer departs to convey Samson's refusal to the Philistine lords, Samson is granted time to interact with the Chorus and the opportunity to gain more of the wisdom that patience brings. By the time the Officer returns, Samson will have learned his lesson.

The first word that the Chorus speaks after the Officer's departure is highly revealing, recalling the opening line of Sonnet 19: "Consider" (1348), the Chorus encourages him, reminding him of the increasingly tense situation between him and the Philistines. Again demonstrating his movement toward patience, Samson does consider the Chorus's words, and it is his thoughtful, reflective attitude that enables him to recognize the call of God in, ironically, the Philistine lords' command. At the beginning of their conversation, however, Samson remains rightly skeptical of attending Dagon's feast, and in his words we see the reappearance of the parable of the talents.

> Shall I abuse this Consecrated gift
> Of strength, again returning with my hair
> After my great transgression, so requite
> Favor renew'd, and add a greater sin
> By prostituting holy things to Idols;
> A *Nazarite* in place abominable
> Vaunting my strength in honor to thir *Dagon*? (1354–60)

Samson is legitimately concerned about improperly using his great God-given talent to abet a pagan event and thus once again dishonor the talent giver and himself. But the irony of Samson's concern is that if he maintains his convictions without "considering" the Chorus's words, he actually risks burying his talent in the ground. By listening to the Chorus, however, and leaving open the possibility of serving God in this bizarre situation, Samson takes the part of the waiting workers in the parable of the laborers; and his willingness to accept this unlikely call, ironically, empowers him ultimately to fulfill both parables.

During his discussion with the Chorus, and amid great internal struggle, Samson begins to sense this call from God. Here, at the eleventh hour, having stood without significant physical movement for the duration of the drama, Samson, in his developed patience, submitted to God's written law, is able to discern the inner authority of God's Spirit that prompts him to follow a call that that appears to transgress the written law.[36] Having just affirmed that one who displeases God because of "the fear of Man . . . / Shall never, unrepented, find forgiveness" (1374, 1376), he says,

> Yet that he may dispense with me or thee
> Present in Temples at Idolatrous Rites
> For some important cause, thou needst not doubt. (1377–79)

We can see from Samson's use of "dispense"—a word that suggests a monetary image and again recalls the parable of the talents—that he continues to desire to be used by God; indeed, he hopes that God himself will gain a "profit" of sorts through him, in that God's longtime investment in Samson will once again "yield dividends" against the Philistines. After the Chorus speaks of its own inability to understand how all this will take place, Samson continues:

> Be of good courage, I begin to feel
> Some rousing motions in me which dispose
> To something extraordinary my thoughts.
> I with this Messenger will go along,
> Nothing to do, be sure, that may dishonor
> Our Law, or stain my vow of *Nazarite*.
> If there be aught of presage in the mind,
> This day will be remarkable in my life
> By some great act, or of my days the last. (1381–89)

In the short time between the Philistine Officer's departure and return, Samson's growth in patience—a patience that he understands may culminate in his death—has given him the wisdom to sense God's call, to know how to maintain faithful purity in a potentially compromising situation, and to recognize the enormity—and probably the finality—of the service that awaits him. In addition, he demonstrates patience's humility in suffering by agreeing, like Christ himself, to be led by his captors to serve as a lowly form of entertainment—because Samson is convinced of God's call now to labor for his glory. That his mission will be blessed by God is confirmed by the Chorus, which, at his departure, says,

> Go, and the Holy One
> Of *Israel* be thy guide
> To what may serve his glory best, and spread his name
> Great among the Heathen round:
> Send thee the Angel of thy Birth, to stand
> Fast by thy side. (1427–32)

The Chorus's words again echo Sonnet 19, recalling Patience's words that "who best / Bear his mild yoke, they serve him best" (10–11). In his humility, Samson now demonstrates that he is one who bears (typologically) the "mild yoke" of Christ. And because he acts for the glory of Israel's God, he serves him—and his glory—best. The second part of the Chorus's blessing also reflects the sonnet's language. The Chorus commands that Samson, who will finally achieve his mission only by continuing to "stand and wait" at the feast itself, be given the Angel of the Lord (generally equated with God himself) "to stand / Fast by thy side." Even as Samson stands and waits on God, God will stand and wait with him. With such an ally, the blind, patient Samson will use his God-given talent as never before.

Manoa's Misunderstanding

After he leaves with the Officer, Samson's patience and his increasing sensitivity to God's call become all the more clear in light of the comments Manoa makes when he returns to the scene. Having heard Manoa's resolve to ransom Samson's freedom and care for his son for the rest of his days, the Chorus remarks, "Thou in old age car'st how to nurse thy Son, / Made older than thy age through eyesight lost" (1488–89). The Chorus here again speaks more truly than it knows. To be sure, Samson's blindness disables him and makes him dependent in one obvious sense. But this is not the only sense in which he is now "older than" Manoa "through eyesight lost." Samson's blindness has given him wisdom beyond his own years, certainly beyond anything that Manoa possesses. In contrast to Samson's willingness to be employed by God in unusual ways, Manoa continues to insist that God must heal Samson in order to use him. Manoa declares,

> I persuade me God had not permitted
> His strength again to grow up with his hair
> Garrison'd round about him like a Camp
> Of faithful Soldiery, were not his purpose
> To use him further yet in some great service,
> Not to sit idle with so great a gift
> Useless, and thence ridiculous about him.
> And since his strength with eyesight was not lost,
> God will restore him eyesight to his strength. (1495–1503)

Manoa's illogical statement proves a foil to the wisdom of Samson's words before Samson departs for the feast. Indeed, even as Samson in his patience places himself in a situation where he may fulfill both parables, Manoa's words make it sound as if Samson is incapable of fulfilling either one without the restoration of his sight. From Manoa's perspective, a blind Samson can do nothing but "sit idle"—not waiting to be called but in a posture of perpetual inactivity, with no expectation ever of serving. Manoa having determined this, Samson's gift/talent of strength consequently must be perpetually "Useless." Ironically, in expecting God to perform the miracle of reversing Samson's blindness, Manoa places limitations on God—and, for that matter, on Samson. To think that God must heal Samson in order to use him is, we may say, shortsighted, and this belief reveals Manoa's ignorance of how his son has grown and matured since Manoa's departure early in the drama.

Samson's Death: Patient Waiting and the Service of Manifold Destruction

The Messenger's report of Samson's heroic death confirms both Samson's new gift of patience and his fulfillment of both parables. The Messenger relates that Samson's role as the Philistines' entertainer was humiliating from the beginning:

> At sight of him the people with a shout
> Rifted the Air clamoring thir god with praise,
> Who had made thir dreadful enemy thir thrall. (1620–22)

The Messenger also notes, however, that Samson's reaction to all this was one of self-control and dignity: "He *patient* but undaunted where they led him, / Came to the place" (1623–24, emphasis added). This patience in suffering, we soon discover, is also exactly what enables him to come to the advantageous position in which he soon finds himself. We may surmise that if Samson had responded to the crowd's glee by attacking them, he would have been subdued after doing comparatively little damage. By exercising his new gift of patience, however, he is given the opportunity to inflict maximum destruction upon his enemies.[37]

Significantly, Samson's final act of heroism, the Messenger tells us, is set up by his standing and waiting:

> At length for intermission sake they led him
> Between the pillars; he his guide requested
> (For so from such as nearer stood we heard)
> As overtir'd to let him lean a while
> With both his arms on those two massy Pillars
> That to the arched roof gave main support
> . . . .
> And eyes fast fixt he stood, as one who prayed,
> Or some great matter in his mind revolv'd. (1629–34, 1637–38)

Samson is brought to the pillars during the "intermission"—a time during which people wait in expectation for what comes next but during which nothing significant is supposed to happen. And, obviously, Samson's own posture during this time is to stand and wait—and to pray. It is during this final time of standing and waiting that Samson receives his final call from God.

Indeed, the degree to which Samson at this point is in step with the Spirit of God has been observed by a number of critics. John Spencer Hill writes that Samson's destruction of the temple "is an act of responsive choice, a free action in which the will of the instrument co-operates with, and is submerged in, the will of God." Similarly, Albert R. Cirillo sees this point as a critical juncture in Samson's "movement . . . from darkness to light." "At this moment," Cirillo comments regarding Samson's silent prayer, "Samson achieves his closest communion with God, as the actual intense light of noon becomes the inner light which displaces the darkness of his despair."[38] More recently, in a study that portrays Samson as the violent champion of Israel's terrifying God—a God whom the Semichorus calls "our living Dread" (1673)—Michael Lieb contends that here Samson "implement[s] the full force of God's awesome power. . . . He is 'our living Dread' incarnate."[39] Relating Lieb's concept to the parables in question, we may say that Samson, in receiving this late, final call from his master, now being fully subsumed in God's will and power, uses his God-given talent of strength to its greatest conceivable degree.

In what are quoted as his final words, Samson calls attention to the two talents that now allow him to perform his final act. He tells the Philistines that he has performed according to their orders, "as reason was, obeying" (1641); now, however, he will perform another act, "to show you of my strength, yet greater" (1644). These words outline the two-step process of Samson's final act. First, in his obedience to their initial command, he exercises reason. Clearly, this use of reason was brought about by his patience while suffering humiliation. And the outcome, as we have already seen, is to bring him to his current place of advantage next to the pillars. Second, he uses his strength, his famous gift, to complete his final act. But he could not properly use this primary talent had he not exercised his newer one— that of patience, or patient reason.

Upon hearing this news, the Chorus, addressing the dead Samson, paraphrases Judges 16:30 by proclaiming that in his death "thy slaughtered foes [are] in number more / Than all thy life had slain before" (1667–68). It is part of the biblical account that, in his blindness, Samson slew more of Israel's enemies than he ever had when he could see. This in itself is perhaps enough for us to affirm that Samson fulfills the parable of the talents nobly, having not hidden his great gift but exercised it in a way that yields exponentially greater returns. Milton's Samson, however, also fulfills the parable in a much more subtle way. Upon his death, we see that Samson has actually doubled his talents. He had been given the gift of strength, and not only has he resisted the temptation to forsake that gift for a life of ease; he has added to his gift of strength the gift of patience, ultimately fulfilling Milton's ideal of "the better fortitude / Of Patience and Heroic Martyrdom." As we have seen, it is Samson's patience that prevents him from squandering his strength on various offending parties throughout the drama; furthermore, patience enables him to stand and wait for God's call, to follow when that call begins, to stand and wait again—in just the right place—in the midst of that call; finally, patience enables him to hear the final divine command to act, to complete the call he has been given. Again, we see both the parable of the laborers and the parable of the talents at work here, with the patience needed to fulfill the parable of the laborers enabling him also to fulfill the parable of the talents with his final act of strength.

The last words of *Samson Agonistes* are spoken by the Chorus, whose speech, as Michael Spiller observes, Milton uses to direct his audience's understanding of Samson, his final actions, and his legacy.[40] The Chorus proclaims God's faithfulness toward his chosen people, Samson in particular, whom it describes as God's "faithful Champion" (1751). These words recall those of the master in the parable of the talents to each of his profitable employees—"Well done, good and faithful servant"—they are the opposite of the master's rejection of the unprofitable servant with whom Milton so famously identified. We sense that Milton's Samson will also receive a favorable eternal welcome. Yet we also recognize that such a welcome is not the result of Samson's consistent obedience. Having squandered his early blessings, Samson was made to stand idle for a time—but only, in the end, to show forth God's grace and faithfulness in even greater ways, and, we should add, to bless Samson himself in previously unknown ways.[41] It is Samson's position as one of the late-called laborers that affords him his new gift of patience. And it is patience that enables him to use his strength in unprecedented ways, for Samson offers both talents to the Lord who originally gave him only the first—Samson, ironically, like the good and faithful servants, has doubled his talents. Truly, it is Samson's unexpected participation in the parable of the laborers that enables him to fulfill positively—and not negatively—the parable of the talents.[42]

3

Abdiel and the Son

Milton's Ideal Relationship with the Two Parables
in Paradise Lost and Paradise Regained

The previous chapter's analysis of Samson demonstrates Milton's representation of the resolution of his sometimes tortured relationship with the
parable of the talents—a resolution finally achieved only by the grace given
through the parable of the laborers. More idealized representations of
Milton's relationship with the parable of the talents are seen in his depiction
of the loyal angel Abdiel in *Paradise Lost* and the Son in *Paradise Regained*.
Abdiel best represents Milton's image of the ideal servant of God, whose
fidelity is unswerving, who unflinchingly sides with the righteous cause
against all opposition, whose faithfulness is unequivocally rewarded by the
God he so loyally serves. Because Abdiel's faithful service is so resoundingly
consistent, he does not require the mitigating grace of the parable of the
laborers that is so needed by Milton in his 1633 letter "To a Friend," by the
autobiographical speaker of Sonnet 19, and by Milton's Samson. And yet
both Abdiel and the Son, in their unfallen natures, manifest the perfect ideal
between the parable of the talents and the parable of the laborers, in a
manner reminiscent of, yet transcending, how Milton balanced those two
parables in his 1633 letter.

Abdiel: "Servant of God, Well Done"

The connection between Abdiel and the commended servants in the parable
of the talents is straightforward: The Father's words to Abdiel upon his
arrival at God's throne following Abdiel's rebuke of Satan—"Servant of
God, well done" (6.29)—clearly reflect the parable's master's words to his
profitable employees: "Well done, good and faithful servant" (Matt. 25:23;

cf. 25:21). But, as we shall see, elements of the parable of the laborers are also evident and, as with Milton's Samson, the connection between the two parables and Abdiel is demonstrated in part by the similarities between the language of Sonnet 19 and words pertaining to the loyal angel.

Abdiel—who demonstrates, as Sharon Achinstein writes, such "familiar Miltonic themes" as "absolute loyalty to God, persistence in the face of public rebuke, solitary resistance, bold speech acts," and "a desire to convince through argument"—has long been viewed by critics as a character with whom Milton strongly identifies.[1] This identification is affirmed forcefully by James Holly Hanford: "Of all the angels, Abdiel, apostate from the ranks of Satan, is most completely representative of Milton in this phase of his personality. We have seen the poet building up in himself from childhood the ideal of the just man, isolated from his fellows, indifferent to their scorn, adhering to the lofty principles of his own nature, and dependent on no reward save God's approval. So Abdiel, fearless in his righteousness, defies the multitude and appears before the throne to enjoy in fullest measure the perfect witness of all-judging Jove."[2] Similarly, Stephen Fallon, who calls Abdiel Milton's "alter ego," sees in Abdiel the fiery rhetorician Milton of the republican *Defenses* and *The Readie and Easie Way*, and he writes that "Abdiel stands in or speaks for the Milton who early and late figured himself as the lone voice of godliness, the lone just man."[3]

Hanford's and Fallon's comments broadly connect Milton to Abdiel, but Abdiel's rebukes of Satan in books 5 and 6 offer additional insight into Milton's close relationship with the loyal angel. These passages suggest a correlation between Abdiel's disdain for Satan's presumed monarchy and Milton's support of the Puritan cause. In book 5, Abdiel berates his leader, Satan—who is indignant over the Father's command that the angels worship the Son and foments rebellion in his speech to his angelic squadron—for calling God a tyrannical monarch over the angels, whom Satan claims are "ordain'd to govern, not to serve" (5.802). Abdiel responds that God does not seek to oppress them but is "bent rather to exalt / Our happy state under one Head more near / United" (5.829–31). Abdiel argues that God's magnanimity toward his creations stands in stark contrast to Satan, who amid his bogus cry for equality has "place[d] thyself so high above thy Peers" (5.812). Michael Lieb notes similarities between Abdiel's words and Milton's support of the Puritan rebellion against King Charles, who, "maintaining a false divinity . . . paradoxically corrupts himself and invites destruction."[4]

Seen from this perspective, Milton's rebellion against Charles is no more a rebellion against God's ordained ruler than is Abdiel's rebellion against Satan, who, like Charles, falsely sets himself up as the rightful ruler of his peers. Thus Milton's rebellion, like Abdiel's, is in fact an act of devotion to God, the rightful ruler of all.[5] Along the same lines, Lieb notes the irony of Abdiel's referring "to himself as a 'dissenter' and to the host of God as 'sectarians' (6.145–47)." Obviously, Abdiel and his brethren are loyalists to God even as they dissent against Satan's rebellion. The same principle holds true for Milton and his Puritan allies: "Although the Puritans were looked upon as dissenters and sectarians, they were, in fact, conformists to a higher order, one that not only condoned but commanded holy war in a righteous cause."[6]

The Father commends Abdiel using language taken directly from the parable of the talents: "Servant of God, well done" (6.29). Let us examine the Father's speech, to which Hanford refers in the statement quoted above:

> Servant of God, well done, well hast thou fought
> The better fight, who single hast maintain'd
> Against revolted multitudes the Cause
> Of Truth, in word mightier than they in Arms;
> And for the testimony of Truth hast borne
> Universal reproach, far worse to bear
> Than violence: for this was all thy care
> To stand approv'd in sight of God, though Worlds
> Judged thee perverse. (6.29–37)

Recognizing the connection between Milton and Abdiel, we see in these words the ultimate divine justification for Milton's tireless efforts on behalf of the Puritan cause and truth itself. In the end, whatever the earthly success or failure of Milton's various battles, his final vindication would come from the only one who could judge purely: God himself.

It is hard to accept that Milton could identify completely with Abdiel, not only because of the angel's unswerving purity but also because of his remarkable ability to uphold the righteousness of God without any taint of self-justification or self-defense. Contrasting Abdiel's words to Satan with Sonnet 19, Stanley Fish writes, "Abdiel's acceptance of his uselessness is impressive precisely because it is unconscious. He is able to regard his own superfluousness as a matter of praise and feel no personal injury (sense of injured merit) at all."[7] Fish's words describe Abdiel but not Milton, whose own tender ego displays itself so prominently throughout his polemical tracts. But Abdiel represents Milton's *ideal* servant of God. To be sure, the Milton we see in Sonnet 19 and *Samson Agonistes*, and the tension evident in those works between the two parables, is a more accurate portrayal of Milton's overall character. Nonetheless, we may fairly look at Milton's identification with Abdiel as his own ideal relationship with the parable of the talents, one that demonstrates not only unqualified fidelity to God but also an attitude of pure confidence before God, a certainty of the justice of his cause and his consistent dedication to it, free from the fear of being judged unprofitable by the God who has entrusted him with his noble talents.

Elements of the parable of the laborers are also evident in Abdiel's character, and they buttress, not challenge, Abdiel's role as the ideal servant of God. The connections between Abdiel and the two parables are demonstrated in part by the parallels between Sonnet 19 and the Abdiel narrative. Significantly, as we have seen, Abdiel's initial rebuke of Satan is immediately preceded by Satan's rebellious assertion that he and his yet-unfallen angelic listeners are "ordain'd to govern, not to serve" (5.802). The affinity of the word "serve" with Sonnet 19's final line becomes all the more pronounced in Abdiel's physical response to Satan's speech: Abdiel "St[ands] up" (5.807) to resist and oppose Satan.[8] But given his zealous rhetorical challenge to Satan, does Abdiel "stand and wait"? In a very real sense, he does just that. Although his words are forceful, Abdiel does not challenge Satan physically but rather seeks to persuade him and his fellows, urging repentance.[9] He does not overstep his role by prematurely moving into violent action, which would have been unwise and counterproductive. Rather, he chooses to flee the scene, amid the abuse of his fellows and former leader, to seek the presence of his true master.[10]

When he reaches God's sacred hill, the implicit connections between Abdiel and the parable of the laborers become apparent. The language of Sonnet 19 is again evident when the Father calls Abdiel one who "stand[s] approv'd" (6.36), and indeed at that moment Abdiel stands and waits for his master's call. Here, Abdiel's situation is reminiscent of the last-called laborers in the parable, for he is the final angel to report for military duty against Satan.[11] And yet, paradoxically, he has already been pronounced a good and faithful servant before he enters the battle. In his standing and waiting, he already stands approved, with the blessing received by the faithful servants of the parable of the talents. And when Abdiel joins the legions of angels who oppose the fiend, his active service is unmistakable: after Satan ironically tries to turn the message of the parables and Sonnet 19 on its head—accusing the loyal angels of being those who "through sloth had rather serve" (6.166)—Abdiel refutes Satan, affirms the freedom that comes from serving God, and delivers a mighty blow to Satan's head. Here, in both word and deed, Abdiel personifies the ideal servant of God, one who is equally faithful—and blessed—in both his patient standing and waiting and his explicit and perfectly timed action.

Charles W. Durham observes that Abdiel "deserves to be emulated because he is the only character in the poem except the Son who is praised directly by the Father and because his obedience and love most clearly parallel those of the Son."[12] The parallels between Abdiel and the Son are also evident with relation to parabolic themes. Like Abdiel, the Son in *Paradise Lost* is commended by the Father for his obedience before he takes any concrete physical action in the epic, and his "standing and waiting" is particularly evident in that he does not enter into the war in heaven until called by the Father on its final day. In the war, the Son is indeed the last-called laborer, and, transcending the equal wages of the parable, his reward is not merely equal to those who fought the entire battle but greater than all others. And yet the Son's role as the last-called laborer is superlatively paradoxical. He is the last-called laborer in the war, and his future incarnation as Jesus will follow and fulfill the labors of many prophets and holy persons before him, but in truth he has been laboring with the Father from the beginning, as his role creating the heavens, the earth and its inhabitants (book 7), and the angels (as Abdiel attests in 5.835–41) makes plainly. evident.

The Son's Patient Heroism in *Paradise Regained*

Abdiel's paradoxical heroism in *Paradise Lost* is eclipsed by that of the Son in *Paradise Regained*, another highly self-referential Miltonic character who epitomizes the ideal melding of the good and faithful servant in the parable of the talents and the patient last-called workers in the parable of the laborers. Without directly noting connections between the Son and the figures of these parables, Stephen Fallon astutely observes how Milton wrote himself and his lifelong concerns regarding waiting, preparation, and action into the Son: "The Son's belated public ministry authorizes in retrospect the belatedness that worried the young Milton." "The dialectic within the

Son between readiness and the need for further preparation," Fallon writes, "recalls a familiar move of the young Milton, who claims that he is ready to do great things, worries about belatedness, and trades on the capital of future achievement."[13] As with Abdiel, the Son's heroism reflects the themes and diction of Sonnet 19, particularly its concluding line. Throughout *Paradise Regained*, the Son demonstrates the ideal of a good and faithful servant while standing and waiting. In a monologue before he is led into the wilderness to be tempted by Satan, he remembers how, in his youth,

> victorious deeds
> Flam'd in my heart, heroic acts; one while
> To rescue *Israel* from the *Roman* yoke,
> Then to subdue and quell o'er all the earth
> Brute violence and proud Tyrannic pow'r
> Till truth were freed and equity restor'd. (1.215–20)

Much has been made of the fact that the Son immediately follows these lines by stating his preference to "first" use "winning words to conquer willing hearts, / And make persuasion do the work of fear" (1.221–23), suggesting the Son's basic pacifism in contrast with Samson's brutality in *Samson Agonistes*, although commentators regularly omit the fact that the adolescent Son still desires "to subdue" the "stubborn" (1.226).[14] But we should recognize that the Son's own youthful inclinations toward heroic action and even diplomacy parallel the very temptations that Satan will offer him later in the poem.[15] Moreover, Mary's words to him (1.229–58) do not try to dissuade him from action. Rather, Mary emphasizes his status as the rightful ruler of Israel and indeed, by virtue of his status as the Son of God, the entire world, and she actually encourages action to demonstrate his divine status. She goes so far as to exhort him to "By matchless *Deeds* express thy matchless Sire," and proclaims, "Thy Father is th' Eternal King, who rules / All Heaven and Earth, Angels and Sons of men" (233, 236–37, emphasis added).

But the Son's response to Mary is not to act prematurely but to search the scriptures. His reading of the law and the prophets both confirms his identity as the divine messiah and informs him

> that my way must lie
> Through many a hard assay even to the death,
> Ere I the promis'd Kingdom can attain,

Or work Redemption for mankind, whose sins'
Full weight must be transferr'd upon my head. (1.263–67)

The Son's summary of his immense calling reflects his understanding that his prophesied ministry will involve, paradoxically, active service (note the verbs "attain" and "work") that he does not choose for himself but that will be given to him (his difficult way is laid out before him; mankind's sins are "transferr'd upon" him—the passive obedience of his *patiens* is clearly in view here). And his response is to "wait" for the "time prefixt" (1.269). The active nature of the Son's waiting is hinted at when he says that he is not "dishearten'd or dismay'd" by the burdens he will bear (1.268). He is not passively waiting in a depressed or fearful state. Rather, knowing the prophet Malachi, he anticipates John the Baptist, "who was to come / Before Messiah and his way prepare" (1.271–72; cf. Mal. 3:1), and he actively convinces John to baptize him. The Son's interaction with John demonstrates the paradoxical nature of his ministry. The Son "stands and waits" in good Sonnet 19 fashion for John's appearance, but he knows what he is waiting for, having actively searched the prophets. He receives John's baptism, taking on the characteristic passive posture, but Milton emphasizes his active role in bringing the baptism about. The Gospel of Matthew informs us that Jesus requests that John baptize him in spite of John's initial refusal (3:14–15), but Milton's Son emphasizes the effort expended in convincing John, stating in his meditation that John "was *hardly* ['with difficulty'] won" (1.279, emphasis added).[16]

Immediately following his baptism, the Son receives the approval of his Father, whose voice "from Heav'n" claims him as "his beloved Son" with whom he is "well pleas'd" (1.284–86; cf. Matt. 3:17 and Luke 3:22). The Father's commendation of the Son resembles his commendation of Abdiel in several ways, most significantly in that both Abdiel and the Son receive the Father's approval before they enter into active service against Satan. But if Abdiel's affirmation is directly followed by his successful military confrontation against Satan, the Son's is followed by an extended period of resisting various temptations to act prematurely, all the while exemplifying the heroism of one who serves valiantly by patiently standing and waiting for God's specific call. The Son's obedience to his Father's will is again exemplified as he follows the Spirit into the wilderness and then fasts for forty days, taking no specific action beyond the rigor of this extreme self-denial, even as he recognizes that his Father is preparing him for his future ministry and suffering.[17]

The first temptation Satan offers the Son, following both Gospel accounts, is the temptation to turn stones into bread. But Milton's additions to those accounts make the Son's refusal all the more remarkable. Satan, disguised as a poor, aged shepherd who claims to live among a destitute people, says,

> if thou be the Son of God, Command
> That out of these hard stones be made thee bread;
> So shalt thou save thy self and us relieve
> With Food, whereof we wretched seldom taste. (1.342–45)

Particularly striking is Satan's allusion to Luke 23:39, in which the unrepentant thief on the cross says, "If thou be Christ, save thyself and us." Milton's Satan quotes the thief's final clause exactly, and both Satan's and the thief's words represent similar temptations to illegitimate but seemingly charitable action. Had the biblical Jesus followed the thief's admonition and removed himself and the others from the cross, he would have abandoned his substitutionary atonement for humanity and, ironically, would have saved no one at all.[18] The perverse irony of the unrepentant thief's words becomes all the clearer when Jesus, several verses later, assures the repentant thief of his eternal salvation (23:43). Satan's temptation in *Paradise Regained* follows a similar ideal; unlike the unadorned Gospel accounts, where Satan's attempt to make Jesus turn the stones into bread appeals only to Jesus's physical and emotional self-interest, Milton's Satan appeals to Jesus's pity for the starving people whom the disguised Satan allegedly represents. As in Luke's crucifixion account, however, had Jesus acted on this temptation, he could have saved no one in the ultimate sense. This becomes especially clear when, near the end of the brief epic, the angels celebrate Jesus's victory over Satan; they conclude by saying, "Now enter, and begin to save mankind" (4.635). The Son's role as humanity's savior is contingent upon his resisting Satan's temptations,[19] and in his security as the beloved Son of God—an identity confirmed by the Father's pronouncement at his baptism—Jesus resists Satan's call to act as a temporal savior, choosing instead to stand and wait for the proper time to act as humanity's eternal savior.

The Son's firm understanding of his identity also empowers him to resist Satan's second temptation to act prematurely, and here again we see the Son choose the eternal over the temporal. Satan spends the bulk of book 3 and the first half of book 4 tempting the Son to show forth his power through "premature political solutions" by acquiring kingdoms by conquest and by freeing both Israel and the Romans from oppressive rule,[20] ultimately promising the Son all the world's kingdoms if he will fall down and worship him. The Son rebuffs Satan several times during the course of this temptation, each time emphasizing his security in the promise that all these kingdoms are his by right and that he will actively and eternally rule them in the Father's "due time" (3.182, 440). When Satan urges him to begin his reign immediately, the Son rejects such false urgency; rather, as in book 1, he finds his identity in the written word of God, and he rests in the scripture's promise: "of my reign Prophetic Writ hath told / That it shall never end" (3.184–85); similarly, when Satan offers to help him immediately attain "David's Throne" (4.108) and free oppressed people from the tyrant Tiberius, the Son replies that he knows that "when my season comes" to reign, he will destroy "All Monarchies besides throughout the world," and he reemphasizes that "of my Kingdom there shall be no end" (4.146, 150, 151). Confident in the truth of God's word—the scriptures—and fully aware of Satan's duplicity, the Son is content to stand and wait for his promised time to begin his eternal reign, for his Father's glory. As Emily Griffiths Jones has observed, for Milton and his Son, "True patience . . . can never be politic in the self-seeking sense; Jesus is waiting not for the right time to exercise his own pragmatic providence . . . but for divine providence 'To exercise him.'"[21]

Indeed, in portraying the Son's resistance to Satan's first two temptations, Milton takes care to depict the Son as a hero characterized by patience and active self-control. It is noteworthy that twice in the course of his urging the Son to eat of the sumptuous banquet in the first temptation, Satan urges the "Son of God" to "sit down and eat" (2.368, 377). Beyond Satan's tempting the Son to transgress the Mosaic law and consume unclean foods,[22] what stands out in Satan's repeated invitation is his attempt to have the Son exchange his posture of active standing and waiting on his Father's direction in favor of sitting, resting, and disobediently receiving sustenance and refreshment from his Father's enemy. Indeed, were the Son to choose to "sit down and eat," he would complete his mission of self-denial, figuring, prematurely and perversely, the image articulated in both the Apostles' Creed and the Nicene Creed of the risen and ascended Son, his salvific work on earth completed, who now "sitteth on the right hand of the Father." Had the Son acquiesced in Satan's bidding and sat with him at his banquet, his salvific mission would have concluded in complete failure.

The Son's replies to Satan's urging to "sit down and eat" and his subsequent temptation to "Get riches" and thus command influence (2.427–31) are spoken, respectively, "temperately" (2.378) and "patiently" (2.432), for he is confident in his calling to stand and wait upon his Father. In the final paragraph of book 2, in which Jesus, replying "patiently," offers his final refutation of Satan's first temptation—an elongated temptation to worldly wealth, pleasure, and sensuality—he emphasizes self-control and self-government, extolling him "who reigns himself" as greater than an earthly king, specifically stating twice the need to rule one's own "passions" (2.467, 472) in order to gain genuine nobility.[23] This contrast between patience and passion, repeated again in book 3 when Jesus notes the "honor" of "patient Job" and his "Saintly patience" (3.95, 93) in contrast with those who indulge "in brutish vices" (3.86), may be seen as the contrast between those who, confidently waiting on God for their reward, are characterized by godly patience, and those who, lusting after the rewards of this world, are driven by the passion of the flesh and self-aggrandizement.[24] As various authors have noted, the matter of patience, particularly with respect to the Son's ultimate mission, is of great importance to Milton. Gerald J. Schiffhorst observes that for Milton and others in "the Christian virtue tradition," patience "is the Christian's active response to adversity, the inner strength of those armed with grace who accept suffering while awaiting with an active readiness what Providence will reveal. With its root meaning of suffering, patience leads invariably to the crucified Son of God."[25]

The relationship between passion and patience in *Paradise Regained* can be better understood in relation to the characters of Passion and Patience in part 1 of John Bunyan's *Pilgrim's Progress* (1678), published only seven years after *Paradise Regained* and *Samson Agonistes*. Bunyan's Passion and Patience are two little boys whom the Interpreter shows Christian. Passion, the elder boy, is described as "much discontented" because the boys' "Governor" wants him to "stay for his best things," but Passion "will have all now." Patience, by contrast, "is willing to wait." Passion represents "the men of this world" who "must have all their good things now"; whereas Patience represents the men of the world "which is to come." Patience has "the best wisdom . . . because he stays for the best things."[26] Similarly, Milton's Son's wisdom is grounded in his devotion to his Father's timing, and he rejects the immediate gratification Satan offers through either sensual temptation or military or rhetorical prowess abetted by Satan himself. Moreover, the Son's patient willingness to resist fleshly passion, even amid suffering, qualifies him to endure, sinlessly, his *patiens*, his Passion on the cross. By exercising the wisdom to resist the premature temporal glory Satan offers, the Son will gain "the best things"—eternal glory at his Father's right hand and salvation for those who trust in him.

The Son's final stand against Satan occurs when, at the temple pinnacle, Satan again tempts the Son to immediate action—in this case, an immediate tangible display of his unique relationship to the Father. Satan tells the Son, "*Now* show thy Progeny" by "Cast[ing] thyself down," for God will rescue him "if" he really is the "Son of God" (4.554–55, emphasis added).[27] The Son replies tersely, "Also it is written, / Tempt not the Lord thy God"— words that implicitly affirm his divine status and its attendant power—and Milton's narrator adds to the Gospel accounts by stating that the Son "stood" while speaking and that "Satan smitten with amazement fell" at his words (4.560–62).[28] The connection here between the Son who serves his Father as he stands and waits and the final line of Sonnet 19 are apparent in both the theme and the language describing the Son's victory. Moreover, we see once again that the Son's resisting Satan's temptation is based on his confidence in his eternal standing, in this case his permanent unique position as the Son of God, a position whose truth is secure, for it is based on the scriptures and confirmed by the Father after the Son's baptism—which took place when, at "The time prefix," the Son "waited" (1.269). The Son does not need to "now show [his] progeny" upon the temple pinnacle because, as the angels who attend him proclaim, he is the

> True Image of the Father whether thron'd
> In the bosom of bliss, and light of light
> Conceiving, or remote from Heaven, enshrin'd
> In fleshly Tabernacle, and human form,
> Wand'ring the Wilderness, whatever place,
> Habit, or state, or motion, still expressing
> The Son of God. (4.596–602)

The Son's relationship with the Father is in no way limited by space or time, and so the Son is content to stand and wait for the next occasion on which his Father will have him display the power of that relationship. Ironically, the Son's answer to Satan does show forth his progeny, as both the tempter's overwhelmed response and the angels' song displays. And in this defeat of Satan, the Son shows in no uncertain terms that he serves his Father by standing and waiting, a patient posture that anticipates his final *patiens* and final victory over Satan on the cross,[29] where he again resists the temptation to act prematurely. Having defeated Satan where Adam failed, Milton's Son is content to "private[ly]" return "unobserv'd / Home to his Mother's house" (4.638–39), where, presumably, he will obediently await his Father's next direction for fruitful labor.

Part 2

The Parable of the Wise and Foolish Virgins

Having investigated the far-reaching dynamics of Milton's relationships with the parable of the talents and the parable of the laborers in his early, middle, and late works, we will now investigate Milton's equally pervasive relationship to the parable of the wise and foolish virgins (Matt. 25:1_13). I argue that his identification with the ideal of the wise virgin is persuasively recognizable in his 1642 Sonnet 9 ("Lady that in the prime of earliest youth") and is manifested, both early and late in his poetic career, in the idealized Lady of *A Mask Presented at Ludlow Castle* (also known as *Comus*, 1634); in the departure from wise virginity exhibited by Satan, Eve, and Adam in *Paradise Lost*; and in both the flawless wise virginity of the Son in *Paradise Regained* and Samson's repentant movement toward wise virginity in *Samson Agonistes*.

4

A "Virgin Wise and Pure"

Parabolic Self-Reference in Sonnet 9

Lady that in the prime of earliest youth,
  Wisely hast shunn'd the broad way and the green,
  And with those few art eminently seen
That labor up the Hill of Heav'nly Truth,
The better part with *Mary* and with *Ruth*
  Chosen thou hast; and they that overween,
  And at thy growing virtues fret their spleen,
  No anger find in thee, but pity and ruth.
Thy care is fixt and zealously attends
  To fill thy odorous Lamp with deeds of light,
  And Hope that reaps not shame. Therefore be sure
Thou, when the Bridegroom with his feastful friends
  Passes to bliss at the mid-hour of night,
  Hast gain'd thy entrance, Virgin wise and pure.

Sonnet 9 has not received extensive critical analysis. The few critics
who have commented on the poem have often focused on identifying its
unnamed subject. Prominent suggestions have included Mary Powell,
Milton's first wife (E. A. J. Honigmann, A. N. Wilson, Leo Miller, Leland
Ryken, Edward Jones);[1] Lady Alice Egerton, who played Milton's Lady in
Comus (William R. Parker, Nicholas W. Knight);[2] the mysterious Miss
Davis, whom, according to Edward Phillips, Milton considered marrying
after Mary Powell's desertion (David Masson cautiously proposes this);[3]
the ten-year-old Miss Thomason, the daughter of the subject of Sonnet 14
(John S. Smart); and Mary Boyle Rich (Sara van den Berg).[4] I propose
that while the sonnet does address an actual woman—I will argue for

Mary Powell and for dating the sonnet to just before the Milton-Powell wedding—it also addresses Milton himself.[5] That is, Sonnet 9's Lady is largely Milton's projection of himself during his Cambridge undergraduate years, when he, in his "prime of earliest youth," inhabited the role of the "Lady," a "Virgin wise and pure," who "shunn'd the broad way," endured the criticism of those of lesser virtue, and zealously filled his "odorous Lamp with deeds of light."[6]

Miltonic Self-Address, Milton the Lady, Milton the Wise Virgin

The idea that Milton, while ostensibly addressing another person in a sonnet, is also speaking to himself is not new to Milton scholarship. John Shawcross makes a similar claim in his discussion of Sonnet 20 ("Lawrence of virtuous Father virtuous Son"), asserting that Milton's words to young Lawrence are wholly applicable to Milton himself.[7] Moreover, Milton's identification with the chaste Lady of Sonnet 9 is strikingly consistent with both his self-professed identity as the virginal "Lady of Christ's College" and his implicit and persistent identification with the ideal of the wise virgin, a composite of the wise virgins of the parable of the wise and foolish virgins (Matt. 25:1–13), to whom Sonnet 9's Lady is explicitly compared throughout the sestet. By examining a number of Milton's early writings, we may see both his unashamed celebration of chastity and his identification with the figure of the Lady, who personifies the wise practice of virginity. This identification is seen explicitly in his Sixth Prolusion and implicitly in the Lady of A Mask Presented at Ludlow Castle (also known as Comus). Finally, this identification culminates in Milton's address to the Lady of Sonnet 9, a wise virgin who represents both Milton's retrospective projection of himself in the "prime of earliest youth" and his long-awaited soul mate, a seventeen-year-old bride-to-be who is about to wed a still idealistic poet twice her age. Additional insight from Milton's divorce tracts—probably written in the years immediately following Sonnet 9's composition and in whose context we may situate the sonnet—and from his portrayals of Adam and Eve and the angel Abdiel in Paradise Lost make this seemingly novel proposal entirely plausible. It is to this end that I make reference to many critical studies in this chapter, for I contend that my reading of Sonnet 9 actually situates itself comfortably amid any number of established readings of Milton's works. Indeed, in this part of the book, I hope to demonstrate that Sonnet

9 may play an important role in our greater understanding of Milton's life and larger body of writings.

That the sonnet's Lady is explicitly identified with the wise virgins of the parable strengthens the argument that Milton himself is an object of address in Sonnet 9. Milton clearly had a propensity to identify himself with certain parabolic figures, most famously, as we have seen, the unprofitable servant in the parable of the talents (Matt. 25:14–30), but also the last-hired laborers in the parable of the laborers (Matt. 20:1–16) and, as we shall see in chapter 8, the scribe in the parable of the householder (Matt. 13:52). The notion that Milton identified himself with the ideal wise virgin is entirely consistent with his established identification with other parable figures.[8] We should also be aware that Milton's identification with the female subjects of the parable of the wise and foolish virgins is not unusual in light of early modern Bible commentary. In what is probably the best-known exposition of that parable, the 1659 tract *The Parable of the Ten Virgins*, the Puritan pastor Thomas Shepard asserts that the ten virgins of the parable represent "all visible saints" and that the five wise virgins represent true believers.[9] Shepard's line of thought is similar to that of John Calvin, who distinguishes the wise virgins as those who are "faithful in perseverance [in their faith]," and that of Matthew Poole, who calls the wise virgins "pious souls" and the foolish ones "hypocrites and formal professors." This teaching is also seen in the 1662 commentary of the Puritan pastor John Trapp, who asserts that the wise virgins are those with "true faith in their hearts" and the foolish virgins "empty casks, barren fig-trees, pretenders only to the power of godliness."[10] And Milton himself, alluding to the parable in *Eikonoklastes* (1649), writes that a man's *"spiritual defects"* in prayer cannot be made acceptable to God "by another man's abilities"; instead, Milton admonishes him "not to walk by another man's Lamp, but to get Oyle into his own" (*CPW*, 3:552). In any event, Milton and the aforementioned divines each apply the figures of the virgins not only to females but to church members in general, be they true or false professors of faith. Indeed, Milton's identification with the wise virgins in Sonnet 9 places him in line with established contemporary modes of biblical interpretation.[11]

Milton's preoccupation with chastity is evident in accounts of his personal life and in his prose writings. His sobriquet at Cambridge—"The Lady of Christ's College"—was given to him not only for his daintily handsome, fair appearance[12] but also, very probably, for his decision not to indulge in sexual pursuits "common to the male college student."[13] Young Milton deeply valued maintaining his virginity amid the temptations of college life, and the fact that his classmates would give him such a dubious nickname shows that he met with considerable derision for this decision. Moreover, Milton's 1642 tract *An Apology for Smectymnuus*, written, like Sonnet 9, just before his marriage to Mary Powell, forcefully declares his convictions on male chastity: "If unchastity in a woman whom Saint *Paul* termes the glory of man, be such a scandall and dishonour, then certainly in a man who is both the image and glory of God, it must, though commonly not so thought, be much more deflouring and dishonourable. In that he sins both against his owne body which is the perfecter sex, and his own glory which is the woman, and that which is worst, against the image and glory of God which is in himselfe" (*CPW*, 1:892). Milton's intense conviction on this subject is all the more noteworthy, as Stevie Davies comments, because he lived "in an age when female chastity was obligatory but male chastity a joke." Tellingly, a bit later in the same tract, Milton compares himself to Electra as he argues against the prelates, writing, "A *wise Virgin* answer'd her wicked Mother" (*CPW*, 1:905, emphasis added).[14]

The Lady of Christ's College and Prolusion 6

Analysis of Milton's Cambridge years also lends credence to the idea of his identification with his own female poetic characters. In an insightful discussion of Milton's collegiate gender identification, Michael Lieb notes that the epithet

> The Lady of Christ's was . . . an identity through which Milton became known to others and a result of which he was made to struggle with the whole notion of femininity such a designation implied. As an aspect of that struggle, Milton was obligated to justify himself not only to his compeers but to himself as an individual at once male and yet exhibiting characteristics that would prompt others to identify him as a female. Milton took the epithet to heart. At stake for him was what became the dilemma of an incipient bisexuality crucial to his own sense of self and essential in his formative outlook.[15]

Lieb, John Shawcross, and others pay close attention to Milton's Sixth Prolusion, which he probably wrote in 1628 during the summer before his

senior year and presented before his classmates during that summer vaca-
tion. The overt "gender bending" of this Latin speech—and I contend that
Milton's "bisexuality" is in fact a rhetorical device that he manipulates for
his own rhetorical purposes, as opposed to an accurate description of his
sexual orientation—offers strong precedent for a reading of Sonnet 9 that
sees its Lady as representing both Mary Powell and Milton himself.[16]

In delivering the prolusion, Milton plays the role of the master of cere-
monies who "salts," or initiates, his fellow students. In this capacity, it was
traditional for the "senior sophister" to play the part of a "Father" lecturing
his "Sons."[17] The manner in which Milton uses this part as "Father" to
address his own sexuality is striking indeed; among other things, as Barbara
Lewalski notes, the "defiantly chaste" Milton "jokes about the irony of his
change of title from 'Lady' to 'Father,' a title assuming sexual experience."[18]
Milton's nickname was sufficiently known among his peers that he could
discuss it as a point of mirth; he used this occasion as an opportunity to
defend himself against this epithet, though he never renounced it. Indeed,
he almost seems to revel in the bisexual puns that the nickname affords him,
as when he asks facetiously:

> How does it happen that I have so quickly become a Father? Good heavens,
> what a prodigy this is, more astonishing than any recorded in Pliny! Have I
> slain some serpent and incurred the fate of Tiresias? Has some Thessalian
> witch poured magic ointment over me? Or have I been violated by some god,
> like Caeneus of old, and won my manhood as the price of my dishonour,
> that I should be thus suddenly changed from woman into man? Some of late
> called me "the Lady." But why do I seem to them too little of a man? . . . It is,
> I suppose, because I have never brought myself to toss off great bumpers like
> a prize-fighter, or because my hand has never grown horny with driving the
> plough, or because I was never a farm hand at seven or laid myself down full
> length in the midday sun; or last perhaps because I never showed my virility
> in the way these brothellers do. But I wish they could leave playing the ass
> as readily as I the woman. (CPW, 1:283–84)

Milton's discussion of himself in relation to the mythological figures of
Tiresias and Caenus is especially noteworthy in relation to his own struggle
for gender identity. Both Tiresias and Caenus had their genders changed
by the gods. And although Milton distances himself from any association
with such transgender—and sexually charged—characters, he delights in

exploiting his title as "the Lady" as an opportunity to mock his audience, and he adamantly defends the very characteristics that earned him the nickname, including his carefully guarded virginity. While he could have changed all of these characteristics with little effort, he notes that his detractors are inescapably trapped in their own boorishness. Although he defends his own masculinity, we have every reason to believe that he would rather continue being "the Lady of Christ's College" than alter his chaste behavior so as to conform to such men's expectations. Milton's rhetorical antics present a curious subject of inquiry with relation to larger discussions of gender in early modern studies. We might postulate that the easy manner in which Milton embraces both his identity as "the Lady" and his role as the "Father" suggests that at this early stage of life he self-consciously resisted the kind of "male sexual anxieties" that Stephen Greenblatt and Andrew P. Williams observe as commonly manifesting themselves in the writings of Shakespeare and other early modern male authors. At the same time, one could convincingly argue, as Lieb does, that Milton's banter in this prolusion is a rather stark manifestation of such "masculine anxiety," in spite of his attempt to obfuscate such anxiety with his jocular speech.[19]

The Lady of *A Mask* and the Lady of Sonnet 9

The image of Milton's brothel-frequenting classmates reappears in the persons of Comus and his rowdy crew, even as Milton's identification with the wise and virginal Lady reappears in the Lady of *A Mask*, Milton's masque celebrating the heroic chastity of the Lady, who successfully resists the seductive advances of Comus, the son of Bacchus and Circe who has taken the Lady captive when she, separated from her two brothers, is wandering lost in a dark forest. Numerous authors have connected the masque's Lady with Milton himself.[20] Lieb maintains that *A Mask* is a "dramatic representation" of both "the anxiety made evident in the gender reversals of the Sixth Prolusion" and Milton's "terrible sense of being victimized by an alien universe." Lieb writes, "the Lady of Christ's assumes his role as the Lady of the masque."[21] As we shall see, it is by no means an overstatement to apply these views also to the Lady of Sonnet 9. Indeed, the Lady of *A Mask*, in the preservation of her chastity (a term Milton "used interchangeably" with "virginity" "throughout *A Mask*")[22] and virtue, reflects not only the autobiographical Milton but also the Lady of Sonnet 9, who in turn reflects the wise virgins of the parable.

Milton's use of the parable of the virgins in Sonnet 9 is obvious, but we also may observe its implicit pervasiveness in the masque. Thematically, the intense emphasis on the Lady's virginity in and of itself brings the parable to mind, especially in light of the close connection between the Lady's wisdom and "the sage / And serious doctrine of Virginity" (786–87). The Lady's role as the "wise virgin" is emphasized all the more in light of her foil, Comus, who is both a fornicator whom she calls a "Fool" (663) and a "mock bridegroom"[23] whose rhetorical effort to deflower the Lady includes his ironic invitation that she "Be wise, and taste" his seductive potion (813). The persistent thematic presence of the "wise virgin" in the masque makes us even more acutely aware of the connection between the two works. Another connection can be seen in the language used by the masque's Lady, her Elder Brother, and the Attendant Spirit to describe her. While she wanders in the woods, the Lady tells herself that because she has a "virtuous mind," she is ever attended by "pure-ey'd Faith," "Hope," and "Chastity" (211–15). Later, the Elder Brother assures the Second Brother by associating their sister with "Virtue" and "Wisdom's self" (373–75), before extolling her "Chastity" and "Virgin purity" (425, 427). Speaking to the brothers, the Attendant Spirit calls her "my Virgin Lady" (507). Similar language can be seen in lines 2, 7, and 14 of Sonnet 9.

The sonnet's diction also echoes important structural themes of the masque. The masque's Lady, because of the darkness, has lost her way. She admits that her "unacquainted feet" are unable to navigate "the blind mazes of this tangl'd Wood" (180–81); she has, on a physical level, unintentionally left the "narrow way" of life and now unwittingly walks perilously close to the "broad . . . way that leadeth to destruction" (Matt. 7:13). In spite of this, because of her conduct as a wise virgin, she is able to resist the evil that pervades the "gloomy covert [thicket] wide" (945) where Comus holds her captive. Similarly, the sonnet's Lady "Wisely hast shunn'd the broad way" (2). The sonnet goes on to note that the Lady accompanies "those few . . . / That labor up the Hill of Heav'nly Truth" (3–4). These lines parallel the symbolic journey of the masque's Lady. At the opening of the masque, the Attendant Spirit laments the large majority of people who are

> Unmindfull of the crown that Virtue gives
> After this mortal change, to her true Servants
> Amongst the enthron'd gods on Sainted seats. (9–11)

He goes on to contrast the ignorant majority with the worthy few, represented most explicitly in the masque by the Lady:

> Yet some there be that by due steps aspire
> To lay their just hands on that Golden Key
> That opes the Palace of Eternity:
> To such my errand is . . . (12–15)

The Christianized Platonic ascent described here and in the sonnet is further demonstrated in the Lady and her brothers' allegorical journey through the dark woods to their "Father's residence" (947) in Ludlow Castle—a "towered" residence that is "perched on a cliff."[24]

The link between *A Mask* and Sonnet 9 is of great value in supporting the notion that Milton addresses both himself and Mary Powell in the sonnet. Milton's self-address in the sonnet is suggested, however unwittingly, by Anna Nardo, when she compares Sonnet 9's Lady both to Milton himself in his prose writings and to several other self-representations found in some of Milton's most self-referential characters:

> The "Lady" [of Sonnet 9] finds herself in a situation which Milton came to know well and which he would later recreate as the plight of many of his major characters: she is alone in her virtue and assailed by detractors. Like the lonely young lover [the speaker of Sonnet 1] who hears only the "rude Bird of Hate," the misunderstood pamphleteer [Milton in his 1643–45 tracts in favor of divorce for reasons of incompatibility] surrounded by a "barbarous noise," Abdiel jeered at by Satan's army, the Son [of *Paradise Regained*] and Samson patiently enduring the taunts of Satan and Harapha—the virtuous lady waits among fretful critics for a reward that will bring her out of isolation to a communal celebration with "the Bridegroom with his feastful friends."[25]

Nardo's comments are significant for both what they express and what they leave out. It is curious, in light of the Sixth Prolusion and other early writings, that Nardo essentially restricts Milton's ability to relate the sonnet's Lady's situation to his experiences in mature manhood. We can supplement Nardo's comment by adjusting her own words: The "Lady" finds herself in a situation that Milton *already* knew well, and which he already had depicted in his collegiate prolusions and his *Mask Presented at Ludlow Castle*. Milton's open acknowledgment of his classmates' dislike is already evident even in his First Prolusion, which suggests that the rejection of his classmates stemmed largely from his moral rectitude. In any event, we can safely assert that Milton, from an early age, saw himself as a person his adversaries would view contemptuously, one whose "growing virtues [would] fret their spleen."

Nardo does not mention the parallels between the Lady of Sonnet 9 and the Lady of A Mask, but we may note them here. Besides their common title of "Lady," both share in the experience of being mocked for their virtue, both are zealous in this virtue, both are noted for their wisdom, both are committed to their virginity, and, I would contend, both are associated with Milton's parabolic ideal of the wise virgin. Significantly, in addition to the self-referential speaker of Sonnet 1, each poetic character whom Nardo does compare to the Lady of Sonnet 9—Abdiel, the Son, and Samson—is a character in whom, like the Lady of A Mask, Miltonic self-representation has been noted by various critics.[26] Milton's perception of himself as one whose virtue is mocked and belittled manifests itself consistently throughout his work, including Sonnet 9.

Abdiel and the Lady of Sonnet 9

The connection between the sonnet's Lady and the Milton-like Abdiel is particularly striking when we examine the language Milton uses to describe both figures. Sonnet 9 tells its addressee that, in spite of the disdain of others, "Thy care is fixt and zealously attends / To fill thy odorous Lamp with deeds of light" (9–10). Similarly, Abdiel—whose "zeal" is mentioned four times in the twenty lines Raphael uses to describe him in book 5 of Paradise Lost— addresses Satan "in a flame of zeal" (5.807); later, God tells Abdiel that in spite of bearing "Universal reproach," "all thy care [was] / To stand approv'd in sight of God" (6.34, 35–36); we are also told that Abdiel is "bent on highest deeds" (6.112). The Lady "labor[s] up the Hill of Heav'nly Truth" (4), whereas Abdiel, after resisting Satan, is taken "to the sacred hill," where God honors his work for "the Cause / Of Truth" (6.25, 31–32; earlier, Raphael says that Abdiel did not "swerve from truth" [5.902]). Just as the Lady's zealous deeds "Hast gain'd [her] entrance" to "the Bridegroom" Christ (14, 12), Abdiel's obedience has brought him a personal audience with the Father. The speaker commends the Lady for choosing "The better part" (5); God commends Abdiel for fighting "The better fight" (6.30).

Abdiel's rebuke to Satan also echoes, both positively and negatively, the words and themes of Sonnet 9. The Lady, called a "Virgin wise and pure" (14), is lauded for her "virtues" (7); Abdiel calls Satan a "fool" (6.135) and "unwise" (6.179) and chides him for his failed "Virtue" (6.117). In addition, the Lady's shunning of the "broad way" as she ascends "the Hill of Heav'nly Truth" (2, 4) contrasts with Satan's "erring, from the path of truth remote" (6.173). Finally, just as the Lady is associated with "those few" (3) who persevere in holiness, Abdiel, as he informs Satan, is one of the "few" who choose rightly "when thousands err" (6.148). We may reasonably suggest that the writer who identified so strongly with Abdiel found a comparable connection with the sonnet's Lady.

Sonnet 9, Mary Powell, and *The Doctrine and Discipline of Divorce*

As we move now to analyze Sonnet 9's connection to Milton's divorce tracts and Adam and Eve's relationship in *Paradise Lost*, we do well to review the argument for Mary Powell being the addressee of Sonnet 9, written just before her and Milton's marriage in May 1642—a marriage preceded by a courtship of less than a month, their meeting occasioned by his visit to her father's home in Forest Hill in order to settle a long-standing debt that Richard Powell owed Milton. The strongest defense of this position, and one that to the best of my knowledge has never been refuted, is offered by Leo Miller. Throughout his article, Miller discusses the implausibility of the other women generally put forth as the subject of the sonnet. He dismisses the view that the Lady was Alice Egerton, noting that in 1642 the twenty-three-year-old Egerton was "hardly in the prime of earliest youth";[27] he expresses incredulousness at the idea that Milton would address the sonnet's frankly sexual subject matter "to a neighbor's ten-year-old little girl [Miss Thomason]";[28] and he considers preposterous the notion that, some months after Mary Powell's desertion, Milton would tell "Miss Davis, who probably knew his wife's name, 'the better part with *Mary* chosen thou hast.'" Miller contends that Mary Powell fits the sonnet's subject very well, and he postulates that Milton, very soon before their wedding, wrote the poem to comfort Mary amid the mockery of "scoffing village maidens" who ridiculed her choice to wed a Puritan twice her age. Dividing Mary, the wise virgin, from her foolish peers, Milton invokes the perfect scriptural image, one that "permits him to play with his double entendres of being escorted after the feasting at the mid-hour of night in customary country fashion to the bridal chamber." The sonnet's closing phrase, "Virgin wise and pure," would be an "inconceivable, impertinent" way to address "just any girl," but "most appropriate" for Milton's young bride "on the eve of their vows."[29]

Miller's argument seems entirely plausible, as do the insights of A. N. Wilson, who avers that Sonnet 9 portrays a Mary—who already displays "a quiet and natural innocence" and "a desire for godliness and sobriety"— that an idealistic Milton "can educate her into becoming."[30] Barbara K. Lewalski (making no reference to the sonnet) also notes that Milton, still quite naïve about women and holding unexamined expectations about "a young bride's malleability and subjection to her husband," probably assumed "that, once married, Mary would be eager to share his interests and conform herself to his ways."[31] Lewalski's comments call to mind Milton's comment in *The Doctrine and Discipline of Divorce* (1643, second edition 1644)—the tract he began writing shortly after Mary's desertion—that chaste men are often unaware "that the bashful muteness of a virgin may oft-times hide all the unlivelines & naturall sloth which is really unfit for conversation" (*CPW*, 2:249), a phrase often seen as autobiographically linked to Milton and Mary.[32] In any event, Wilson suggests that Mary "appealed to the teacher in Milton,"[33] and we may suggest that she also appealed to the virgin Lady in Milton, one who saw in her both the purity of his youth—retained into his present manhood—and an innocent wisdom that would blossom under his tutelage.

Miller also argues "that there is no valid reason whatsoever" to date Sonnet 9 after Mary's desertion shortly after their June (most scholars suggest May) 1642 marriage (composition dates anywhere from May 1642 to 1645 have been suggested); and, noting the disputed ordering of Sonnets 11 and 12, he takes issue with the notion that the sonnet must be dated after Sonnet 8, "Captain or Colonel," which was probably written in November 1642.[34] Dating Sonnet 9 to 1642 certainly fits well with the idea that it addresses both Milton and Mary Powell. In examining the time period in which Milton composed this sonnet, and the temporal and literary perspective from which he wrote it, we are aided by Honigmann's rebuttal of Smart's contention that the Lady of Sonnet 9 was a girl approximately ten years old: "As Milton's two first lines could refer *back* to the lady's earliest youth she need not have been as 'very young' as Smart held."[35] Honigmann makes this point to bolster his own assertion that the sonnet is addressed to Mary Powell, but his point is even more helpful in legitimizing the idea that Milton is referring simultaneously to *his own* youthful "prime." In considering this point, we may note the *OED*'s definition of "prime of youth" as "the springtime of human life . . . from about 21 to 28 years of age," and Woodhouse and Bush point out that this definition of "*prime of youth* was repeatedly used to distinguish this period from *prime* as the period of greatest perfection and vigour."[36] In light of the *OED*'s definition of "prime of youth," we may recognize that the "prime of *earliest* youth" (my emphasis) fits perfectly well with Milton's age as an undergraduate at Christ's College (roughly sixteen to twenty) as well as to Mary Powell's age (seventeen) when she married Milton.

In this sense, the temporal ambivalence of the opening two lines of the sonnet allows Milton to refer to both himself and his bride simultaneously. Honigmann observes that "the oblique allusions to marriage would have special point if the poet and the 'Lady' were themselves about to marry";[37] how much more meaningful would such allusions be for the idealistic and naïve poet who, having also lived chastely throughout his life, now believed he had found his ideal soul mate—one whose dedication to Christ, virginity, and virtue matched his own, one with whom he could now await the return of the bridegroom Christ in marital chastity, sharing in, to quote *The Doctrine and Discipline of Divorce*, the "meet and happy conversation" that "is the chiefest and noblest end of mariage" (*CPW*, 2:246) and enjoying "the soul's union and commixture of intellectual delight" (2:339). If Milton composed Sonnet 9 with both Mary and himself in view, we can appreciate how susceptible Milton was to unrealistic expectations of the partnership he and Mary would enjoy. We can imagine him, during their brief courtship, projecting onto her the sophisticated virtue of his own youth and seeing her as his great earthly reward from God for his own chaste faithfulness. We can see him applying to their anticipated life together the statement the broken-hearted Milton made soon thereafter, in *The Doctrine and Discipline of Divorce*, that "God's doing ever is to bring the due likenesses and harmonies of his workes together" (2:272). As John Halkett and James Grantham Turner have demonstrated, the idealistic portrayal of marital compatibility that Milton offered in the divorce tracts was at odds with other Puritan representations of marriage. Many of these representations celebrated marriage's function in offering companionship, but they were more interested in how marriage could grow the church through procreation, and in its being the proper outlet for sexual desires and a source of domestic support.[38] Milton's particular vision of marriage, founded on "the likeness of personal disposition,"[39] makes the idea that Sonnet 9 addresses both Mary Powell and himself all the more plausible.

Mary Powell and Mary of Bethany

A word is in order about the potentially problematic matter of associating Mary Powell with the biblical women of the sonnet's fifth line. The Lady of the poem is said to have "Chosen" (6) "The better part with *Mary* and with *Ruth*" (5). Dayton Haskin, who argues for no particular woman as Milton's subject in Sonnet 9, asserts that "in seventeenth-century England, Mary and Ruth were often thought to be complex figures of considerable experience, and the moral propriety of their conduct was disputed." Moreover, he suggests that "it was not easy to assimilate these women to the wise virgins of Matthew's parable." Regarding the biblical Mary, Haskin's concerns center around the popular association between Mary the sister of Martha—whom Christ commended for having "chosen that good part" of sitting at his feet instead of helping Martha in household service (Luke 10:38–42), an episode to which Milton explicitly alludes in Sonnet 9—and Mary Magdalen, "out of whom went seven devils" (Luke 8:2) and who was commonly associated with the sinful woman who anointed Jesus's feet at the home of Simon the Pharisee in Luke 7:36–50, a passage that, Haskin notes, was read as part of the liturgy of the feast of Mary Magdalen. The association between Mary the sister of Martha (generally called Mary of Bethany) and Mary Magdalen was brought about by conflating Luke 7:36–50 with John 12:1–11, which tells of Martha's sister anointing Jesus in a similar manner; Haskin writes that "the conflation of Marys continued to show up frequently in sixteenth- and seventeenth-century popular devotion."[40] We should ask whether Milton would associate the "Virgin wise and pure" who was his bride-to-be with a woman assumed to have been a prostitute.

In response to such a concern, we should emphasize that the conflation of the two Marys, first introduced in 591 in a sermon by Gregory the Great and part of the Roman Church's liturgy for nearly fourteen centuries thereafter (although never accepted in the Eastern Church),[41] was rejected by the Reformed and Puritan tradition with which Milton aligned himself. Significantly, the feast of Mary Magdalen had actually been absent from the

Anglican liturgy for some ninety years by the time Milton composed Sonnet 9. The feast, present in the 1549 *Book of Common Prayer* (though it never conflated Mary Magdalen with Mary of Bethany), was omitted from the 1552 *BCP*—very probably because many Reformed divines did not accept even that Mary Magdalen was the woman of Luke 7:36–50[42]—and was not reinstated until the second half of the twentieth century. At the same time, the feast remained in Roman Catholic liturgy, and the *Missale Romanum* of 1570 reaffirmed the medieval composite of Mary Magdalen and Mary of Bethany.[43] Simply put, the "composite Mary" was a popish innovation and, despite some Anglican sympathizers, was in Milton's time primarily associated with Catholic devotion. It seems unlikely that the independent-minded Milton would have allowed this Roman conflation, rejected by the English Church, to keep him from comparing his beloved Mary and her virtuous actions with Mary of Bethany and her choice to sit at Christ's feet.

Not surprisingly, biblical commentators in the Reformed tradition also rejected quite resolutely the conflation of the two Marys.[44] Instead, these commentators associated the anointing of Jesus by Mary of Bethany with the anointing by the unnamed woman recorded in Matthew 26:6–13 and Mark 14:3–9, an episode that their writings explicitly describe as separate from the Luke 7:36–50 anointing.[45] Significantly, each account of the episode recorded in John 12, Matthew 26, and Mark 14 highlights Jesus's commending Mary for going to extravagant lengths to honor him—the ointment with which she anointed Jesus cost some three hundred denarii, approximately a year's wages—in spite of the protests of the disciples (John 12:4 specifies Judas), who object that the ointment could have been sold and the money given to the poor. Here again, in her pious extravagance, Mary is praised for choosing "the better part," and Calvin's commentary on this episode applies Christ's defense of Mary "to all who make triumph in holiness": "Godly men are often criticized and indeed openly condemned unjustly, men who know themselves to be in good conscience, doing nothing other than at God's bidding: they are reckoned proud when they despise the world's judgment and are content with the approval of God alone. It is a hard temptation, and one almost impossible to resist—the crushing effect of a general, though false, consensus against us."[46] Calvin's words show clearly why Mary of Bethany, who persisted in good deeds in spite of the derision of ungodly onlookers, would be an eminently appropriate figure to commend to both his bride-to-be and himself, and would be entirely consistent with the figure of the righteous, virginal, oft-mocked hero with whom Milton himself identified. We may also surmise that if any ignorant persons, subscribing to faulty, papist-influenced biblical interpretation, chose to confuse this Mary and the repentant prostitute of Luke 7:36–50 and thus cast aspersions on his beloved, the idealistic poet would have allowed them to "fret their spleen" in their self-righteous foolishness. Moreover, it is easy to imagine that, in Milton's eyes, Mary Powell displayed the characteristics, during their brief courtship, of this biblical Mary; perhaps she sat quietly to hear his words of wisdom; no doubt her choice to devote her life to him demonstrated how extravagantly she valued him, the mockery of her foolish peers notwithstanding.[47]

Haskin's caveat regarding Milton's association of the sonnet's Lady with Ruth can also be answered in light of contemporary biblical commentary. Haskin notes "Ruth's astonishing sexual initiative" with Boaz, Ruth's kinsman-redeemer who would become her husband, and he cites Matthew Poole's view that Ruth's mother-in-law, Naomi, encouraged Ruth to approach Boaz because Naomi did not trust "God's Providence."[48] This mild critique of Naomi notwithstanding, Poole is careful to commend Ruth herself. Naomi was aware of "the wisdom and sobriety both of Boaz and Ruth," he says, and in approaching Boaz, Ruth used "no words or gestures which might provoke his lust; wherein she showed her temperance and modesty." Trapp affirms that Naomi's advice to "Serve God's providence by demanding marriage of him" was "in those days, and in Ruth's case . . . neither unlawful nor immodest (Deut. xxv)." Trapp writes of Ruth's purity in grand terms, with regard to both her reputation and her behavior; he notes that in Boaz's city, Ruth was praised as "eminently and eximiously virtuous," and, commenting on Ruth 3:14—"she lay at his feet until the morning"—Trapp writes, "A rare example of chaste and virtuous behavior!"[49] Indeed, as Hughes points out and Flannagan repeats, Ruth "traditionally exemplified Christian womanhood," a position affirmed by various seventeenth-century divines.[50] Moreover, Milton's offering the widow Ruth as an exemplum for the never-married Mary Powell is also in line with established early modern practice, for Ruth's example was commended to every Christian woman, be she "wife, or maid, or widow."[51] Once again, were any person to look askance at Milton's beloved because of her association with this biblical figure, that person would only be displaying ignorance inspired by envy.

Mary Powell and Ruth

The connection between Sonnet 9's Lady and Ruth also supports the case that the Lady in the sonnet is Mary Powell. "The better part" that Ruth has chosen includes both her decision to forsake her homeland, its gods, and its potential husbands to follow Naomi back to Israel (Ruth 1:14–17) and her decision to seek marriage to the much older Boaz instead of pursuing "young men" (3:10).[52] From Milton's perspective especially, both of Ruth's choices find parallels in Mary's choice of Milton: she is leaving her parents' home and the family's royalist politics, and its attendant version of Anglicanism, and turning away from any potential suitors in that religious tradition to follow the Puritan Milton; and her choice to marry a man twice her age mirrors Ruth's choice of Boaz. In addition, Boaz's role as a kinsman-redeemer who will provide financial security for both Ruth and the destitute Naomi is echoed in Milton's relationship with Mary and her family. Mary's father, Richard Powell, was indebted to Milton, and Lewalski remarks that Richard—who "never paid" the thousand-pound dowry he promised Milton—"was no doubt eager to encourage a prospective son-in-law who might afford him some needed forbearance in financial matters."[53]

Milton and Mary, Adam and Eve

The imagery Milton uses to portray marriage in *Paradise Lost* further supports the notion that he would have anticipated his marriage with Mary as a divinely wrought union between him and a "likeness" of himself.[54] This idea is especially compelling when the epic is read in conjunction with Milton's later divorce tract *Tetrachordon* (1645), specifically its discussion of relevant biblical passages, and if we keep in mind both William Kerrigan's contention that Milton identifies strongly with both Adam and Eve[55] and the various critics who have seen parallels between Adam and Eve and Milton and Mary Powell.[56] There is also the insight of the many critics who have seen Adam's attraction to Eve as narcissistic in nature, a notion that finds its parallel in the dual address of Sonnet 9. Indeed, James W. Stone's observation that "Adam may be said to be captivated narcissistically by the perfect image of himself that he sees reflected in Eve" seems entirely applicable to the sentiment of the sonnet, particularly in light of Milton's view of marriage as articulated in the divorce tracts.[57]

Paradise Lost celebrates a spiritual union that exceeds what is explicitly presented in Genesis or other biblical texts but is fairly consistent with other Reformed commentators' discussions of Adam and Eve—although we must note that Milton's requirement that contemporary couples essentially emulate such oneness in order to constitute a legitimate marriage clearly exceeds the expectations of other commentators. When Adam narrates the creation of Eve to Raphael—the angel God has sent to Eden to warn Adam of Satan's evil intent—he tells how God presented Eve to him, describing her as "Thy likeness, thy fit help, thy other self, / Thy wish, exactly to thy heart's desire" (8.450–51). In Genesis, God describes the woman he is about to create as "an help meet for" Adam (2:18), and the idea that Eve is Adam's "likeness" is derived from God's earlier pronouncement that "man" would be created "after our likeness" (1:26). But Genesis makes no suggestion that Eve is Adam's "other self," nor is such terminology used elsewhere in the Bible to describe married couples.[58] In *Tetrachordon*, however, Milton lays out this position in some detail, arguing that the original Hebrew for "help meet" describes "*another self, a second self, a very self it self*" (*CPW*, 2:600). Milton's discussion of this verse has some parallels with the commentary of Trapp, who describes Adam's "help meet" as "one in whom he may see himself, and that may be to him as an *alter-ego*, a second self."[59] But Milton goes beyond Trapp in insisting that such a priori "fitnes" be prescriptive for married couples. While the biblical texts offer no expectation that a man's wife-to-be will correspond "exactly to [his] heart's desire," *Tetrachordon* affirms that a "help meet" will have "effectuall conformity of disposition and affection" to her husband; and, having stated that Eve was made in Adam's "image," "not so much in body, as in unity of mind and heart," Milton's tract affirms that God instituted such "love and solace and meet help" as "the soul" "of matrimony" as a perpetual "ordinance" (*CPW*, 2:600, 602, 603). *Tetrachordon* goes on to celebrate the idea that married couples will have a "liknes" to each other expressed by "fitness of mind and disposition," indeed asserting that couples who are genuinely married are not merely physically "one flesh" but also "one minde" (*CPW*, 2:605, 610). Such high expectations for marital compatibility, which exceeds that of other Puritan commentators, lend additional credence to the idea that the Lady addressed in Sonnet 9 is both Milton and Mary.

Adam goes on to tell Raphael how he called Eve "Bone of my Bone, Flesh of my Flesh, my Self / Before me" (8.495–96); Adam also describes married couples as "one Flesh, one Heart, one Soul" (8.499). These statements recall Eve's earlier recollections of how Adam called her not only his "flesh" and "bone," but also "Part of my Soul" and "My other half" (4.483, 487, 488). Here again, Milton's Adam goes beyond what the biblical text suggests regarding marital intimacy. In Genesis 2:23, Adam indeed declares Eve to be "bone of my bones, and flesh of my flesh"; but Genesis makes no mention of Eve's being Adam's "self," although John Calvin's commentary on this verse states that she is, in relation to Adam, "as it were, another self."[60] Milton's Adam also expands on Genesis 2:24, which declares that a man "shall cleave unto his wife: and they shall be one flesh." The physical union of being "one flesh" described in Genesis does not explicitly declare man and wife to be "one heart" or "one soul," although certain Reformed and Puritan commentators do make such statements, albeit none so strongly as Milton. Giovanni Diodati, commenting on Genesis 2:24, sees "one flesh" as meaning "one person, united in body, in soule, in covenant, and indissoluble community."[61] Poole writes that this unity means that the couple is "entirely and inseparably united, and shall have as intimate and universal communion, as if they were one person, one soul, one body," adding, "this first institution shows the sinfulness of divorces."[62] By contrast, Milton argues throughout his discussion of Genesis 2:24 in *Tetrachordon* (*CPW*, 2:603–13) that a married couple that lacks such unity does not actually have an authentic marriage and thus should be permitted to divorce. In any event, the gap between Adam's extrabiblical celebration of Eve's sameness to himself in *Paradise Lost* and the actual Genesis account lends a disturbing credibility to Julia Walker's hostile response to Adam's celebration of "my Self / Before me." Walker writes, "As Adam gazes at Eve he is doubly metamorphosed: he becomes that Medieval Narcissus figure transfixed by the image of his beautiful self and he loses sight of God." Could a similar assessment be offered of Milton himself in his self-representation in Sonnet 9? If so, can Milton's narcissistic idolatry toward his own godly wise virginity in the sonnet explain his self-justifying rhetoric—in the name of fidelity to scripture and genuine piety, in the face of his blatant divergence from Christ's injunctions in Matthew 5:31–32 and 19:6–9—in the divorce tracts that he began publishing the year after Mary Powell's desertion?[63]

That Milton has Adam declare such spiritual and emotional union the pattern for future couples indicates that Adam—and Milton himself—considered such oneness to be the normative state between husband and wife, however tainted by the Fall.[64] Milton viewed such experiential oneness not simply as a normative description of marriage but as an actual prerequisite for a couple to be considered legitimately married in the first place. Commenting on Matthew 19:5 in *Tetrachordon*, Milton calls attention to Jesus's abbreviated citation of Genesis 1:27 and 2:24, noting that Jesus omits the verses in between, which "containe the noblest and purest ends of Matrimony, without which attain'd, that conjunction hath nothing in it above what is common to us with beasts" (2:648). When this statement is combined with his discussion of those verses—some of which I cite above—we recognize that Milton considered such emotional and spiritual "oneness" the appropriate expectation for any marriage that would transcend animal relations. This notion of oneness grounded in spiritual and intellectual likeness—a unity achieved by initial compatibility rather than by a married couple's concerted effort toward closeness—is again not in line with the general Puritan expectations of Milton's age. Even Poole's idealistic commentary has an exhortative tone, seeing such hopeful oneness as both a goal to be reached and—as with Diodati's comments—a barrier against divorce regardless of the extent to which it is achieved. The influential William Whately ironically told discontented spouses, "Thou art indeed married to an ill companion"—"thy wicked flesh"—and he urged such persons to focus on reforming themselves to achieve marital happiness.[65] Furthermore, as Edmund S. Morgan has noted, Puritan divines recognized the difficulties endemic to marriage and encouraged people to bear with the weaknesses of their spouses. Thomas Thatcher advised his audience to "Look not for Perfection in your relation," for "God reserves that for another state where marriage is not needed." Similarly, John Oxenbridge encouraged his audience to be realistic, "limiting the expectation," keeping in mind that they "mary a child of Adam."[66] Daniel Rogers reminded his readers that "Offences . . . wil arise," and he recommended that couples, after fighting, "should outstrip the other afterward, in humiliation and Repentance!"[67] In his study of the Puritans, theologian J. I. Packer notes that "the Puritan ethic of marriage" consists of finding a partner "whom you *can* love steadily as your best friend for life, and then to proceed with God's help to do just that."[68] This contrasts with Milton's insistence that "matrimony is dependent on harmony of natures rather than will."[69]

As we have seen, Milton's stress on "harmony of natures" as the prerequisite for a genuine marriage is entirely consistent with the suggestion that Milton was addressing Sonnet 9 not only to his fiancée Mary Powell but to himself. Indeed, when we view the sonnet in light of both his divorce tracts and the poetic works discussed here, the notion of the sonnet's dual address loses its novelty. It stands to reason that the former "Lady of Christ's College," older but still idealistic, would anticipate that his own bride-to-be would be a Lady like himself, a Lady in harmony with the ideal of the wise virgin he himself strove to attain, a wise virgin in her own right. A partnership that enjoyed "meet and happy conversation" between Lady and Lady was the sort of marital union that Milton envisioned for himself and Mary, and his idealism is reflected in the dual address of Sonnet 9.

A final connection between Sonnet 9 and *Paradise Lost* can be seen late in the epic's final book, when Eve, having just awakened, recites an unrhymed sonnet to Adam immediately before they must depart from Eden. Although the couple has lost the prelapsarian bliss that earlier characterized their relationship, Eve's enduring commitment to the husband with whom she is now reconciled is expressed in words that, as Cheryl H. Fresch has noted, recall Ruth's commitment to Naomi in Ruth 1:16:

> but now lead on;
> In mee is no delay; with thee to go,
> Is to stay here; without thee here to stay,
> Is to go hence unwilling; thou to mee
> Art all things under Heav'n, all places thou. (12.614–18)

Eve's words to Adam parallel the Lady's choice of "The better part with Mary and with Ruth," and, in an observation pertinent to matters of gender in Sonnet 9, Fresch points out "the intriguing complications of gender issues in marriage which are embedded in the Old Testament narrative of Ruth cleaving unto Naomi and going on to marry Boaz, father of Obed" (the grandfather of David and an ancestor of Christ).[70] Moreover, although Fresch makes no mention of Sonnet 9, her words regarding Adam and Eve apply equally, if not even more powerfully, to the dual addressees of the sonnet, particularly in light of the sonnet's final three lines: "As Adam and Eve enter upon their postlapsarian (and patriarchal) human marriage, they are also—together—entering upon their mystic marriage with Christ, and within that mystic union they are not so much 'called to their parts' as they are called to their single part—their cojoint role as the bride."[71] Indeed, the wise virgin of Sonnet 9 can perhaps best be seen as the single part that is the anticipated union of John and Mary, having gained, together as one, entrance into union with the bridegroom Christ.[72]

5

The Wise Virgin in Action
The Lady of A Mask

Having now established Milton's personal identification with the ideal of the wise virgin in the parable of the wise and foolish virgins, his self-referential connection to the Lady of Sonnet 9, his self-referential connection to the Lady of *A Mask Presented at Ludlow Castle*, and the various thematic connections between the Lady of *A Mask* and the Lady of Sonnet 9, we can investigate *A Mask* more fully, using the rubric of the wise virgin. Several aspects of the ideal of the wise virgin, as analyzed in relation to Sonnet 9, pertain directly to *A Mask* and Milton's implicit self-representation therein. These include the Reformed belief that the wise virgins of Matthew 25:1–13 represented the true, invisible Christian Church and its individual members; the biblical (and Miltonic) connection between sexual purity, genuine piety, and true wisdom; and the corresponding connection between sexual immorality, idolatry, and foolishness. Moreover, as I discuss below, the Lady represents the ideal of the unmarried wise virgin who looks forward to chaste marriage (both allegorically with Christ and literally with an appropriate future husband), just as Adam and Eve represent, for a time, the ideal of wise virgins within the bonds of chaste marriage, a topic explored in the next chapter.

Before beginning extended analysis of *A Mask*, a summary of the work is in order. The masque, first performed on Michaelmas night 1634 before John Egerton, earl of Bridgewater and then president of Wales, focuses on the virgin Lady (originally played by the earl's daughter, fifteen-year-old Alice Egerton), separated from her brothers (originally played by Alice's eleven- and eight-year-old brothers) as they travel through a dark wood on their way to their father's castle. As she wanders, the Lady is tricked by the enchanter Comus, the son of Bacchus and Circe, who, disguised as a humble shepherd, promises to help reunite her with her brothers. The scene then shifts to the Lady's brothers, the Elder Brother assuring the distressed Younger Brother that the Lady is armed with the "hidden strength" (415) of chastity, which will protect her from whatever evil persons might seek to assail her. The brothers are met by an Attendant Spirit, disguised as their father's shepherd, sent by heaven to aid them, who prepares to lead them to the Lady, advising them how to rescue her from Comus. Meanwhile, the Lady is at Comus's castle, frozen by his magic to an enchanted chair, surrounded by Comus and his followers, humans who earlier drank of his potion and whose countenances have been transformed to those of animals. Comus seeks to persuade the Lady to drink his potion, assuring her of the pleasure that awaits her, but she resists, rejecting his perverse logic and affirming "the sage / And serious doctrine of Virginity" (786–87). The brothers and the Spirit break in, chasing off Comus and his entourage, but, failing to take Comus's wand, they cannot free their sister from the chair. The Spirit summons the virgin nymph Sabrina, who frees the Lady. The scene then shifts to Ludlow Castle, where, amid dancing and singing, the Spirit presents the Lady and her brothers to their parents as he celebrates virtue's victory "O'er sensual Folly, and Intemperance" (975) and sings of "Celestial *Cupid*" and "his dear *Psyche*," whom he will make "his eternal Bride" (1004, 1005, 1008).

The Lady, the Church, and the Individual Christian

Building on the argument that Cupid and Psyche represent Christ and his church, various scholars have made the case that Milton's self-referential Lady represents both the church and the individual Christian. Alice-Lyle Scoufos argues convincingly that Milton draws heavily from several dramas from the twelfth and sixteenth centuries whose subject is the woman wandering in the wilderness in Revelation 12. Particularly significant to Milton are the 1538 Latin drama *Pammachius*, by the German Protestant reformer Thomas Kirchmayer, and the 1556 Latin drama *Christus Triumphans: Comoedia Apocalyptica*, by the English martyrologist John Foxe. In both of these dramas, the woman wandering allegorically represents "the congregation of the faithful"—the invisible church—"who will be rewarded ultimately with marriage to the Heavenly Bridegroom," as anticipated in Revelation 19:7 and 21:2, 9–10. Significantly, the name of Kirchmayer's heroine is Veritas—the mystical (invisible) church, for Kirchmayer held that Ecclesia, "the visible church," "had been seduced by Rome."[1] In Foxe's drama, the woman wandering, named Ecclesia, is met at the end of her journey by a chorus of five lamp-bearing wise virgins, Ecclesia's bridesmaids, who clothe her in preparation for the coming of the divine bridegroom. That these wise virgins represent genuine Christians within the larger visible church is reflected in their concluding admonition to the audience, which they implicitly advise to imitate themselves—and thus the faithful Ecclesia—instead of the foolish, sleeping virgins in the parable: "Spectators, now you see the bride decked out and all things in readiness. Nothing remains except the bridegroom himself, who will bring the final catastrophe to our stage. When that will happen none will say for sure. The poet has shown you what he could. And he earnestly advises you not to be unprepared, lest the bridegroom, when he comes, reject you as you sleep."[2] According to Scoufos, Milton's Lady "is the stock character, Ecclesia, but she is also further defined by Milton's careful control: her purity is analogous to that of the Holy Virgin, but unlike the mother of Christ (the Roman Catholic view of the church) she is vulnerable to ruin. Her Protestantism, like that of Kirchmayer's Veritas, is stressed through her insistence upon 'pure ey'd faith.'" Scoufos sees Milton's Lady as "an allegorical representation of the English Church" and also an "English Puritan" whose faith is demonstrated by her "moral stamina," "virtuous will," and "chaste decisions."[3]

Building on Scoufos's work, Catherine I. Cox also notes the allegorical connection between the masque's Lady and the unnamed woman of Revelation 12, but she emphasizes the deep resonance between *A Mask* and the early modern Protestant interpretation of the Song of Songs (Canticles), whose bride, "symbolizing the church or the individual Christian soul, is typically described as a pilgrim or a wandering woman." Cox notes the similarities between Milton's masque and various sixteenth- and seventeenth-century poems based on Canticles, and commentaries on Canticles, that cite these common themes: "Lost in the wilderness, the bride is tempted by idolatry and sensual appetite, drawn away from Christ, her true husband, by a false bridegroom (sometimes a tyrannical husband, or, like Comus, a false shepherd), pulled down and held immobile by sin, and finally freed by her intense faith and Christ's love of her."[4] Cox suggests that Milton's masque depicts "the cleansing, perfecting, and glorifying of the saint, ongoing in this life, reach[ing] final consummation at the Apocalypse."

Cox's observations are particularly remarkable when one considers the genre in which Milton chose to depict the sanctification of the saint that Cox describes. As Lauren Shohet points out, the masque was "the very genre that Puritan critics most explicitly indict as 'wanton.'" Shohet quotes Lucy Hutchinson, who specifically associated masques with fornication, incest, and adultery. Shohet writes that, in Hutchinson's view, masques and their attendant "sexual lewdness" were "signs of impending (revolutionary) apocalypse," among the entertainments designed "to keep the people in their deplorable security, till vengeance overtook them."[5] By contrast, Milton's Christian masque, as we shall see, urges its audience to exercise chastity of mind and body in anticipation of the believer's final union with the ultimate Wise Virgin, Christ.

The Lady's Vulnerability, Chasity, and the Critics

The journey of Milton's Lady is complex, and throughout the masque she demonstrates both a fierce commitment to chastity and a susceptibility to weakness, error, and, according to Cox, even sin. Cox argues that as an allegorical representation of both the "visible church" and the "individual Christian," the Lady is "paradoxically spotless and soiled."[6] My own interpretation of the Lady, which agrees with Scoufos and others, is that the Lady represents the invisible church and its individual members[7] and recognizes the Lady's human weakness and need for outside deliverance. At the same time, in keeping with her place as Milton's largely ideal self-representation of the wise virgin, she at no point falls into outright sin, although she does, at least initially, fall into error because of weakness.

The Lady's opening monologue ironically alludes to the parable of the wise and foolish virgins as she states her susceptible condition. At one point she addresses the "thievish Night" and asks it,

> Why shouldst thou, but for some felonious end,
> In thy dark lantern thus close up the Stars,
> That nature hung in Heav'n, and fill'd their Lamps
> With everlasting oil, to give due light
> To the misled and lonely Traveller? (195–200)

It is curious that the virgin Lady describes her circumstances with this particular image. "Nature," with a diligence that resembles the wise virgins of the parable, has filled the lamps of the stars with "everlasting oil"; nature has not been negligent, but rather has been faithful in providing sufficient resources for the aid of travelers. But nature's plenty has been thwarted by the "thievish Night," which is somehow able to overwhelm the well-trimmed lamps of the stars.

The result of this darkness, obviously, is that the Lady has lost her way; she admits that her "unacquainted feet" are unable to navigate "the blind mazes of this tangl'd Wood" (180, 181). She has, on the physical level, left the "narrow . . . way" of "life" and now unwittingly walks perilously close to the "broad . . . way, that leadeth to destruction" (Matt. 7:14, 13—note again Milton's prominent use of this passage in Sonnet 9, line 2). The immediate result is that she becomes easy prey for Comus, disguised as a kindly shepherd, acting the part of the parabolic wolf "in sheep's clothing" (Matt. 7:15). Comus, whom William Shullenberger calls a "mock bridegroom,"[8] can also be seen as a travesty of the bridegroom in the parable of the virgins—when he spots the Lady, he declares, "I'll speak to her / And she shall be my Queen" (264–65). Deceived by his ostensible charity, the Lady agrees to trust and accompany Comus both because of his disguise as a humble shepherd and because she recognizes that the "scant allowance of Star-light" (308) prevents her from finding the "readiest way" (305) to the place where he says her brothers are. As Cox observes, the Lady's being temporarily deceived by Comus finds parallels in the church's susceptibility to the deceptions of false teachers and other spiritual imposters.[9]

Cox affirms that the Lady's ordeal with Comus indicates the "persecution" of the true church and its susceptibility to "spiritual error," and although the former is certainly true, I believe that the phrase "spiritual error" must be used very cautiously with regard to the Lady. Cox suggests that the Lady's early spiritual error is twofold, consisting of her choice to move toward the unseen revelers she hears (see 169–81) and her decision to accompany the disguised Comus after he says he was so "awe-struck" by her brothers—whom he claims to have seen—that he "worshipt" them (301, 302). Cox writes that the lost Lady's decision to "rely on the guidance of the rude worshippers" she hears "indicates a momentary failure to trust in God's providence."[10] Cox is perhaps correct, but the Lady's lapse, if that is what it is, is only "momentary." Significantly, she does not come into contact with the revelers either before or during her initial meeting with the disguised Comus, and there is good reason to believe that, had she seen them, she would not have approached them for aid, a supposition corroborated by the fact that Comus appears to her incognito.

Cox's second point is more intriguing. Cox states that the disguised Comus's praise of her brothers "is clearly idolatrous" and that his hyperbolic words, which "should serve to warn the Lady," actually "serve to seduce" her.[11] An argument can certainly be made that Comus's hyperbole should have tipped off the Lady that something was amiss. At the same time, we must keep in mind that Comus's approach is directly preceded by her recognition that "the Supreme good" (217)—that is, the "Christian God"[12]—"Would send a glist'ring Guardian, if need were / To keep my life and honor unassail'd" (219–20), and by her prayerlike song for aid in finding her brothers (230–43). One could argue that had she rejected the kindly shepherd's offer of help, she would be rejecting God's providential answer to her prayer, insofar as she can discern that answer. One could further argue that the shepherd's hyperbolic response to her brothers, however idolatrous, need not undermine or compromise his seemingly genuine desire to help her. The lost and frightened Lady is accepting the aid of a kindly if too easily impressed man who knows both the woods and the location of her brothers.

We should also acknowledge that the Lady's mistake is precipitated by the dark night, and it is significant that, despite the plentiful supply of oil in nature's "Lamps," the stars are all too easily obscured by another natural factor—plentiful cloud cover. The effect of this physical darkness is that the Lady loses her physical way. She cannot find her brothers without assistance; the absence of natural light makes her vulnerable to Comus's deception. She is also physically vulnerable in her hunger and exhaustion. As J. Martin Evans points out, she is separated from her brothers because they have gone "to bring [her] Berries" or other available "cooling fruit" (186) while she rests.[13] Her situation reveals no moral or spiritual fault of her own. Rather, it demonstrates the limits of nature and natural light in safeguarding the individual traveler against the harms of this world, be they physical or spiritual. For all her moral strength, the Lady—like the church or the Christian—is never intended to be autonomous. In the opening lines of the masque, the Attendant Spirit states that "Sovran Jove" sent him to "defen[d] and guard" the Lady and her brothers (41, 42). And of course the Lady's brothers—who can be interpreted as ministers of the church or "representatives of virtuous male chastity"[14]—have been unsuccessful guardians.

Clearly, the Lady is now in serious physical danger and will soon be assaulted spiritually. But we come to recognize that even in her solitude, and susceptibility on the physical level, she is protected spiritually by the power of her chaste virginity.

Even before she is accosted by the disguised Comus, the Lady's own words reveal her awareness of this protection. In her lost state, she finds herself already assaulted by "A thousand fantasies / . . . / Of calling shapes and beck'ning shadows dire" that "throng into my memory" (205, 207, 206).[15] Despite this psychological onslaught, she maintains a strong, perhaps even naïve overconfidence:

> These thoughts may startle well, but not astound
> The virtuous mind, that ever walks attended
> By a strong siding champion Conscience.—
> O welcom pure-ey'd Faith, white-handed Hope,
> Thou hov'ring Angel girt with golden wings,
> And thou unblemish't form of Chastity,
> I see ye visibly, and now believe
> That he, the Supreme good, t'whom all things ill
> Are but as slavish officers of vengeance,
> Would send a glist'ring Guardian, if need were,
> To keep my life and honor unassail'd. (210–220)

Although, on a physical level, the Lady is alone and cannot see, on a spiritual level she has both sight and protection. Because she has a "virtuous mind," she is ever attended by "pure-ey'd Faith" (note the similarity of this language to Sonnet 9, lines 7 and 14), "Hope," and "Chasity"; and she is able to see these forms "visibly," and proclaims the continual protection of "the Supreme good" to defend her from all evil, a protection that finds its ultimate fulfillment in the person of Sabrina, the virgin nymph who eventually rescues the Lady.

The protection afforded the Lady by her chastity is also articulated by the Elder Brother, who has earlier suggested that the "sexually unfledged Lady" is "an embodiment of Wisdom."[16] He tells the Second Brother that because of her "chastity," she "is clad in complete steel" and that, furthermore, "No savage fierce, Bandit, or mountaineer / Will dare to soil her Virgin purity" (420, 421, 426–27).[17] It is worthwhile to note the obvious: that for all her and her brother's confidence, the Lady's virtuous chastity does not prevent her from falling for Comus's deception (265–330). Rosemund Tuve observes that the Lady's virtue does not give her the ability "to see through to the true nature of that which . . . simply says it is other than it is."[18] The Lady is undoubtedly in a very dangerous situation. But I cannot agree with Blaine Greteman that the Elder Brother's description of chastity is, as it pertains to the Lady, "painfully, embarrassingly wrong."[19] Certainly, the Elder Brother's words are exaggerated, unimaginative, and terribly naïve, and perhaps he overstates his sister's supposedly invulnerable protection in an attempt to console himself for his own shortcomings as her protector.[20] Moreover, significantly, his words obviously cannot be said to apply to chaste persons beyond the masque's allegory.[21] At the same time, the Elder Brother's claims are not technically disproved by Comus's initial deception of the Lady or by his subsequent rhetorical machinations. As William Kerrigan has noted, "The fate of the well-protected Lady seems to bear out the extreme doctrines of the Elder Brother."[22]

The Lady and Comus: Wise and Foolish Rhetoricians

But to give the Elder Brother's assertion any credence, an important distinction must be made. The Lady is not the victim of the kind of savage assault that the Elder Brother speaks of but is tempted by a more sophisticated force, one that does not attempt to besmirch her chastity through raw physical power. (Indeed, one may logically surmise that in Milton's view, following that of Augustine and Aquinas, a completed sexual assault, lacking the consent of the victim, could not cause a true loss of the victim's virginity.)[23] As far as Milton's masque is concerned, chastity cannot be taken away without the consent of the chaste. And this is why the rubric of the wise virgin is so germane to a proper understanding of the Lady's character. For while the Lady can be deceived by physical appearance and Comus's pretense of "simple hospitality,"[24] she remains, through wisdom, steadfast in her resistance to Comus's overt assault upon her chastity.[25] In this assault, Comus's chosen method of seduction is verbal—that of logical argumentation. As Louis Schwartz writes, "Comus' primary interest [is] the Lady's will, rather than simply the use of her body (he wants her to choose to use her body in a particular way)."[26] Comus thus attempts to belittle the Lady's dedication to chastity by showing her that chastity is anything but wise, and that her resistance to his sexual advances is a foolishly illogical waste of nature's bounty. The Lady answers Comus in kind, and with vehemence—the first word she speaks in her captive state is "Fool" (662)—and her address to Comus clearly sums up her opinion of him and his philosophy. But the Lady's judgment here is indicative of a much larger phenomenon that characterizes their dialogue. Their discourse is ultimately an argument over what is wise and what is foolish. The Lady's position as a wise virgin, obviously, stands in stark contrast to Comus's lewd venality. From her perspective, which represents the biblical association of fools with moral looseness, wickedness, idolatry, verbal folly, and a pathetically misguided self-confidence in their own incorrect positions,[27] Comus is a fool indeed. She and Comus argue from two entirely different perspectives, two entirely different paradigms concerning the foundation of wisdom itself. Their conflict is not the dichotomy that Georgia B. Christopher suggests when she argues that Comus attempts "to penetrate faith with reason." The problem is not with reason per se but with the perverse and consequently foolish nature of Comus's reason and conduct. By contrast, the wise virgin Lady articulates pure wisdom, which is grounded in her faithful chastity. As Susan Felch notes, the "conflict between Comus and the Lady pits the wisdom of the world against the wisdom of God."[28]

The Lady, held captive bodily by Comus's spell as he seeks to tempt her with his potion, takes as her foundation the heavenly, the eternal, the transcendental. This perspective is clear from her opening words to Comus:

> Fool, do not boast,
> Thou canst not touch the freedom of my mind
> With all thy charms, although this corporal rind
> Thou hast immanacl'd, while Heav'n sees good. (662–65)

The Lady's words are remarkable, not so much for her oft-quoted affirmation of the freedom of her mind despite bodily imprisonment as for her appeal to an unyielding standard of rightness over and above both her bodily weakness and the power of Comus's physical entrapment and relentless rhetoric. The Lady's appeal to heaven and its eternal standard of goodness establishes from the outset the basis of all her convictions and actions. Her audience, to be sure, will be engaged by the struggle that follows, but the Lady's position is as constant and immovable as heaven itself. She will not be swayed by the so-called wisdom of Comus's seduction, however enticing it may appear to certain critics, because its foundation is "earthly, sensual, devilish" (James 3:15); it is of the world, and it ultimately reveals Comus as the very fool the Lady first recognized him to be. Needless to say, neither side can persuade the other, for Comus and the Lady speak from two entirely different perspectives that effectively prevent any change of mind. As Stanley Fish asserts, Comus and the Lady "do not merely hold different points of view but live in different universes."[29]

Whereas the Lady's argument is founded on eternal principles, Comus's rests on transitory things: emotion, sensation, comfort. The initial words of his rebuttal seek to neutralize her indignant appeal:

> Why are you vext, Lady? why do you frown?
> Here dwell no frowns, nor anger, from these gates
> Sorrow flies far: See, here be all the pleasures
> That fancy can beget on youthful thoughts,
> When the fresh blood grows lively, and returns
> Brisk as the *April* buds in Primrose-season. (666–671)

Comus makes no attempt to answer the Lady on her terms, on the level of the eternal principle to which she holds. Instead, he tries to undermine her disgust by showing that it's illogical. In essence, he is saying, "this is a happy place and free of anger; therefore, you shouldn't be angry."

After laying down this emotional base, Comus moves to the next stage of his seduction by logic: he tries to show the Lady that by dint of her misguided convictions, she is the cause of her own unhappiness:

> Why should you be so cruel to yourself,
> And to those dainty limbs which nature lent
> For gentle usage and soft delicacy?
> But you invert the cov'nants of her trust,
> And harshly deal like an ill borrower
> With that which you receiv'd on other terms,
> Scorning the unexempt condition
> By which all mortal frailty must subsist,
> Refreshment after toil, ease after pain,
> That have been tir'd all day without repast,
> And timely rest have wanted; but, fair Virgin,
> This will restore all soon. (679–90)

Once again, Comus does not address the Lady's recourse to heavenly principle. Instead, he introduces his own principle, that of nature as distinctly separate from the heavenly. Comus simply accuses the Lady of being unnatural, of betraying nature itself, with the result that she is now in pain. Fortunately, all these bad feelings can be reversed if the Lady will merely stop resisting the natural order of things. That a "fair Virgin," after a lifetime of chastity, should submit to Comus's advances is, after all, as natural and appropriate as any sort of rest or pleasure after significant toil or pain. The supposed naturalness of the Lady's gently letting go of her chastity is reinforced, as Shullenberger points out, by the slowed pacing of these lines, their pauses, and "the alternation of consonant rhymes that quietly seal off" lines 685 to 690. Comus's speech here "is a hypnotic incantation that seeks to produce the spiritual condition of exhaustion and relaxation."[30]

Whatever the attractiveness of Comus's appeal, it is not surprising that he fails to persuade Milton's Lady. Nor is it surprising that she makes no attempt to rebut his argument point by point. Instead, her rhetorical tactic is to proclaim the fundamental falseness of his person and perspective. Her diction is especially revealing here, not only of her utter disdain for her captor but also of the unflinching tenacity with which she holds to her own convictions. In the thirteen lines that follow, the Lady levels eight accusations of dishonesty against Comus. She calls him a "false traitor" who has "banish't" "truth and honesty" from himself by means of his "lies" (690–92). He is a "foul deceiver" who has "betray'd" her "credulous innocence" by means of "vizor'd falsehood and base forgery" (696–98). He seeks to "trap" her "With lickerish baits fit to ensnare a brute" (699–700). In spite of all his efforts, she utterly spurns his "treasonous offer" (702). In the end, she acknowledges that Comus, being a despicable character in the first place, really cannot help but spew such fallacious garbage. In words that recall Jesus's denunciation of the Pharisees, the Lady proclaims, "none / But such as are good men can give good things" (702–3).[31] This statement transcends the need for a logical rebuttal of Comus's argument. Her point to Comus is simple: You, being a "false traitor" (and then some), are utterly incapable of offering me any goodness; therefore, I know that what you are offering is as evil and deceptive as you are.

The Lady adds to this moral dismissal the following statement, which speaks volumes as to why she is not enticed by his allurements:

And that which is not good, is not delicious
to a well-govern'd and wise appetite. (704–5)

These words sum up the utter incompatibility of their persons and positions. Comus genuinely thinks that he is offering the Lady something delectable and irresistible. Her response is the most flagrant of insults to her assailant. She does not even give him the satisfaction of thinking that she needs to struggle to resist him. Rather, being a wise virgin, she simply does not find his enticements attractive in the first place. The emotional energy she expends against him is not the product of an aroused libido, as several critics have argued, but the overflow of her moral outrage.[32]

That Comus simply cannot comprehend the Lady's perspective is evident in his immediate response to her denunciation.

O foolishness of men! that lend their ears
To those budge doctors of the *Stoic* Fur,
And fetch their precepts from the *Cynic* Tub,
Praising the lean and sallow Abstinence. (706–9)

Once again, Comus's words betray his complete nonengagement with the Lady's otherworldly frame of reference. It is clear that she does not think her convictions are based on the teachings "of men"—still less would she see them as based on the atheistic or agnostic philosophies of the Stoics or the Cynics. The ascetic practices of these philosophies are indeed appropriate targets for Comus's verbal onslaught. The problem is that the Lady's philosophy is neither Stoical nor Cynical. Comus's arguments make good sense within the natural parameters that he lays out. But the Lady's steadfastness is never based on nature or natural reasoning but on divine principle. It is a mistake, however, to assume that because the Lady resists Comus's sensual temptations she is therefore also opposed to pleasurable things, including sexual relations, in their proper context.[33] The feast at the masque's conclusion, with its celebration of marital sexuality, attests to this. Maryanne Cale McGuire notes that "for Puritans chastity did not imply asceticism. Rather, the Protestant doctrine of stewardship made the rule of chastity a correct use of the world rather than a flight from it. . . . But commitment to God must inform and when necessary take precedence over all earthly delights and loves." Moreover, as John Leonard points out, citing R. M. Frye and John Calvin, "'virginity,' in Puritan usage, could include marriage."[34] The

Lady opposes Comus's seduction because the pleasure he offers is offered within the idolatrous—and thus foolish—context of immorality.[35]

All of this, of course, is lost on Comus, who proceeds even more strongly than before to accuse the Lady of manifold crimes against nature, even to the point that he charges her with blasphemy against the nature-focused deity to whom he alludes. Comus ironically alludes rather prominently to several biblical passages, turning them on their heads and making a mockery of the Judeo-Christian ethic at the heart of the Lady's chaste convictions. After speaking eloquently about how nature has generously sprinkled the earth with her plentiful bounty, Comus says,

> If all the world
> Should in a pet of temperance feed on Pulse,
> Drink the clear stream, and nothing wear but Frieze,
> Th'all-giver would be unthank't, would be unprais'd,
> Not half his riches known, and yet despis'd,
> And we should serve him as a grudging master,
> As a penurious niggard of his wealth,
> And live like Nature's bastards, not her sons,
> Who would be quite surcharg'd with her own weight,
> And strangl'd with her waste fertility. (720–29)

Comus's diatribe reveals itself as particularly ironic and misguided in that the biblical passages he alludes to celebrate temperance and discipline as the necessary path to right relationship with a holy God. Comus's mockery of the idea of drinking clear water and "temperate" feeding "on Pulse [vegetables]" alludes to the first chapter of Daniel, where Daniel and the other exiled Jewish youths in the Babylonian court, in an effort not to defile themselves with ceremonially unclean food, forego the king's rich food in favor of a diet of "pulse to eat, and water to drink" (1:12). The irony of Comus's allusion to Daniel, as A. S. P. Woodhouse and Douglas Bush point out, is that "Daniel and his companions are not the worse but the better for this abstinence (which refutes Comus' assumption), and their virtue is supported by God, who gives them wisdom and knowledge of a higher order."[36] The foolishness and blasphemy that Comus associates with temperance is, through his manipulative allusion, revealed to be something altogether different from what he makes it out to be. Curiously enough, the four "wise virgins" of Daniel are made wiser still by their self-control; and their temperance, far from being an affront to the Creator, is an act of the greatest reverence. Their devotion to God, demonstrated in their faithfulness to Jewish dietary restrictions, is met with clear blessings, to which the book of Daniel attests.

In line 727, "And live like Nature's bastards, not her sons," Comus also alludes to Hebrews 12:8: "But if ye be without chastisement . . . then are ye bastards, and not sons."[37] In a manner similar to the passage in Daniel 1, the larger context of Hebrews 12 celebrates obedient self-denial and hardship as the pathway to God's blessing. The author encourages his audience to imitate Jesus, "who for the joy that was set before him endured the cross" (12:2). Such an image certainly turns Comus's notion of pleasure inside out, in that Jesus pursued joy by means of his obedient acceptance of painful persecution ordained by God himself. Similarly, while the author of Hebrews acknowledges that "no chastening for the present seemeth to be joyous, but grievous," he assures his readers that "afterward it yieldeth the peaceable fruit of righteousness unto them who are exercised thereby" (12:11). In stark contrast to Comus's carpe diem message, the biblical passage to which he alludes promises enduring contentedness to those who would forego transitory pleasures in favor of the discipline of God. Especially devastating to Comus's celebration of unbridled pleasure is the specific admonition in Hebrews to diligently follow "holiness," a practice that will prevent becoming a "fornicator" (12:14, 16). Patently contrary to Comus's message, sexual indulgence is the impediment, not the path, to God's blessings.

Comus's most bizarre biblical allusion, however, in light of Milton's larger body of work and the themes discussed in part 1 of this study, is his use of imagery from the parable of the talents to support his brief for copulation:

> List Lady, be not coy, and be not cozen'd
> With that same vaunted name Virginity;
> Beauty is nature's coin, must not be hoarded,
> But must be current, and the good thereof
> Consists in mutual and partak'n bliss,
> Unsavory in th' enjoyment of itself. (737–42)

Comus's argument from trade, if taken to its logical conclusion, presents persons who are the most sexually active, presumably with multiple partners, as being those who serve nature best, for such persons are vehicles of blessing to as many as possible.[38] One can almost imagine the scenario of Comus's nature-deity, at the end of time, pronouncing to each of her most promiscuous subjects, "well done, good and faithful servant." In any event, Comus becomes increasingly forceful in his attempt to prove that a "wise virgin" is an oxymoron. The final line of this speech admonishes the Lady to "think" and "be advis'd"—it is only logical for her to pursue the sort of revelry Comus advocates. She is "but young yet" (755), and it stands to reason that she should seize the day.

When Comus finishes, the Lady replies that she would rather not even grace him with an answer, but since he has delivered such a bogus polemic, she will "answer a fool according to his folly" (Prov. 26:5). What she finds particularly deplorable is that, although Comus's premises are untrue to the core, they are disguised as rational argument. His entire diatribe is thus an insult to her identity as a wise virgin; she even suggests that she would be less offended had he simply attempted to overcome her through mere sensual temptation. As it is, she is utterly disgusted

> that this Juggler
> Would think to charm my judgment, as mine eyes,
> Obtruding false rules prankt in reason's garb.
> I hate when vice can bolt her arguments,
> And virtue has no tongue to check her pride. (757–61)

Thus the wise Lady considers herself duty-bound to defend not simply the ideal of chastity but also reason itself.

At this point, and for the only time in their exchange, the Lady chooses to answer Comus along his own lines of argumentation. To be sure, as she does so she approaches the subjects of nature and the power behind it from a completely different framework than he does, but it is significant that for once she does not simply dismiss him as a "fool" or "false traitor" but— though she insults him here as well—meets his argument head on:

> Imposter, do not charge most innocent nature,
> As if she would her children should be riotous
> With her abundance; she, good cateress,
> Means her provision only to the good
> That live according to her sober laws
> And holy dictate of spare Temperance:

> If every just man that now pines with want
> Had but a moderate and beseeming share
> Of that which lewdly-pamper'd Luxury
> Now heaps upon some few with vast excess,
> Nature's full blessings would be well dispens't
> In unsuperfluous even proportion,
> And she no whit encumber'd with her store,
> And then the giver would be better thank't,
> His praise due paid, for swinish gluttony
> Ne'er looks to Heav'n amidst his gorgeous feast,
> But with besotted base ingratitude
> Crams, and blasphemes his feeder. (762–79)

The Lady's argument for temperance is especially valuable in understanding her character in relation to the subject of exploitive sexuality that Comus has pressed so aggressively. By redefining the proper enjoyment of nature's bounty in terms of egalitarian moderation, the scheme the Lady describes here easily translates into her ideal of appropriate, chaste sexual expression: marital monogamy.[39] Although neither marriage nor sexuality is explicitly mentioned, this is because the Lady answers Comus in his own terms here. Her diction, however, makes clear her sentiments. Those "just m[e]n" who now "pine with want" could be satisfied with their rightful share; those—like Comus himself—who indulge in "lewd" excess upset nature's balance and "blaspheme" the one who is giver of all. These lines are also particularly germane to Milton's own identification with the Lady and his self-representation in A Mask. We easily can imagine the young Milton, not far removed from his days at Cambridge, recalling the promiscuity of many of his peers and lamenting that such behavior shattered for them the Christian ideal of a newly married couple entering their nuptials as virgins. We can also imagine that Milton, choosing in obedience to his God to remain chaste and lonely, longed for companionship, resented those who indulged in such behavior, and felt himself and those like him personally harmed by sexual practices that upset the divine ideal that "Nature's full blessings would be well dispens't / In unsuperfluous even proportion."[40]

In any event, these lines demonstrate that the Lady's dedication to chastity and virginity is hardly the obnoxious prudishness that some critics see.[41] A few basic points can be articulated: first, it is patently absurd to conclude that because a young woman (or man) desires to remain a virgin before marriage, she (or he) is thus hostile to the idea of sex altogether. The celebration of married love seen in the masque's closing song (discussed below) alone should refute such an interpretation. Indeed, it seems myopic to argue that because the Lady rebuffs a would-be rapist, she would not in the future enjoy wedded love with her husband. Within the commitment to chastity that the Lady embraces as part of her overall worldview, virginity is, quite simply, the only appropriate option for her in her unmarried state. It should hardly be noteworthy that a wise virgin like the Lady would rebuff the likes of Comus. It is, again quite simply, the only proper choice that she can make. If we view her situation with any perspective at all, we will appreciate her victimized circumstances enough to withhold any wrongheaded judgments against her.

Having logically rebutted Comus's "argument from nature," the Lady returns to her previous tactic of dismissing him on grounds of character. Here, perhaps even more powerfully than anywhere else in the masque, it is clear that the Lady and Comus are arguing from completely different frames of reference. Comus has not yet realized this, but the Lady is fully aware of it:

> Shall I go on?
> Or have I said enough? To him that dares
> Arm his profane tongue with contemptuous words
> Against the Sun-clad power of Chastity
> Fain would I have something to say, yet to what end?
> Thou hast nor Ear nor Soul to apprehend
> The sublime notion and high mystery
> That must be utter'd to unfold the sage
> And serious doctrine of Virginity,
> And thou art worthy that thou shouldst not know
> More happiness than this thy present lot.
> Enjoy your dear Wit and gay Rhetoric
> That hath so well been taught her dazzling fence,
> Thou art not fit to hear thyself convinc't. (779–92)

Although she goes on to say quite a lot, her point is that there is really no point in wasting her breath—Comus just doesn't get it, and he can't get it.

He has lowered himself to a state that prevents his understanding.[42] To understand "the sage / And serious doctrine of Virginity" requires holiness utterly alien to Comus. David Gay hears in these lines the echo of 1 Corinthians 2:14, where Saint Paul writes that "the natural man receiveth not the things of the Spirit of God: for they are foolishness unto him: neither can he know them, because they are spiritually discerned."[43] As Merritt Hughes has noted, the "high mystery" the Lady mentions alludes to "the mystery of godliness" that Saint Paul writes of in 1 Timothy 3:16; Hughes also connects the phrase with Milton's own assertion in his *Apology for Smectymnuus* concerning "the doctrine of holy Scripture unfolding those chaste and high mysteries ... that the body is for the Lord and the Lord for the body" (*CPW*, 1:892—Milton is quoting 1 Cor. 6:13, which asserts more completely, "Now the body is not for fornication, but for the Lord; and the Lord is for the body").[44] We may also recognize the connection to Paul's description of marriage as "a great mystery" that parallels the relationship between Christ and the church (Eph. 5:32) and Milton's own affirmation in *Colasterion* that marriage is "the mystery of Joy" (*CPW*, 2:749).

But whether the "mystery" the Lady refers to is seen in terms of unmarried virginity, chaste marriage, or both, Comus is very far from understanding any notion of godliness characterized by abstention from fornication. Instead, Comus is portrayed as one who has fallen progressively further away from any possibility of apprehending such mysteries. Indeed, not only can he not comprehend such sacred notions, but he is also incapable of properly exercising natural reason, as is demonstrated in his just-refuted polemic concerning nature's bounty. In this, Comus resembles those described by Saint Paul, who, in their irreverence toward God, "professing themselves to be wise ... became fools" (Rom. 1:22). Paul goes on to connect wrong thinking about God to sexual misconduct:

> [They] changed the glory of the uncorruptible God into an image made like to corruptible man, and to birds, and fourfooted beasts, and creeping things. Wherefore God also gave them up to uncleanness through the lusts of their own hearts, to dishonour their own bodies between themselves: Who changed the truth of God into a lie, and worshipped and served the creature more than the Creator.... For this cause God gave them up unto vile affections ... (1:23–26a) And even as they did not like to retain God in their

knowledge, God gave them over to a reprobate mind, to do those things which are not convenient, being filled with all unrighteousness, fornication, wickedness . . . (1:28–29a)

That Milton had this passage in mind when writing *A Mask* is shown in the Attendant Spirit's description of Comus's entourage, whose "human count'nance, / Th' express resemblance of the gods," has been, through imbibing Comus's potion, "chang'd / Into some brutish form of Woolf, or Bear / Or Ounce, or Tiger, Hog, or bearded Goat" (68–71). The bestial foolishness of Comus's followers, who have rejected God's image in themselves (Gen. 1:26–27) in favor of Comus's idolatrous licentiousness, is revealed in how they boast that, with their animal visages, they are "more comely than before" (75).[45] Even more significant is how the sexually degenerate, idolatrous Comus genuinely thinks himself wise—and the Lady foolish—while he espouses specious reasoning that the wise virgin Lady easily refutes. (Indeed, Comus displays upside-down thinking and denial of reality from his initial entrance with his companions, when he utters such phrases as, "What hath night to do with sleep?" and "'Tis only day-light that makes sin" [122, 126].) Just as the Lady's wisdom and dedication to chastity are intricately linked, so too are Comus's commitment to "free love" and his overall portrayal as a fool. As a foolish fornicator (for lack of a better term), he is the perfect foil to Milton's wise virgin.

To be sure, Comus does recognize a supernatural force behind the Lady's words, which he describes as "set off by some superior power" (801). But this recognition only inspires him to accost her more forcefully. His final lines demonstrate his fundamental conception of wisdom, morality, and the foundation of authority upon which one ought to base conduct. He mocks the Lady's words as "mere moral babble, and direct / Against the canon laws of our foundation" (807–8). The issue of which "canon laws" Comus refers to has been the subject of much debate, with many critics contending that Milton is mocking the canon laws of the Church of England here.[46] Whatever ecclesiastical ridicule this statement may imply, Comus flagrantly exhibits how foreign to him the Lady's belief system and moral standards are. He simply doesn't know what to make of the Lady; he is genuinely bewildered. Comus's worldview remains strong to the end: "Be wise, and taste" (813). For Comus, the notion of a "wise virgin" is an oxymoron indeed—any virgin is a foolish virgin—but he can cure the Lady of her foolish virginity if she would only drink his potion and receive his so-called wisdom.

The Lady's Rescue, the Virgin Sabrina, and Eternal Marriage

Of course, the Lady never tastes Comus's concoction, and at just this point her brothers enter and drive off Comus and his followers. Some comment is warranted, however, regarding whether Comus, at the time of the rescue, is on the verge of physically compelling the Lady to drink his potion. Critics who suggest that Comus is about to force her to drink make this point to demonstrate the limits of the protective power of her chastity. Debora Shuger argues that Comus's "ability to make her sit and drink exposes the limits on 'the Sun-clad power of Chastity.'" And Theresa DiPasquale writes, specifically in response to the Elder Brother's belief that chastity will repel "brute violence" (451), "Neither chastity *nor* wise eloquence is sufficient to protect against 'brute' coercion, be it sexual or ecclesiastical. The Lady is thus saved from having Comus's libertine/prelatical cup forcibly pressed to her lips only by the entrance of her brothers."[47]

There are a few problems, however, with this position. First, despite critics' inferences, there is nothing in Milton's text to indicate conclusively that Comus is about to force the Lady to drink when the brothers enter. Significantly, the rather detailed stage directions that immediately follow "Be wise, and taste" say nothing of the sort. And there is nothing about the words "Be wise, and taste" that suggests that physical force is about to follow. The words could just as well begin a new series of rhetorical thrusts by which Comus will "try her yet more strongly" (806). Moreover, the phrases at the end of Comus's previous two speeches to the Lady sound equally threatening but are not followed by physical action. Comus's declaration "This will restore all soon" (690), spoken while holding his glass, could just as well immediately precede a physical attempt to make her drink, but it does not; so could "be adviz'd; you are but young yet" (755), but it does not.

It is also inaccurate to suggest that the brothers' rescue of the Lady is somehow unrelated to the power of her chastity. Significantly, early in the masque, the Lady links her chastity to her belief that "the Supreme good," if necessary, "Would send a glist'ring Guardian . . . / To keep my life and honor unassail'd" (217, 219–20). And this is exactly what happens. The brothers' rescue is directed by the Lady's "glist'ring Guardian," the Attendant

Spirit, who ensures that both her "life and honor" are "unassail'd." In my view, the Lady's chastity—including the divine favor she enjoys as a result of it—does indeed protect her throughout the masque, and thus demonstrates the accuracy of both her and the Eldest Brother's early pronouncements concerning chastity's power.

In any case, the limits of the Attendant Spirit's power are evident in his inability to free the Lady from Comus's throne, to which she remains frozen. The Spirit calls on the virgin nymph Sabrina for help. Sabrina's ensuing rescue of the Lady reinforces both the image of the wise virgin that pervades *A Mask* and the theme of chastity's power and the favor given to those who wisely maintain their virginity. Sabrina, whom the Spirit describes in words that recall the Lady of Sonnet 9—she is "a Virgin pure" (826)—was herself a mortal young maiden whose chaste virtue brought about her rescue from destruction.[48] The Spirit explains that in her mortal life, Sabrina was a "guiltless damsel" who, being unjustly pursued by "her enraged stepdam *Guendolen*, / Commended her fair innocence to the flood / That stay'd her flight with his cross-flowing course" (829–32). After drowning, she was revived by sea nymphs and their father, Nereus, and then "underwent a quick immortal change" and was "Made Goddess of the River" (841–42). Unlike the Lady's initial rescuers, Sabrina, the immortal virgin whose typological resemblance to Christ—the ultimate wise virgin—has been recognized by various critics,[49] is able to free the Lady from Comus's "marble venom'd seat" and the "gums of glutinous heat" (916–17) that hold her fast.[50] Sabrina's virgin power enables her to free the Lady; she breaks Comus's spell after touching his envenomed throne with her "chaste palms moist and cold" (918). Milton emphasizes that it is the Lady's chastity that draws Sabrina to rescue her; the Attendant Spirit tells the brothers that "maid'nhood she [Sabrina] loves, and will be swift / To aid a Virgin, such as was herself, / In hard besetting need" (855–57). After she answers the Spirit's call for aid, Sabrina herself tells him, "'tis my office best / To help ensnared chastity" (908–9). Indeed, Sabrina, even more completely than the Attendant Spirit, fulfills the Lady's belief that her chastity will inspire "the Supreme good" to send the guardian she might need (215–20).

It is fitting that the virgin Lady, who allegorically represents both the faithful individual Christian and the faithful church, would be rescued by the virgin Sabrina, who allegorically represents Christ. Cox writes, "The freeing touch of Sabrina thus rewards the Lady's fidelity just as Christ's grace touches and frees his bride."[51] And after the Lady and her brothers return to their father's house[52]—where the Attendant Spirit's celebration of the children's triumph "O'er sensual Folly, and Intemperance" (975) once again reinforces the theme of wise virginity and virtue over the foolishness of debauched living—a final allegorical representation of Christ and his relationship to the church and its individual members is offered. In his epilogue, the Attendant Spirit celebrates the eternal marriage of Cupid and Psyche:

> But far above in spangled sheen
> Celestial *Cupid* her fam'd son advanc't,
> Holds his dear *Psyche* sweet entranc't
> After her wand'ring labors long,
> Till free consent the gods among
> Make her his eternal Bride,
> And from her fair unspotted side
> Two blissful twins are to be born,
> Youth and Joy; so *Jove* hath sworn. (1003–11)

This image marks the masque's culmination of its allegorical portrayal of the Lady representing both the faithful church and its faithful individual members. The allegorical significance of this image is suggested by the Attendant Spirit's parenthetical admonition to his mortal audience before he begins speaking of both divine-mortal couples: "(List mortals, if your ears be true)" (997). These words echo those of Jesus after he has spoken (but before he has explained) the parable of the sower in Mark 4: "He that has ears to hear, let him hear" (4:9). Like Jesus, the masque's Spirit has a message for his audience that both depends on his audience's spiritual readiness and transcends the image he lays out before them,[53] and here Milton incorporates the "long tradition" of those "who saw in the classical story of Psyche and Cupid an adumbrated account of the human soul's search for God." Recognizing Milton's "celestial Cupid" as representing Christ, Scoufos observes that Milton "uses the wedding of Psyche and the god of love to depict the eternal bliss of the marriage of the Lamb and his Bride" found in Revelation 19:7–9. Scoufos notes parallels between *A Mask* and Foxe's *Christus Triumphans*, observing that in the first act of Foxe's drama, Christ weds Psyche, the individual soul, and in the final act weds Ecclesia, the church. Milton, however, "believed that the individual soul *was* the church, alone or in communion. His Lady represents both Psyche and Ecclesia in one figure."[54]

John Leonard, who also affirms that Milton's Psyche represents both the individual soul and the church, adds that Milton's description of Psyche and Cupid's marriage celebrates earthly as well as heavenly marriage, noting that the phrase "fair unspotted side" (1009) alludes to Ephesians 5:25–28: "Husbands, love your wives, even as Christ also loved the church, and gave himself for it; that he might sanctify and cleanse it with the washing of water by the word, that he might present it to himself a glorious church, not having spot, or wrinkle, or any such thing; but that it should be holy and without blemish. So ought men to love their wives as their own bodies." Leonard affirms that this allusion "implies continuity between marriage in heaven and marriage on earth,"[55] and this continuity serves to refute the arguments of scholars who have asserted that Milton himself took a vow of lifetime celibacy or that the Lady's refusal of Comus's sexual advances constitutes a wholesale rejection of sexuality per se. In Cox's view, "the celestial betrothal of the epilogue, rather than the earthly riches of Comus's earlier argument, signifies God's manifold bounty. For her constancy and zeal, Milton's Lady is promised solace and joy in human marriage. However, like 'unspotted' Psyche, who triumphs by her 'wand'ring labors long' (1006–9), she, and indeed all of God's faithful disciples, must await the more blissful and ecstatic union—the divine nuptial that exists beyond 'the green earth's end' (1014)."[56]

Milton's honoring of unwed celibacy, earthly marriage, and heavenly marriage in A Mask is entirely consistent with Sonnet 9, and his belief that virginity and chastity are ideals applicable to both singleness and marital monogamy is reflected throughout Paradise Lost. The masque's Lady is a wise virgin on many levels: she is chaste, she intelligently refutes the arguments of her would-be seducer, she recognizes the goodness of sexuality in its proper context. Like the virgins of the parable, her mind remains awake as she awaits the divine bridegroom with whom she, representing both the church and its faithful members, will unite in eternal matrimony. Like the Lady of Sonnet 9, her wise virginity in singleness prepares her for the wise virginity of marital fidelity with a worthy husband both here and hereafter.

6

Wise Virginity Lost in *Paradise Lost*

If Milton's *Mask Presented at Ludlow Castle* celebrates the ideal of the wise virgin, *Paradise Lost* (1667, 1674) offers a more complex depiction of that concept. As Stephen Fallon has recognized, the portrayal of Adam and Eve in Milton's great epic demonstrates Milton's investment of himself in their moral complexity.[1] *Paradise Lost* contains no explicit reference to the parable of the wise and foolish virgins, but the principle of the wise virgin is evident in the unfallen state of Adam and Eve, who demonstrate wisdom in direct proportion to their commitment to chastity of mind and body. Milton's portrayal of Adam and Eve as wise virgins reflects his belief, discussed in the previous chapter, that chastity and virginity encompass not only abstinence by unmarried persons but also faithful monogamy by married couples. This belief is emphasized in *Paradise Lost* before the Fall when, although Adam and Eve have made love, Milton's narrator uses the capitalized adjective "Virgin" to describe Eve (see 5.296, 8.501, and 9.270). After the Fall, however, she is not described as "virgin" again. In short, Milton depicts Eve and Adam as wise virgins who descend into foolishness through their respective acts of wrong thinking and behavior as they submit to vanity and passion rather than godly reason. Eve's status as a wise virgin is destroyed through her unwise choice to leave her husband and seek forbidden wisdom, while Adam becomes foolish by ceasing to display watchful vigilance, ultimately exchanging the pure wisdom of God for a self-deceiving wisdom of his own invention. Having lost paradise, Adam and Eve begin their return to wisdom as they return to following God's word and, in the end, are given hope through a vision of redemption that will take place through the ultimate wise virgins—Jesus and his mother, the Virgin Mary.

Satan's Perverse Fall from Wisdom and Purity

A brief look at Satan (another of Milton characters whom numerous critics have considered self-referential)[2] and his own fall from his position as a wise virgin is in order at the outset. Particularly important is what Satan's hapless daughter, Sin, recounts to him when they meet unexpectedly in his journey out of hell in book 2. She is the issue of "the monstrous pregnancy of narcissistic Satan."[3] Her bizarre birth took place, she tells him, while he and the other soon-to-be rebel angels "combin'd / In bold conspiracy against Heav'n's King" (2.750–51), at which time, she says, "Out of thy head I sprung" (2.758)—"like a masturbatory fantasy," in the words of Edward Le Comte.[4] Satan's bringing forth of Sin, then, results from the self-serving plan of rebellion that he has concocted as "the biblical archetype of the self-obsessed malcontent."[5] To Satan, this plan is wise, for it will liberate him and his followers from God's tyranny and enable them to live on his terms.

Satan's rebellion, for which he offers an ontological justification based on his claim that the angels were "self-begot, self-raised" (5.860) rather than created by God, later inspires the loyal angel Abdiel, who speaks for God, and ultimately for Milton himself, to call Satan a "fool" (6.135), one who in his entire scheme "err'st" (6.172), who is "from the path of truth remote" (6.173). Further, Abdiel describes Satan as both "unwise" and "not free, but to thyself enthrall'd" (6.179, 181). Abdiel recognizes that Satan, for all his foolishness, pursues his plan under the banner of wisdom, and he sees that Satan's "wise" plan is in essence an act of unfaithfulness; Satan's conspiracy is adultery, as it were, against God almighty, and Abdiel charges him with perversion. In calling Satan self-enthralled, Abdiel recognizes the "licentiousness" of the "liberty" of which Satan boasts,[6] a charge that Abdiel implicitly reinforces when he tells Satan that he "*lewdly* dar'st . . . upbraid" Abdiel and the faithful angels' "minist'ring" (6.182, emphasis added).[7]

This connection between sexual perversion, the perversion of wisdom, and the rebellion against God is unmistakable in light of Satan's rape of Sin.[8] Continuing to recount their previous relationship, Sin recalls to Satan how she, "familiar grown, / . . . pleas'd" her father,

> and with attractive graces won
> The most averse, thee chiefly, who full oft
> Thyself in me thy perfect image viewing
> Becam'st enamor'd, and such joy thou took'st

With me in secret, that my womb conceiv'd
A growing burden. (2.761–67)

The sexual perversion we see here, besides involving the obvious elements
of rape and incest, also includes another manifestation of the self-"enthrall'd"
Satan, "the narcissist who loves himself only."[9] Indeed, As John Mulryan
observes, "Satan is self-impregnated, or self-raped, making love to himself
and then to his daughter, the product of his incestuous mind."[10] Sin notes
that he is "enamor'd" by seeing his own "perfect image" in her, and his perverted self-love/lust explicitly confirms that he chooses love of self over love
of God, which he rebelliously renounces. This perverted choice is entirely
consistent with Satan's narcissistic character; as F. T. Prince notes, "It is
appropriate that Satan's love should spring from a mirror-like reflection of
himself."[11] His rape of Sin explicitly manifests his perverse, self-focused
affections, demonstrating acutely that his rebellious, ungodly wisdom is
inextricably linked with infidelity. Like the Fall of Adam and Eve that follows, Satan's fall from the wisdom of God is simultaneously a fall from
chastity.

Eve and Adam: Wise Virgins Unfallen

We are thus aware of Satan's perversions when we first encounter the chaste
couple Adam and Eve. Milton depicts them as pure manifestations of God's
image, and, in their unfallen glory, perfect representations of Milton's ideal
of the wise virgin.

Godlike erect, with native Honor clad
In naked Majesty seem'd Lords of all,
And worthy seem'd, for in thir looks Divine
The image of thir glorious Maker shone,
Truth, Wisdom, Sanctitude severe and pure,
Severe, but in true filial freedom plac't. (4.289–94)

The grandeur, dignity, and innocence of the first couple and their relationship to God contrasts starkly with the account of Satan and Sin. Being made
in God's image, they reflect his wisdom and purity; and their nakedness, far
from being associated with lust, accentuates their "Majesty."[12] These lines
display Milton's conviction that innocence and purity—both spiritual and

sexual—are perfectly compatible with wisdom, and that whatever knowledge Adam and Eve may be deprived of by God's prohibition against eating from the Tree of Knowledge, such ignorance in no way detracts from the wisdom their creator has given them.[13]

The couple's first recorded interaction reveals a wisdom based on their contented submission to God and Eve's contented submission to Adam. Adam quickly demonstrates his unfallen understanding of God, his created order, and their privileged place in it. Surveying creation's beauty and their happiness, he recognizes and tells Eve that "the Power / That made us, and for us this ample World" must "Be infinitely good" (4.412–14); seeing the blessings God has lavished on them as his special creations and chosen rulers over the earth, Adam recognizes God's command not to eat of the Tree of Knowledge as "One easy prohibition" (4.433). Delighting in their wondrous situation, he lovingly exhorts Eve and himself to "ever praise him," "extol / His bounty," and follow their "delightful task" of caring for the garden (4.436–37).[14] Adam's recognition of God's created order demonstrates a simple yet profound wisdom—evident even at his first waking moments (see 8.277–82), which, as we shall see, contrasts with his illogic in book 9.

Newborn Eve: The Threat of Foolish Self-Love and Her Initial Wise Choice

Eve recognizes that her position in the created order complements Adam's, and her understanding of their relationship's hierarchy demonstrates her own unfallen wisdom.[15] She states that they ought to praise their maker, adding that she enjoys "So far the happier Lot" because she is privileged to be with Adam, who is "Preëminent by so much odds" (4.446–47). She proclaims that she was "form'd" "for" Adam and "from" him, "flesh of [his] flesh" (4.440–41); "without" Adam, her existence is "to no end." She calls Adam "my Guide / And Head" (4.442–43), and she relates to him her first moments and their subsequent meeting, emphasizing that she acquired a right perspective on herself when she became united to him. The most curious, and critically most controversial, part of her initial self-awareness occurs when she becomes entranced by her own reflection in a lake:

> As I bent down to look, just opposite,
> A Shape within the wat'ry gleam appear'd
> Bending to look on me, I stared back,

> It started back, but pleas'd I soon return'd,
> Pleas'd it return'd as soon with answering looks
> Of sympathy and love; there I had fixt
> Mine eyes till now, and pin'd with vain desire . . . (4.460–66)

These lines, clearly alluding to Ovid's account of Narcissus in *The Metamorphoses*, have elicited voluminous critical commentary, ranging from readings that celebrate Eve's innocent wonder to those suggesting that Eve here shows herself as partly fallen well before eating the forbidden fruit in book 9. I see this scene as simultaneously foreboding and hopeful, a demonstration of Eve's potential to fall into the very self-love that leads her to sin even as it celebrates her ability to freely exercise the "reasoned choice" to follow God's instruction and begin a loving marriage with Adam.[16] Eve's potential for narcissism, like Satan's, is evident from the start; indeed, Eve's relating that she was "pleas'd" by her reflection ominously echoes Sin's reminding Satan that he was "pleas'd" by her (2.262), a detail probably recognized by Satan, who watches and hears the couple's conversation. Unlike Satan, however, Eve's attraction here does not "bringeth forth sin" (James 1:15); rather, Eve allows her unfallen self-enthrallment to be broken by the divine voice of wisdom, which she obediently follows. The voice instructs:

> What thou seest,
> What there thou seest fair Creature is thyself,
> With thee it came and goes: but follow me,
> And I will bring thee where no shadow stays
> Thy coming, and thy soft imbraces, hee
> Whose image thou art, him thou shalt enjoy
> Inseparably thine. (4.467–73)

Despite her initial inclination to return to her reflection, God's words inspire Eve to replace her incipient narcissism with the love of Adam, a love characterized by a hierarchy of wisdom. Any unwise desire for her own beauty gives way to a proper understanding of the preeminent place of the wisdom given, in Milton's Eden, to Adam, and the perfection of her happiness begins when she willingly "yield[s]" to him. "From that time," she says, she has recognized

> How beauty is excell'd by manly grace
> And wisdom, which alone is truly fair. (4.489–91)

Having moved away from the threat of foolish self-love and chosen to unite with Adam, Eve from this moment becomes a wise virgin and a happy bride. This is not a result of the wisdom that she possesses in isolation from Adam, but of her recognition of and submission to Adam's wisdom, a progress into wisdom predicated on her earlier willingness to recognize and submit to the voice of God. The inextricable link between wisdom, properly placed faith and love, submission, fidelity, sexual purity, and happiness is integral to the scheme of Milton's Eden, and it is these elements' right relationships that Satan attacks during his subsequent rhetorical assaults upon Eve.

Julia Walker, Eve's "Absence of Self," and the Scope of Miltonic Self-Representation

At this point, in the larger context of Milton's penchant for self-representation in his characters, let us examine briefly the criticisms of Eve's character that Julia Walker offers in *Medusa's Mirrors*. Walker specifically laments Eve's "absence of self," lack of sight, and lack of any knowledge of herself:

> What does Eve see? Not herself. Not God. Not Adam as "her image" remembered from the lake. Milton's narrative of Eve, like Ovid's narrative of Medusa, presents female power only as the object of the actions of a god or the gaze of a man. The figure that supposedly generates the reflection is, in Milton's text, curiously absent. Her fictive presence and her physical attributes are necessary for the narrative, but the narrative itself is Adam's, is God's, is Milton's. Eve, in *Paradise Lost*, is the reflection of the perceptions of these men, not of herself.[17]

It is not my purpose to agree or disagree with Walker's assessment, but I would argue that Walker's dissatisfaction with Milton's depiction of Eve is really dissatisfaction with his representation of himself in Eve. Milton's Eve, that is, like the idealized Lady of Sonnet 9 (see chapter 4) is not an autonomous individual but a reflection of the expectations of the idealized and disturbingly narcissistic male self-representation who constructs, beholds, and delights in her as a reflection of his delight in himself. If Eve is in fact Milton's idealized self-representation (who completes his Adamic self-representation by virtue of Adam's seeing in her "my Self / Before me" [8.495–96]), then Walker's concerns are, curiously enough, validated by my own study, a strange admission that I offer as a scholar whose fundamental approach to Milton is very different from Walker's.

But perhaps I concede too much here; perhaps Milton's self-representation in Eve is not so thoroughgoing as to deny her the selfhood that Walker claims Eve lacks. Indeed, readers' centuries-long fascination with Milton's Eve seem to argue against Walker's contention. And the fact that most of that fascination centers around passages in which Eve resists, or at least appears to resist, patriarchal expectations—(the encounter with her reflection in the lake; her transgressive dream encounter with the Satanic angel with whom she seems to share the forbidden fruit, and their subsequent exhilarating flight; her determined plan to separate from Adam to tend Eden more efficiently; her fatal choice to eat the apple; her deadly decision to offer the fruit to Adam)—strongly suggests in Eve an autonomy that argues against Walker's reading. I submit that Milton's construction of Eve moves far beyond the limitations of the Eve who is enveloped by Adam's narcissistic desire for her and encompasses the wondering, the imaginative, the adventurous, the rebellious, the heartbroken, the repentant, and, in the end, the submissive to God and his word individual who embodies Milton's own complex and multifaceted being.

Satan in Eden: Sexual Jealousy and Perverted Wisdom

Returning to book 4, we see that Satan's jealousy of Adam and Eve's relational and sexual happiness,[18] and his disgust at their cheerful submission to the God whose authority he seeks to usurp, are matched by his sin-darkened inability to comprehend the possibility that the couple might remain happy in spite of God's prohibition against their eating from the Tree of Knowledge. Ruminating on this prohibition, Satan muses upon God's unfairness and lack of sense: "Knowledge forbidd'n? / Suspicious, reasonless" (4.515–16). But discerning that disobeying this command will lead to the couple's ruin, Satan resolves:

> I will excite thir minds
> With more desire to know, and to reject
> Envious commands, invented with design
> To keep them low whom Knowledge might exalt
> Equal with Gods; aspiring to be such,
> They taste and die: what likelier can ensue? (4.522–27)

We see here the twisted and self-contradictory logic in which Satan's fallen mind indulges. On the one hand, Satan resents God's prohibition, indicting God on behalf of the ignorant couple whom he has deprived of the knowledge that would make them godlike. On the other hand, the prohibition being what it is, Satan happily uses this "unfair" restriction to tempt Adam and Eve to their deaths.[19]

Satan's words reveal the fraudulence of the wisdom he proffers. Clearly, his stated concern for the man and woman is another manifestation of his own self-love; in his aim to rescue them from the confines of Eden, he seeks to rob them of the bliss he has witnessed. The desire to "rescue" them from paradise makes no sense, of course, nor does the "knowledge" with which he seeks to tempt them. Satan sees that Adam and Eve possess an innocent wisdom, and it is clear, ironically, that his offer of "knowledge" is in fact a temptation to foolishness—the foolishness of rebelling against God. But we should not expect Satan to make sense; indeed, it makes perfect sense that he makes no sense. For in his own perverse rebellion against God, Satan forfeited the divinely given wisdom Adam and Eve now enjoy, and the residual manifestation of his God-given wisdom—his evil wit—now exists only to further the destruction Satan carries within himself. Not surprisingly, the temptation he concocts is a temptation to fall into the same sin that he has. There is a bizarre consistency in Satan's pattern of sinful reproduction. He has produced Sin, his own evil image, full-grown from his own head. And he has proceeded to rape and produce offspring by her. Similarly, he has produced in his angelic followers sinful offspring in his own image, and now he seeks to do the same to the first couple.

The Unfallen Lovemaking of Wise Virgins

Adam and Eve soon display the connection between the innocent wisdom of unfallen, faithful obedience and chaste, unfallen sexuality. Eve exemplifies this when she responds to Adam's invitation to rest (and, implicitly, to make love):

> My Author and Disposer, what thou bidd'st
> Unargu'd I obey; so God ordains,
> God is thy Law, thou mine: to know no more
> Is woman's happiest knowledge and her praise. (4.635–38)

Expressing a view of knowledge utterly contrary to Satan's, Eve demonstrates an innocent wisdom in her unquestioning obedience to her husband, an attitude that, in Milton's portrayal, springs from a proper obedience to God and thoroughly contradicts Satan's rebellious nature. In Adam's company, Eve has all the wisdom she needs.[20] She is able to think rightly about herself, him, God, and creation; she enjoys right relationship with God, humanity, and nature. She is, in all respects, a wise virgin, a state confirmed by the joyous sexual relations in which she and Adam soon partake—relations which consummate, paradoxically, their wise virginity.

Milton's subsequent description of wedded love is remarkable for its celebration of both the wisdom and the purity that characterize the sexual relationship Adam and Eve enjoy.[21] Significantly, Milton's narrator makes a smooth transition from the couple's "adoration pure" of God to a defense of marital sexuality, which "God declares / Pure" (4.737, 746–47). The narrator uses the vehicle of the first couple's unfallen marriage bed to extol marital love as a whole, and Milton's self-referential voice manifests itself prominently here. While addressing "wedded Love" (4.750), he declares, "By thee adulterous lust was driv'n from men" (4.753), stressing that such love is "Founded in Reason, Loyal, Just, and Pure" (4.755). These lines offer an idealized celebration of marital sexuality in both its prelapsarian and postlapsarian contexts, arguably even eliding the distinction. There is no question that Milton presents marital sexual relations as genuinely redemptive, contrasting them with perverse forms of sexuality against which marital sex offers protection (see 4.765–770).

The narrator also punctuates this description of marital bliss with a brief inclusion of the figure Love (another name for Cupid), an inclusion that recalls to us the image of Cupid offered at the end of *A Mask Presented at Ludlow Castle*:

> Here Love his golden shafts imploys, here lights
> His constant Lamp, and waves his purple wings,
> Reigns here and revels. (4.763–65)

Just as the figure of Cupid in *A Mask* is recognized as tantamount to Christ,[22] a similar ideal is evident here. Milton's narrator, having lauded marital love as God's gift to humanity, now melds classical and Christian images of divine love, recalling both the arrows of Cupid and the marriage between Christ and his church, supplemented with the image of the "constant Lamp," which fulfills and transcends the yet-burning lamps of the wise virgins who await the bridegroom Christ. Implicitly, Milton's narrator recognizes all who properly enjoy marital sexuality as wise virgins in the broad sense, and such persons are given ultimate expression in the figures of Adam and Eve, on the one hand, and Christ and his church, on the other.[23]

Perhaps the narrator's most revealing expression of the connection between wisdom and sexual chastity is articulated at the close of the bower scene:

> Sleep on
> Blest pair; and O yet happiest if ye seek
> No happier state, and know to know no more. (4.773–75)

Milton says, in effect, that the couple enjoys the most perfect pleasure possible—marital lovemaking—and that just as such happiness is preserved by not seeking greater happiness (which does not exist, though one could be deceived into thinking it does), the highest form of knowledge is the wisdom to reach no further—a wisdom that Satan and his followers fell from heaven for want of. The consequence of reaching for knowledge beyond human grasp is both the loss of happiness of the postlapsarian state and a fallen intellect. The admonition "know to know no more" offers an obvious double entendre, encompassing both sexual and cerebral knowledge and implicitly connecting readers to Genesis 4:1, which states that "Adam knew Eve his wife" (cf. Gen. 4:25). This relationship between sexual and cerebral knowledge also foreshadows the method of temptation that Satan uses to seduce Eve. To "know to know no more" expresses the very essence of Milton's unfallen wise virgin, for it displays an innocent obedience to God that preserves both perfect prelapsarian wisdom and sexual happiness.[24]

Eve's Dream: Satan's First Assault on Wise Virginity

Witnessing Adam and Eve's joy in love tortures Satan, who begins to work toward their downfall by directly assaulting their unfallen wisdom and sexuality as they sleep. Satan's whisperings into the ear of the sleeping Eve resemble a seduction, as he attempts

to reach
The Organs of her Fancy, and with them forge
Illusions as he list, Phantasms and Dreams.

Satan also attempts to inspire in Eve

distemper'd, discontented thoughts,
Vain hopes, vain aims, inordinate desires
Blown up with high conceits ingend'ring pride. (4.801–3; 807–9)

These lines are sexually charged; Le Comte notes that the "venom" (4.804)
Satan speaks into her is "like semen, the seed of illicit thoughts,"[25] his words
working against the narrator's warning to "know to know no more." The
discontent that Satan sows within Eve's unconscious mind includes temptation both cerebral and sexual, playing on Eve's vulnerability to vanity and
leading her away from the ideal of the wise virgin. And Satan's seduction
of the sleeping Eve is effective because, with her rational capacities lying
dormant but her fancy awake,[26] she can be attracted to the evil phantasm
Satan proffers even as she is incapable of rationally resisting this attack.

Imaginative Seeds of Self-Love and Adultery

When the distraught Eve tells Adam of her dream the next morning, she
confirms Satan's seductive intent. From the first detail of her report, the
adulterous nature of her "sexual dream" is evident.[27]

Methought
Close at mine ear one call'd me forth to walk
With gentle voice, I thought it thine; it said,
Why sleep'st thou, Eve? now is the pleasant time. (5.35–38)

The lines that follow, in which the voice tells of the "love-labor'd song" of
the bird and declares that Eve is "Nature's desire" (5.41, 45), solidify the
sexual nature of the voice's call. Indeed, Satan "woos her like a Cavalier and
husband substitute."[28] In fairness to Eve, she believes the voice is Adam's;
the narrator, having only a little before celebrated Adam and Eve's lovemaking, does not disapprove of Eve's rising to meet what she thinks is her
husband's invitation to make love again at a different location. At the same
time, however, the voice's words reveal a degree of flattery that appeals to

Eve's natural susceptibility and crosses into the realm of idolatry. The voice tells her,

> Heav'n wakes with all his eyes,
> Whom to behold but thee, Nature's desire,
> In whose sight all things joy, with ravishment
> Attracted by thy beauty still to gaze. (5.44–47)

These words heap praise on Eve that rivals the praise owed to God—and readers can compare this inappropriate praise of Eve to the praise all nature offers God in 5.153–208—and yet the dreaming Eve does not question it, even when Adam is nowhere to be found. Although Eve cannot be blamed for her nonrational decision-making process in sleep, if she were able to exercise her reason fully, she might recognize the illogic of Adam's voice speaking idolatrous flattery. Of course, she is not able, and drawn by such flattery, she continues to search for the unseen speaker. Satan capitalizes here on Eve's vulnerability to self-love, and as a master of flattery he woos her skillfully. There is something insidious, indeed horrifying, going on here. In attacking her in her vulnerability—something he is aware of only by virtue of the words of love she spoke to Adam—Satan draws her away from her proper likeness (that is, Adam, from whom she is made in God's image) and draws her toward himself, the original narcissist, who hopes to use her vulnerability to make her into his fallen image.

Unsurprisingly, the voice's idolatrous sexuality leads Eve to an idolatrous representation of the Tree of Knowledge. Eve reports that the tree seemed "Much fairer to my Fancy than by day" (5.53), and she beholds beside it "One shap'd and wing'd like one of those from Heav'n" (5.55). Once again, the dreaming Eve cannot exercise the full capacity of her reason. At this point, an awakened Eve might ask this angel, "Who are you? Where is my husband? Didn't you also hear his voice? Were you impersonating him?" But she does not.[29] In fact, there is no further mention of Adam in her dream. Instead, Eve focuses her attention on the tree and her new companion. At this point the angel makes explicit the temptation to forbidden knowledge using words that make the tree become "an object of libidinous temptation":[30]

> O fair Plant, said he, with fruit surcharg'd,
> Deigns none to ease thy load and taste thy sweet,
> Nor God, nor Man; is Knowledge so despis'd?

> Or envy, or what reserve forbids to taste?
> Forbid who will, none shall from me withhold
> Longer thy offer'd good, why else set here? (5.58–63)

The angel employs a perverse logic here that in its ostensible benevolence sets itself up against the explicit command of God, and, hailing the higher knowledge offered by the tree, contradicts the admonition to "know to know no more." Eating the fruit, the angel calls Eve to do likewise, employing words aimed to disrupt her contented bliss with Adam. He tells Eve,

> happy though thou art,
> Happier thou may'st be, worthier canst not be:
> Taste this, and be henceforth among the Gods
> Thyself a Goddess, not to Earth confin'd,
> But sometimes in the Air, as wee, sometimes
> Ascend to Heav'n, by merit thine, and see
> What life the Gods live there, and such live thou. (5.75–81)

Having aroused Eve from the perfect contentment of her marital love-making, the dream angel tempts her with assurances of superior happiness and supernatural knowledge. He then approaches Eve closely to tempt her with the fruit, and her account of what happens next employs sexually charged language to describe both his actions and her response:

> So saying, he drew nigh, and to me held,
> Even to my mouth of that same fruit held part
> Which he had pluckt; the pleasant savory smell
> So quick'n'd appetite, that I, methought,
> Could not but taste. Forthwith up to the Clouds
> With him I flew, and underneath beheld
> The Earth outstretcht immense, a prospect wide
> And various: wond'ring at my flight and change
> To this high exaltation; suddenly
> My Guide was gone, and I, methought, sunk down,
> And fell asleep. (82–92)

Although Eve herself has not sinned in the experience of this dream,[31] her dream is nonetheless a kind of dual seduction that ultimately leaves her vulnerable to the actual temptation of book 9. For the self of Eve's dream is seduced on two levels: first, although the text does not explicitly say that she ate, Eve's narrative suggests that she was seduced into eating the fruit of the Tree of Knowledge, thus violating God's clear prohibition;[32] equally important, however, the dreaming Eve is seduced away from regarding Adam as her sole intimate companion. In effect, the angel of the dream replaces Adam. He successfully draws Eve from her marriage bed by imitating Adam's amorous call, but once Eve is with him, he no longer attempts to imitate Adam; rather, she seems to forget, quite on her own, the husband for whom she had been searching.

Eve's fascination with, and even sympathy for, the angel is evident in her verbal and nonverbal responses to his speaking of, eating, and offering her the forbidden fruit. Having observed him verbally defy and actively transgress God's prohibition, she recounts, "mee damp horror chill'd / At such bold words vouch with a deed so bold" (5.65–66). Eve's words suggest a dark sexual attraction to the angel, and, conspicuously, she casts no negative judgment on his defiant speech or his consumption of the fruit. Rather, she refers to both his words and his action as "bold," a word indicating "showing or requiring courage; daring, brave," a word that is often used "with admiration emphasized,"[33] and the same word that Adam uses in 9.921 to describe Eve's eating of the fruit as he is in the process of justifying his "resolution ... to Die" with Eve (9.907). Furthermore, the angel's "dr[awing] nigh" and holding "Even to [Eve's] mouth" the fruit is a sexual advance that she does not resist. Their flight together mirrors the exhilaration of lovemaking, and her response upon its climactic ending—to sink down and fall asleep—mirrors its conclusion. A. B. Chambers, though he denies that Eve herself sins, acknowledges that "Eve's fancy receives a suggestion of sin, it delights, and it consents."[34]

In the course of the dream, the angel has given Eve things that Adam cannot rightly offer her: praise of her appearance that effectively supplants the praise of God; an example of one who, for ostensibly noble purposes, questions the very commands of God; the opportunity to become truly divine and an accompanying moral rationalization for disobeying God's prohibition; an exhilarating, passionate flight to the heavens that transcends the first couple's God-given physical boundaries. The angel is someone new, intriguing, exciting, and attractive to Eve. Indeed, Eve's dream is significant not only for weakening her psychologically and setting her up for Satan's temptation in book 9; it also provides an attractive precedent for the separation scene upon which the success of Satan's temptation ultimately depends. The seeds of discontent in Eve's relationship with Adam have been planted, and one wonders, after Eve's "dream date" with the angel, whether Adam and his rational obedience to God will ever fully satisfy her again.[35]

Adam's Insufficient Response

Adam's response to Eve is both tender and pedantic, demonstrating some understanding but also a confusion that reflects his inexperience and a hesitance to confront the danger at hand. He recognizes the dream as a threat, not only to Eve's individual well-being but also to their union. He recognizes the dream as "uncouth" and "of evil sprung" (5.98), and he wisely notes the primacy of "Reason" over "Fancy" even as he recognizes fancy's potential to deceive (see 5.100–113). He advises Eve:

> be not sad.
> Evil into the mind of God or Man
> May come and go, so unapprov'd, and leave
> No spot or blame behind: Which gives me hope
> That what in sleep thou didst abhor to dream,
> Waking thou never wilt consent to do. (5.116–21)

Adam's words here and elsewhere in this speech reveal naïveté and a failure to exercise vigilance.[36] He recognizes the dream as evil but cannot yet comprehend the origin of such evil.

The presence of evil seems illogical to Adam; he recognizes that Eve is pure, and that it would thus be nonsensical for such evil to spring from within her unsolicited, but he does not consider that Eve's dream might have been placed in her by a malevolent outside source. Even after Raphael's visit detailing Satan's rebellion and malevolence, Adam shows no awareness that the dream might have been satanically inspired. Indeed, even in book 9, when he allows Eve to separate from him, he never sufficiently recognizes Eve's and his own vulnerability to this evil from without. Moreover, Adam speaks a fair amount about reason and the need for the various faculties, fancy included, to work within reason's parameters. But he never questions Eve—who in sleep was clearly attracted to the angel—to make sure that her "Fancy" is being properly subordinated to her "Reason." Rather, he articulates the rather irresponsible assumption that Eve's faculties will take care of themselves when she is awake. But this is problematic; Adam should know better, and he probably does. As William B. Hunter comments, "Adam's cheerful explanation must have fallen a little flat on his own ears, for Eve's physical state indicated an internal disorder."[37] Perhaps, in spite of his own knowledge, he does not appreciate fully the degree to which Eve's fancy needs reason's guidance, something he should recognize from her original vulnerability to self-love. Moreover, Adam does not acknowledge his own responsibility to provide her with such rational direction. Instead, he naïvely assumes that because she is "Created pure" (5.100), she is rationally sufficient in herself. Adam ignores that it was because of her initial union with him that she moved from displaying narcissistic tendencies to articulating chaste wisdom.[38]

Adam also makes the naïve assumption that Eve fully rejects all aspects of her dream. With the possible exception of "how glad I wak'd / To find this but a dream!" (5.92–93), Eve says nothing to indicate that she did, as Adam claims, "abhor to dream" all these things. Given that even in their prelapsarian state Adam and Eve are capable of recognizing good and evil,[39] it seems a weak excuse to argue that Adam, in his unfallen innocence, is unable to recognize his wife's implicit attraction to the angel and what he offers. Unlike Adam, we recognize that Eve did not fully "abhor to dream" her encounter with the angel, and David Aers is right to take Adam to task for failing to ask Eve about her feelings concerning the dream and failing to recognize "her pleasure" in experiencing it.[40] Furthermore, despite Adam's assurance that she "never wilt consent to do" such a thing when awake, we know with certainty that not only she but Adam himself will soon consent to such disobedience. Ironically, Adam talks a good deal about wisdom even as he exercises so little of the wise vigilance characteristic of the wise virgins of Matthew's parable. Adam's problem—for which Raphael, the angel God sends to warn Adam of Satan's evil machinations, later admonishes him—is his tendency to overestimate Eve's autonomous rational capacities and underestimate his own role in directing her. If they are to remain wise virgins, Adam must exercise appropriate leadership, the very thing he progressively fails to do.

Failures to Wisely Watch: Adam's Susceptibility and Raphael's Warnings

Adam's misrepresentation of Eve manifests itself explicitly when he speaks with Raphael in book 8. Raphael has spent books 5 and 6 telling Adam and

Eve of Satan's rebellion, Abdiel's noble resistance against him, the ensuing war in heaven, and the rebels' defeat by the power of the Son, who casts them into hell. Book 7 consists of Raphael's narrative of the Son's subsequent creation of the world. Near the beginning of book 8, Eve departs to tend her flowers, expecting Adam to tell her whatever the angel tells him thereafter (see 8.40–57). Adam inquires at length about astronomy and the possibility of life on other planets, a subject Raphael eventually cuts off, admonishing Adam to "be lowly wise" (8.173), perhaps suggesting to readers that Adam should at this time concentrate on protecting Eve and himself from the Satanic threat at hand rather than such speculations. At Raphael's request, Adam tells the story of his first day of existence, a joyous episode that leads to his first meeting with God and culminates in God's creating Eve, whom God describes as "Thy likeness, thy fit help, thy other self, / Thy wish, exactly to thy heart's desire" (8.450–51). Adam responds to Eve's presence by declaring her "Bone of my Bone, Flesh of my Flesh, my Self / Before me" (8.495–96). As noted in chapter 4, Adam's declaration here echoes Genesis 2:23, even as the words "my Self / Before me" are nowhere to be found in the biblical text and give rise to Julia Walker's charge—also discussed in chapter 4—that Adam is already displaying here a narcissistic infatuation with Eve that displaces his love for God.[41] Although I would argue that Adam, like Eve fascinated with her reflection in the lake, does not sin in this declaration, it does reveal his own susceptibility to narcissistic self-love, a susceptibility that develops into transgression, as we shall see.

This concern notwithstanding, Adam's first encounter with Eve begins appropriately enough. In fact, their initial meeting reveals significant elements of the wise virgin theme implicit in the bower scene of book 4. Adam describes Eve as one endowed with "Innocence," "Virgin Modesty," and "virtue" (8.501–2), who responds to the "pleaded reason" of his courting (509–10). In addition, Adam relates how the "Ev'ning Star" had lit "the Bridal Lamp" for their initial lovemaking (519–20). Adam also tells of the unique joy their divinely ordained sexual relationship gives him. After this point, however, Adam begins to waver from right reason. While he acknowledges that Eve is "inferior" to him "in the mind" (541) and that her "inward Faculties" less resemble God's than his do (542–44), he also admits that his understanding of such matters falters "when I approach / Her loveliness" (546–47). On such occasions, Adam reports,

> so absolute she seems
> And in herself complete, so well to know
> Her own, that what she wills to do or say,
> Seems wisest, virtuousest, discreetest, best;
> All higher knowledge in her presence falls
> Degraded, Wisdom in discourse with her
> Loses discount'nanc't, and like folly shows;
> Authority and Reason on her wait,
> As one intended first, not after made
> Occasionally; and to consummate all,
> Greatness of mind and nobleness thir seat
> Build in her loveliest, and create an awe
> About her, as a guard Angelic plac't. (8.547–59)

Raphael is displeased with Adam's effervescent report, and whatever our emotional sympathies toward Adam, we may recognize problems with his rationale.[42] Indeed, Adam's words ironically contradict Eve's earlier statements celebrating "How beauty is excell'd by manly grace / And wisdom, which alone is truly fair" (4:490–91), a rational understanding that helped free her from her initial narcissistic impulse toward her reflection. Here in book 8, however, Adam shows himself susceptible to a kind of idolatry of Eve's beauty. Adam's potential for such idolatry overlaps with his potential for narcissism; it also resembles Eve's own inclination toward narcissism, but it is far more treacherous in that it attributes to Eve, by virtue of her beauty alone, a degree of wisdom that far exceeds her natural capacities. Adam's incorrect thinking causes him to overestimate Eve's rational capabilities and moral rectitude and to underestimate his responsibility to guide her in the way of wisdom, a responsibility that necessitates his own vigilant exercise of wisdom, a vigilance that again shows signs of waning.

Indeed, we should consider Adam's comments to Raphael in relation to his earlier (under)reaction to Eve's dream. Both speeches exhibit Adam's passivity and misplaced confidence in Eve's self-sufficiency, a confidence that betrays a failure to exercise the husbandly role of leader and protector in which Eve so delights in book 4. Adam's speech concerns Raphael all the more because Adam extols Eve's supposed "complete[ness]" and superior wisdom, virtue, and discretion, even though he has just said that she is in fact intellectually inferior to him. Adam's speech reveals his willingness to entertain emotionally what he rationally knows to be untrue.

Raphael—who has previously told Adam, in Eve's presence, to "warn / Thy Weaker" about Satan and to "fear to transgress" (6.908–9, 912)—now sternly chides Adam for his problematic affections:

> be not diffident
> Of Wisdom, she deserts thee not, if thou
> Dismiss not her, when most thou need'st her nigh,
> By attribúting overmuch to things
> Less excellent, as thou thyself perceiv'st. (8.562–66)

Raphael recognizes that Adam's tendency to "dismiss" "Wisdom" in favor of his feelings and perceptions can weaken his rational faculty, eventually leaving him without wisdom's protection when he might need it most. Raphael also recognizes that in spite of Adam's ostensible magnanimity toward Eve, his obsequious admiration will wreak havoc on her attitude toward him. Raphael warns Adam that Eve and her beauty are "worthy well / Thy cherishing, thy honoring, and thy love, / Not thy subjection" (8.568–70). He continues:

> weigh with her thyself;
> Then value: Oft-times nothing profits more
> Than self-esteem, grounded on just and right
> Well manag'd; of that skill the more thou know'st,
> The more she will acknowledge thee her Head,
> And to realities yield all her shows;
> Made so to adorn for thy delight the more,
> So awful, that with honor thou may'st love
> Thy mate, who sees when thou art seen least wise. (8.570–78)

Simply put, if Adam fails to exercise wisdom in his estimation of and relationship with Eve, he will lose both wisdom and Eve.[43] Of course, Raphael's warning foreshadows exactly what happens in book 9 when Adam, yielding to (though not persuaded by) Eve's dubious logic, permits and even exhorts Eve to separate from him. But in these earlier scenes, Adam's dubious thinking process anticipates his passive release of Eve into Satan's deception. Her dream has eroded her resistance, but having learned of her dream, Adam has not vigilantly protected her. And his words to Raphael demonstrate that he has not been thinking rightly. Raphael warns him, in the words of Marjorie Hope Nicolson, "to learn the difference between true love and passion."[44] Passion subdues reason; true love is based in reason and works in conjunction with it, as Raphael goes on to explain:

> In loving thou dost well, in passion not,
> Wherein true Love consists not; Love refines
> The thoughts, and heart enlarges, hath his seat
> In Reason, and is judicious, is the scale
> By which to heav'nly Love thou may'st ascend,
> Not sunk in carnal pleasure. (8.588–93)

True love, chaste love, is the companion of wisdom and leads to God himself. Passion, by contrast, impedes reason and leads one away from God. One is wise, the other is foolish; one secures the position of the wise virgin, the other jeopardizes it.

Adam does not recognize sufficiently that everything Raphael says here is crucial to his and Eve's destinies; rather than discuss with Raphael strategies for wise resistance of the enemy, he continues to pursue the topic of lovemaking, inquiring whether or not angels make love (8.614–18). His focus is not on securing wisdom and God's proper order of things. And although he does not sin or lose paradise until late in book 9, his inaction makes Eve and himself vulnerable to attack, and his unwise failure to lead erodes Eve's respect for him. Bowers observes that "[Eve's] revolt will reach its crisis only when Adam in his unwisdom has abdicated his proper function of superior and of command."[45] But this abdication has been developing for some time before Adam and Eve's separation and subsequent tragedy. Adam's passivity in books 5 and 8 paves the way for the first couple's fall.

Unwise Separation

As noted above, Adam and Eve's separation is largely the result of Adam's giving in to Eve's inferior logic.[46] The irony, as she herself attests in book 4, is that Eve learns right thinking from Adam. As William Madsen remarks, "at the crucial moment . . . Adam forgets the lesson he has taught Eve."[47] Moreover, the logic Eve employs while seeking to persuade Adam to "divide our labors" (9.214) demonstrates the influence of her Satan-inspired dream. The principle Eve advocates concerning the increased efficiency of divided labors resembles the dream angel's rationale behind the rightness of Eve's eating the forbidden fruit: that if men become gods, good "more abundant grows" (5.72). It is hardly coincidental that Eve uses the angel's logic while trying to separate from Adam. After all, her encounter with the angel is what makes Eve comfortable with the idea of separation. As Robert Wiznura has observed, Eve's dream "opens up the possibility of the false autonomy offered by Satan, an autonomy predicated on action and disobedience."[48] And now Eve employs the logic, the seeming wisdom, of her dream seducer. That she echoes the angel's argument implicitly confirms the obvious: that she no longer views Adam and his immediate presence as the logical prerequisite for her well-being, and believes that her life may be enriched by pursuing some experience apart from him. Indeed, the "wisdom" she employs here is a precursor to her spiritual adultery.

Adam's response to Eve, like his response to her dream, demonstrates a knowledge of reason even as he ultimately fails to act on this knowledge. While careful not to dismiss Eve's ideas, Adam recognizes that their constant companionship brings both joy and wisdom, and that they should not hastily sacrifice it. Noting the connection between relational joy and wisdom, Adam says that the desire for efficient work need not "debar" (9.236) them from

> this sweet intercourse
> Of looks and smiles, for smiles from Reason flow,
> To brute deni'd, and are of Love the food,
> Love not the lowest end of human life.
> For not to irksome toil, but to delight
> He made us, and delight to Reason join'd. (9.238–43).

Adam recognizes here that, in unfallen Eden, there is a harmonious connection between the delight of human interaction and rationality, and his words resemble Raphael's connection between true love and reason. While Eve advocates the division of labor in strictly utilitarian terms,[49] Adam understands that God's purpose for their work in the garden is multifaceted; it is an exercise that engages the complementary faculties of delight and reason, best conducted within relational community. At this juncture,

Adam has stated his point well enough, but he quickly defers to Eve's inferior logic, saying,

> But if much converse perhaps
> Thee satiate, to short absence I could yield.
> For solitude sometimes is best society,
> And short retirement urges sweet return. (9.247–50)

Again, this statement reveals the damage Eve's dream has done to their relationship. Adam has made a convincing argument for the rightness of their staying together, but he seems to recognize that Eve is not content with the status quo; as Mary Jo Kietzman puts it, "Adam seems newly aware of the distance which separates him from a very complicated Eve." He demonstrates insecurity and "uncertainty," and his words betray his hope that if he allows her a "short absence," their interaction will be more "sweet" upon her "return."[50]

Wise Warnings, Problematic Arguments, Unwise Permission

But after speaking these words, Adam quickly recognizes how problematic any separation would be. He states his "other doubt" (9.251)—the "malicious Foe" (9.253) of whom Raphael warned. This foe "Env[ies] our happiness" (9.254) and, Adam surmises, watches for a chance to assault them when they are separate, since he is "Hopeless to circumvent us join'd, where each / To other speedy aid might lend at need" (9.259–60). Having outlined this threat, Adam urges Eve to "leave not the faithful side / That gave thee being, still shades thee and protects" (9.265–66). In expressing these concerns, Adam again speaks rationally, but he does not convince Eve.

In fact, his words offend Eve, who considers his concern both unfair and illogical. She is incredulous that Adam fears that her "firm Faith and Love / Can by his [their foe's] fraud be shak'n or seduc't" (9.286–87), and hurt that Adam could have "misthought of her to thee so dear" (9.289). Of course, given Eve's dream, her disconcerting fascination with it, and her standoffish attitude toward him, Adam has every reason to doubt Eve's capacity to resist seduction while alone. This, along with Satan's proximity and Adam's responsibility as Eve's protector, again validate his concern. It seems that Eve is "misthinking" about Adam, not vice versa. Even more revealing of her faulty logic is the dubious statement upon which she bases much of her argument. She claims that they need not fear Satan's "violence," because they are *not capable of death or pain* (9.282–83, emphasis added). Eve's words here display a serious misunderstanding of the extent of Satan's power and machinations, for they limit to the physical realm Satan's threat to the couple. Moreover, her words contradict warnings that both Raphael and God himself have given Adam. At the end of book 6, Raphael, in Eve's presence, cautions Adam that Satan's punishment for his disobedience is "Eternal misery" (6.904). He urges Adam to learn from Satan's "terrible Example the reward / Of disobedience," and implores him to "remember, and fear to transgress" (6.910–12). Having already warned Adam that an envious Satan plots to "seduce" him "from obedience" (6.901–2), Raphael instructs him to "warn / Thy weaker" (6.908–9). Moreover, Adam later tells Raphael of God's warning that if he should transgress by eating from the forbidden tree, "inevitably thou shalt die" (8.330). Clearly, Eve's statement is dangerously inaccurate; Adam knows it, and he ought to instruct Eve regarding God's and Raphael's warnings.

But Adam makes no attempt to correct Eve's misrepresentation of their condition. Rather, wishing to undo the injury that his words have caused Eve, he implicitly assents to her statement. He replies "with healing words" (9.290) and addresses her as "immortal *Eve*" (9.291). "Immortal," for the present, accurately describes Eve, yet Adam's language seems improper, and so does his pronouncement of Eve as free "from sin and blame entire" (9.292). Although this statement too is true (for now), Adam is fully aware that Eve is capable of sin and of dying, and painfully cognizant of the threat of a foe who seduced a third of the angels into sin and damnation. He has these facts on good authority. Simply put, this is no time for the flattery in which Adam indulges here. Displaying an attitude that foreshadows his decision to eat the forbidden fruit, Adam seems more concerned with preserving the couple's immediate comfort than with protecting her (and his) long-term well-being. He is, it seems, favoring the concerns of passion over those of true love.

Continuing in the same manner, his ensuing argument is characterized by an apologetic, even obsequious tone, and he does not even to attempt to disabuse Eve of her misplaced confidence.

> Not diffident of thee do I dissuade
> Thy absence from my sight, but to avoid

> Th' attempt itself, intended by our Foe.
> For hee who tempts, though in vain, at least asperses
> The tempted with dishonor foul, suppos'd
> Not incorruptible of Faith, not proof
> Against temptation: thou thyself with scorn
> And anger wouldst resent the offer'd wrong,
> Though ineffectual found: misdeem not then,
> If such affront I labor to avert. (9.293–302)

Adam, whose earlier statements displayed, for the most part, the force of logic, offers here "a trivial argument"—an illogical "concern for appearances"—and then resorts to more flattery and avoids the uncomfortable reality of the situation.[51]

It appears that Adam is deceiving himself. Just a few lines later he notes that their "Enemy" (9.304) was able to "seduce / Angels" (9.307–8). Why, then, would he now suggest that his only real concern is that Eve would "resent" and be "anger[ed]" by the necessarily "ineffectual" "offer'd wrong" this enemy might attempt? By avoiding the obvious—that any enemy who could seduce angels en masse would have a very good chance of seducing a solitary Eve—Adam reduces his argument from a substantive effort to protect his wife to mere patronizing fluff. His words to Eve are in fact an insult. What he winds up saying, in effect, is, "I know that our foe won't be able to harm you, but I don't even want to have to suffer the indignation of his trying to. That might upset you, and I want to prevent that." In attempting to remove the sting of his earlier remarks, Adam both overstates Eve's self-sufficiency and suggests that the potential damage their foe can inflict on her is a mere wound to her sensibilities. His attempt to prevent such an inconsequential attack comes off as more priggish than chivalric, and his words only strengthen Eve's resolve to venture out on her own. Perhaps the most unfortunate aspect of Adam's condescending lines is that they effectively nullify the remainder of his speech, which is actually quite substantive. In an echo of the parable of the wise and foolish virgins, Adam tells Eve that just as in her presence he becomes "More *wise*, more *watchful*, stronger" (9.311, emphasis added), he hopes that she feels likewise empowered when with him.[52] Significantly, he asserts that they both display the characteristics of the parabolic wise virgins better when they are together than when they are alone. They are, as it were, the oil in each other's lamp.

Eve responds with increased offense and decreased logic. The illogic in her reply, however, takes its cue from her husband's own dubious remarks. She accuses Adam of thinking poorly of "her Faith sincere" (9.320); "she hears him trying to reduce her,"[53] and in arguing for the rightness of her proposed solitary work, says:

> But harm precedes not sin: only our Foe
> Tempting affronts us with his foul esteem
> Of our integrity: his foul esteem
> Sticks no dishonor on our Front, but turns
> Foul on himself; then wherefore shunn'd or fear'd
> By us? who rather double honor gain
> From his surmise prov'd false, find peace within,
> Favor from Heav'n, our witness from th' event. (9.327–34)

Obviously, Eve both underestimates Satan and overestimates her and Adam's powers of resistance. But her logic notably builds on that offered by Adam. Since he has argued that he simply doesn't want Eve to suffer the insult of whatever temptation might be offered, she appropriately answers that such temptation, when rebuffed, will not dishonor the one tempted but rather the tempter himself, and will result in substantial rewards— "double honor"—for those who expose their foe as an ineffectual villain.[54] The irony of all this is that, within the nonsensical rubric Adam has constructed, Eve's logic here makes perfectly good sense. She is working from the assumption that they will not—indeed, cannot—fall. Thus Adam's inordinate plea for caution insults not only her but God himself, for it effectively portrays Eden as a fraud (9.337–41).

Adam responds with an eloquent polemic that echoes God's words to Raphael in 5.235–45; he asserts that God created "Nothing imperfecst" (9.345), but also notes that "God left free the will" (9.351). Despite their secure situation, it is

> yet possible to swerve,
> Since Reason not impossibly may meet
> Some specious object by the Foe suborn'd,
> And fall into deception unaware,
> Not keeping strictest watch, as she was warn'd. (9.359–63)

Adam again uses the language of the parable here, with line 363 echoing
Matthew 25:13 and Jesus's admonition to imitate the wise virgins. To think
oneself, whatever God's blessing, to be above falling is simply unwise; to
"watch" against evil is to be wise. Thus Adam warns:

> Seek not temptation then, which to avoid
> Were better, and most likely if from mee
> Thou sever not: Trial will come unsought. (9.364–66)

Once again, Adam makes a convincing argument, and we can only wonder
whether Eve might have stayed had his persuasion been matched with a
gentle authoritative finality.

But there is neither finality nor authority in Adam's statement. Instead,
again presumably inspired by his desire that their relationship be without
friction, a desire motivated by passion, not genuine love, he gives Eve an out:

> But if thou think, trial unsought may find
> Us both securer than thus warn'd thou seem'st,
> Go; for thy stay, not free, absents thee more;
> Go in thy native innocence, rely
> On what thou hast of virtue, summon all,
> For God towards thee hath done his part, do thine. (9.370–75)

Adam "collapses into linguistic disarray" here, displaying "torturous syntax,"
capitulating to "nonsense." At this point, as William G. Riggs observes,
Adam "no longer speaks with God-like authority"; rather, he has "recast
himself as an injured and petulant lover."[55] Riggs's comments may be contrasted with those of Gordon Teskey, who writes, "Adam's statement, 'thy
stay, not free, absents thee more,' is to my mind the truest in the poem.
Doing anything against your own will and good judgement, to please someone else, is slavery and morally destructive to both parties."[56] But Adam's
statement, couched in insecurity, not wisdom, is not truly an affirmation of
Eve's free will—which Adam's earlier arguments in favor of her staying in
no way threatened—but rather an abdication of his role as her wise and
vigilantly watchful protector, a role particularly crucial in their present
perilous circumstances.

The irony here is that, in his dubious "appeal to the principle of
freedom"—an appeal, Anthony Low notes, that is "as flawed as Eve's earlier
appeal to the value of trial and experience"[57]—Adam releases Eve into the

most perilous danger just when his argument has been most convincing. Perhaps he comforts himself in the thought that the last line he has spoken reflects the very words that Raphael spoke to him the evening before: "Accuse not Nature, she hath done her part; / Do thou but thine" (8.561–62). Adam is simply passing on the wisdom from heaven to his wife, and if it is good enough for him, it should be good enough for her. The problem is that Adam cannot do *his* "part" by simply telling Eve to do *her* "part." In trying to do so, Adam is abdicating his responsibility as Eve's husband under the pretense of an equality that simply does not exist in Milton's Eden. When Raphael tells Adam to "warn / Thy weaker" (6.908–9), the angel is serious about Eve's being "weaker" than Adam. And it is obvious that by "warn" he does not mean that Adam should make his case only to end by saying, "but do what you think best." The point, of course, is that Adam is supposed to know best—and not only to know best but to present his knowledge to his "weaker" in a convincing manner.

This role, however, has become problematic for Adam, influenced as he is by passion. As is evident from his words in book 8, although on some level Adam accepts Eve as his "weaker," he continues to be affected by his exchange with Raphael:

> when I approach
> Her loveliness, so absolute she seems
> And in herself complete, so well to know
> Her own, that what she wills to do or say,
> Seems wisest, virtuousest, discreetest, best;
> All higher knowledge in her presence falls
> Degraded, Wisdom in discourse with her
> Loses discount'nanc't, and like folly shows;
> Authority and Reason on her wait. (8.546–54)

These lines play themselves out in book 9; but it is Adam himself, not Eve, who brings about their fulfillment. Various critics have criticized Adam for abandoning his role as Eve's leader and protector. Anthony Low writes, "when unfallen Adam lets Eve go, he abdicates a position of natural and loving, not expedient, authority. His duty is to command what is right."[58] For Adam to command Eve's obedience in this way would be no more tyrannical than God's prohibition against eating from the Tree of Knowledge in the first place. (And critics who claim that Adam would have been out of order to command such a thing mimic Satan's criticism of God.) In any event, as Low, Dennis Danielson, and Stanley Fish have noted, such a command by Adam would not have violated Eve's free will—but it might very well have prevented the Fall.[59] Low continues in words discomfiting to modern sensibilities but faithful to Milton's larger narrative: "Had Adam insisted on obedience, Eve would still have had the choice of disobeying. Perhaps she would have eventually done so. It seems more likely, however, that she expected Adam's prohibition and was taken by surprise at his sudden consent." Going on to assert that Eve's "dependence on Adam" and his "guidance" is basic to her character as Milton develops it," Low concludes that "Adam errs when he permits her to have her way, and abdicates his proper responsibilities."[60]

That Adam's own words to Eve are ultimately responsible for Eve's departure is evident from her response:

> With thy permission then, and thus forewarn'd
> Chiefly by what thy own last reasoning words
> Touch'd only, that our trial, when least sought,
> May find us both perhaps far less prepar'd,
> The willinger I go. (9.378–82)

These lines are preceded by the narrator's comment that Eve "Persisted, yet submiss" (9.377). The word "submiss" emphasizes that Eve, whatever her ostensible independence of thought, remains in a sense curiously deferential to her husband. She departs from him, she says, with his "permission," and her rationale for doing so is buttressed by the concessive statements he has just spoken. This point must not be missed: Eve's separation from Adam is predicated on Adam's own words, on Adam's own departure from the logic of God that he employed only sentences before. There is no concrete reason to believe that Eve would have left had he been more vigilant in his position.[61] And there is a bizarre similarity between this separation and the separation that took place in Eve's dream in book 4: both are brought about by Eve's following, so to speak, the voice of Adam. In dismissing Eve, Adam has relinquished his God-given role as protector. He has ceased to be watchful and wise, and he has placed them both in positions where it will be increasingly difficult to exercise watchfulness or wisdom. Adam's words have set up Eve, a now unprotected and, being alone, less wise virgin, in a position where she is vulnerable. All the while, Satan, her spiritual seducer, lies in wait.

Satan's Seduction

The serpent's temptation of Eve can rightly be called a seduction,[62] and we see in their conversation preceding her eating of the forbidden fruit the manner in which the serpent's flattery overcomes Eve's exercise of reason. Furthermore, just as Eve was freed from her initial self-attraction by her coming together with Adam, so too in the temptation does Eve, apart from Adam's protection, give in decisively to reawakened narcissistic impulses. This dangerous reversion is inevitably accompanied by a loss of right thinking about herself, Adam and her relationship to him, and God himself—the very sort of right thinking she gained through her initial union with Adam. Not surprisingly, Satan's appeals to Eve's vulnerability to self-love are accompanied by assaults on her thinking concerning God, Adam, and herself.

Even before he speaks, Satan's flattery is evident. The serpent stands before Eve "in gaze admiring . . . bow[ing]," "Fawning . . . lick[ing] the ground whereon she trod" (9.524, 526). The deceptive nature of Satan's flattery becomes especially manifest when he speaks. While all his initial words to Eve are suspicious, several statements are patently false and even idolatrous. The purpose of such statements, from the first, is to draw Eve away from her loyalties to Adam and to God and to replace them with an increased focus upon herself. In his opening sentence, Satan addresses Eve as "sovran Mistress" (9.532); he goes on to call her the "Fairest resemblance of thy Maker fair" (9.538); he tells her that "all things" her "Celestial Beauty adore" (9.539–40), and says that she

> shouldst be seen
> A Goddess among Gods, ador'd and serv'd
> By Angels numberless, thy daily Train. (9.546–48)

The serpent's word choice ought to make Eve suspicious from the start. His use of the word "sovran" is a clear indication that he is tempting Eve into self-idolatry. Prior to this scene, "sovran" appears thirteen times in *Paradise Lost*, all of them in reference to God himself.[63] The serpent's language also assumes polytheism, something that Eve seems not to notice but that is significant because it is within the context of polytheism that Satan articulates his deceptive doctrine concerning God's and Eve's respective degrees of deity.[64] For if one implicitly accepts the notion of polytheism, as Eve seems to do in the ensuing conversation, the idea of one's actually being or becoming a god is all the more plausible, as is the idea that the God of Eden is merely a deity whose benevolence is limited to his own interests and who is threatened by the thought of another's obtaining wisdom that could rival his own. The temptation to spiritual adultery is evident here as Satan attacks Eve's vulnerability to narcissism and builds on the emotional adultery he began to effect in her dream.

Satan also uses flattery to undermine Eve's belief that Adam is the closer of the two of them to God's image. Even as Adam tells Raphael about how "weak" he is "Against the charm of [Eve's] Beauty's powerful glance" (8.532–33), he acknowledges not only that she is "th' inferior, in the mind / And inward Faculties" (8.541–42), but that "In outward also" she is "resembling less"

> His image who made both, and less expressing
> The character of that Dominion giv'n
> O'er other Creatures. (8.543–46)

Eve herself essentially states this position when she recalls that after she received Adam's hand in their initial meeting, she

> from that time see[s]
> How beauty is excell'd by manly grace
> And wisdom, which alone is truly fair. (4.489–91)

Satan, of course, is aware that Eve came to this view only upon uniting with Adam. And Satan knows that Eve's initial impression of Adam was that he was "less fair" (4.478) than the image of herself in the lake. The Eve whom the serpent now encounters, her hand decisively withdrawn from her husband's (9:385–86), is vulnerable to returning to her former self-focus and to receiving uncritically the serpent's pronouncement that she is the "Fairest resemblance of thy Maker fair." Most heinous of all is the serpent's claim that "all things living" and "Angels numberless" adore her. The verb "adore" is used thirteen times previously in the epic, and each time it is used to refer to the worship of God or pagan deities, including Satan himself in 4.89.[65] Satan's plan of spiritual adultery escalates here.

The claim that angels ought to adore Eve should be especially suspect, and enough to awaken her suspicion and inspire her outright rejection of the serpent's words. They do not, however, because Eve, in her solitude, is not exercising her significant but limited rational capacities. Instead, her emotional faculties are unchecked by reason. Riggs asserts that Satan, as in Eve's dream, "appeals to Eve's 'fancy,' to her impulse to conjoin, to her self-centering attraction to the world as mirror or extension of herself."[66] Consequently, she is already well on her way to being seduced; we are told that "Into the Heart of *Eve* his words made way" (9.550). The serpent's blasphemy is not of concern to her; the only thing that seems noteworthy to Eve is that the serpent can speak, a phenomenon, curiously enough, she calls a "miracle" (9.562).

The serpent attributes this "miracle" to his eating of the "fair Apples" (9.585) of "A goodly Tree" (9.576); the result of this eating, he reports, is the "Strange alteration" (9.599) within him: a dramatic increase in "Reason" and the acquisition of "Speech" (9.600). The serpent goes on to emphasize that the most joyous of his newly acquired faculties is the ability

> to come
> And gaze, and worship thee of right declar'd
> Sovran of Creatures, universal Dame. (9.610–12)

As before, his flattery takes the form of idolatry, and the more deeply his charming words enter Eve's heart, the more open she becomes to a different theology altogether. Furthermore, even as she accepts the serpent's flattery and the ideas that accompany it, she at no point questions the believability of the serpent's story, even though she is aware that a powerful enemy is at large.

The Logic of Transgression

When the serpent brings her to the Tree of Knowledge, Eve for the first time recognizes that *its* fruit is the fruit he claims has given him his new power. Initially, she resists—she tells the serpent that "of this Tree we may not taste nor touch" (9.651), noting that this is the only command that God has given her and Adam and that the penalty for transgression is death (9.661–63). But Eve has been weakened—by her dream, by her separation from Adam, by the serpent's flattery and the worldview that accompanies it.

The serpent's appeal at this point builds on this weakness, and his argument makes sense to one who has accepted his earlier flattery. The serpent enters into a short, worshipful address of the tree (beginning, "O Sacred, Wise, and Wisdom-giving plant / Mother of Science" [9.679–80]) before speaking to Eve directly. Addressing her as "Queen of this Universe" (9.684), he aggressively attacks the very suggestion that God should punish the eater of the wisdom-giving fruit, a fruit that can offer a "happier life" by imparting the "knowledge of Good and Evil" (9.697). His words cast doubt on the most fundamental notion of God's justness, his proper authority over his creation:

> God therefore cannot hurt ye, and be just;
> Not just, not God; not feared then, nor obey'd:
> Your fear itself of Death removes the fear.
> Why then was this forbid? Why but to awe,
> Why but to keep ye low and ignorant,
> His worshippers. (9.700–705)

The serpent's logic here rips away the very essence of Eve's previous conception of her benevolent maker. She is susceptible to such logic because her reception of his earlier flattery has already confused the fundamental issue of her place as a subject of God. If she is in fact "Queen of this universe," and if all nature and the angels themselves adore her, then who is this God to keep her from the knowledge of good and evil? And how can such a God be just, or even worthy of the superior position he assumes?

The serpent continues. God knows, of course, that those who eat of the fruit "shall be as Gods" (9.708); but what of it? Why would it offend God "that Man should thus attain to know" the knowledge of good and evil (9.726)? Can it hurt him?

> Or is it envy, and can envy dwell
> In heav'nly breasts? these, these and many more
> Causes import your need of this fair Fruit.
> Goddess humane, reach then, and freely taste. (9.729–32)

The serpent uses his own question to invert Eve's rapidly decaying understanding of God. When the serpent asks, "can envy dwell / In heav'nly breasts?," his insinuation is: "God must be envious of you; this being the case, can he really be God?" And this suggestion only confuses Eve further. Paul Hammond points out that Satan's "series of rhetorical questions . . . seem to offer [Eve] the freedom of a response . . . but in reality they are freighted with a predetermined answer."[67] Were Eve at this point thinking rightly, she could have responded, "No, of course envy cannot dwell in

heavenly breasts, so stop bringing up this absurd notion that God is envious." But she does nothing of the sort. Her thoughts concerning God have
been turned upside down, just as her thoughts about herself have been
inverted. By the time the serpent addresses Eve as "Goddess humane," we
sense that she essentially has come to believe that she is superior to God
himself, or at least entitled to eat the fruit this dubious God has forbidden.

The narrator's comments reveal that Eve's mind has been changed by
means of her emotions. We are told that the serpent's words "Into her *heart*
too easy entrance won" (9.734, emphasis added—and we notice the narrator's underscoring of this point in that this line essentially repeats 9.550),
and that his "persuasive words" seem to her "impregn'd / With Reason . . .
and with Truth" (9.737–38). At the same time, we see her physical appetite
conspiring with her susceptibility to flattery to influence her thinking and
her actions. As noon draws near, within Eve

> wak[es]
> An eager appetite, rais'd by the smell
> So savory of that Fruit, which with desire,
> Inclinable now grown to touch or taste,
> Solicited her longing eye. (9.739–43)

Eve is simultaneously experiencing overloads upon her emotions, her reason, and her physical appetite, and she fails to resist this collective assault.
Rather, she seems to embrace it all too easily.

Self-Deception, Self-Justification, Self-Exaltation

Eve's ensuing address to the tree is a speech of "self-deception" that makes
clear that she has crossed over into Satan's way of thinking.[68] Copying the
serpent, she addresses the tree in a manner that borders on idolatry, an
idolatry that will manifest itself fully after she eats the fruit moments later.
The logic she exhibits in her address also emulates the rationale of the
serpent. Demonstrating that her conception of God has become entirely
inverted, she tells the tree that God's "forbidding / Commends thee more,
while it infers the good / By thee communicated, and our want" (9.753–55).
The fruit, far from being a bane to be avoided, now becomes, by virtue of
God's prohibition, the epitome of goodness for humanity. A little later she
says, "this Fruit Divine" is "the Cure of all" (9.776), another statement that

reveals the degree to which her previous way of thinking has been sup-
planted by Satan's. Claiming that the fruit has "virtue to make wise," she
asks, just before reaching forth and eating the fruit, "what hinders, then /
To reach, and feed at once both Body and Mind?" (9.778–79). The answer
now, of course, is nothing, for Eve has been convinced of a new reality in
which wisdom has been utterly redefined, committing the "basic error" of
"assuming that knowledge is synonymous with wisdom," departing from the
biblical truth that "the beginning of wisdome is the fear of the Lord"[69] and
the narrator's admonition to "know to know no more." Failing to be wise,
she now embraces the full corruption of her person.

After her "lustful act" of eating the apple,[70] Eve puts her newfound
"wisdom" into practice by actively worshipping the tree. Again demonstrating the extent to which the serpent's flattery has affected her mind, Eve
opens her address with the words "O Sovran, virtuous, precious of all
Trees / In Paradise" (9.795–96). It is no coincidence, given Satan's previous
mock worship of Eve, that she now uses the word "sovran"—once reserved
for God—to describe the tree. Her praise of the tree is justified, she claims,
because through it she "grow[s] mature / In knowledge as the Gods who
all things know" (9.803–4), and because it has rescued her from her "ignorance" and "op'n'st Wisdom's way" (9.809). These statements are notable not
only for their polytheism. As Milton's readers would have recognized, Eve
acts the part here of the self-deceived idolatrous fools whom Paul describes
in his Epistle to the Romans. These individuals, "Professing themselves to
be wise . . . became fools" (Rom. 1:22), and "worshipped and served the
creature more than the Creator" (1:25). C. S. Lewis comments on the vulgar
irony of Eve's behavior: "She who thought it beneath her dignity to bow to
Adam or to God, now worships a vegetable." And Garrett A. Sullivan Jr.
notes a similar absurdity about the woman who separated from Adam in
order to care for Eden's overgrown vegetation more efficiently: "After the
Fall, Eve worships, rather than prunes or tends, a plant."[71]

But given that she has been following Satan, we should not be surprised
by such ironic reversals. Eve's act of idolatry, Lewis writes, "thus completes
the parallel between her fall and Satan's"; both Satan and Eve have succumbed to the temptation of self-love. As Michael Lieb observes, for Eve,
the forbidden fruit is "the projection of herself"; upon eating it, "The figure
at the water's edge has been seduced into copulating with her reflection."[72]
Like Satan, Eve makes love to her own image. Like Satan, she is no longer

a wise virgin. Like Satan, Eve follows her own sin by seeking the perverse conversion of her existing community.

Regarding her marriage to Adam, Eve's immediate concern is whether she ought to share with him the fruit that has given her this newfound "power" (9.820), and this question reveals the effect that her transformation has had upon her once-contented mind. Adam has been replaced by Eve's own ambitions. In her idolatrous worship, she tells the tree, "Experience, next to thee I owe, / Best guide" (9.808–9). This title was previously reserved for Adam, whom she had called "my Guide / And Head" (4.442–43). At this point, she thinks it may be best to keep her power for herself. To do so, she speculates, would "add what wants / In female sex," would all the more "draw his Love" (9.821–22), and would

> render me more equal, and perhaps,
> A thing not undesirable, sometime
> Superior: for inferior who is free? (9.823–25)

This Eve differs sharply from the Eve of book 4, who proclaimed herself to "enjoy / So far the happier Lot" (4.445–46) by being coupled with the superior Adam. It is only when Eve recognizes that if God has seen her disobedience, "Death" indeed may "ensue" (9.827), and she decides to share the fruit with Adam, for whom she now proclaims unswerving love.[73]

Knowing Better

When Eve recounts her experience to Adam, he immediately understands the tragedy that has befallen her, and thus also himself. His description of Eve as "Defac't, deflow'r'd, and now to Death devote" (9.901) is as accurate as it is sad. But Adam quickly decides to share Eve's fate. Announcing, "Certain my resolution is to Die" (9.907), he cries out to Eve that he cannot endure the loneliness of life without her:

> I feel
> The link of Nature draw me: Flesh of Flesh
> Bone of my Bone thou art, and from thy State
> Mine never shall be parted, bliss or woe. (9.913–16)

From this determination, rooted in an idolatry that places Eve above God, Adam embarks on a process of self-deception that emboldens him to pursue

to the end the suicidal course upon which he now sets himself. As the
narrator makes clear, Adam, unlike Eve, is not deceived by an outside agent
but acts "Against his better knowledge" (9.998). As he completes his descent
from wise virgin to self-deceived fool, Adam employs language that reflects
both Satan's deception and Eve's credulity. He begins by praising his
"advent'rous Eve" for her "Bold deed" (9.921)—essentially the same phrase
Eve used to describe her Satanic dream angel's eating of the forbidden fruit
(5.66). Adam's approving use of these words adds credence to the notion
that Eve was indeed attracted to the "deed so bold" of the dream angel.
Similarly, he echoes Eve's argument that even as the serpent ate of the fruit
and "yet lives" (9.932) in a higher capacity, so too should its alleged transformation inspire them to eat and "attain / Proportional ascent, which
cannot be / But to be Gods, or Angels Demi-gods" (9.935–37). Adam's
self-deception here mirrors Eve's deception by Satan, though its agent differs. Both deceptions are seductions, but Adam, enamored with Eve and
controlled by passion instead of wisdom and chaste love, allows himself to
be seduced by his own desires, a fall into foolish self-love even worse than
Eve's own eating of the apple.[74]

The Glory of (Self-)Love

Adam's foolish choice, often mistaken as a grand display of love for Eve but
in reality a self-deceived "love that is self-love,"[75] displays itself explicitly in
the final words he speaks before he eats the apple:

> So forcible within my heart I feel
> The bond of Nature draw me to my own,
> My own in thee, for what thou art is mine;
> Our state cannot be sever'd, we are one,
> One Flesh; to lose thee were to lose myself. (9.955–59)

Although Adam's decision to die with Eve has been called "heroic charity"
and even Christlike,[76] Adam articulates an idolatry of self that manifests
itself in the person of Eve, an idolatry that continues the pattern of narcissism that characterized the respective falls of Satan and Eve and that
tragically gives in to the susceptibility to narcissistic idolatry suggested by
his initial celebration of Eve as "my Self / Before me" (8.495–96).[77] Adam's
decision is the tragic upshot of the self-deception that inspired him to

permit Eve to separate from him in the first place. In both instances, Adam, choosing passion for Eve over godly reason, convinces himself to allow Eve's inferior logic to prevail on him for the sake of preserving their relationship in the short term. And in each case, it is not Eve's but Adam's own words that allow unwise choices. The separation having occurred with his own permission, Adam now convinces himself that his only choice is whether to live on without Eve or meet death with her. Milton notes that, from Adam's perspective, the situation "*seem'd* remediless" (9.919, emphasis added).

But *was* the situation really "remediless"? The extent to which passion now controls Adam can be seen more fully when we consider that there was a rational *and* loving alternative for Adam. As various critics have suggested, had Adam prioritized faithfulness to God over devotion to Eve and self, he might have "interceded with God on her behalf" and begged for mercy and forgiveness for Eve.[78] Most compellingly, Dennis Danielson and John Leonard have both argued that Adam, being yet sinless, could have offered to die in Eve's place, after which God might well have resurrected him.[79] But Adam does not trust God enough to make this appeal. His lack of wisdom here again indicates that Adam does not eat the fruit out of love for Eve—he does so out of love for himself.[80] The self-deception of his words gives him away.

When Adam eats the fruit, the couple consummates their sin with the first lustful human sexual act, what the narrator calls the "the Seal" "of thir mutual guilt" (9.1043). This event is clearly the antithesis of the blessed lovemaking described in book 4, and upon its conclusion the couple recognize, as they look upon each other, "how op'n'd" "thir Eyes" now are and "How dark'n'd" "thir minds" have become (9.1053–54). The "guilt and dreaded shame" (9.1114) that ensue are followed by violent quarreling, and we see that "Understanding" and "Will" are "both in subjection now / To sensual appetite" (9.1127–29). Adam and Eve's full descent from wise virginity now consummated, they continue to argue, blaming each other for the Fall that has taken place.[81]

The Humble Return to Wisdom

Although the ideal of the wise virgin within Adam and Eve is destroyed upon their fall into sin, and although Adam fails to offer himself for Eve in a way that would have prefigured the sacrificial act of the ultimate Wise Virgin, Jesus Christ, Adam and Eve's movement toward redemption in the remainder of the epic directly relates to behavior that anticipates, obeys, and places faith in Christ. In book 10, Eve's words to the still scornful Adam—her well-meaning but ineffectual offer to ask God that judgment "from thy [Adam's] head" be "remov'd" and instead "may light / On me . . . / Mee mee only" (10.934–36)—have often been described as Christlike.[82] Similarly, Adam, softened by Eve's humble repentance, wishes, though he knows it is now impossible, that Eve's sin be "forgiv'n" and "That on my head all might be visited" (10.956, 955). More important, although Adam knows that neither he nor Eve can now die for the other's sins, he recognizes that the words spoken by the Son during his curse of the serpent, Satan, the *protoevangelium*—that Eve's seed will "crush his head" (10:1035)—anticipate a victory over Satan, through their offspring, that precludes Eve's wrong-headed idea that they should kill themselves so as to end the curse on mankind. Adam's recognition of the word of God and its implications begins to reverse the effects of his earlier disobedience of God's word and propels him to initiate his and Eve's prayer of repentance that concludes book 10.[83]

Adam's incipient faith in Christ reaches fuller development when Michael instructs him, while Eve sleeps, before the couple's expulsion from Eden. When Michael tells him of the coming "King *Messiah*," virgin-born and sired by "The Power of the most High" (12.358–71), Adam joyfully recognizes him as "The Seed of Woman: Virgin Mother" (12.379) and as "the Son / Of God most High" (12.381–82); moreover, he recognizes his role as this One's original progenitor. Speaking directly to this future "Virgin Mother," and celebrating his connection with her, Adam proclaims,

> Hail,
> High in the love of Heav'n, yet from my Loins
> Thou shalt proceed, and from thy Womb the Son
> Of God most High; So God with man unites. (12.379–82)

As Michael unfolds history before them, Adam comes to a fuller understanding of both the ills the world will face and the hope offered through the promised savior. Having finally been shown Satan's ultimate defeat and the promise of the "New Heav'ns," "new Earth," and the "endless" ages of

"Joy and eternal Bliss" "founded in righteousness and peace and love" (12.549, 551, 550), Adam offers his own final reflections:

> Greatly instructed I shall hence depart,
> Greatly in peace of thought, and have my fill
> Of knowledge, what this Vessel can contain;
> Beyond which was my folly to aspire.
> Henceforth I learn, that to obey is best,
> And love with fear the only God, to walk
> As in his presence, ever to observe
> His providence, and on him sole depend,
> . . . .
> Taught this by his example whom I now
> Acknowledge my Redeemer ever blest. (12.557–64, 572–73)

Michael replies, "This having learnt, thou hast attain'd the sum / Of wisdom; hope no higher" (12.575–76). The archangel's affirmation of Adam's words and of the paramount "wisdom" of godly obedience indicates the degree to which Adam's new understanding of and faith in his coming savior has transformed him from the despairing, self-deceived man who fell into foolish disobedience. Michael continues:

>   only add
> Deeds to thy knowledge answerable, add Faith,
> Add Virtue, Patience, Temperance, add Love,
> By name to come call'd Charity, the soul
> Of all the rest; then wilt thou not be loath
> To leave this Paradise, but shalt possess
> A paradise within thee, happier far. (12.581–87)

Michael's admonition to pursue "Charity" as the crown of virtue recalls the Lady of *A Mask Presented at Ludlow Castle* and her dedication to "Faith," "Hope," and "Chastity" (213, 215, cf. 1 Cor. 13:13). It also recalls A. E. Dyson's observation that in *A Mask*, "Chastity is more than an isolated virtue; it is symptomatic of spiritual wholeness and the life of grace."[84] With Dyson's words in mind, we may equate the Lady's "Chastity" with the "Charity" Michael now exhorts Adam (and, by extension, Eve) to display. By pursuing faithfully the true love of God and each other, the first couple, in spite of their fallen condition, may again act the part of wise virgins, knowing God's blessing and offering hope to the race that will be the bittersweet fruit of their devotion.

The newly awakened Eve also recognizes her part in this promised redemption. Pledging her unfailing loyalty to Adam in the difficult life beyond Eden that now awaits them, Eve gains solace in the company of her husband, "Who for my wilful crime art banisht hence" (12.619). She too gains hope, recognizing her restored relationship with Adam as inextricably linked to the anticipated savior in whom she now places her faith:

> This further consolation yet secure
> I carry hence; though all by mee is lost,
> Such favor I unworthy am voutsaf't,
> By mee the Promis'd Seed shall all restore. (12.620–23)

As Anne-Julia Zwierlein has observed, Eve's anticipation of "the real pregnancies [she] will carry to term—ultimately leading to the birth of Christ" counteracts Satan's "sinister version of male pregnancy"—his birthing and rape of Sin.[85] Eve's repentant return to a life of wise virginity will bring about the birth of the ultimate Wise Virgin, Christ, who in his perfect obedience to the Father will conquer the sin first initiated by Satan's original act of disobedient self-love and redeem sinful humanity's inheritance of Eve's and Adam's subsequent acts of disobedient self-love.

The poem's final picture of Adam and Eve is one of tearful harmony and hope. They have lost their innocence, they have lost paradise, and yet they also recognize that within them lives the redemption of humanity. Instructed now in the wisdom of obedience, they depart from Eden. Even as they leave the blessed bowers in which they enjoyed their original lovemaking, they leave Eden "hand in hand" (12.648), and their continued union displays the continued blessing of God and the hope of the race they will now procreate. Moreover, their enduring loyalty to each other—a loyalty that is once again submitted to the love of God and not passion—reveals that they are once again acting as wise virgins. To be sure, they are scarred, and they will give birth to a scarred and painfully fallen race. But they are also the recipients of divine grace. The final image of them, "hand in hand" as they depart from Eden, is also an image of them "hand in hand" taking the first steps in their lifetime journey of redemption. Their journey, in the end, leads toward heaven—and, Michael tells them, its "Joy and eternal Bliss" (12.551). While the conclusion of *Paradise Lost* does not quite leave us with a picture of the marriage of God and his people envisioned in Revelation 19:7–9, it does, in its language, hint at it. For we know that the "eternal bliss" enjoyed by the virgin church of God in the new heaven and new earth will exceed the joys that Adam and Eve knew in their unfallen "blissful Bower" (4.690), which they entered "hand in hand" (4.689). The bliss they now journey toward is heavenly, eternal, consisting in the rapturous love of God himself, and ultimately made possible by the seed of their now-fallen union of love. With this hope in mind, even in their shadowy understanding, our handed couple may indeed know "A paradise within . . . happier far" (12.587).[86]

7

Perfect and Recovered Virginity in
Paradise Regained and *Samson Agonistes*

Having discussed the fall from and partial recovery of wise virginity by Eve and Adam in *Paradise Lost*, let us now examine the theme of wise virginity in the protagonists of Milton's final two poems, the Son in *Paradise Regained* and Samson in *Samson Agonistes*. In these two characters Milton portrays, respectively, the ideal, perpetually unsullied divine Wise Virgin, and one whose repentance from sexual foolishness enables him to be restored to wisdom and God's blessing. In this sense, Milton's self-referential Son and Samson demonstrate Stephen Fallon's contention that the two protagonists represent, respectively, Milton's idealized self-representation and his more realistic self-representation as a flawed but redeemed man.[1]

The Son of *Paradise Regained* and Perfect Wise Virginity

Paradise Regained contains no explicit reference to the parable of the wise and foolish virgins, but the poem's brief dramatization of things pertaining to the Son's sexuality certainly portrays the Son as the apex of wise virginity. This portrayal is first seen during the poem's council in hell, at which Satan, having just witnessed John baptize Jesus and the Father "pronounc[e] him his beloved Son" (1.32), tries to devise temptations to thwart the Son's salv- ific mission. Significantly, before anyone else speaks, Satan suggests that the Son is above falling by sexual means. Stating that "*Adam* by his Wife's allurement fell," he observes that Adam was "to this Man inferior far" (2.134–35). Nonetheless, the first demon to reply is the sensual Belial, who encourages Satan to "Set women in his eye" to entangle the Son's heart "in Amorous Nets," noting that "wisest *Solomon*" became an idolater through the charms of his heathen wives (2.153–72). Satan quickly rebuffs Belial, reminding him that "he whom we attempt is wiser far / Than *Solomon*" (2.205–6). Satan's diction here is crucial to Milton's presentation of the Son as wise virgin. Satan echoes Matthew 12:42, in which Jesus, speaking of himself to the Pharisees, says, "a greater than Solomon is here." The change from "greater" to "wiser far" demonstrates Milton's oft-noted emphasis on the connection between wisdom and sexual restraint; Satan's confidence in the Son's ability to resist sexual temptation is synonymous with his recognition that the Son possesses a wisdom of self-control and a devotion to God that far exceed those demonstrated by Solomon.[2] And Satan's larger reply to Belial also emphasizes this connection between wisdom and sexual purity. Satan contrasts the Son's "more exalted mind" to the "weak minds" that, plagued by "fond [i.e., foolish] desire," are seduced by sensual charm (2.206, 221, 211). Satan articulates here Milton's own belief that the Son epitomizes the ideal wise virgin.

Despite Satan's disdainful response to Belial's suggestion, his subsequent banquet temptation includes the implicit homosexual and heterosexual temptations represented by the banquet's servers, described as "Tall stripling youths rich clad, of fairer hew / Than *Ganymede* or *Hylas*" (2.352–53) and

> Nymphs of *Diana's* train, and *Naides*
> With fruits and flowers from *Amalthea's* horn,
> And Ladies of th' *Hesperides*, that seem'd
> Fairer than feign'd of old. (2.355–58)

In recent decades, critics have paid significant attention to the homosexual temptation represented by the "Tall stripling youths."[3] I believe it best to consider these youths as part of what Barbara Lewalski calls "the panorama of refined sexual pleasure offered to Christ," included within the larger array of sensual temptations that Milton has the Son experience in order to demonstrate, in the words of Phillip Rollinson, that he "was *fully* tempted in every way that a human can be tempted."[4]

But in spite of the seemingly overwhelming sweep of temptation, sexual and otherwise, before him, the Son's response is remarkable in that it demonstrates how little any of it fazes him. His succinct rejection of the temptation is spoken "temperately" (2.378), an adverb that the *Oxford English Dictionary* defines in this context as "With self-restraint; without passion or violence; dispassionately," and, remarkably, as "chastely."[5] Implicit in the *OED*'s definition is the sense that the Son's dispassionate response is connected to his chastity, a quality of the Son that the poem does not emphasize but that, like his patience, is nonetheless a significant aspect of his sinless character. Milton's text suggests that although sexual temptation is offered to the Son, it does not present a serious challenge. In the words of Eric Song, "these objects of attraction hardly register at all as genuine temptations."[6] Jesus's dispassionate response does not directly address the sexual aspects of Satan's banquet, although they are implicitly included when Jesus says, "Thy pompous Delicacies I contemn, / And count thy specious gifts no gifts but guiles" (2.390–91).

The Son's easy rejection of sensual allure is in keeping with that of the nobler men who, as Satan tells Belial, "with a smile made small account / Of beauty and her lures, easily scorn'd / All her assaults, on worthier things intent" (2.193–95). The Son's wise purity confirmed, Satan offers no further sexual temptation. He will pursue other means instead: "manlier objects" by which to "try / His constancy, with such as have more show / Of worth, of honor, glory, and popular praise" (2.225–27). Satan hopes to appeal to the Son's pride, enticing him with the prospect of conquering tyrants and freeing oppressed nations, of attaining the learning of the pagans, of ruling the world (albeit via servitude to Satan himself).[7] But the Son's wise purity proves equally effective in resisting these temptations.

The Son's rejection of sexual temptation recurs near the end of book 2, when, comparing the nobility of an earthly king to that of a self-governed individual, he tells Satan,

> Yet he who reigns within himself, and rules
> Passions, Desires, and Fears, is more a King;
> Which every wise and virtuous man attains:
> And who attains not, ill aspires to rule
> Cities of men, or headstrong Multitudes,
> Subject himself to Anarchy within,
> Or lawless passions in him, which he serves. (2.466–72)

Although the Son's triumph over sensuality appears effortless, these lines apply to all who would pursue virtuous self-government, for anyone who is truly wise will conquer the "Passions" that bring a man, however outwardly noble, into the bondage of foolish devotion to pleasure. Milton's word choice here recalls Adam's fall by way of passion even as it anticipates Milton's depiction of Samson as a man imprisoned by his choice to give himself over to "pleasure and voluptuous life" (*Samson Agonistes*, 534). Of the three characters, it is the Son who, by making the right choice in every case, epitomizes the wise virginity that Milton explores throughout his writings.

Samson and Recovered Wise Virginity

If the Son in *Paradise Regained*, with his "unassailable chastity," is the exemplum of such self-government, Milton portrays Samson as one who, having exhibited its opposite, seeks to attain wisdom by rejecting the sensuality that has enslaved him.[8] Samson, in contrast to the ideal wise virgin of the Son, is explicitly portrayed in *Samson Agonistes* as one whose failure to exercise wisdom is directly connected to his foolishness in the sexual realm. Indeed, from the outset Samson describes himself as one whose tragic sexual weakness for his Philistine wife Dalila is connected to his want of spiritual wisdom.[9]

Samson's Recognition of His Foolishness

It is clear that Samson's foolishness and sexual enthrallment are inextricably linked, as we see in the first three scenes of the play—his opening soliloquy, his first conversation with the Chorus, and his conversation with his father, Manoa. In each scene, Samson describes himself in terms of his unwise conduct with Dalila. Early in the drama, Samson laments that he "weakly to a woman" (50) revealed the secret of his strength:

> O impotence of mind, in body strong!
> But what is strength without a double share
> Of wisdom? Vast, unwieldy, burdensome,
> Proudly secure, yet liable to fall
> By weakest subtleties, not made to rule,
> But to subserve where wisdom bears command. (52–57)

And in his first speech to the Chorus, Samson calls himself a "Fool" for having "divulg'd the secret gift of God / To a deceitful Woman" (201–2); he suggests that he is "sung and proverb'd for a Fool / In every street" (203–4)— having become an "example" to men "to listen to wisdom and beware of the harlot"[10]—and he complains that his share of "wisdom" is "nothing more than mean" (207). A bit later he laments his "fond wish" (228) of taking Dalila as his wife. And in his first speech to Manoa, Samson speaks of his "folly" (377) for revealing, against his better judgment, his secret "to a woman, / A *Canaanite*, my faithless enemy" (379–80). He bewails the "servile mind" that displayed the "foul effeminacy" of his sexual slavery to Dalila (412, 410), displaying not "a grain of manhood" when he "yielded" and "unlock'd her all my heart" (408, 407) after sexual intercourse, a time "when men seek most repose and rest" (406). Fallon notes that Samson's "oral promiscuity" is largely responsible for his loss of a "chastity" that "must be regained,"[11] and although the ensuing loss of manhood represented by Samson's shaving and blinding has been noted by various critics, Samson himself asserts that his "effeminacy" and loss of "manhood" are the result of his acts of sexual and oral looseness that preceded his subsequent physical deprivations.[12]

Samson's oft-stated remorse concerning his unwise marriage to Dalila contrasts with his silence regarding his first marriage to the woman of Timna, a contrast that speaks against John T. Shawcross's theory that Milton portrays both of Samson's marriages as misguided and not from the Lord.[13] But most significantly, Samson's repeated self-deprecation demonstrates Milton's emphasis on the connection between wisdom and sexual purity and, conversely, that between foolishness and sexual misconduct. As with Satan and Adam and Eve, Samson's foolishness, though manifested in sexual misconduct, is ultimately the foolishness of infidelity to God—the belief that the self-deluding wisdom of one's selfish desires is somehow wiser than God's explicit command to shun marriage with infidels (Deut. 7:3–4). In chapter 10 I discuss in detail how Samson's renewed commitment to the written word of God coincides with his redemptive progress and directly precedes his being called again by God to act as his champion. Here, I merely seek to demonstrate that Samson's rejection of sinful sexuality, his movement toward the ideal of the wise virgin, is a significant and necessary aspect of his redemptive progress.[14]

Samson's Wise Resistance of Dalila

Samson's movement toward the wisdom of sexual purity is displayed in his interaction with his estranged wife, Dalia. Although I will examine only small portions of their conversation, Samson's movement toward wisdom can be seen both in his recognition of Dalila's motive in attempting to reconcile and in the snare of sensuality in which she tries to entrap him. His resistance to Dalila's machinations, his ability to recognize and reject her deception, is reminiscent of the Son's words to the disguised Satan in their initial encounter in *Paradise Regained*: "I discern thee other than thou seem'st" (1.348). If Fallon is right to see Samson as a broken, fallible, but ultimately victorious variant of the ideal figure of the Son, then Samson's resistance to Dalila is a movement toward both redemption and Christlike conduct, the precursor to his once again hearing God's call to begin his people's deliverance.

Samson's rejection of Dalila and her enticements parallels his repudiation of the pagan values into which his marriage led him, and a larger spurning of pagan licentiousness on behalf of Israel as a whole. As Jackie DiSalvo observes, "Samson's [earlier] misplaced devotion to his beautiful, sensual wife parallels the Philistines' idolizing of Dagon in drunken, carnal festivities held in an elaborately ornamented temple." DiSalvo argues that "Dalilah serves as a kind of temple prostitute" for the fertility god Dagon, and postulates that such idolatrous dissipation was commonly practiced by the men of Judah who failed to aid Samson's efforts against the Philistines, a practice suggested, DiSalvo writes, by Samson's accusation that Judah has been "by thir vices brought to servitude" (269), through their "accommodation with their pagan conquerors." Samson's situation, she concludes, parallels Milton's position in 1671 "as the prophet of a Puritan culture threatened with decimation by the seductive orgies of the Restoration."[15] For Samson, then, the challenge of resisting Dalila's overtures ultimately gives him the opportunity to "begin to deliver Israel out of the hand of the Philistines" (Judg. 13:5), not only militarily but sexually as well.

Early in their conversation, Samson speaks to Dalila in the language of discernment, demonstrating his ability to see beneath surface appearances. He speaks of her "wonted arts" and "feign'd remorse" (748, 752). Samson has been criticized for his harsh words toward Dalila,[16] but his harshness may be seen as self-protection against her wiles, his recognition that even the "wisest and best men" are liable to be taken in by pretended "peniten[ce]" (759–61), condemned

> to wear out miserable days,
> Entangl'd with a pois'nous bosom snake,
> If not by quick destruction soon cut off
> As I by thee, to Ages an example. (762–65)

Samson's words here are remarkable in that even though his choices have caused him to be "sung and proverb'd for a Fool," a negative example "to Ages," he is determined to learn from his mistakes and not repeat them. Despite his harshness, Samson displays humility and a movement toward wisdom by learning from his own foolish past.

Dalila indeed makes "an alluring case for reconciliation with Samson," and "her magnificence and rhetorical skill" demonstrate that she is still a formidable temptation to Samson.[17] Michael Lieb argues that Dalila employs "a consummate rhetoric of seduction,"[18] and her temptation becomes explicitly sexual when she claims that she only betrayed him because she wanted him home with her instead of at "liberty" to embark on "perilous enterprises," leaving her "at home" alone to "Wail" his "absence" (803–6). She continues by offering an alluring alternative to both his previous freedom and his current labor:

> Here I should still enjoy thee day and night
> Mine and Love's prisoner, not the *Philistines'*,
> Whole to myself, unhazarded abroad,
> Fearless at home of partners in my love. (807–10)

But Dalila's desire that Samson should become her sex slave fails to take him in. He sees her deception for what it is, calling her a "sorceress" who speaks "cunningly" (819); he admits that, in his "folly," he has been "false" to himself (825, 824); he challenges her claim that she betrayed him for "Love" and calls her actions nothing more than a "furious rage / To satisfy thy lust" (836–37). In both his ability to distinguish between love and lust and his reasoned choice to resist her demand for sexual intimacy, Samson displays the traits of a wise virgin.

He continues to resist when Dalila declares that she will "intercede" (920) with the Philistine lords so that she can take him from prison to be with her, where, she claims,

> my redoubl'd love and care
> With nursing diligence, to me glad office,
> May ever tend about thee to old age
> With all things grateful cheer'd, and so supplied,
> That what by me thou hast lost thou least shall miss. (923–27)

But Samson again sees through this deceit, and his answer demonstrates wisdom in distinguishing between truth and deception in matters of sexuality. He tells Dalila not to think him "unwary" enough to "again" be "caught" in her "snare" (930, 932, 931):

> I know thy trains
> Though dearly to my cost, thy gins, and toils;
> Thy fair enchanted cup, and warbling charms
> No more on me have power, thir force is null'd,
> So much of Adder's wisdom I have learn't
> To fence my ear against thy sorceries. (932–37)

As Fallon observes, this reference to Dalila's "fair enchanted cup" connects her with Circe even as Samson divorces her,[19] and his reference to "Adder's wisdom" recalls Christ's admonition to his followers to be "wise as serpents,"[20] an admonition coupled with the command to be "innocent as doves" (Matt. 10:16, Geneva Bible). In exercising such wisdom in resisting Dalila's enticements, Samson also displays sexual innocence, conforming to the ideal of the wise virgin by refusing her "invitation to enter the emasculating bower of bliss," recognizing and rejecting the "carnal effeminacy" he succumbed to earlier, and freeing himself to pursue again "heroic chastity," "heroic manhood," and "godly intimacy" with the Lord.[21] He succeeds in "overcoming" Dalila's "encircling linguistic entanglements" and her "equally spurious rhetoric embodied in a feminine non-language of tears and sighs."[22] His resistance is all the more impressive when one considers that, in his blind and captive state, the opportunity to live out the rest of his days in sexual luxury might be attractive indeed. And yet, like the Lady of *A Mask Presented at Ludlow Castle*, Samson remains firm by refusing the offer of a false freedom through sensuality.[23] Indeed, recognizing that the counterfeit freedom Dalila offers would cause him to "live uxorious to [her] will / In perfect thraldom" (945–46), Samson sees his prison, by comparison, as "the house of Liberty" (949).

After Samson forgives her from a distance, Dalila departs, but not before comparing herself to Jael smiting Sisera; announcing her fame among the Philistines, she revels in her victory over Samson, her nation's enemy (982–90). Her boasting in triumph reveals the duplicity of her previous show of compunction and of her claim that the Philistines compelled her to betray him (850–70). As Thomas Kranidas puts it, "It was for glory, and the exercise of power in lust that would contribute to that glory, that Dalila visits Samson and attempts to reseduce him."[24] For its part, the Chorus observes Dalila's adeptness at hiding her true character, calling her "a manifest Serpent by her sting / Discovered in the end, till now conceal'd" (997–98). But it is worth noting that Samson, in his renewed exercise of wisdom, recognizes earlier than the Chorus the motives beneath Dalila's false rhetoric of love.

Passion and the Wisdom of Self-Mastery

Ultimately, Samson's resistance to Dalila is a victory not so much over her as over his "former self," which he "subjected to his bodily passions and desires." As Bryan Adams Hampton observes, Samson's sexual resistance evidences "a pouring out of selfish desire in order to be filled with God's desires," a "temper[ing]" of "his sexual passions" so that not Dalila but "YHWH becomes his lover."[25] Samson's victory over his former self attests to the transformation and purification of his character and his consequent readiness to again stand on the written word of God and obey the call of God's Spirit, a phenomenon I discuss at more length in chapter 10.

Samson's implicit status as a repentant and renewed wise virgin, set free from the clutches of foolish sexual thralldom, is suggested near the drama's end by Manoa,[26] who predicts that Samson's memory will "inflame" "all the valiant youth" "To matchless valor" (1739, 1738, 1740), and announces that

> The Virgins also shall on feastful days
> Visit his Tomb with flowers, only bewailing
> His lot unfortunate in nuptial choice,
> From whence captivity and loss of eyes. (1741–44)

The allusion here to Judges 11:37–40—in which Jephthah's soon-to-be-sacrificed daughter asks her father's permission to go with her friends to "bewail [her] virginity," a practice that became a yearly custom for the young women of Israel—places Samson in the perpetual company of the virgins, who honor his memory while "only bewailing" Samson's "unfortunate" choice of Dalia. But it is Samson's wise decision to free himself from what Martin Mueller calls "his overwhelming passion for" Dalila that enables him to move forward in the redemptive process that culminates in his final victory over the Philistines. Indeed, as Mueller suggests, the development of Milton's drama suggests that the Chorus's concluding lines about God's dismissing his servants with "calm of mind all passion spent" apply, above all, to Samson himself.[27] Significantly, as Judith H. Anderson has noted, in the Renaissance understanding of the word, "passion is simply a loss of rational self-control."[28] And such a loss indeed characterized Samson in his libido-driven marriage to Dalila and subsequent betrayal of God's secrets. As Roy Flannagan's reading of this line observes, Aristotelian catharsis takes place in an audience when "a potentially harmful passion is purged, for the betterment of the citizen and the state."[29] Having witnessed Samson's decision to turn from the foolishness of sensual passion to the wisdom and self-control of purity, the audience is admonished to go and do likewise.

Part 3

The Parable of the Householder

Divine Inspiration by Way of Virtue and Purity

Our discussion of Milton and the ideal of the wise virgin necessarily precedes our analysis of Milton and the parable of the householder (Matt. 13:52), a parable with which, as we shall see in chapter 8, Milton explicitly identifies in an effort to demonstrate the biblical and spiritual legitimacy of his daring exegesis of scripture regarding divorce. Milton's self-representations as the wise virgin had to precede his self-representations as the Spirit-guided parabolic householder because, in Milton's view, the prophet-poet's gifts of spiritual inspiration and insight can be attained only through the long-standing chastity, moderation of appetite, and overall purity of conduct that come from wisdom gained through self-control and laborious learning. This conviction is evident even in Milton's earliest writings. In Elegy 6 (December 1629), written to Charles Diodati just after Milton's twenty-first birthday, Milton, who "locates himself with the epic and hymnic poets,"[1] writes that an epic/hymnic poet (in contrast with the often self-indulgent lyric poet) must "have a youth chaste and free of crime, and an austere character, together with a good name; such a person is a prophet-priest, dressed in holy vestments and bathed in holy waters, prepared to face the angry gods" (63–66).[2]

These ideas are repeated in *Il Penseroso*, probably written in 1631, in which Milton's self-referential speaker pledges his allegiance to the "sad

Virgin" (103) goddess Melancholy, one associated with "calm Peace and Quiet, / Spare Fast, that oft with gods doth diet, / And hears the Muses in a ring, / Aye round about *Jove's* Altar sing" (45–48). The spiritual insight to be gained from such allegiance to Melancholy is attested to in the final 22 lines of the poem:

> But let my due feet never fail
> To walk the studious Cloister's pale,
> And love the high embowed Roof,
> With antic Pillars massy proof,
> And storied Windows richly dight,
> Casting a dim religious light.
> There let the pealing Organ blow
> To the full voic'd Quire below,
> In Service high, and Anthems clear,
> As may with sweetness, through mine ear,
> Dissolve me into ecstasies,
> And bring all Heav'n before mine eyes.
> And may at last my weary age
> Find out the peaceful hermitage,
> The Hairy Gown and Mossy Cell,
> Where I may sit and rightly spell
> Of every Star that Heav'n doth shew,
> And every Herb that sips the dew;
> Till old experience do attain
> To something like Prophetic strain.
> These pleasures *Melancholy* give,
> And I with thee will choose to live. (155–76)

For the young Milton, being a prophet-poet was inextricably linked with fidelity to the chaste, studious, and moderate lifestyle discussed in both these works. And the claims of Elegy 6 and *Il Penseroso* are consistent with the words of the Attendant Spirit in *A Mask Presented at Ludlow Castle* (1634), which differentiate the mass of earthly minded humanity with the "some"—best exemplified by the virgin Lady of that work—who "by due steps aspire / To lay their just hands on that Golden Key / That opes the Palace of Eternity" (12–14). Such spiritual elitism is echoed in Sonnet 9

(1642), the self-referential address of which celebrates the "Virgin wise and pure" (14) who "Wisely hast shunn'd the broad way and the green, / And with those few art eminently seen, / That labor up the Hill of Heav'nly Truth" (2–4). All of these writings promise or suggest the special divine access given to "those few" who, by purity, self-sacrifice, and assiduous labor, faithfully pursue the narrow way of wise virginity.

This perspective is reinforced in *The Reason of Church-Government* (February 1642) where, at the end of his lengthy, bizarrely self-referential preface to book 2—which has already celebrated the "divine inspiration" (*CPW*, 1.802) given to biblical prophets and ancient poets (see 1.802–3, 816–17) and exhibited Milton's almost neurotic obsession with the parable of the talents (see 1.804–5)—Milton proceeds to anticipate, in the context of an unexpected proposed "covnant" with his audience, the inspired epic poetry he hopes to produce by making proper use of his gifts:

> Neither doe I think it shame to covnant with any knowing reader, that for some few yeers yet I may go on trust with him toward the payment of what I am now indebted, as being a work not to be rays'd from the heat of youth, or the vapours of wine, like that which flows at wast from the pen of some vulgar Amorist, or the trencher fury of a riming parasite, nor to be obtain'd by the invocation of Dame memory and her Siren daughters, but by devout prayer to that eternall Spirit who can enrich all utterance and knowledge, and sends out his Seraphim with the hallow'd fire of his Altar to touch and purify the lips of whom he pleases. (*CPW*, 1.820–21)

Milton adds that the epic poet must pursue "industrious and select reading, steddy observation, [and] insight into all seemly and generous arts and affaires" (*CPW*, 1.821), even as he acknowledges that his venture into polemical writing for the sake of the church prevents him temporarily from "beholding the bright countenance of truth in the quiet and still air of delightfull studies" (*CPW*, 1.821–22). Significantly, Milton's allusion here to Isaiah 6:6–7, with its image of the prophet having his lips purified by the seraph in anticipation of his prophetic ministry, again reinforces Milton's theme of purity as a prerequisite for the divine enlightenment necessary for composing his anticipated epic poem.[3] In this passage, moreover, Milton publicly presents himself as one who already possesses such purity.

Divorce and Self-Exoneration

Given what happened next in Milton's life, the bitter irony of his remarkably public self-representation is stunning. How could he continue to represent himself publicly as a morally chaste and pure poet-prophet in light of Mary Powell's desertion a month or two after their wedding in May 1642—a wedding, as I argued in chapter 4, that he anticipated in Sonnet 9, in which he addressed both Mary and himself as "Virgin wise and pure" (14)? As we turn to Milton's identification with the spiritually enlightened and scriptur-ally astute scribe/householder of the parable of the householder, an iden-tification demonstrated explicitly in both the anonymously published first edition (August 1643) and the second edition (February 1644) of *The Doctrine and Discipline of Divorce* (hereafter *DDD*), we may see that Milton takes pains to affirm his status as a pure virgin, a status no doubt challenged by his marital failures and his unorthodox insistence upon the biblical rightness of divorce for reasons of incompatibility.

Milton's insistence on his moral purity appears early in the first edition of *DDD*. "Many who have spent their youth chastely," he writes, "are in some things not so quick-sighted, while they haste too eagerly to light the nuptial torch."[4] Although Milton does not write in the first person in *DDD* when he describes the suffering of those trapped in bad marriages, his self-presentation in that tract has been the subject of considerable critical dis-cussion and it is entirely reasonable to analyze *DDD* with Milton's own situation in mind.[5] Significantly, in the statement just quoted, Milton both affirms his moral purity and uses it to exonerate himself from any taint of sin regarding his ill-fitting marriage. This moral exoneration persists when he writes of the man in such a marriage that "both the hate which now diverts him and the loneliness which leads him still powerfully to seek a fit help, has not the least grain of a sin in it." He calls Moses's permission to divorce in Deuteronomy 24:1 God's "pure and chaste law." Milton repeats these claims in the tract's second edition.[6]

In each of these passages, Milton connects chastity and moral purity with the appropriateness of divorce. He first affirms his purity when he says that chastity, not any sin on his part, explains his situation as one in an ill-fitting marriage. Significantly, Milton is even willing to concede here that the chaste virgin might, because of innocence and inexperience, lack relational wisdom. He argues that the married chaste man—now wiser by dint of his unfortunate marriage—should have liberty to exercise his new relational wisdom without any threat to his chaste status, as the second quotation above suggests. In that passage, Milton—no doubt anticipating accusations of an ungodly and even adulterous attitude—affirms the sinlessness of both his hatred toward his present wife and his longing for marriage with a more appropriate wife. He goes on specifically to describe the Mosaic permission to divorce as "chaste," a remarkable claim given Jesus's statement that "Whosoever shall put away his wife, except it be for fornication, and shall marry another, *committeth adultery*" (Matt. 19:9, emphasis added).

All of this is significant in light of the persona that Milton creates for himself in *DDD* as a divinely aided exegete of scripture, a persona created largely from his explicit identification with the parable of the householder, addressed at length in chapter 8. In brief, Milton must affirm his unbroken association with chastity or risk invalidating his status as a pure prophet-poet. Milton's self-exoneration in *DDD* should be seen not merely as a means of morally validating his hope for divorce and future marital happiness but also as a rhetorical strategy by which he preserves his lifelong goal to be an inspired epic poet.[7]

The Spirit and "th' Upright Heart and Pure"

The other works I discuss in part 3 also display a kind of self-representation in which moral purity precedes the spiritual inspiration and insight of the parabolic householder. As I discuss in chapter 9, Milton implicitly continues his identification with the parable when, as the self-referential narrator of *Paradise Lost* and *Paradise Regained*, he presents himself as able to perform through the Holy Spirit's inspiration and guidance "Things unattempted yet in Prose or Rhyme" (*PL*, 1.16)—that is, biblically based narratives that expand significantly on biblical texts and yet remain faithful to the revealed scriptures. But the Miltonic narrator, while directly imploring the Spirit to instruct him in knowledge that only the Spirit can offer, also writes, "Thou O Spirit, that dost prefer / Before all Temples th' upright heart and pure" (*PL*, 1.17–18). The narrator directly implies here that his continued moral purity is a prerequisite for the unprecedented spiritual inspiration he will receive. Later, in chapter 9, I discuss how the characteristics of the parabolic householder are evident in *Paradise Regained* in Milton's narrator and in his self-referential Son and Mary, the two biblical characters whose chastity and purity are most above reproach. Finally, in chapter 10, I discuss how Milton's self-referential Samson in *Samson Agonistes* plays the role of the parabolic householder in his repentant submission to Mosaic law and his consequent ability to discern the "rousing motions" of the Spirit, which prompt him to perform at Dagon's temple. Significantly, both Samson's bravely articulated recommitment to the written law and the spiritual discernment that follows are necessarily preceded by his chastened commitment to moral purity, demonstrated, as we saw in chapter 7, by his wise rejection of Dalila's temptations to a life of indolence and sensual pleasure. Indeed, like Adam and Eve's process of redemption in *Paradise Lost*, Samson's attitude as a repentant wise virgin paves the way for a clearer understanding of and obedience to the word of God, an obedience that gains Samson the inspiration of the householder.

8

"Out of His Treasury Things New and Old"
The Doctrine and Discipline of Divorce *and* De Doctrina Christiana

In *Milton's Burden of Interpretation*, Dayton Haskin writes extensively about the parable of the talents (Matt. 25:14–30) as a place of self-identification for Milton. Although the recognition of Milton's self-conscious connection with that parable is not new, Haskin advances the issue considerably. Especially helpful is his emphasis on Milton's anguished relationship with that parable; equally instructive is his incisive discussion of how Milton interpreted the talents in the parable to be both "the Word of God itself *and . . .* the natural abilities of those to whom the Word had been entrusted."[1] When we recognize that Milton's relation to the parable was not merely that of a poet seeking to live up to his vocational calling but also that of a biblical interpreter keenly aware of the awesome burden on those called to "rightly divid[e] the word of truth" (2 Tim. 2:15), we gain a greater understanding of the enormous hermeneutical concerns that inform Milton's perception of himself as a prophet-poet.

The magnitude of such hermeneutical concerns is illustrated powerfully by Milton's identification with another biblical parable, one that has received little attention in Milton scholarship. The parable of the householder, or the master of the house (to use what appears to be Milton's own English translation), appears prominently both in *The Doctrine and Discipline of Divorce* (DDD) and in his posthumously discovered Latin theological treatise, *De Doctrina Christiana* (DDC); and the self-confidence that Milton exhibits in his identification with the figure of the householder offers us a valuable complement to Milton's anguished identification with the unprofitable servant of the parable of the talents. The parable of the householder appears in Matthew 13:52; it is the final parable in a series of eight in that chapter. The previous seven parables are Jesus's well-known "parables of the kingdom of heaven," including the oft-quoted parable of the sower. Upon completing these parables of the kingdom, Jesus asks his disciples, "Have ye understood all these things?" After they reply in the affirmative, Jesus tells the brief parable of the householder: "Therefore, every scribe which is instructed unto the kingdom of heaven is like unto a man that is an householder, which bringeth forth out of his treasure things new and old." Milton's contemporary, the Reformed Bible commentator Matthew Poole, asserts that the parabolic householder represents capable ministers of the Gospel, whom Poole describes as "men mighty in the Scriptures, well acquainted with the writings of the Old and New Testament, and the sense of them; men that have a stock of spiritual knowledge, able readily . . . to speak to men and women's particular cases and questions."[2] Clearly, the parabolic householder is one who properly understands Jesus's most intricate teachings in light of the Hebrew scriptures and in turn passes such knowledge on to his own audience. Keeping this definition in mind as we examine Milton's personal connection with the parable of the householder, we see a Milton who self-consciously portrays himself as a New Testament model of an ideal biblical interpreter, a man whose careful analysis uncovers new insights from the Bible, insights present all along but hitherto ignored, neglected, and misinterpreted.

The Miltonic Householder in *The Doctrine and Discipline of Divorce*

Milton's self-conscious identification with the parable of the householder is discernible throughout *DDD*. The verse (in presumably his own translation, slightly different from the Authorized King James Version and partially quoted in this chapter's title) appears on the title page of the August 1643 tract as an epigraph, and the association the reader is to make with the anonymous author seems clear enough.[3] In the February 1644 second edition of *DDD*, however, Milton includes his initials directly above the epigraph. This placement has the effect of rendering even more dramatically Milton's own association with the parable, and Haskin rightly asserts the strong probability that Milton himself was responsible for its presence on the tract's title page.[4] Milton's acute degree of identification with the householder appears even more clearly when we consider the parable's use in another important contemporary tract, the posthumously published *Exam-*

ination of the Theses of Dr. Francis Gomarus Respecting Predestination by James Arminius (1645). In his preface to the *Examination*, Stephen De Courcelles pronounces Arminius "the living effigy of that Scribe" described in Matthew 13:52.[5] Here, as in *DDD*, a clear and honorable association is made between an author and the scribe in the parable of the householder. The obvious and important difference is that, in Arminius's case, this honorable association is made by someone else. A similar phenomenon is seen in the preface to Jonathan Edwards's *The Distinguishing Marks of a Work of the Spirit of God* (1741). There, William Cooper states that "the reverend author is known to be a scribe instructed unto the kingdom of heaven."[6]

In any event, the reader need merely read the complete title of *DDD* to begin making connections between Milton's tract and the parable in question. The complete title of the 1644 edition is *The Doctrine & Discipline of Divorce; Restor'd to the good of both Sexes, from the bondage of CANON LAW, and other mistakes, to the true meaning of Scripture in the Law and Gospel Compar'd. Wherein also are set down the bad consequences of abolishing or condemning of Sin, that which the Law of God allowes, and Christ abolisht not* (*CPW*, 2:221). Milton, acting the part of the parabolic householder/master of the house, will be bringing out of his treasury things new and old. On the one hand, his teachings are new: they contradict canon law and church tradition of most every sort. On the other hand, they are old; according to Milton, they are in fact "the true meaning of Scripture." Milton is not inventing a new doctrine or a new scripture but recovering scripture's original meaning, which has been obfuscated by centuries of corrupted church teaching. His exegesis relies not on outside scholarly influence but on the Holy Spirit, the one who inspires the "internal scripture" that confirms the external text, which Milton later discusses in *DDC*. As Douglas Trevor notes, Milton presents himself here "as a self-authored, divinely aided exegete" who insists "that an accurate, 'true' sense of the Bible is obtained through solitary reading, where God alone presumably aids one in one's understanding."[7] Milton's use of Matthew 13:52 differs from the prefaces to Arminius's and Jonathan Edwards's works in his clear emphasis on recovering a scriptural truth that has been lost in the course of church history. Both De Courcelles and Cooper highlight the erudition of the "scribe" in question, not the restoration of the doctrine championed. Cooper, in fact, does not even quote the second part of the parable, which mentions "things new and old." Milton, however, takes pains to use the parable as a justification for the controversial contents of the pamphlet, a point recognized by Lowell W. Coolidge, who in his editorial commentary points out that Milton's phrasing in the title indicates his "attempt from the onset to forestall charges of innovation."[8]

The second half of the pamphlet's title also reflects the theme of the householder. Milton's title affirms that the legality of divorce he advocates is "that which the Law of God allowes, and Christ abolisht not." Again, the hermeneutical task of the householder is apparent. On the one hand, he brings forth "new" treasure—a teaching that ostensibly supersedes the teachings of Christ himself! On the other hand, it is truly something "old," a teaching affirmed by Mosaic law that, if we only examine the scripture rightly, we will see that Christ never abolished at all. Thus Milton the householder, in his argument for divorce, puts forth a revolutionary doctrine only in initial appearance. In reality, he is merely affirming a biblical teaching that has been the consistent affirmation of the whole of scripture. Indeed, just as Christ came not "to destroy the law, or the prophets ... but to fulfil" (Matt. 5:17), the householder appears to elucidate this fulfillment for the benefit of the church at large.

Fidelity to Scripture and the Principle of Charity

It is crucial that we recognize that Milton sees what he is doing as testimony to his utter fidelity to the scripture itself. Indeed, although to immediate appearances he is bringing out something new from his treasury, it is in reality a precious old treasure, one that the householder Milton is uncovering, polishing, and showing forth in its original splendor. Haskin's words about *DDC* speak just as powerfully to this situation in *DDD*: "The so-called 'heresies' which have elicited praise or condemnation depending upon the predilections of modern critics are first and last a function of [Milton's] serious attempt to adhere to 'the Bible only.'"[9] As a modern-day fulfillment of the parable of the householder, Milton is "instructed unto the kingdom of heaven" by the scriptures themselves, and it is his God-given duty to interpret and present them with absolute fidelity.

Both Milton's self-proclaimed fidelity to scripture and Haskin's incisive recognition of it fly in the face of the influential assertion of Arthur Barker, who in his analysis of *DDD* states that "the centre of reference in the divorce tracts . . . shifts from the revealed will of God to the rights of the particular believer."[10] Although Barker's contention is a popular approach not only to *DDD* but to Milton's writings as a whole, this is not how Milton presents himself or his exegesis in *DDD*. On the contrary, his declaration of the authority of scripture and his total faithfulness to the scriptural text is clearly quite emphatic. R. Kenneth Kirby raises the legitimate question whether Milton "was really conscious of the liberties he was taking with currently accepted principles of interpretation." But it is equally fair to question Kirby's matter-of-fact statement (following Barker) that "Milton found it necessary to sacrifice Scriptural precedent to reason."[11] Barker's and Kirby's claim that reason, not fidelity to scripture, was Milton's ultimate hermeneutical principle, I contend, fails to recognize adequately the intensely mystical nature of Milton's self-proclaimed prophetic office and his belief that the inner scripture of the Spirit within him ultimately led him to the "true meaning" of the external scripture of the Bible.[12]

Rather than affirm the view that *DDD* is a "reason-based" tract, I assert that both Milton's devotion to the external scripture and his persona as the parabolic householder in *DDD* support Stanley Fish's discussion of that work. Fish believes that Milton's unorthodox teachings on divorce spring from his conception of God. Milton perceives that God's principal intention in instituting marriage is to combat loneliness, not mere lust, and he thus argues that a marriage that fails to assuage loneliness is not binding. This argument, Milton says, coincides with his hermeneutical principle (which Milton claims to derive from Saint Paul) that "the way to get a sure undoubted knowledge of things, is to hold that for truth, which accords most with charity" (*CPW*, 2:340; an earlier emphasis on charity is apparent on pp. 228–33, in the tract's introductory address to Parliament).[13] Fish avers that Milton goes on to interpret all scripture concerning marriage and divorce from this preconceived framework, and that Milton's conclusions on the subject spring from his original notion of God as a deity who "is always disposed toward charity," whose purpose for marriage is to alleviate loneliness, and who, in his supreme charity, permits divorce between persons for whom an ill-advised marriage failed to produce the blessed companionship a genuine marriage would have provided.[14] I believe that Fish's argument is strengthened if we place Milton's perceptual tendencies within the framework of his identification with the householder.

Indeed, within the larger hermeneutical principle of charity that informs *DDD*, the "things old" that Milton brings out of his treasury are not simply his recovery of the proper doctrine of divorce; they encompass a proper perception of God altogether, as well as a proper perception of the whole of scripture. As he exercises the role of the householder, Milton's (ostensibly) "new" treasure concerning the legitimacy of divorce on grounds of incompatibility brings to light the larger principle that the "old" treasure of God and his word always displays the supreme divine attribute of charity.

Milton's recovery of the proper biblical understanding of divorce also rescues him from the charges of licentiousness leveled against him by contemporary opponents.[15] As Stephen Fallon observes, throughout *DDD*, Milton "distances himself from any spot or blame, and derives his authority from his purity."[16] Significantly, the purity Milton claims for himself in *DDD* buttresses his identification with the wise virgin, a purity necessary for him to exercise the prophetic office implicit in *DDD* and explicit, as we shall see, in *Paradise Lost*.

Returning to Barker's and Kirby's contention regarding the preeminence of reason in *DDD*, we can recognize that the conclusions Milton draws from his notion of "the rule of charity" follow a certain logical progression that some might label "rational." But this fact hardly makes Milton the champion of reason that he is often portrayed to be, and it is wrong to think that adherence to reason ultimately leads him to assert positions that appear contrary to the plain meaning of the very scripture he wishes to uphold. Rather, Milton, playing the role of the parabolic householder, is better understood as a prophet who sees himself as having attained the spiritual insight needed to properly divide the word of God in ways that centuries of interpreters, in their spiritual blindness, have missed. Indeed, his novel exegesis in *DDD* can be seen as rational only in the sense that any rational argument is derived consistently from Milton's preconceived framework of charity. But it is this preconceived framework, not reason per se, that drives Milton throughout *DDD*. We must ask, for example, how "reasonable" it is to assert utter fidelity to scripture while at the same time arguing against its plain meaning. Surely Fish is correct that in *DDD* Milton subjects scripture to "an interpretation so strenuous that even the word 'manipulation' is too mild to describe it."[17]

The True Meaning of Scripture

Throughout his 1644 preface to *DDD*, Milton implicitly places himself in the tradition of reformers who, at various times in biblical and church history, played the role of the householder in bringing out of the treasury of scripture things new and old. At one point he compares his recovery of the "ancient and most necessary, most charitable, and yet most injur'd, Statute of *Moses*" to that of the rediscovery of the Mosaic scriptures during King Josiah's reign (*CPW*, 2:224). The intent behind this comparison is straightforward: the lost book of the law was indeed new to the people of Judah, to whom the scriptures had been lost for generations; nonetheless, what was freshly given to them was truly the old treasure of the Mosaic law, and the fact that it had been lost all those years made it no less valid. Rather, its ageless, divinely bestowed truths had the power to revive God's people once more. In the same way, Milton's rediscovery of the proper doctrine of divorce would have the power to revive and release those unfairly bound by canon law in an inappropriate marriage.

Toward the end of the preface, Milton aligns himself with Jesus, and compares his opponents, who are misguided by "Custom and Prejudice" (*CPW*, 2:232), to the Pharisees. When Milton considers "the little that our Saviour could prevail about this doctrine of Charity against the crabbed textuists of his time," it is "no wonder" that he has his own pedantic opponents on the subject of divorce (*CPW*, 2:233). He is "confident that who so preferrs either Matrimony, or other Ordinance before the good of man and the plain exigence of Charity, let him professe Papist, or Protestant, or what he will, he is no better than a Pharise, and understands not the Gospel: whom as a misinterpreter of Christ I openly protest against" (*CPW*, 2:233). In his identification with Christ's trials, Milton not only demonstrates his absolute confidence in his own righteousness; he also claims a special affinity with the mind of Christ, such that he is able to transcend the written code even as he maintains his total fidelity to the word of God and Christ himself. Employing rhetoric reminiscent of Jesus's affirmation that "the sabbath was made for man and not man for the sabbath" (Mark 2:27), Milton represents himself not as one boldly employing the tools of reason but as one whose unique understanding of the "doctrine of Charity" places him in the role the ideal householder, who may properly imitate the perfect incarnation of charity himself.[18]

Much later in *DDD*, in book 2, chapter 20, Milton continues his emphasis on charity by linking charity's "guidance" with the illumination of the
"Spirit," as he once again declares that his analysis of scriptural teaching on
divorce has liberated the church from centuries of misunderstanding concerning the teachings of Jesus. The passage is worth quoting at length:

> [Charity's] unerring guidance and conduct [I] having follow'd as a loadstarre
> with all diligence and fidelity in this question, I trust, through the help of
> that illuminating Spirit which hath favor'd me, to have done no every da[y's]
> work: in asserting after many ages the words of Christ with other Scriptures
> of great concernment from burdensom & remorsles obscurity, tangl'd with
> manifold repugnances, to their native lustre and consent between each other:
> heerby also dissolving tedious and *Gordian* difficulties, which have hitherto
> molested the Church of God, and are now decided not with the sword of
> *Alexander*, but with the immaculate hands of charity, to the unspeakable
> good of Christendom. (*CPW*, 2:340)

Milton's affirmation here of the Spirit's "illuminating" his hermeneutical
recovery of Christ's true teachings on divorce demonstrates explicitly that
Milton viewed his work as the parabolic householder in *DDD* as inspired
by the Holy Spirit. Moreover, his close association between the Spirit's
illumination and charity's "guidance" suggests that, in his pervasive references to charity in *DDD*, he is implicitly connecting this charitable work
with the Spirit's guidance. This passage anticipates both Milton's affirmation
in *DDC* that his scriptural analysis is guided by the Holy Spirit and his
invocations of the Spirit's aid in *Paradise Lost* and *Paradise Regained*. Indeed,
throughout Milton's explicit and implicit self-representations as the parabolic householder, he clearly depicts his work of bringing forth "things new
and old" as illuminated by the Holy Spirit.

The Miltonic Householder and *De Doctrina Christiana*

Milton's identification with the householder appears prominently again in
DDC, and the similarity between his treatments of the parable in *DDC* and
DDD suggests how deeply ingrained was his understanding of himself as
a Spirit-inspired exegete of the truth of scripture. In the opening chapter
of *DDC*, Milton invokes the parable to justify his methodology in composing the work: "I do not teach anything new in this work. I aim only to assist

the reader's memory by collecting together, as it were, into a single book, texts which are scattered here and there throughout the Bible, and by systematizing them under definite headings, in order to make reference easy. This procedure might well be defended on grounds of Christian prudence, but in fact a more powerful command in its favor is that apparently it fulfils God's own command: Matt. xiii.52: *"every scribe who has been instructed in the kingdom of heaven, is like a householder who brings out of his treasure new and old possessions"* (CPW, 6:127–28). As in DDD, Milton uses his identification with the parabolic householder here as a scriptural mandate for his entire work and, implicitly, for the numerous heterodox teachings therein. As in DDD, he represents himself here as one who is not engaging in theological innovation but simply summarizing the basic teaching of the Bible. And as in DDD, he contrasts his use of the Bible alone with the accumulated layers of church tradition. In the passage that immediately precedes the one quoted above, Milton admonishes his audience to follow his example and seek true Christian doctrine "not among philosophizing academics, and not among the laws of men, but in the Holy Scriptures alone and with the Holy Spirit as guide" (CPW, 6:127). Here again the householder manifests himself, for Milton is clearly championing the original meaning of the scriptures against the accretion of centuries' worth of fallible human teaching, thus bringing out of his treasure things new and old via the Spirit's guidance.

Milton's prominent use of the parable of the householder in DDC is all the more significant when we consider its complete absence in most of the important works of systematic theology of his day, including Calvin's *Institutes of the Christian Religion* and the two books of theology generally considered the most influential on DDC, William Ames's *Medulla Theologica* and Johannes Wollebius's *Compendium Theologiae Christianae*. Nor is Matthew 13:52 cited anywhere in the collected *Works of James Arminius*, another notable absence considering Arminius's influence on Milton's theological thought.[19]

Another significant parallel to DDD occurs in book 1, chapter 30 of DDC, titled "Of the Holy Scripture," in which the parable of the householder makes another appearance, this time to reinforce Milton's argument that "every believer," because "he has the spirit" and thus "the mind of Christ," is entitled to interpret scripture for himself (CPW, 6.583). Milton goes on to assert that "anyone endowed with the gift of teaching, *every teacher of the* law [Latin *omnis scriba*—"every scribe"] *who has been instructed in readiness for the kingdom of heaven*, Matt. xiii.52," is "entitled to interpret the scriptures for others in public" (*CPW*, 6:584). Echoing his affirmation in *DDD*, Milton says that points of theological confusion should be settled "from that same Spirit operating in us through faith and *charity*" (*CPW*, 6:586, emphasis added). In the next paragraph, Milton begins his well-known discussion of the "double scripture" that God gives believers in the Gospel. This "double scripture" consists of the "external" scripture of the Bible and the "internal scripture of the Holy Spirit" which Milton calls "the pre-eminent and supreme authority" (*CPW*, 6:587). This passage has often been cited as proof of Milton's limited commitment to the biblical text, but such claims are highly problematic. Milton clearly sets his affirmation of the superior "internal scripture" against such worldly authorities as churches, magistrates, popes, councils, and other "human traditions" (*CPW*, 6:591). But Milton's conviction on this subject simply is not what has been called his "free[ing] himself from that last infirmity of noble Protestants—subservience to holy writ";[20] such sentiment conflicts with Milton's affirmation that "we believe in the whole scripture because of that Spirit which inwardly persuades every believer" (*CPW*, 6:590), a statement that echoes the Westminster Larger Catechism (1647).[21] Remembering Haskin's admonition that Milton's "heresies" display his "attempt to adhere to 'the Bible only,'" we can see that the heterodox teachings of *DDC* are in fact Milton's genuine effort to draw his doctrine, in his own words, "from the Sacred Scriptures alone" (*CPW*, 6:125). As he implies in *DDD*, Milton asserts here that the Spirit itself will guide us to a proper interpretation of the Bible, an interpretation that will necessarily depart at points from the uninspired orthodoxies of fallible men.[22]

Internal Scripture and Old Treasures

That said, we may again recognize the workings of the parabolic householder in the heterodoxies that Milton champions in *DDC*. It is fair to say that Milton brings out (ostensibly) "new" treasures throughout his work by means of the various controversial doctrines he sets out. At the same time, his stated concern is that of the "old" treasure of the "external" scriptures and, in light of *DDC*'s chapter 30, of the "internal" scripture given to each believer by the Holy Spirit. These treasures, of course, have been available for ages; it is the role of the householder, however, to bring out such possessions from his treasury, that his audience may see them with new eyes. To be sure, Milton wanted his readers to examine the biblical text for themselves, jettisoning the weight of church tradition in favor of the internal scripture of the Spirit. Such readers, not those constrained by human laws and councils, would themselves be fit conduits of the Spirit and imitators, like Milton, of the supreme Householder, Christ himself.

Milton's final citation of the parable of the householder is of less consequence than his previous ones, but it attests to his association of the householder with the responsibility of the minister of the Gospel to expound the word in a meaningful way. In the final chapter of *DDC*, Milton lists Matthew 13:52 under his discussion of ministers' "duties towards men in general" (*CPW*, 6.805). The verse is quoted without additional comment, but its inclusion is revealing in that it implicitly admonishes ministers of any sort to interpret the external scriptures through the power of the internal scripture, breaking free from the constraints of custom so that they may bring forth treasures both new and old. For their ideal model, of course, such ministers need look no further than Milton himself.[23]

Milton's use of and identification with the parable of the householder gives us a greater understanding of his perception of himself as a divinely called biblical exegete. By identifying himself with the householder of Matthew 13:52, Milton can claim that his biblical interpretation transcends the corruption of church traditions and recaptures the pure, original meaning of the scriptures themselves. It is especially significant that Milton uses the parable of the householder so prominently in *The Doctrine and Discipline of Divorce* and *De Doctrina Christiana*, two works in which his own exegetical conclusions clash so significantly with orthodox Christian teaching. By aligning himself with the householder, Milton aligns himself with the words that Jesus used to describe the ideal teacher of scripture; by assuming this prophetic mantle, Milton presents himself, against all others, as a teacher anointed by the Spirit and by Jesus himself. Such a teacher, to be sure, would be at odds both with the scribes and Pharisees of Jesus's day and the accumulated church tradition of Milton's own. He would, however, be on the side of the true meaning of the scripture itself. For Milton, such an ally would indeed be sufficient.

9

Milton's Epic Narrators and the Son and Mary in *Paradise Regained*

Having established Milton's explicit identification with the parabolic house-holder in *The Doctrine and Discipline of Divorce* (DDD) and *De Doctrina Christiana* (DDC), we may now consider how such identification manifests itself implicitly in his late major poems. It is no overstatement to say that *Paradise Lost* in its entirety is an extended demonstration of Milton's acting in the capacity of the parabolic householder. He is, after all, retelling scripture and expanding upon it, and he places himself in an advantageous position over the original author of Genesis in that he can write of humanity's creation and fall from a distinctly New Covenant perspective. In this, Milton's autobiographical epic narrator resembles very strongly the characteristics that Dayton Haskin recognizes in Milton's self-referential Mary in *Paradise Regained*, discussed later in this chapter; indeed, the Miltonic narrator throughout *Paradise Lost* "exercises the authorly roles of preserving, interpreting, and combining diverse texts into a unique personal synthesis."[1] This chapter first addresses the narrator's invocations at the beginning of books 1, 3, and 7, because they illustrate most overtly Milton's prophetic identification with the householder who brings forth treasures new and old.

The Narrator of *Paradise Lost*: Householder Extraordinaire

Milton's persona as one who retells the scripture manifests itself in *Paradise Lost*'s opening lines, when Milton's narrator addresses his heavenly muse:

> Of Man's First Disobedience, and the Fruit
> Of that Forbidden Tree, whose mortal taste
> Brought Death into the World, and all our woe,

With loss of *Eden*, till one greater Man
Restore us, and regain the blissful Seat,
Sing Heav'nly Muse, that on the secret top
Of *Oreb*, or of *Sinai*, didst inspire
That Shepherd, who first taught the chosen Seed,
In the Beginning how the Heav'ns and Earth
Rose out of *Chaos*: Or if *Sion* Hill
Delight thee more, and *Siloa's* Brook that flow'd
Fast by the Oracle of God; I thence
Invoke thy aid to my advent'rous Song,
That with no middle flight intends to soar
Above th' *Aonian* Mount, while it pursues
Things unattempted yet in Prose or Rhyme.
And chiefly Thou O Spirit, that dost prefer
Before all Temples th' upright heart and pure,
Instruct me, for Thou know'st; Thou from the first
Wast present, and with mighty wings outspread
Dove-like satst brooding on the vast Abyss
And mad'st it pregnant: What in me is dark
Illumine, what is low raise and support;
That to the highth of this great Argument
I may assert Eternal Providence,
And justify the ways of God to men. (1.1–26)

Milton's self-consciousness as the reteller of the Genesis narrative shows forth powerfully throughout this passage. In his first line, he introduces "Man's First Disobedience" and the loss of paradise. His retelling of Genesis and his connection with Moses are explicit in his echo of the English Bible's opening words, "In the Beginning" (1.9), even as he tells of Moses's instruction of the Israelites. David Daiches recognizes Milton's implicit self-identification here as "the inspired spokesman of God before the elect of England," just as Moses was the inspired spokesman of elect Israel. Daiches sets his observations in the context of Milton's historical situation: "One must remember the Puritan tendency to identify the English as latter-day Israelites, God's second chosen people: Milton is the neo-Moses and his audience are the neo-Israelites, 'the chosen Seed.' The multiple identifications set up in these lines relate not only to Milton's personal ambitions as poet-prophet but also to the whole context of seventeenth-century religious and political argument."[2]

We may also recognize in Milton's lines a message that transcends his immediate nationalistic concerns. His scope is universal. From the start, he speaks of "*Man's* First Disobedience" and its consequence upon "the *World*" (1.1, 3, emphasis added). And if Moses's role was to teach "the chosen Seed" of Israel, then Milton's goal is to instruct the elect of any nation that might read his epic, for he states plainly that he seeks to "justify the ways of God to *men*" (1.26, emphasis added).[3] Also adding to this universal scope is how Milton speaks of the Holy Spirit, whose aid he now invokes. He tells of the "Heav'nly Muse" that inspired Moses "on the secret top / Of *Oreb*, or of *Sinai*" (1.6–7), but, in an implicit reference to the Spirit's expanded ministry in the Christian era, Milton adds that the Spirit now "dost prefer / Before all Temples th' upright heart and pure" (1.17–18), words that recall Milton's persistent need throughout his writings to identify as a wise virgin in order to attain the spiritual insight necessary to write the epic he now composes.[4] Clearly, Milton is seeking, and sincerely believes that he is receiving, special inspiration from the Spirit.[5] And yet this same Spirit dwells in and instructs all worthy hearts, and we may presume that Milton expects his readers to receive the Spirit's aid as they embark on reading his inspired epic.

From the start, Milton makes his reader aware that his retelling of the Genesis account goes beyond Moses's sparse narrative, not merely in length but also in its fullness of spiritual perspective. In the opening lines, he summarizes the whole of the biblical redemptive story, noting the deadly consequences of the "loss of *Eden*" but adding, "till one greater Man / Restore us, and regain the blissful Seat" (1.4–5). Milton's epic, unlike Genesis, is told in light of the full canon of scripture, and (contrary to Thomas Ellwood's famous statement) tells of paradise regained as well as paradise lost. Milton also claims access to a source of inspiration that goes beyond Moses's. As William Kerrigan notes, "through a sequence of biblical places, the poet alludes to sources of inspiration progressively more perfect" in which he "summarizes the progressive revelation of God to His people."[6] God first reveals himself to Moses in the burning bush of Exodus 3, "on the secret top / Of *Oreb*" (1.6–7); later on, God reveals himself more fully to Moses on "*Sinai*" (1.7), where he meets with Moses and gives him the law. The word of God is manifested completely in the incarnate Christ, who heals the man born blind at *"Siloa's* Brook that flow'd / Fast by the Oracle of God" (1.11–12).[7]

Milton's progressive allusions here show him as inheriting the prophetic Spirit that has recorded the history of redemption. Kerrigan points out that Milton calls the temple of Jerusalem "the Oracle of God" and thus "emphasizes prophetic rather than institutional Christianity," demonstrating that he "wishes to participate in the prophetic history of the private motions of God." Milton aspires "to continue the sequence, becoming a new vessel for the Word."[8] Unlike Moses's, Milton's inspiration is not limited by location but is contingent on his right relationship with God. As noted above, the Spirit, in the Christian era, "prefer[s] / Before all Temples th' upright heart and pure" (1.17–18). It is fitting, then, that Milton, who in his later years belonged to no organized church, should gain the inspiration of the Spirit, which is unconcerned with physical or ecclesiastical religious structures. As one whose purity has been established through his consistent identity with the parabolic virgin—a condition, as noted earlier, not altered but rather upheld by his *DDD*—Milton implicitly announces here that he is a supremely well qualified conduit for the Spirit's continued dwelling and inspiration, fulfilling at last the aspirations he articulated in Elegy 6 and *Il Penseroso*.[9]

Milton's Spiritual Inspiration and Scripture

Kerrigan discusses the problematic relationship between *Paradise Lost* and the Bible. Does Milton, for example, make use of Genesis "only to exceed that account"? Kerrigan also raises the possibility that Milton is not only "imitating" Moses but actually "competing with" him.[10] We should explore seriously the implications of Milton's boast of his "advent'rous Song" (1.13) pursuing "Things unattempted yet in Prose or Rhyme" (1.16). Is he claiming here to go beyond not merely secular authors but Moses as well? This seems likely in light of the line's context. To be sure, Milton's reference to soaring "above th' *Aonian* Mount" (1.15) suggests, as Roy Flannagan notes, "Milton's challenge to classical Greek and Roman epic and to Renaissance epic";[11] at the same time, Milton has just made fairly extensive reference to Moses's Spirit-inspired writings, and in line 17 he begins his address to the Spirit, telling of the Spirit's preference for "th' upright heart and pure," beseeching the Spirit to "Instruct" him, and recalling Moses's image in Genesis 1:2, which describes the Spirit's presence at the world's creation (1.19–22).

The Spirit's presence "from the first" is what enables the Spirit now to "Instruct" Milton about the events involving the creation and, presumably, the fall of angels and of man (1.19). Milton asks the Spirit, "What in me is dark / Illumine" (1.22–23), a request that transcends a blind poet's request for poetic "sight." Milton beseeches the Spirit to show him those things that he cannot know apart from special inspiration—the happenings in Eden, heaven, and hell that, encompassing matters well beyond the first three chapters of Genesis, Milton could not access through the existing scriptures. If he is to create his detailed, far-reaching epic, he needs the inspiration of the same Spirit that instructed Moses. And given that the Spirit now reveals itself in progressively fuller ways, Milton considers it sensible that the Spirit now will enable him to write these "Things unattempted yet in Prose or Rhyme."

Milton's aspirations for his "great Argument" include his plan to "assert Eternal Providence / And justify the ways of God to men" (1.24–26). This ambition is clearly part of why Milton seeks the Spirit's aid, and it is another manifestation of Milton's hope to go beyond Moses himself. One thing Genesis does not offer is an explanation for its happenings. Of course, centuries of commentators had attempted such explanation, but Milton seeks to vindicate God's ways not by commentating upon a limited existing text but by creating a narrative that owes its creation, ultimately, to the same Spirit that gave Genesis to Moses.[12] Milton's narrative, unlike Moses's, makes clear the reasons behind so many previously unknown theological matters, including but not limited to God's representation of predestination and free will, the fall of the angels, the psychological motivations behind Adam's and Eve's transgressions, and how the events concerning humanity's fall fit into the totality of God's redemptive plan. Just as readers of *Paradise Lost* would find themselves more completely instructed in the ways of God than would readers of Genesis 1–3, it would be sensible to assert that in *Paradise Lost* the Spirit has inspired a work that surpasses Moses's writings.

Kerrigan quotes the opening of Andrew Marvell's dedicatory poem "On Paradise Lost," in which Marvell describes how Milton's epic unsettled him deeply at first.

> When I beheld the Poet blind, yet bold,
>   In slender Book his vast Design unfold,
> *Messiah* Crown'd, God's Reconcil'd Decree,
> Rebelling Angels, the Forbidden Tree,
> Heav'n, Hell, Earth, Chaos, All; the Argument
> Held me a while misdoubting his Intent,
> That he would ruin (for I saw him strong)
> The sacred Truths to Fable and old Song
> (So *Sampson* grop'd the Temple's Posts in spite)
> The World o'erwhelming to revenge his sight.[13]

Here, Marvell addresses the very appropriate concern that, given *Paradise Lost's* opening lines, with its "great Argument" and cosmic ambition to move beyond Moses's writings, the conscientious reader must necessarily wonder whether Milton intends to "ruin" the "sacred Truths" by supplanting them with his epic. As Kerrigan writes, "if the poet claims higher inspiration than Moses, it seems distressingly easy to conclude (let rude ears be absent) that the epic intends to be a document superior to a portion of Holy Scripture."[14]

We might ask, however, whether Milton intends to overtake the Bible, or does he mean rather to synthesize it and bring forth its meaning in its totality? *Paradise Lost* does, after all, make use of "both the inspiration of Sinai and the inspiration of Siloa" and addresses both creation and redemption.[15] Clearly, Milton goes beyond Genesis, but he does so by using the whole of scripture, an observation Joseph Addison essentially made in 1712.[16] It is hard to believe that Milton sees himself in any kind of competition with Moses, and it is doubtful that he "claims a higher inspiration than Moses," as Kerrigan asserts; rather, he sees himself as inspired by the same Spirit in a complementary role. Of course, the notion of a poet's seeing himself as complementing scripture is in itself audacious, but the distinction is significant. Milton sees himself, through the inspiration of the Spirit, bringing to light what was previously veiled, or less explicit, in the scripture, but he does not believe that he is teaching "anything new in this work" (*CPW*, 6:127) any more than he does in *DDD* or *DDC*. Rather, the epic's invocation, once again, demonstrates the workings of the Miltonic householder. He brings forth out of his treasure things new and old, offering his readers the ancient truths of scripture in a new way. In the words of Barbara Lewalski, Milton "does not consider the Spirit's inspiration a matter of special, mystical illumination making his poem a second Scripture, but rather as sanctioning and aiding the exercise of his authorial gifts in interpreting and representing [his] subjects." Lewalski compares such poetic inspiration—the "inspired guift of God" that Milton discusses in *The Reason of Church-Government* (1:816) and then practices in *Paradise Lost*—to the Spirit-inspired sermons (also called "prophesyings") of the seventeenth century, citing the orthodox Puritan William Perkins's sermon manual *The Arte of Prophesying* (1592) as exemplary of this contemporary view of the Spirit's relation to the preacher's prophetic task.[17]

I suggest that Milton's view of his inspiration lies somewhere between Kerrigan's notion of Milton's creating a new scripture and Lewalski's view that Milton's inspiration is analogous to that of preachers like Perkins. It must be stressed that, although they clearly sought the Holy Spirit's guidance in preparing and delivering their sermons, orthodox preachers like Perkins did not claim to offer their audiences extrabiblical, previously unseen visions of heaven, hell, and Eden. With this caveat in mind, Kari Boyd McBride and John C. Ulreich's claim regarding Milton and Aemilia Lanyer is worth considering: "Both poets . . . submit themselves to the poetry of the Spirit—not the authority of the literal Biblical word, but of the Word that has been revealed through their diligent inquiry and which they reinscribe as Biblical poetry."[18] Keeping in mind Milton's consistent critique, throughout *DDD*, of those who follow an overly "literal" scriptural hermeneutic, McBride and Ulreich's claim rings true. But we must always remember that for Milton, resistance to an overly literal view of scripture in no way suggests a lack of fidelity to scripture's larger message. Indeed, in putting forth his poetic visions with the Spirit's inspiration, Milton does not see himself at odds with the existing scriptures but rather as reinforcing them, even as in *DDD* he insists that his inspired, charitable interpretations of biblical teachings on divorce represent (and indeed recover, as *DDD*'s 1644 title page declares) "the true meaning of Scripture" (*CPW*, 2:221).

Consequently, Milton's professed fidelity to scripture in no way reduces his prophetic ambitions. Jason Rosenblatt notes that book 3's narrator "assumes a role analogous to the role of Moses" in that "he aspires to a vision of the timeless realm of light."[19] The Miltonic narrator does, in the words of Isabel MacCaffrey, deal in the realm of "divine epistemology, the ways whereby men can know, or come to know, God."[20] Rosenblatt points out the manner in which both Exodus and the invocation in book 3 address themes of both "initiation and revelation" and "obstruction and concealment." Toward the end of his invocation in book 3, the blind Miltonic narrator asks the "Celestial Light" he addresses to "Shine inward" and "plant eyes" in his "mind" "that I may see and tell / Of things invisible to mortal sight" (3.51–55). After uttering this prayer, the narrator describes "th' Almighty Father" (3.56) and his heavenly court, and then presents God's dialogue with "His only Son" (3.64). Milton's heavenly depiction makes manifest far more than anything Moses reveals in Exodus. Rosenblatt observes that "the Sinai narrative employs the imagery of covering," including Moses's being surrounded by a thick cloud (Exod. 19:9), being hidden by God's hand (Exod. 33:22), and having his radiant face obscured by a veil (Exod. 34:33–35).[21]

Milton's narrative, however, uncovers many of the very things that Moses's Exodus could not reveal. The dialogue between Father and Son includes, among other things, the Father's discussion of predestination and free will. The theology espoused in these lines is, of course, more explicit than that in the Bible, but it is also, as Maurice Kelley has pointed out, a parallel representation of the doctrines of predestination and free will discussed in Milton's DDC.[22] So, while Milton boldly depicts God the Father expounding the theology that reflects Milton's own position, he is simply presenting, like everything else taught in DDC, only what, he says, the scriptures themselves teach. Again, Milton's depicting such theology as flowing directly from the Godhead is certainly something "new," something audacious, something that transcends in its comprehensiveness the efforts of previous writers—including Moses—and something that requires, as we have seen, the inspiration of God himself. At the same time, all that the Godhead speaks and does in *Paradise Lost* is ultimately only what the scriptures themselves teach in one form or another, which becomes all the more evident when we read Milton's epic with an eye to DDC, as Kelley does throughout *This Great Argument*.[23] The ingenious manner in which Milton presents biblical concepts may be elongated, but, to Milton, it is not capricious. Rather, these concepts are the work of the Miltonic householder, who in his newfound presentation of ancient truths offers his audience a genuine depiction of biblical content, and "bringeth out of his treasury things new and old" (Matt. 13:52, Milton's translation in CPW, 2:221).

The invocation in book 7 reveals a similar phenomenon. Among other things, this invocation prepares readers for Raphael's narration to Adam and Eve of the creation of the world. Here, Milton's autobiographical narrator addresses the "Goddess" "Urania"—persuasively identified by Stevie Davies and William B. Hunter as the Holy Spirit[24]—beseeching her to inform him what happened when "The affable Arch-angel" Raphael "forewarned / *Adam*" against "Apostasy" (7.41–43). The narrator also announces that Raphael will tell readers "how this World / Of Heav'n and Earth conspicuous first began" (7.62–63)—another matter that for our narrator requires divine inspiration. As Kerrigan writes, "Milton cannot sing of Creation unless the Spirit who presides over Creation also presides over the creation of his song."[25] It is indeed curious that Milton's narrator chooses to offer, through Raphael, a retelling of a retelling of creation and the prohibition on eating from the forbidden tree. Raphael serves as a kind of intermediate householder, telling Adam and Eve for the first time the story of creation, a story that Milton's narrator in turn relates to his "fit audience . . . though few" (7.31) and that builds considerably on the foundational text of Genesis 1.

Although book 7 contains the last of Milton's narrator's direct invocations to his heavenly guide, we recognize in the ensuing books, amid their multifaceted retellings of biblical events, the continued presence of the Miltonic householder. Books 8, 9, and 10 are, of course, an extended retelling of Genesis 2 and 3. And books 11 and 12 outline, through the words of the archangel Michael (another intermediate householder), the whole of biblical salvation history, offering a comprehensive framework in which to place the ongoing consequences for the human race of Adam and Eve's original transgression, climaxing with an account of Christ's redemption offered for the sins of the world.[26] The narration of these chapters relates directly to the opening lines of book 1's invocation, where the narrator announces his intention to sing not only of the "loss of *Eden*" but also of "one greater Man" who would "Restore us, and regain the blissful Seat" (1.4–5). We see that the highlights of salvation history that Michael reveals in books 11 and 12 put the events of Genesis 3 in the perspective of the whole of scripture, and thus the epic surpasses Moses in its comprehensive scope. But despite the panoramic perspective of books 11 and 12, Milton's narrators ultimately teach nothing but "the Bible only," simply offering biblical content in a context that, while demonstrating Milton's own inspiration by the Holy

Spirit, reflects the parameters of the existing biblical scriptures. In this sense, the invocations of books 1, 3, and 7, which introduce and set up the larger scheme of retelling the scriptures in a way that is representative of the entire epic, also highlight, from the beginning, the narrator's role as the parabolic householder, who, in all that he does throughout *Paradise Lost*, "bringeth out of his treasury things new and old."

The Narrator of *Paradise Regained*: Scripture and Inspiration

Having examined the parabolic householder in the invocations of *Paradise Lost*, let us turn briefly to this phenomenon in *Paradise Regained*. The Miltonic narrator's only invocation in *Paradise Regained*, appearing at the beginning of the brief epic, repeats the aforementioned pattern of the narrator's asking the Spirit's inspiration to tell that which has not been told. Significantly, Milton addresses "Thou Spirit who ledst the glorious Eremite [Jesus] / Into the desert" (1.8–9). This address is particularly germane to Milton's poetic retelling of Luke 4:1–11, which begins, "And Jesus being full of the Holy Ghost returned from Jordan, and was led by the Spirit into the wilderness" (4:1). The narrator prays here to the same Spirit that orchestrated the events of Jesus's temptation and inspired the Gospel witness who recorded them. Moreover, as Lewalski astutely notes, "Milton cannot make this poem unless the Spirit prompts him as it prompted the Son to interpret properly the relevant texts and stories" in his rhetorical combat against Satan.[27] Milton asks the Spirit to help him to record

> deeds
> Above Heroic, though in secret done,
> And unrecorded left through many an Age,
> Worthy t' have not remain'd so long unsung. (1.14–17)

Again, the pattern of the Miltonic householder is evident. The incidents he is about to relate are both new and old, occurring long ago but now shared for the first time.

As with *Paradise Lost*, the question of whether Milton believes he is composing a new scripture must be addressed. For Joseph Wittreich, the answer is clear: *Paradise Regained* is "not a revision or even [a] recasting" of the Gospel accounts but "a new revelation."[28] Wittreich's verdict is at odds with Allan H. Gilbert's much more conservative but no less unequivocal

pronouncement of nearly a century before. Gilbert's reading of the relation-
ship between *Paradise Regained* and the canonical scripture resembles
Joseph Addison's discussion of *Paradise Lost* and the Bible. According to
Gilbert, Milton, in describing Jesus's temptations, "follows the narrative of
Luke's Gospel without alteration, and without adding anything not directly
evolved from it"; indeed, in his "expan[sive]" rendition of the "second temp-
tation" of Luke 4, "Milton adheres to the letter of the biblical account."
Gilbert notes that Calvin asserts in his commentaries on the synoptic
Gospels that Jesus endured many more temptations than the Bible records.[29]
Moreover, Elizabeth Marie Pope observes that the idea that Satan's temptations of Christ were far more numerous than those recorded by the
evangelists was part of the commentary tradition from Origen through John
Lightfoot and Lancelot Edwards.[30] In this sense, Milton's narrative is con-
sistent with the established commentary tradition.

And yet that tradition does not claim to narrate for us elaborately developed details extrapolated from Luke's compressed summaries. Milton's
poem does make such claims, crediting the Spirit's inspiration, and so, as
with Kerrigan's claims regarding *Paradise Lost*, Wittreich's assertion that
Milton offers a new scripture cannot be easily dismissed. And yet in *Paradise
Regained*, as in *Paradise Lost*, the intention of the Miltonic householder
remains consistent. In the end, although his interpretation of Jesus's temptations is uniquely his own, Milton (to reference once again the opening
chapter of *DDC*) does "not teach anything new in this work" (*CPW*,
6:127)—nothing, at least, that would somehow undercut or supersede the
overall message of Luke's account. And surely Wittreich overstates his case
when he avers without explanation that Milton's brief epic is not "even [a]
recasting" of the Gospel narrative. Nonetheless, Milton's Spirit-inspired
retelling of the scripture goes beyond any commentary's claims or preten-
sions. In the end, Milton's approach to biblical interpretation can be
described in the same way that Michael Lieb has described Milton's theology: as "sui generis"—unique and a type of its very own.[31]

Paradise Regained: The Son and Mary as Exemplary Householders

Having seen the parabolic householder in *Paradise Regained*'s narrator, we
may see him manifested there also by Mary and the Son. As Dayton Haskin

has shown, Milton depicts Mary as one who receives, considers, and relates to her son the information she has received from God and his servants.[32] Building on Luke's description (in 2:19 and 2:51) of Mary as one who "ponder[s]" and "ke[eps]" "in her heart" the various proclamations she hears about and from Jesus that attest to his being the Son of God and the messiah, Milton portrays her as a kind of ideal receptacle of divine knowledge who, by virtue of her conscientious "pondering," can understand the messages she has received and in turn use this information and her meditative methodology to train her son and enable him to recognize his divine identity and mission.[33] Mary thus plays the role of the parabolic householder in that she, taking in information from the Hebrew scriptures as well as from contemporary prophets, digests what she has received and brings forth knowledge for the New Testament dispensation that amounts to treasure both new and old.

Mary's Hermeneutical Influence on the Son and His Scriptural Self-Knowledge

Before Milton gives us an extended account of Mary's own ponderings, he shows us, through the account of the Son, Mary's influence on the Son's reception of and interpretation of the Hebrew scriptures. Having been led by the Spirit into the wilderness, the Son recalls events that have led to his current situation. He remembers his childhood and his early hunger for the scriptures, a hunger that culminated in his visit, unbeknownst to Mary and Joseph, to the temple in Jerusalem (Luke 2:46–50):

> When I was yet a child, no childish play
> To me was pleasing, all my mind was set
> Serious to learn and know, and thence to do
> What might be public good; myself I thought
> Born to that end, born to promote all truth,
> All righteous things: therefore I above my years,
> The Law of God I read, and found it sweet,
> And made it my whole delight, and in it grew
> To such perfection that, ere yet my age
> Had measured twice six years, at our great Feast

I went into the Temple, there to hear
The teachers of our Law, and to propose
What might improve my knowledge or their own. (1.201–13)

This passage is well known for its likely self-referential connection to Milton's own youth; more immediately, however, it displays the Son's portrait of himself as one who, through his contact with both the written scriptures and the teachers of the law, might gain a greater understanding of God's truth.[34] Although commentators differ concerning the extent of the divine attributes Milton's Son displays, the Son's words here are consistent with Luke's statement, following Jesus's temple visit, that "Jesus increased in wisdom" (Luke 2:52).[35] Milton's Son, however, portrays his greatest human teacher not as an expert in the law but as his mother, Mary.

Continuing in his reminiscences, the Son tells of his early aspirations to use persuasion, and if necessary force, "To rescue *Israel* from the *Roman* yoke," "to subdue and quell o'er all the earth / Brute violence and proud Tyrannic pow'r," and to allow "truth" and "equity" to flourish (1.217–20; see 217–26). He then relates his recollections of Mary's encouragement:

These growing thoughts my Mother soon perceiving
By words at times cast forth, inly rejoic'd,
And said to me apart: High are thy thoughts
O Son, but nourish them and let them soar
To what height sacred virtue and true worth
Can raise them, though above example high;
By matchless Deeds express thy matchless Sire. (1.227–33)

Mary's loving admonition to the Son, which George H. McLoone describes as her effort to "reform" his "consciousness and voice" through "prophecy,"[36] is continued in a lengthy speech in which she tells him of his divine parentage and of the angelic visitation, in which the angel Gabriel told her that the child she would bear "shouldst be great and sit on *David's* Throne" and rule a "Kingdom" with "no end" (1.240–41). She tells him of the incidents surrounding his birth in a humble manger, the star-guided visitation of the wise men, and Simeon's and Anna's prophetic announcements in the temple, all of which pronounced his messianic identity (1.242–58).

Noteworthy in Mary's speech is her admonition that Jesus "nourish" his thoughts and have them grow to their full measure through right understanding of his identity as the Son of God and the foretold messiah. She describes the events of the first two chapters of Matthew and Luke, scriptures that, when Mary proclaims them, are still in oral form. Significantly, these are events to which Mary had privileged access as an eyewitness—the very events that she herself has "pondered" or "kept" in her heart. The word "nourish" is significant in relation to Mary in that it closely resembles the meaning conveyed by the Greek words translated "pondered" (*symballousa*) or "kept" (*dietērei*) in Luke 2:19 and 2:51. Indeed, Mary encourages her son to have the same attitude that she has toward the events of his life: to nurture and value them, and to add to them greater knowledge that will in turn give him a more perfect understanding of the events themselves, all of which ultimately point to his divine identity.

The Son's response to Mary's encouragement is to return to the Hebrew scriptures and examine them in light of her revelations.

> This having heard, straight I again revolv'd
> The Law and Prophets, searching what was writ
> Concerning the Messiah, to our Scribes
> Known partly, and soon found of whom they spake
> I am; this chiefly, that my way must lie
> Through many a hard assay even to the death,
> Ere the promis'd Kingdom can attain,
> Or work Redemption for mankind, whose sins'
> Full weight must be transferr'd upon my head. (1.259–67)

Here, the Son's reception of Mary's New Testament revelation, combined with his reexamination of the law and prophets, provides him with not only a recognition of himself as the messiah the Hebrew scriptures describe— with the Son's self-recognition of his deity strongly suggested by the enjambed "I am" immediately followed by a caesura at the beginning of line 263—but also with a rather detailed understanding of the nature of his ministry, one that will not involve his earlier aspirations of political liberation but rather his suffering, death, and redemptive bearing of humanity's sins.[37] The significance of Mary's influence on the Son is articulated by Marjorie Hope Nicolson, who notes that at the conclusion of his lengthy monologue—even as he declares that he must begin a public ministry that "best becomes / The Authority which I deriv'd from Heaven" (1.288–89)—"he still seems to be following his mother's teaching, rather than remembering his own life in Heaven." Nicolson's observation is superior to that of Stanley Fish, who neglects to mention the Son's growth in wisdom through Mary's intervention and his own subsequent return to the scriptures, writing that the Son "sees from the inside out, immediately and without process."[38] Fish's point is valid only in the sense that the Son has reached such a level of spiritual insight as a result of the process Mary has taught him.

The Son's skillful ability to produce a new and superior interpretation of the scriptures as a result of his new revelation demonstrates his exercise of the hermeneutic of the parabolic householder. Like the householder, the Son "bringeth forth out of his treasure things new and old" (Matt. 13:52). Obviously, his recognition that he is the divine messiah and his understanding of the nature of his ministry are new things, or treasures; at the same time, they are new observations taken from the old things/treasure of Hebrew scripture; the Son is simply bringing forth with new clarity—and manifesting bodily—the truths that have been there all along.

Although space limitations prevent a detailed analysis of the Son's defeat of Satan and his temptations, which is narrated in the remainder of *Paradise Regained*, the Son's use of Hebrew scripture to thwart Satan is an extended manifestation of the Son as the ideal parabolic householder. One example in particular displays his use of scripture in a way that demonstrates striking continuity with his realization of his messianic identity and mission: In Satan's final temptation, having taken the Son to the highest place on the temple in Jerusalem, Satan exhorts him to "show thy progeny" (4.554), daring him to

> Cast thyself down; safely if Son of God:
> For it is written, He will give command
> Concerning thee to his Angels, in thir hands
> They shall up lift thee, lest at any time
> Thou chance to dash thy foot against a stone. (4.555–59)

Satan's perverse use of Psalm 91:11–12, the last of his temptations to sinful action,[39] is answered by the Son's succinct response: "also it is written, / Tempt not the Lord thy God" (4.560–61), words that cause Satan to fall "smitten with amazement" (4.562). The Son's authoritative use of Deuteronomy 6:16 shows that he is the ultimate householder, one who applies the Mosaic law to himself, recognizing, even more completely than he did in his earlier days, that "of whom [it] spake / I am" (1.262–63). Indeed, the Son's declaration here is his "long-awaited demonstration of divinity," his fullest, most powerful, and first nonsolitary "claim to participate in the Godhead," the moment that he "achieves full knowledge of himself."[40] But if the Son's fullest understanding and display of his deity occurs when he quells Satan at the end of the poem, this event is the culmination of the self-recognition he receives from reading the scriptures in light of the New Testament knowledge given him by Mary years before.

Mary as a Householder: Storing and Pondering

As I have noted here and in chapter 3, many scholars have recognized Milton's identification with the Son of *Paradise Regained*. But this identification becomes all the more curious when we recognize it in relation to the character of Mary. We have seen how her exhortation that her son "nourish" his thoughts is reminiscent of Luke's account of Mary's own resolution to keep/ treasure in her heart the events and words that surrounded his birth, infancy, and childhood. In book 2 of *Paradise Regained*, Milton builds on Luke's words to portray Mary as a kind of "storehouse" of God's teachings, one whose method of collecting and "pondering" spiritual truths resembles the parabolic householder of Matthew 13:52.

Book 2 contains a scene in which Mary recollects the events surrounding the birth, infancy, and childhood of her son. Milton describes Mary as she sees others returning from John the Baptist's service at the Jordan River. Unaware of his confrontation in the desert with Satan, she wonders why Jesus is not among them, and her concern prompts her reminiscences. She recognizes that his disappearance must indicate that he is now taking part in an event of tremendous import. Linking the present with her memory of her young son's going off by himself to the temple at Jerusalem, she says to herself,

> But where delays he now? some great intent
> Conceals him: when twelve years he scarce had seen,
> I lost him, but so found, as well I saw
> He could not lose himself; but went about
> His Father's business; what he meant I mus'd,
> Since understand; much more his absence now
> Thus long to some great purpose he obscures.

But I to wait with patience am inur'd;
My heart hath been a storehouse long of things
And sayings laid up, portending strange events.
    Thus *Mary* pondering oft, and oft to mind
Recalling what remarkably had pass'd
Since first her Salutation heard, with thoughts
Meekly compos'd awaited the fulfilling. (2.95–108)

In the first part of this excerpt, Mary reflects on her habitual practice of receiving information, actively thinking on it, and eventually understanding it in light of additional information that is later received and pondered. Although she initially could not comprehend what the twelve-year-old Jesus meant when he said he "went about / His Father's business" (see Luke 2:49: "Wist ye not that I must be about my Father's business?"), she reports that "what he meant I mus'd, / Since understand." Her response to her initial failure to understand her young son's meaning is to "muse" over his words, a process that eventually allows her to "understand" their full meaning in light of events that continue to unfold before her. Haskin notes that "mus'd" is probably used here as a substitute for the Authorized Version's "pondered" (Greek *symballousa*). He investigates the rich lexical range of Milton's word choice by noting the varied meanings of "muse" in the *Oxford English Dictionary*: "By Milton's time its older senses (*OED*, 5; 6) of 'To wait or look expectantly' and 'To murmur; to grumble, complain' were obsolete. Still, as a reminder of the divergent responses to God's promises made by the Israelites during their wanderings through the wilderness, these meanings are part of the background to the activities of both mother and son. Another sense of the word (*OED*, 2) implies 'be[ing] at a loss,' and this perfectly befits the context in which Mary now finds herself. For her . . . the experience of missing something turns out to be an inspiration."[41] We may further recognize, with Haskin, the connection between Mary's "pondering" God's word and its meaning and a similar sort of "pondering" of the scriptures that is claimed by the author of *DDC*, a phenomenon that enables "Milton's Mary" to emerge "as a portrait of the responsible reader."[42] Such conscientious processing of the divine messages she receives is what empowers her to graduate from a state of confusion to one of understanding; furthermore, she has confidence that just as this process of reception, pondering, and subsequent understanding has borne fruit in the past, it will do so in the present situation of Jesus's absence, a mystery that now "await[s] the fulfilling" (2.108). Mary's progression to understanding is one that she imparts to others, most significantly her son—a phenomenon seen in her earlier exhortation in book 1. In the same way, her methodology may be seen as a tacit exhortation to the audience of *Paradise Regained* as a whole, an exhortation that is echoed in *DDC*, a document that implicitly claims for itself a methodology of reading the scriptures that reflects Mary's.[43]

Also particularly important is Mary's statement "My heart hath been a storehouse long of things / And sayings laid up, portending strange events" (2.103–4). Like Milton himself, Mary is not one who merely waits "for further clarification of the texts that she does not understand"; rather, she "actively seeks out meaning." As Haskin demonstrates, the contemporary usage of the word "storehouse" suggests a highly active connotation. "The *storehouse*," he writes, "(sometimes described as a 'chest' or a 'vessell') served as the standard image in rhetorical treatises for the container in which the topics, or places, were kept." In addition, "storehouse" was often used as the English translation of the Latin *thesaurus*, as translators would be "emphasizing more than they might by the word *treasury* the functional aspect of the collection." Haskin observes that the storehouse/treasury of Mary's heart thus gives her a distinct resemblance to the ideal theologian/scribe that Milton cites in defense of his organizational method in *DDC*, that of the householder of Matthew 13:52: "every scribe who has been instructed in the kingdom of heaven, is like a householder who brings out of his treasure new and old possessions" (*CPW*, 6:127–28, italics omitted). As Haskin notes, "This assimilation of Mary's heart to a thesaurus, upon which the scribe then draws to produce a work at once old and new, makes a sort of signature in Milton's poem, even as it validates the storyteller's method."[44] Milton's identification with Mary is evident in this implicit connection between her interpretive method and his own, a method that she passes on to her son, and one that Milton himself hopes to disseminate among his readers. "Milton presents Mary as one who mediates the Word—first to Jesus himself, then to the New Testament writers, and ultimately to Christians in every age," writes Haskin. "Beyond this, he has painted in her a portrait of the artist. She exercises the authorly roles of preserving, interpreting, and combining diverse texts into a unique personal synthesis. In this way Milton's Mary anticipates the activity of other bearers of the Word, that is, of both the evangelists like Luke and latter-day poets like Milton himself."[45]

Mary's example as a mediator of God's word shows that she as much as the Son is a figure with whom Milton identifies as a fellow parabolic householder. In addition, Mary's role as one who, in Haskin's words, is "preserving, interpreting, and combining diverse texts into a unique personal synthesis" has great personal relevance to Milton himself, something particularly evident when we consider that these processes are exactly what he undertakes in both his polemical tract *DDD* and his theological treatise *DDC*, as well as in his poetic retellings of biblical events, *Paradise Lost*, *Paradise Regained*, and *Samson Agonistes*, processes he undertakes most self-consciously in *Paradise Lost*, as just discussed. And surely such a personal synthesis also takes place in *Paradise Regained*, where the events of the fourth chapter of Luke are retold in a manner that highlights not only the Son's epic struggle against Satan but also, and even more significantly for our purposes, the conspicuously Miltonic figures of Mary and her Son and their thoughtful "musings" upon the biblical texts that they receive and subsequently re-create. Indeed, Milton's deep connection to the Son and Mary may be seen as an extension of his identification with the parabolic householder of Matthew 13:52. For throughout *Paradise Regained*, both the Son and Mary show themselves—like Milton himself—to be readers, hearers, thinkers, and teachers who, as they process the information they have been given from various sources, bring forth out of the treasuries of their hearts and minds "things new and old."

10

Internal and External Scripture
in *Samson Agonistes*

Having discussed the careful, meditative hermeneutic of the householder in the blameless Son and the exemplary Mary of *Paradise Regained*, let us conclude our study of examining a more controversial manifestation of the householder in the person of Milton's self-referential protagonist in *Samson Agonistes*, specifically concerning the matter of immediate spiritual revelation from God and whether Samson discerns accurately God's "promptings." Milton raises this question by portraying Samson's relationship with direct spiritual revelation as potentially delusional, even as the drama portrays direct spiritual revelation as a legitimate means of divine communication that, when correctly understood, can lead to redemption. Ultimately, *Samson Agonistes* suggests a Hebrew deity whose leading may finally be known by the genuine servant of God who has first demonstrated obedience to the divine commands codified in the written scripture. As we shall see, it is Samson's renewed obedience to the Mosaic law he once flouted that enables him to recognize immediate revelation through the Spirit and be used by God to accomplish his greater scriptural will.

Throughout the drama, the matter of immediate revelation is addressed in conjunction with the question of whether such revelation can be trusted if it goes against the explicit teachings of the written scriptures. As readers learn early in the drama, Milton's Samson had been, before the drama began, the recipient of divine inspiration, believing rightly that God had led him to marry his first Philistine wife, the woman of Timna, even though marrying a Canaanite woman went against Mosaic law (Deut. 7:3–4). Paradoxically, Samson's violation of this clear scriptural command accomplishes God's broader commandment in written scripture, for, as we shall see, this marriage enables him to obey the larger sense of the law. In this sense,

Samson plays the role of the parabolic householder, for he acts like one who, in the words of Jesus's parable, "bringeth forth out of his treasure things new and old" (Matt. 13:52). That is, while the leading of God's Spirit to do such a thing goes against a seemingly plain scriptural command, and so seems to be a "new" interpretation altogether, if it accomplishes God's larger scriptural design, then in obeying this controversial leading of the Spirit, Samson is in fact accomplishing what is commanded in the larger scope of the written scripture, and thus acting in obedience to the genuine meaning of the Bible.

If we embrace the perspective of the larger Miltonic canon, we may see that this idea is consistent with Milton's argument in *The Doctrine and Discipline of Divorce* that although his teachings on divorce seem to violate Jesus's prohibitions against divorce in Matthew 5:31–32 and 19:6–9, they are in fact directed by charity and perfectly in accord with the larger biblical mandate regarding charity, which Jesus never overturned. But Samson's status as a genuine householder has been compromised by his disobedient choice to marry Dalila, a choice that was prompted, it turns out, by his libido and arrogance. Thus, in his past discernment of God's supposed "leadings" in his two marriages, Samson proved himself to be first a successful and then an unsuccessful householder and interpreter of special revelation: he properly recognized God's true will and promptings in his first marriage; but later, deluded by his own lust and presumption, he mistook his unlawful desire for Dalila as God's again leading him to marry a Philistine woman. By the end of the drama, however, we see Samson as a restored servant of God, one who fulfills the role of the householder in ways that surpass his original recognition of God's command; indeed, when the chastened Samson demonstrates unswerving fidelity to the written law, he is enabled to discern divine promptings and thus to obey God in ways that transcend the letter of the law even as they fulfill the law's greater purpose.

Israel's God as Divine Householder

Samson's role as a householder and a wise recipient of unmediated revelation in *Samson Agonistes* is predicated on the Hebrew God's supreme role as the ultimate Householder, who may freely command that his servants break his written law in order to accomplish a higher purpose. Just after

Samson tells how God inspired him to marry the woman of Timna, the Chorus describes God in terms highly reminiscent of our earlier discussions of the householder, celebrating God's freedom to act in contravention of his written law in order to accomplish his will, thus delivering an implicit rebuke of those who would call God unjust for his ostensibly contradictory commands:

> Yet more there be who doubt his ways not just,
> As to his own edicts, found contradicting,
> . . . .
>
> As if they [the doubters] would confine th' interminable,
> And tie him to his own prescript,
> Who made our Laws to bind us, not himself,
> And hath full right to exempt
> Whom so it pleases him by choice
> From National obstriction, without taint
> Of sin, or legal debt;
> For with his own Laws he can best dispense.
> He would not else who never wanted means,
> Nor in respect of th' enemy just cause
> To set his people free,
> Have prompted this Heroic *Nazarite*,
> Against his vow of strictest purity,
> To seek in marriage that fallacious Bride. (300–301, 307–20)

The Chorus's depiction of God's approach to his own written law resembles Milton's discussion in *De Doctrina Christiana* (*DDC*) of the superiority of the internal scripture over the external, written scripture. In his chapter "Of the Holy Scripture," Milton writes, "The pre-eminent and supreme authority [over the scripture of the Bible] ∴ is the authority of the Spirit, which is internal" (*CPW*, 6:587). If Milton considers this the case for individual persons, then it is clearly all the more so for God himself. Although Milton's teachings in *DDC* concerning the identity of the Holy Spirit are certainly heterodox, he does affirm that the Holy Spirit is "a minister of God . . . produced, from the substance of God" (6:298).[1] Thus, if the Holy Spirit within the believer prompts him to act against the written scripture, the believer is not acting on his own but has been prompted by God himself. In his supreme freedom, God may choose to work in a way that ostensibly violates his written word, yet in doing so the overall spirit and integrity of the written text is upheld, not undermined. This is certainly the case with Milton's Samson.

At this point, we might ask how such action by God can be reconciled with Milton's cautious and strategic pronouncement that he does "not teach anything new" in *DDC* (*CPW*, 6:127). Furthermore, how can God's seemingly unscriptural promptings in *Samson* be reconciled with Dayton Haskin's insightful comment that Milton's heterodoxies are, in effect, his attempt to uphold "the Bible only"?[2] Such questions may seem unanswerable at first—until we realize that the Chorus's lines are in fact an apologia for the book of Judges itself. Judges 14:4 asserts that Samson's demand that his parents procure him the woman of Timna for his wife "was of the LORD, that he sought an occasion against the Philistines: for at that time the Philistines had dominion over Israel." This verse ought to strike us as odd, because Samson's allegedly God-given desire appears to contradict Deuteronomy 7:3, where the Israelites are commanded not to intermarry with the foreigners among them, for such unions would lead to idolatry. This prohibition is reinforced in Judges 3:5–7, which links intermarriage and idolatry. Why, then, would God use such a seemingly contradictory method later in Judges to accomplish his purpose? Milton's orthodox contemporary, Matthew Poole, writes in his commentary on Judges that "this action of Samson's, though against common rules, seems to be warranted . . . principally by the instinct and direction of God." Addressing Samson's violation, Poole writes that such "pollution" was a "necessary dut[y] . . . being contracted by Divine instinct and direction, and in order to God's honour, and therefore dispensed with by the author of that law, and required by him for his service."[3] In other words, Poole explains, God may freely inspire his servants to act in ways contrary to the written law in order to accomplish his higher purpose.

Although some have suggested that Milton's sympathies for matters of "internal scripture" can be connected with his possible theological affinities with religious radicals, including "Ranters, Quakers, antinomians,"[4] Milton's position in *Samson Agonistes* on whether divine inspiration can override the written law is similar to that of the conservative Poole, an adherent of *jure divino* Presbyterianism, which held that "churches must not endorse measures that were not positively sanctioned by the Scriptures."[5] According to Milton's Chorus, God has perfect freedom to disregard such a prohibition because he "made our Laws to bind us, not himself" (309). Furthermore, the Chorus tells us that such disregard on God's part does not actually contradict his law; to the contrary, it is another dimension of his employing of it. "For with his own Laws he can best dispense," the Chorus says (314). The meaning here of the word "dispense" (a word also used by Poole), as Roy Flannagan notes, is to "administer justice," not, as we might think, "get rid of."[6] In other words, in his infinite wisdom, God, in going above his law, is actually administering it perfectly.[7] Although Milton's text is not specific, we may surmise that God's seeming transgression of his own law is in fact a fulfillment of his overall intention behind that specific prohibition. Deuteronomy 7 begins: "When the Lord thy God shall bring thee into the land whither thou goest to possess it, and hath cast out many nations before thee, the Hittites, and the Girgashites, and the Amorites, and the Canaanites, and the Perizzites, and the Hivites, and the Jebusites, seven nations greater and mightier than thou; and when the Lord thy God shall deliver them before thee, thou shalt smite them, and utterly destroy them; thou shalt make no covenant with them, nor shew mercy unto them" (7:1–2). These verses are immediately followed by the prohibitions against intermarriage and idolatry in 7:3–4. Thus the command that God seemingly has violated with respect to Samson and the woman of Timna is actually predicated upon both his commandment to destroy these same nations and his promise to enable the Israelites to do so. Since the prohibition against intermarriage with these nations is subordinate to the command to destroy them, it seems likely that Milton reasoned that the external scripture was in no way violated by God's free act in this situation.

Divine Prompting, Marriage, and Self-Deception

Having established the theological framework for Samson's inspiration, let us examine his own view of such divine promptings. Early on, Samson tells the Chorus about the supernaturally ordained circumstances of his first marriage:

> The first I saw at *Timna*, and she pleas'd
> Mee, not my Parents, that I sought to wed,
> The daughter of an Infidel: they knew not
> That what I motion'd was of God; I knew

From intimate impulse, and therefore urg'd
The marriage on; that by occasion hence
I might begin *Israel's* Deliverance,
The work to which I was divinely call'd. (219–26)

Samson's description of his divine "impulse" to marry the woman is, as we might expect, consistent with both the Chorus's statement about God's freedom to work "above" his law and Milton's discussion of the superior "internal scripture" of the Spirit in *DDC*. Although Samson's parents, knowing only the external scripture of the law, are concerned about his choice, Samson's perception of the internal scripture of God's Spirit overrides this prohibition and enables him to act toward God's ultimate goal to bring about "*Israel's* Deliverance" from the Philistines. That Samson is indeed obeying God's Spirit when following this "intimate impulse" is demonstrated by the Spirit's repeated empowerment of the Hebrew champion in his decisive victories over the Philistines in Judges 14 and 15. In marrying the woman of Timna, Samson recognizes and follows a genuine "motion" from God, and we see that this new revelation of the internal scripture brings about the more encompassing command of written scripture, the destruction of the Canaanites.[8] Because he walks in obedience to God's Spirit in this first marriage decision, Samson does not violate the law here but acts as a vessel through which God sovereignly "dispenses" with his law. Samson is guiltless "Of sin" (313).[9]

But even though Samson acts as an obedient householder in his first marriage, such rare divine promptings do not give the recipient unfettered freedom to override the law. Samson's description of his allegiance to the "internal scripture" of the Spirit is immediately followed by an admission that reinforces Milton's commitment to "the Bible only." Telling of his ill-fated marriage to Dalila, Samson contrasts his former promptings with his recent transgressions:

I thought it lawful from my former act,
And the same end; still watching to oppress
Israel's oppressors: of what now I suffer
She was not the prime cause, but I myself. (231–34)

Samson condemns himself here for his own presumption in violating the written law. We learn later from his father, Manoa, that with Dalila Samson also "didst plead / Divine impulsion prompting how [he] might'st / Find some occasion to infest [Israel's] Foes" (421–23). By the time he speaks these lines, however, Samson has recognized that, in the case of Dalila, he "had rationalized a 'motion' from self and . . . symbolically violated the trust of God."[10] With his first wife, Samson had received a special prompting from God that did in fact "exempt" him from the "National obstriction" against marrying a Canaanite, thus leaving Samson "without taint / Of sin" (310–13). But then Samson used his earlier prompting as a pretext to marry a second Philistine. In his arrogance, he "thought lawful" that which was clearly unlawful in the written scripture. Simply put, Samson, in his pride and self-indulgence, in "his presumption and lust,"[11] mistook the promptings of his libido for those of the Spirit—a testimony to how Milton's ideal of the parabolic householder is thwarted when the would-be householder strays from the ideal of the wise virgin. Samson, still basking in the military success that followed his previous marriage, no doubt further justified his decision with the belief that marriage to Dalila would bring about further conquest in the name of the Lord.[12] But in his self-reflection and contrition—which includes, as discussed in chapter 7, his wise rejection of the life of sensual indulgence Dalila offers him earlier in the drama—Samson displays an altogether different attitude. Here, he upholds the written scripture fully, recognizing that he may diverge from it only when God's own Spirit clearly overrides a specific portion of the written law to bring about a greater principle within it.

Samson's Chastened Rededication to the External Scripture

Samson's suffering for his miscalculations with Dalila makes him cautious about any further violations of God's law. He displays his new devotion even as God prepares him once again to ostensibly violate the written scripture. After the Philistine Officer conveys his lords' command that Samson entertain them at Dagon's feast, Samson replies that he cannot, for "Our Law forbids at thir Religious Rites / My presence" (1320–21). Samson is probably alluding to Exodus 23:24a, "Thou shalt not bow down to their gods, nor serve them."[13] As his discussion with the Chorus upon the Officer's departure reveals, Samson guards against transgression. He refuses to go to Dagon's feast even though the Chorus makes three logical arguments in favor of his attendance: (1) the Philistine lords might respond harshly to his obstinacy (1348–53); (2) Samson is already serving the "Idolatrous" Philistines in his current labor (1363–64); and (3) Samson's service at Dagon's feast would not really be idol worship, for "Where the heart joins not, outward acts defile not" (1368). Samson, however, is as steadfast in his resistance to them as he was to the Officer, returning their arguments with notably pious rebuttals. Now a man of patience, Samson is not being egotistically obstinate. Rather, his resistance reflects his renewed commitment to the external law of Israel's God, a devotion that qualifies him again to be a conduit for the internal scripture of the Spirit.[14]

Samson, having just stood his ground against the Chorus's arguments, now suddenly reveals that God could still use him—or any of them—at the feast of Dagon:

> Yet that he may dispense with me or thee
> Present in Temples at Idolatrous Rites
> For some important cause, thou needst not doubt. (1377–79)

Milton's use of the word "dispense" here again attracts our attention. Hughes notes that the term "dispense with" in this case means "arrange to remit a penalty for a person so that he may do a forbidden act."[15] Thus God may choose now to "dispense" his law in a way that will "dispense with" Samson—even though Samson ostensibly breaks God's law—in order to accomplish God's higher purpose of destroying the Philistines (see again Judg. 7:1–2). Here we see what Leonard Mustazza recognizes in Samson's taunting of the giant Harapha: that Samson's adroit use of language "turns out to be the prelude to direct heroic action,"[16] an action that, to quote John M. Steadman, is "the logical culmination of a spiritual process rather than . . . the effect of purely external causes."[17] Once again, God's intervention and Samson's role as the householder come into play. At this point, we trust that Samson will be able to recognize God's promptings: in his mature state he has gained an unswerving commitment to God's external scripture; as a result, he now has the wisdom to discern and follow the internal scripture of the Spirit. Here, argues Robert Fallon, Samson "stands ready, empty of self, to receive the divine command, which comes as 'rouzing motions.'"[18]

Rousing Motions and Reverence for God's Law

Samson's report to the Chorus of this divine command displays his recovered spiritual assurance:

Be of good courage, I begin to feel
Some rousing motions in me which dispose
To something extraordinary my thoughts.
I with this Messenger will go along,
Nothing to do, be sure, that may dishonor
Our Law, or stain my vow of *Nazarite*. (1381–86)

As he receives these "rousing motions"—strikingly reminiscent of the "some strong motion" that prompts Milton's Son in *Paradise Regained* to go into the wilderness to be tempted by Satan (1.290; and note that all three Gospel accounts of Jesus's temptations say that the Spirit "led" or "driveth" him "into the wilderness")[19]—Samson shows himself a mature householder and servant of God. Far from the reckless man who used a "leading" as pretense to break the Mosaic law, Samson now describes his obedience to the internal scripture of the Spirit as fundamentally consistent with that of the external law.[20] Indeed, even as Samson's aforementioned probable remembrance of the first half of Exodus 23:24 probably prevented him from initially accompanying the Philistine Officer to Dagon's feast, so too might his memory of the remainder of the verse—"but thou shalt utterly overthrow them, and quite break down their images"—inspire him to go to the festival after all. Samson twice more repeats his resolve to keep the written scripture before he departs (1408–9, 1423–25).

In light of Samson's clear progress regarding the external scripture, we can answer Stanley Fish's following caveat: "the reader who remembers the history of Samson's 'rousing motions' may be wary of labeling these new motions 'of God.'" We may label them as such because Samson, in his transformed fidelity to external scripture, now properly recognizes the signs of the internal scripture of God's Spirit upon him. From this perspective, I disagree with Fish's suggestion that the "rousing motions" play a part "in Samson's breaking free of the Law's bondage."[21] Rather, it is the law itself that gives Samson guidance to restrain his carnal "motions" and, from the perspective of such restraint, to discern the "rousing motions" as genuinely being from God. In this sense, Mary Ann Radzinowicz is only partly correct in asserting that Samson "announc[es] his resolution to answer to nothing but the inner authority of his own sense of God."[22] Rather, Samson's "inner authority" is submitted to the whole of the external law of God, and because of this, he is able to discern when this "inner authority"—prompted by God himself—may command him to ostensibly transgress some aspect of that external law.[23] Here again a comparison to the Son in *Paradise Regained* is instructive. Although his situation does not exactly parallel that of the repentant Samson, we may note that Milton's Spirit-led Son also demonstrates the ability to disregard a portion of the Hebrew scripture in favor of a larger truth therein; indeed, his final defeat of Satan occurs when he successfully thwarts the tempter's misuse of the letter of the external scripture by his own superior obedience to the truth of that same external scripture (4.551–71).[24]

"Of My Own Accord": Samson's Obedience to God's Spirit

When the Messenger comes to report Samson's final actions to Manoa and the Chorus, he states neither that Samson prostrated himself before the Philistine god nor that he maintained his purity by assiduously avoiding any action that could be perceived as spiritually defiling. Rather, the Messenger recounts that Samson, before his last act of heroic destruction, "perform'd" (1626) for the Philistines' entertainment. Significantly, such a performance is exactly what the Officer initially commanded of Samson, a command that Samson initially refused because of his loyalty to the Mosaic law. Samson's "performance," however, is sanctified because it is done in obedience to the leading of God's Spirit that begins with the "rousing motions" Samson describes before he departs.

We see further indications that, to the end, Samson is being guided by the Spirit-given internal scripture that enables him to transcend certain isolated details of the written scripture in order to obey the overall message of that scripture. The Messenger says that, while leaning against the temple pillars, with "eyes fixt fast he stood, as one who pray'd, / Or some great matter in his mind revolv'd" (1637–38); Samson then makes the following declaration, which immediately precedes his destruction of Dagon's temple:

> Hitherto, Lords, what your commands impos'd
> I have perform'd, as reason was, obeying,
> Not without wonder or delight beheld.
> Now of my own accord such other trial
> I mean to show you of my strength, yet greater;
> As with amaze shall strike all who behold. (1640–45)

The degree to which Samson, at this point, is in step with the Spirit of God has been observed by a number of critics. John Spencer Hill writes that Samson's destruction of the temple "is an act of responsive choice, a free action in which the will of the instrument co-operates with, and is submerged in, the will of God."[25] Similarly, Albert R. Cirillo sees this point as a critical juncture in Samson's spiritual "movement . . . from darkness to light." "At this moment," Cirillo comments regarding Samson's silent prayer, "Samson achieves his closest communion with God, as the actual intense light of noon becomes the inner light which displaces the darkness of his despair."[26] More recently, in an essay that portrays Samson as the violent champion of Israel's terrifying God—a God whom the Semichorus calls "our living Dread" (1673)—Michael Lieb contends that Samson "implement[s] the full force of God's awesome power. . . . He is 'our living Dread' incarnate."[27] As Lieb's essay makes clear, the God with whom Samson identifies so closely is deeply disturbing to the modern reader. Such disturbance, however, should not prevent us from recognizing the profound identification Samson achieves here with the God who empowers his final act.[28]

Lieb's argument for Samson's intimate identification with God is based on the assertion that in his declaration to the Philistines, Samson employs "the discourse of God," specifically in announcing that his final display of strength would be done "of my own accord" (1643). Connecting Samson's "of my own accord" with God's own oath formula—*biy nishba'ti* ("by myself [or of my own accord] I have sworn")—in the Hebrew scriptures, Lieb writes that "the Miltonic Samson in effect subsumes within himself the divine role implied by the phrase *biy nishba'ti.*"[29]

While Lieb's argument uses Samson's "of my own accord" to highlight his intense connection with God, the same phrase has been used by Joseph Wittreich, both in *Interpreting "Samson Agonistes"* and more recently and much more extensively in *Shifting Contexts*, to portray an unregenerate Samson who acts here on his own, apart from divine directive.[30] For scriptural evidence, Wittreich cites John 11:49–50, where the high priest Caiaphas tells the council, in response to their statements about Jesus, "Ye know nothing at all. Nor consider that it is expedient for us, that one man should die for the people, and that the whole nation perish not." Wittreich emphasizes that John then comments that Caiaphas speaks here "not of his own accord" (11:51) (the Authorized King James Version of John 11:51 reads, "this he spake not *of himself*" [emphasis added; Greek *aph autou*].) Wittreich continues: "that is, he acts after divine intervention, under the influence of divine inspiration. . . . *Of his own accord* denies the agency of God which NOT *of his own accord* credits him."[31] But Wittreich's reductive assessment of the Greek prepositional phrase that Wittreich and the Revised Standard Version render as "of his own accord" is not consonant with the New Testament itself. Jesus demonstrates this most clearly in John 10:18, where he tells his listeners, "No man taketh it [my life] from me, but I lay it down *of myself* [*ap ematou*]. I have power to lay it down, and I have power to take it again. *This commandment have I received of my Father*" (emphasis added). Here, Jesus uses the same Greek phrase (altered only for the first person) to indicate that a decision he was making "of myself" (or "of my own accord" in the RSV) was also clearly being done in response to God's command. This verse is especially important to our understanding of Milton's Samson—and his phrase "of my own accord"—because Samson was routinely seen as a type of Christ by Milton's contemporaries.[32]

We should also note that in the only two New Testament verses where the Authorized King James Version actually uses the phrase "of his own accord," both instances use it in a way that clearly portrays such action as resulting from divine impulsion. In Acts 12:10, the gate leading to the city opens for Peter "of his own accord" (New International Version, "by itself"); Peter is being led from jail to safety by "the angel of the Lord" (Acts 12:7; cf. 12:7–11). The other instance is in 2 Corinthians 8:16–17, where Paul reports the following: "But thanks be to *God, which put the same earnest care into the heart of Titus* for you. For indeed he accepted the exhortation; but being more forward, *of his own accord* he went unto you" (emphasis added). Here again, the agent who acts "of his own accord" is inspired by God himself. In light of these examples, the argument that Samson's acting "of [his] own accord" necessitates his acting apart from divine direction is hardly persuasive.[33] Rather, Samson's use of this phrase provides us with compelling evidence that the "rousing motions" of which he speaks are indeed from God.[34] In turn, Samson, "of [his] own accord," chooses to obey God's promptings. As Phillip J. Donnelly observes, "The decision by a repentant, trusting conscience to obey a divine command is free, and that is why—still allowing for other multiple levels of irony—Samson insists that he acts 'of [his] own accord' (1643). Although responding to divine prompting, Samson's response nevertheless requires an act of will, trust, and effort on his part."[35] And as Sharon Achinstein writes, Samson's words and actions show him to be "a morally free agent" whose "willing compliance to God's laws" and "actions of the will" demonstrate his "cooperation with the divine."[36]

The Semichorus also declares that Samson, though physically blind, acted "With inward eyes illuminated / His fiery virtue rous'd / From under ashes into sudden flame" (1689–91). These lines, particularly the notion that the "illuminated" Samson's virtue was rous'd, recall Samson's previous reference to the "rousing motions" that originally led him to accompany the Philistine Officer to the temple festival. Indeed, Samson's decisions to follow the Officer, perform at the festival, and pull down the temple's pillars, are all motivated by the same overarching leading of the Spirit—the "internal scripture" of which *DDC* speaks. In his obedience unto death, the spiritually renewed Samson again plays the role of the parabolic householder who "bringeth forth out of his treasure things new and old," allowing the new revelation of internal scripture to guide him to a more perfect adherence to the external law of God. Samson's obedience also demonstrates his resignation to the sovereign will of God, a resignation so unlike his earlier self-indulgence. This obedient resignation enables Samson to be used, once again, as God's instrument of judgment upon the Philistines; it also permits the Chorus to rightly call the once faithless Samson God's "faithful champion" (1751).

Introduction

1. Paul Ricoeur, "Listening to the Parables of Jesus," in *The Philosophy of Paul Ricoeur: An Anthology of His Work*, edited by Charles E. Reagan and David Stewart (Boston: Beacon Press, 1978), 239–45, quoted at 245.

2. For a valuable discussion of this practice generally and of Milton's participation in it, see Dayton Haskin, *Milton's Burden of Interpretation* (Philadelphia: University of Pennsylvania Press, 1994), 1–53.

3. I note such critics throughout this book, but the most thorough analysis of this topic is Stephen M. Fallon, *Milton's Peculiar Grace: Self-Representation and Authority* (Ithaca: Cornell University Press, 2007).

4. Stephen I. Wright, "Parables," in *Dictionary for Theological Interpretation of the Bible*, edited by Kevin J. Vanhoozer et al. (Grand Rapids: Baker Academic, 2005), 559–62, quoted at 560.

5. See James H. Sims, *The Bible in Milton's Epics* (Gainesville: University Press of Florida, 1962); Kitty Cohen, *The Throne and the Chariot: Studies in Milton's Hebraism* (The Hague: Mouton, 1975); James H. Sims and Leland Ryken, eds., *Milton and Scriptural Tradition: The Bible into Poetry* (Columbia: University of Missouri Press, 1984); Mary Ann Radzinowicz, "How Milton Read the Bible: The Case of *Paradise Regained*," in *The Cambridge Companion to Milton*, edited by Dennis Danielson, 2nd ed. (Cambridge: Cambridge University Press, 1999), 202–18; Regina Schwartz, "Milton on the Bible," in *A Companion to Milton*, edited by Thomas N. Corns (Oxford: Blackwell, 2001), 37–54; Phillip J. Donnelly, *Milton's Scriptural Reasoning: Narrative and Protestant Toleration* (Cambridge: Cambridge University Press, 2009); Leland Ryken, *The Apocalyptic Vision in "Paradise Lost"* (Ithaca: Cornell University Press, 1970); Timothy J. O'Keefe, *Milton and the Pauline Tradition: A Study of Theme and Symbolism* (Washington, D.C.: University Press of America, 1982); Youngwon Park, *Milton and Isaiah: A Journey Through the Drama of Salvation in "Paradise Lost"* (New York: Peter Lang, 2000); Mary Ann Radzinowicz, *Milton's Epics and the Book of Psalms* (Princeton: Princeton University Press, 1989).

6. Barbara Kiefer Lewalski, *"Paradise Lost" and the Rhetoric of Literary Forms* (Princeton: Princeton University Press, 1985), 6.

7. Klyne R. Snodgrass, *Stories with Intent: A Comprehensive Guide to the Parables of Jesus* (Grand Rapids: Eerdmans, 2008), 10; Madeleine I. Boucher, *The Parables* (Wilmington, Del.: Michael Glazier, 1981), 13.

8. John W. Sider, "The Parables," in *A Complete Literary Guide to the Bible*, edited by Leland Ryken and Tremper Longman III (Grand Rapids: Zondervan, 1993), 422–35, at 423.

For a detailed discussion of analogy in relation to *parabolē* in the synoptic Gospels, see John W. Sider, "Proportional Analogy in the Gospel Parables," *New Testament Studies* 31 (1985): 1–23.

9. Klyne R. Snodgrass, "Parable" in *Dictionary of Jesus and the Gospels*, edited by Joel B. Green and Scot McKnight (Downers Grove, Ill.: InterVarsity Press, 1992), 591–601, quoted at 593.

10. Sider, "Parables," 423, 424.

11. A helpful summary of what had been the scholarly consensus appears in Craig L. Blomberg, *Interpreting the Parables*, 2nd ed. (Downers Grove, Ill.: InterVarsity Press, 2012), 19–23. The first edition of this influential study was published in 1990. This point is developed in the following section on the history of parable interpretation.

12. C. H. Dodd, *The Parables of the Kingdom* (1935; rev. ed., New York: Scribner's, 1961), 16.

13. Blomberg, *Interpreting the Parables*, 52.

14. Informative studies discussing the history of parable interpretation include Norman Perrin, *Jesus and the Language of the Kingdom: Symbol and Metaphor in New Testament Interpretation* (Philadelphia: Fortress Press, 1976), 89–193; Warren S. Kissinger, *The Parables of Jesus: A History of Interpretation and Bibliography* (Metuchen, N.J.: Scarecrow Press, 1979), 1–230; Craig L. Blomberg, "The Parables of Jesus: Current Trends and Needs in Research," in *Studying the Historical Jesus: Evaluations of the State of Current Research*, edited by Bruce Chilton and Craig A. Evans (Leiden: Brill, 1994), 231–54; Klyne R. Snodgrass, "From Allegorizing to Allegorizing: A History of the Interpretation of the Parables of Jesus," in *The Challenge of Jesus' Parables*, edited by Richard N. Longenecker (Grand Rapids: Eerdmans, 2000), 3–29; Klyne R. Snodgrass, "Modern Approaches to the Parables," in *The Face of New Testament Studies: A Survey of Recent Research*, edited by Scot McKnight and Grant R. Osborne (Grand Rapids: Baker, 2004), 177–90; and Blomberg, *Interpreting the Parables*, 33–191. Most recently, David B. Gowler, *The Parables After Jesus: Their Imaginative Receptions Across Two Millennia* (Grand Rapids: Baker Academic, 2017), covers the history of parable interpretation in literature, visual art, song lyrics, and film. Surprisingly, he offers no discussion of Milton. Perrin and especially Kissinger are particularly valuable for their coverage through Jeremias. For our present study, of the works cited in this note, only Gowler pays any attention to seventeenth- or eighteenth-century treatments of the parables. In the following paragraphs, my discussions of Clement, Augustine, Aquinas, Luther, Calvin, Trench, and Jülicher are largely drawn from Kissinger, while my discussion of Wrede is drawn from Blomberg, *Interpreting the Parables*.

15. Clement's analysis of the parable of the prodigal son survives in an oration on Luke 15 by Macarius Chrysocephalus (1300–1382).

16. Augustine's exposition of the parable of the Good Samaritan resembles that offered by Origen (185–254) in his homily 34 on the Gospel of Luke.

17. John Calvin, *A Harmony of the Gospels: Matthew, Mark, and Luke*, translated by T. H. L. Parker, edited by David W. Torrance and Thomas F. Torrance, 3 vols. (Grand Rapids: Eerdmans, 1979), 3:39, 38. Aquinas and Luther are quoted in Kissinger, *Parables of Jesus*, 42 and 44.

18. Richard Chenevix Trench, *Notes on the Parables of Our Lord* (London: Kegan Paul, Trench, Trübner, 1906). Trench's hefty book was first published in 1841 and went through fifteen editions by 1886, the year of his death.

19. Adolf Jülicher, *Die Gleichnisreden Jesu*, 2 vols. (Tubingen: J. C. B. Mohr, 1888–89). Incredibly, this immensely influential work has never been translated into English.

20. See William Wrede, *Das Messiasgeheimnis in den Evangelien* (Gottingen: Vanden-hoeck & Ruprecht, 1901). This book was finally translated in 1971 by J. C. G. Grieg as *The Messianic Secret in the Gospels* (Cambridge: James Clarke, 1971).

21. Matthew Black, "The Parables as Allegory," *Bulletin of the John Rylands Library* 42 (1960): 273–87, discusses such inconsistencies.

22. Snodgrass, "Modern Approaches to the Parables," 180.

23. Noteworthy existentialist studies include Ernst Fuchs, *Studies in the Historical Jesus* (Naperville, Ill.: Allenson, 1964); and Eta Linnemann, *Parables of Jesus: Introduction and Exposition* (London: SPCK, 1966). Artistic studies include Geraint Vaughan Jones, *The Art and Truth of the Parables: A Study in Their Literary Form and Modern Interpretation* (London: SPCK, 1964); and Dan Otto Via Jr., *The Parables: Their Literary and Existentialist Dimensions* (Philadelphia: Fortress Press, 1967), a study that cuts across other interpretive categories. Early literary approaches include Robert W. Funk, *Language, Hermeneutic, and Word of God: The Problem of Language in the New Testament and Contemporary Theology* (New York: Harper and Row, 1966); John Dominic Crossan, *In Parables: The Challenge of the Historical Jesus* (New York: Harper and Row, 1973); and Madeleine Boucher, *The Mysterious Parable: A Literary Study* (Washington, D.C.: Catholic Biblical Association of America, 1977), which was an important catalyst for the modified allegorical approach to interpreting the parables. Later examples include John Drury, *The Parables in the Gospels: History and Allegory* (New York: Crossroad, 1985); Charles W. Hendrick, *Parables as Poetic Fiction: The Creative Voice of Jesus* (Peabody, Mass.: Henrickson, 1994); and Warren Carter and John Paul Heil, *Matthew's Parables: Audience-Oriented Perspectives* (Washington, D.C.: Catholic Biblical Association of America, 1998). Studies that emphasize the Palestinian context include two books by J. Duncan Derrett: *Law in the New Testament* (London: Darton, Longman, and Todd, 1970); and *Studies in the New Testament*, vol. 1, *Glimpses of the Legal and Social Presuppositions of the Authors* (Leiden: Brill, 1977); and three by Kenneth E. Bailey: *Poet and Peasant: A Literary-Cultural Approach to the Parables in Luke* (Grand Rapids: Eerdmans, 1976); *Through Peasant Eyes: More Lucan Parables, Their Culture and Style* (Grand Rapids: Eerdmans, 1980); and *Finding the Lost: Cultural Keys to Luke 15* (St. Louis: Concordia, 1992). Ideological studies include William Herzog, *Parables as Subversive Speech: Jesus as Pedagogue of the Oppressed* (Louisville: Westminster John Knox Press, 1994); and Robert Price, *The Widow Traditions in Luke-Acts: A Feminist-Critical Scrutiny* (Atlanta: Scholars Press, 1997), 191–201. As for the idea that the parables are "polyvalent," that term is defined by the *Oxford English Dictionary Online* as "having multiple aspects or meanings; open to a number of different interpreta-tions" (definition 4b). Studies advocating polyvalent readings of the parables include Mary Ann Tolbert, *Perspectives in the Parables: An Approach to Multiple Interpretations* (Philadel-phia: Fortress Press, 1979); and, most important, John Dominic Crossan, *Cliffs of Fall: Par-adox and Polyvalence in the Parables of Jesus* (New York: Seabury, 1980). Bernard Brandon Scott, *Hear Then the Parable: A Commentary on the Parables of Jesus* (Minneapolis: Fortress Press, 1989), largely follows the Jülicher-Dodd-Jeremias tradition but demonstrates openness to allegorical elements in the parables and to polyvalent interpretations.

24. Boucher, *Mysterious Parable*, 20, 21. Boucher also calls allegory a "mode of meaning" (17). It is worth noting that, even before Boucher, literary critics have not generally felt the Jülicher-inspired need to distinguish between parable and allegory, a point illustrated by Michael Murrin's comment that Jesus used "the parabolic discourse of the allegorist." Murrin, *The Veil of Allegory: Some Notes Toward a Theory of Allegorical Rhetoric in the English Renais-sance* (Chicago: University of Chicago Press, 1969), 23.

25. See especially Sider's works "Proportional Analogy" and *Interpreting the Parables: A Hermeneutical Guide to Their Meaning* (Grand Rapids: Zondervan, 1995). Also pertinent to our study are three more works by Sider: "The Meaning of *Parabole* in the Usage of the Synoptic Evangelists," *Biblica* 62, no. 4 (1981): 453–70; "Nurturing Our Nurse: Literary Scholars and Biblical Exegesis," *Christianity and Literature* 32, no. 1 (1982): 15–21; and "Reconstructing the Parables: The Logic of the Jeremias Tradition," *Journal of Biblical Literature* 102, no. 1 (1983): 61–83.

26. Blomberg, *Interpreting the Parables*, 51.

27. Leland Ryken, *How to Read the Bible as Literature* (Grand Rapids: Zondervan, 1984), 143. Ryken's discussions of Jesus's parables, including his defense of a restrained allegorical reading, are found on pp. 139–53 and 199–203, and in Ryken's study *Words of Life: A Literary Introduction to the New Testament* (Grand Rapids: Baker, 1987), 61–77. Ryken's approach to allegory and the parables is strongly influenced by Northrop Frye's classic *Anatomy of Criticism: Four Essays* (Princeton: Princeton University Press, 1957), 89–92.

28. Blomberg, *Interpreting the Parables*, 163. In a related essay, "Interpreting the Parables of Jesus: Where Are We and Where Do We Go from Here?," *Catholic Biblical Quarterly* 53, no. 1 (1991): 50–78, Blomberg makes clear that the modified allegorical approach "in no way implies a return to approaches which gave special meaning to other details ([such as] the fatted calf, the ring, robe, and shoes, etc. [in the parable of the prodigal son]) or which saw the characters in the parable as standing for something other than what would have been intelligible in a *Sitz im Leben Jesu*" (54). Here, Blomberg effectively exposes the false dichotomy, which still persists in some scholarly circles and is articulated by Kevin Mills, "Parables A–Z," *Yearbook of English Studies* 39 (2009): 186–98, of parable interpretation as a choice between viewing "a parable as a realistic narrative with a recoverable *Sitz im Leben*," in the Jülicher tradition, or "as a mystifying allegory of salvation history," in the tradition of the church fathers (195).

29. Blomberg, "Parables of Jesus," 62.

30. Blomberg, *Interpreting the Parables*, 190.

31. See Sider, *Interpreting the Parables*, 21–22; and Snodgrass, *Stories with Intent*, 28–29. Both suggest that each individual parable must be read carefully in its own context to determine how many main points it has.

32. As Snodgrass states in *Stories with Intent*, "Today most of Jülicher's argument has been set aside" (6).

33. Wright, "Parables," 560 (emphasis in original).

34. Gregory J. Laughery, "Reading Jesus' Parables According to J. D. Crossan and P. Ricoeur," *European Journal of Theology* 8, no. 2 (1999): 145–54, quoted at 148.

35. Gregory J. Laughery, *Living Hermeneutics in Motion: An Analysis and Evaluation of Paul Ricoeur's Contribution to Biblical Hermeneutics* (Lanham, Md.: University Press of America, 2002), 185.

36. Crossan, *Cliffs of Fall*, 10 (emphasis in original).

37. John Dominic Crossan, "A Metamodel for Polyvalent Narration," *Semeia* 9 (1977): 105–47, quoted at 107.

38. Laughery, "Reading Jesus' Parables," 149–50. In *Interpretation Theory: Discourse and the Surplus of Meaning* (Fort Worth: Texas Christian University Press, 1976), 54–57, Paul Ricoeur speaks of metaphors' containing a "surplus of meaning" rather than advocating the interpretive "*regressus ad infinitum*" that Crossan allows for.

39. Laughery, *Living Hermeneutics in Motion*, 104.

40. Paul Ricoeur, "Biblical Hermeneutics," *Semeia* 4 (1975): 29–148, quoted at 33, 34 (emphasis in original).

41. Laughery, *Living Hermeneutics in Motion*, 90, 104.

42. Ricoeur, "Listening to the Parables," 245. Elsewhere, Ricoeur applies a similar hermeneutic to reading other biblical texts and texts in general. In "Metaphor and the Central Problem of Hermeneutics," in *Hermeneutics and the Human Science: Essays on Language, Action, and Interpretation*, edited and translated by John B. Thompson (Cambridge: Cambridge University Press, 2016), 127–43, Ricoeur writes that as a reader, "I offer myself to the possible mode of being-in-the-world which the text opens up and discloses to me" (139). According to Lance B. Pape, *The Scandal of Having Something to Say: Ricoeur and the Possibility of Postliberal Preaching* (Waco: Baylor University Press, 2013), for Ricoeur, "The textual world is not primarily a window into other times, places, and events, but a present alternative to the reader's prior settled construal of life and its possibilities" (52). See also Jacob D. Myers, "Preaching Philosophy: The Kerygmatic Thrust of Paul Ricoeur's Philosophy and Its Contributions to Homiletics," *Literature and Theology* 27, no. 2 (2013): 208–26, at 216–20.

43. Ryken, *How to Read the Bible*, 144.

44. Mary Ford, "Towards the Restoration of Allegory: Christology, Epistemology, and Narrative Structure," *St. Vladimir's Theological Quarterly* 34, nos. 2–3 (1990): 161–95, quoted at 195, 194. Cf. Blomberg, "Parables of Jesus," 239.

45. Nehemiah Rogers, *The True Convert, or An Exposition upon the XV Chapter of St. Luke's Gospel* (London, 1632); Benjamin Keach, *Exposition of the Parables in the Bible* (Grand Rapids: Kregel, 1974), 371–72, 375. This book is the retitled reprint of Keach's *An Exposition of the Parables, and Express Similitudes of Our Lord and Saviour Jesus Christ*, originally published, posthumously, in 1856.

46. Keach, *Exposition of the Parables*, 303–28.

47. E.g., the Westminster assemblyman Thomas Gataker (1574–1654), *Shadows Without Substance, or Pretended New Lights* (London, 1646): "we dare not allegorize the Scriptures, where the letter of it yeelds us a cleer and proper sense" (69). My thanks to Leland Ryken, *Worldly Saints: The Puritans as They Really Were* (Grand Rapids: Zondervan/Academie Books, 1986), 145 and 253, for calling my attention to the seventeenth-century theologians cited in this paragraph and its notes.

48. Barbara Kiefer Lewalski, *Protestant Poetics and the Seventeenth-Century Lyric* (Princeton: Princeton University Press, 1979), 122.

49. James Durham, *Clavis Cantici, or An Exposition of the Song of Solomon* (Edinburgh, 1668), 22, 23; cf. John White (1575–1648), *A Way to the Tree of Life, Discovered in Sundry Directions for the Profitable Reading of the Scriptures* (London, 1647): "we grant that some [scriptural] places may have a proper sense, or a mystical or allegorical" (167); but White also warns, "Such Allegoricall senses of Scripture, we must not easily admit, unless the Scripture it self warrant them" (168). For an overreaching but intriguing discussion of the Puritan commitment to allegory, via typology, see Thomas H. Luxon, *Literal Figures: Puritan Allegory and the Reformation Crisis in Representations* (Chicago: University of Chicago Press, 1995). For a more restrained discussion of early modern Protestant use of typology and its connection to allegory, see Lewalski, *Protestant Poetics*, 111–44.

50. William Bridge, *Scripture Light, the Most Sure Light* (London, 1656), 48.

51. John Ball, *A Short Treatise Containing All the Principal Grounds of Christian Religion* (London, 1656), 55.

52. Calvin, *Harmony of the Gospels*, 2:225.

53. Matthew Poole, *A Commentary on the Holy Bible*, 3 vols. (1685; reprint, London: Banner of Truth, 1963), 3:245–46.

54. Calvin, *Harmony of the Gospels*, 3:110, 111.

55. Thomas Shepard, *The Parable of the Ten Virgins Opened and Applied* (1659), in *The Works of Thomas Shepard*, vol. 2 (Ligonier, Pa.: Solo Deo Gloria Publications, 1990), 16.

56. Shepard, 193. Similarly, John Flavel (ca. 1627–1691), in *Husbandry Spiritualized, or The Heavenly Use of Earthly Things* (1669), in *The Works of John Flavel*, vol. 5 (London: Banner of Truth, 1968), calls the foolish virgins "hypocrites towards Christ" (96). Flavel also discusses the parable of the wheat and the tares (Matt. 13:24–30), calling the wheat "the saints" and the tares "hypocrites" (95).

57. Andrew Bromhall, "How Is Hypocrisy Discoverable and Curable?," in *Puritan Sermons, 1659–1689*, vol. 1, edited by James Nichols (Wheaton, Ill.: R. O. Roberts, 1981), 535–52, quoted at 537. Cf. Thomas Watson (1620–1686), *The Godly Man's Picture* (1666; reprint, Edinburgh: Banner of Truth, 1992), which likens the foolish virgins to those who have "the lamp of profession without the oil of grace" (17).

58. Calvin, *Harmony of the Gospels*, 2:286–88; James Ussher, "Romans 6,23: The Wages of Sin is Death," in *Eighteen Sermons Preached in Oxford 1640* (London, 1660), 117–36, quoted at 134. I thank Ryan Hackenbracht, "Milton and the Parable of the Talents: Nationalism and the Prelacy Controversy in Revolutionary England," *Philological Quarterly* 94, nos. 1–2 (2015): 71–93, at 71, for first exposing me to Ussher's sermon.

59. John Bunyan, *The Pilgrim's Progress* (New York: New Family Library, 1972), 145. Bunyan quotes Matthew 25:23.

60. Richard Sibbes, *The Bruised Reed and Smoking Flax* (Edinburgh: Banner of Truth Trust, 1998), 67; Poole, *Commentary on the Holy Bible*, 3:119–20.

61. Matthew Henry, *Matthew Henry's Commentary on the Whole Bible*, vol. 5 (1706; reprint, Iowa Falls: World Bible Publishers, n.d.), 372.

62. John Owen, "Ministerial Endowments the Work of the Spirit," in *The Works of John Owen*, vol. 9, edited by William H. Goold (London: Banner of Truth, 1985), 441–52, quoted at 448.

63. Richard Sibbes, "The Rich Pearl," in *The Complete Works of Richard Sibbes*, vol. 7, edited by Alexander Balloch Grosart (Edinburgh: James Nicholl, 1864), 253–60, quoted at 257, 256.

64. George Swinnock, *The Christian Man's Calling*, in *The Works of George Swinnock*, vol. 1 (1868; reprint, Edinburgh: Banner of Truth, 1992), 30.

65. Calvin, *Harmony of the Gospels*, 2:82–83.

66. Haskin, *Milton's Burden of Interpretation*, 1–28 (on the parable of the talents, see 29–53). Other valuable studies of Bible reading in early modern England include Kate Narveson, *Bible Readers and Lay Writers in Early Modern England: Gender and Self-Definition in an Emergent Writing Culture* (Farnham, Surrey: Ashgate, 2012); Jeremy Schildt, "'In My Private Reading of the Scriptures': Protestant Bible-Reading in England, Circa 1580–1720," in *Private and Domestic Devotion in Early Modern Britain*, edited by Jessica Martin and Alec Ryrie (Farnham, Surrey: Ashgate, 2012), 189–209; and Jeremy Schildt, "'Eying and Applying and Meditating on the Promises': Reading the Bible in Seventeenth-Century England" (PhD diss., University of London, 2008). For an analysis of seventeenth-century British exegetical methods, see Henry M. Knapp, "Understanding the Mind of God: John Owen and Seventeenth-Century Exegetical Methodology" (PhD diss., Calvin Seminary, 2002), 40–138.

67. Sims, *Bible in Milton's Epics*, 202–4 (Abraham), 206–7 (Moses), 153–54 (Joshua), 209–10 (Cain), 174–78 (Esau), 173–75 (Nebuchadnezzar), 178–79 (Belshazzar), 174–75 (Herod), and 180–81 (Judas Iscariot).

68. See O'Keefe, *Milton and the Pauline Tradition*, 291–310, quoted at 291.

69. Radzinowicz, "How Milton Read the Bible," 213–16, quoted at 213; Radzinowicz, *Milton's Epics*, 23–48.

70. Barbara Kiefer Lewalski, *Milton's Brief Epic: The Genre, Meaning, and Art of "Paradise Regained"* (Providence: Brown University Press, 1966); Stella P. Revard, "The Gospel of John and *Paradise Regained*: Jesus as 'True Light,'" in Sims and Ryken, *Milton and Scriptural Tradition*, 142–59.

71. Miriam Muskin, "'Wisdom by Adversity': Davidic Traits in Milton's *Samson*," *Milton Studies* 14 (1980): 233–55; Mary Ann Radzinowicz, *Toward "Samson Agonistes": The Growth of Milton's Mind* (Princeton: Princeton University Press, 1978), 227–60; John Wall Jr., "The Contrarious Hand of God: *Samson Agonistes* and the Biblical Lament," *Milton Studies* 12 (1978): 117–39; Schwartz, "Milton on the Bible."

72. James Holly Hanford, *John Milton, Englishman* (New York: Crown, 1949), 198. More recently, Stanley Fish has discussed the manner in which Milton's "conflicted relationship with the ideal of submission is acted out in the careers of even his most exemplary heroes." Fish, *How Milton Works* (Cambridge, Mass.: Belknap Press of Harvard University Press, 2001), 301.

73. *Specimens of the Table Talk of the Late Samuel Taylor Coleridge*, edited by Henry Nelson Coleridge, 2 vols. (London: John Murray, 1835), 2:240.

74. Fallon, *Milton's Peculiar Grace*, 6.

75. Paul Ricoeur, "The Bible and the Imagination," in *Figuring the Sacred: Religion, Narrative, and Imagination*, translated by David Pellauer, edited by Mark I. Wallace (Minneapolis: Fortress Press, 1995), 144–66, quoted at 166.

76. Laughery, *Living Hermeneutics in Motion*, 104.

77. One valuable perspective on this subject is offered by Kari Boyd McBride and John C. Ulreich, "Answerable Styles: Biblical Poetics and Biblical Politics in the Poetry of Lanyer and Milton," *Journal of English and Germanic Philology* 100, no. 3 (2001): 333–54.

78. Stephen Greenblatt, *Renaissance Self-Fashioning: From More to Shakespeare* (Chicago: University of Chicago Press, 1980), 8–9. See also Margo Todd, "Puritan Self-Fashioning: The Diary of Samuel Ward," *Journal of British Studies* 31, no. 3 (1992): 236–64.

79. Leland Ryken, "Puritan Rhetoric and Biblical Reference in Two Miltonic Sonnets," paper presented at the Midwest Conference on Christianity and Literature, Chicago, March 24, 2001.

80. Charles A. Huttar, "Samson's Identity Crisis and Milton's," in *Imagination and the Spirit*, edited by Charles A. Huttar (Grand Rapids: Eerdmans, 1971), 101–57, at 102.

81. U. Milo Kaufmann, *"The Pilgrim's Progress" and Traditions in Puritan Meditation* (New Haven: Yale University Press, 1966), 200. Kaufmann quotes Henri Talon, *John Bunyan: The Man and His Works*, translated by Barbara Wall (Cambridge, Mass.: Harvard University Press, 1951), 132. Talon is referring here specifically to John Bunyan; Kaufmann applies the observation to Puritans in general.

82. John Calvin, *Institutes of the Christian Religion*, translated by Ford Lewis Battles, edited by John T. McNeil, 2 vols. (Philadelphia: Westminster Press, 1960), 1:35.

83. The degree to which Milton can properly be called a "Puritan" has been challenged by Catherine Gimelli Martin, *Milton Among the Puritans: The Case for Historical Revisionism* (Farnham, Surrey: Ashgate, 2010). Despite Milton's differences with many Puritans, which

Martin appropriately raises, Thomas Fulton, in his review of Martin's book in *Renaissance Quarterly* 65, no. 1 (2012): 307–9, notes that "from [Milton's] perspective—liturgically, politically, and in terms of church government—he was" a Puritan (308). See also the discussion of Milton in various essays in *The Cambridge Companion to Puritanism*, edited by John Coffey and Paul C. H. Lim (Cambridge: Cambridge University Press, 2008). On the difficulty of defining the word "Puritan" precisely, see Alec Ryrie, *Being Protestant in Reformation England* (Oxford: Oxford University Press, 2013), 3–6, 324.

84. Ryken, "Puritan Rhetoric."

85. Haskin, *Milton's Burden of Interpretation*, 2. While we see Milton engage in this practice explicitly in the tension he portrays between the parable of the talents and the parable of the laborers, he engages in it implicitly in his requirement that one be a "wise virgin" before one can become the kind of prophetic "householder" depicted in part 3.

86. Laughery, *Living Hermeneutics in Motion*, 93.

87. Paul Ricoeur, "Toward a Hermeneutic of the Idea of Revelation," *Harvard Theological Review* 70, nos. 1–2 (1977): 1–37, at 30.

88. Leland Ryken noted this tendency in his paper "How Literary Critics Use the Bible," presented at the Southeast Conference on Christianity and Literature, Southern Adventist University, Collegedale, Tennessee, April 7, 2001.

89. See especially Fallon, *Milton's Peculiar Grace*. See also Terry G. Sherwood, *The Self in Early Modern Literature: For the Common Good* (Pittsburgh: Duquesne University Press, 2007), 259–319. For biographies that address Milton's self-presentation, see especially Michael Lieb, *Milton and the Culture of Violence* (Ithaca: Cornell University Press, 1994); John T. Shawcross, *John Milton: The Self and the World* (Lexington: University Press of Kentucky, 1993); A. L. Rowse, *Milton the Puritan: Portrait of a Mind* (London: Macmillan, 1977); and Hanford, *John Milton, Englishman*. For examples of Milton's self-presentation in his *Poems 1645*, see Stella P. Revard, *Milton and the Tangles of Neaera's Hair: The Making of the 1645 "Poems"* (Columbia: University of Missouri Press, 1997); and John K. Hale, "Milton's Self-Presentation in *Poems . . . 1645*," *Milton Quarterly* 25 (1991): 37–48. For an extended study of Milton's self-presentation in his political prose, see Reuben Sanchez, *Persona and Decorum in Milton's Prose* (Madison: Fairleigh Dickinson University Press, 1997); see also Laura Lunger Knoppers, "Milton's *The Readie and Easie Way* and the English Jeremiad," in *Politics, Poetics, and Hermeneutics in Milton's Prose*, edited by David Loewenstein and James Grantham Turner (Cambridge: Cambridge University Press, 1990), 213–25.

90. In no way do I see my effort here as exhaustive. For example, in discussing Milton's relationship with the parable of the talents, much valuable analysis could be done of the character of Adam in *Paradise Lost*. Moreover, I regret that I can only begin to discuss the extent to which *Paradise Lost* and much of *Paradise Regained* demonstrate Milton's deep and thoroughgoing identification with the figure of the parabolic householder.

Chapter 1

1. Dayton Haskin, *Milton's Burden of Interpretation* (Philadelphia: University of Pennsylvania Press, 1994), 33, 2.

2. Haskin does address the relationship between these two parables briefly with reference to *Samson Agonistes*, 169–70. He does so in response to John Guillory's discussion of the two parables in "The Father's House: *Samson Agonistes* in Its Historical Moment," in *Re-membering Milton: Essays on the Texts and Traditions*, edited by Mary Nyquist and

Margaret W. Ferguson (New York: Methuen, 1987), 148–76, at 158–59. For an extended discussion of the tension between the two parables in *Samson*, and its eventual resolution, see chapter 2 of the present study.

3. This date was established by William R. Parker, "Some Problems in the Chronology of Milton's Early Poems," *Review of English Studies* 11, no. 43 (1935): 276–83. Until Parker's article, December 1631 was generally held as the time of composition. William B. Hunter argues for the older view in "The Date of Milton's Sonnet 7," *English Language Notes* 13, no. 1 (1975): 10–14. More recently, John Gouws, "The Date of Milton's Sonnet VII," *Notes and Queries* 57, no. 1 (2010): 39–41, persuasively reaffirms Parker's December 1632 date.

4. Parker discusses the likelihood of Young in "Milton's Unknown Friend," *Times Literary Supplement*, May 16, 1936, 420.

5. William Riley Parker, *Milton: A Biography*, 2nd ed., edited by Gordon Campbell, 2 vols. (Oxford: Oxford University Press, 1996), 1:122. For a persuasive argument that Milton did not finally abandon his youthful aspiration to be an Anglican priest until after Laud's *Constitutions and Canons Ecclesiasticall* were passed by the Convocation in June 1640, see John Spencer Hill, *John Milton: Poet, Priest, and Prophet; A Study of Divine Vocation in Milton's Poetry and Prose* (London: Macmillan, 1979), 27–49. See also Jameela Lares, *Milton and the Preaching Arts* (Pittsburgh: Duquesne University Press, 2001), 16–29.

6. Margo Swiss, "Crisis of Conscience: A Theological Context for Milton's 'How Soon Hath Time,'" *Milton Quarterly* 20, no. 3 (1986): 98–103, quoted at 98.

7. William Perkins, *How to Live and that Well* (London, 1611), 41.

8. Swiss, "Crisis of Conscience," 99; William Whately, *The New Birth* (London, 1618), 158–59.

9. John Owen, "Ministerial Endowments the Work of the Spirit," in *The Works of John Owen*, vol. 9, edited by William H. Goold (London: Banner of Truth, 1985), 441–52, quoted at 448.

10. Haskin, *Milton's Burden of Interpretation*, 28–31, mentions John Bunyan and John Donne, to name only two. Ryan Hackenbracht, "Milton and the Parable of the Talents: Nationalism and the Prelacy Controversy in Revolutionary England," *Philological Quarterly* 94, nos. 1–2 (2015): 71–93, at 76–77, outlines the political use of the parable of the talents by the Smectymnuans and other antiprelatists in the early 1640s.

11. Responding to an earlier version of the present chapter (David V. Urban, "The Talented Mr. Milton: A Parabolic Laborer and His Identity," *Milton Studies* 43 [2004]: 1–18), Stephen M. Fallon goes so far as to argue that Milton uses the parable of the laborers to reverse "the burden of the [parable of the talents] as part of a self-valorizing strategy." Fallon, *Milton's Peculiar Grace: Self-Representation and Authority* (Ithaca: Cornell University Press, 2007), 19n7.

12. Hunter, "Date of Milton's Sonnet," 12.

13. Anna Nardo, *Milton's Sonnets and the Ideal Community* (Lincoln: University of Nebraska Press, 1979), 141.

14. Stephen Booth and Jordan Flyer, "Milton's 'How Soon Hath Time': A Colossus in a Cherrystone," *ELH* 49, no. 2 (1982): 449–67, quoted at 454.

15. See Booth and Flyer, "Milton's 'How Soon Hath Time,'" 455; Haskin, *Milton's Burden of Interpretation*, 114; and Nardo, *Milton's Sonnets*, 143.

16. John Calvin, *A Harmony of the Gospels: Matthew, Mark, and Luke*, translated by T. H. L. Parker, edited by David W. Torrance and Thomas F. Torrance, 3 vols. (Grand Rapids: Eerdmans, 1979), 2:264, 265.

17. Calvin, *A Harmony of the Gospels*, 2:265–66, 289.

18. Parker, *Milton: A Biography*, 2:788–89, 1:126. Barbara K. Lewalski, *The Life of John Milton: A Critical Biography* (Oxford: Blackwell, 2000), 71, suggests late 1637 or early 1638.

19. *The Riverside Milton*, edited by Roy Flannagan (New York: Houghton Mifflin, 1998), 226.

20. Milton's language here probably also reflects the influence of Aristotle's discussion, at the end of his larger discussion of friendship among unequals in *Nicomachean Ethics*, of what children owe their parents. Aristotle's *Ethics*, translated by Martin Ostwald (Upper Saddle River, N.J.: Prentice Hall, 1999), says, "Friendship demands the possible; it does not demand what the giver deserves. In some cases, in fact, it is impossible to make the kind of return which the giver deserves, for instance, in the honors we pay to the gods and to our parents. Here no one could ever make a worthy return, and we regard a man as good if he serves them to the best of his ability" (8.14.1163b15). We may assume that Milton, well aware of both his father's generosity and his own abilities, nonetheless expects that his achievement must be considerable if he is to serve his father "to the best of his ability." On the broader subject of Aristotle's discussion of family friendships, see Elizabeth Belfiore, "Family Friendships in Aristotle's Ethics," *Ancient Philosophy* 21, no. 1 (2001): 113–32.

21. John T. Shawcross, *John Milton: The Self and the World* (Lexington: University Press of Kentucky, 1993), 87, 310. Shawcross quotes his own translation of *Ad Patrem*. See *The Complete English Poetry of John Milton*, edited and translated by John T. Shawcross (New York: New York University Press, 1963), 129.

22. Parker, *Milton: A Biography*, 1:17.

23. J. Milton French, *Milton in Chancery: New Chapters in the Lives of the Poet and His Father* (New York: Modern Language Association of America, 1939), 62–67. For a fuller investigation of usury in Milton's writings, see David Hawkes, "Milton and Usury," *English Literary Renaissance* 41, no. 3 (2011): 503–28.

24. Although it is not the subject of my discussion of *The Reason of Church-Government*, relevant indeed is the observation by Brooke Conti, *Confessions of Faith in Early Modern England* (Philadelphia: University of Pennsylvania Press, 2014), that in that tract Milton tries "to justify the value of a literary life (to himself? to God?) in much the same way that he once attempted to justify it to his father in *Ad Patrem*" (87–88).

25. Lewalski, *Life of John Milton*, 145. My identification of Milton as a "Puritan" acknowledges his sympathy with the broader goals of the Puritan movement without committing Milton to agreement on specific aspects of Puritan theology. See Catherine Gimelli Martin, *Milton Among the Puritans: The Case for Historical Revisionism* (Farnham, Surrey: Ashgate, 2010).

26. Fallon, *Milton's Peculiar Grace*, 88.

27. Hill, *Poet, Priest, and Prophet*, 79 (this paragraph and the next are heavily influenced by 79–81). For discussions of Milton's prophetic identity in *RCG*, see Angela Esterhammer, *Creating States: Studies in the Performative Language of John Milton and William Blake* (Toronto: University of Toronto Press, 1994), 74–87; and Fallon, *Milton's Peculiar Grace*, 88–99.

28. Hill, *Poet, Priest, and Prophet*, 79. Noting the connection to Moses that Milton makes earlier in the tract (see *CPW*, 1:747), Esterhammer, *Creating States*, observes that Milton already "aligns himself with the greatest of the prophets" here (75).

29. Hill, *Poet, Priest, and Prophet*, 79–80.

30. Lewalski, *Life of John Milton*, 149.

31. For a discussion of Milton's crafting his prophetic persona after Jeremiah, see Reuben Sanchez, "From Polemic to Prophecy: Milton's Uses of Jeremiah in *The Reason of Church Government* and *The Readie and Easie Way*," *Milton Studies* 30 (1993): 27–44. This essay is reprinted in Sanchez's *Persona and Decorum in Milton's Prose* (Madison: Fairleigh Dickinson University Press, 1997), 60–76. Brooke Conti, "'That Really Too Anxious Protestation': Crisis and Autobiography in Milton's Prose," *Milton Studies* 45 (2006): 149–86, at 155–56, challenges the idea that Milton is styling himself as a Hebrew prophet, noting that his self-focused concerns are not in line with that prophetic tradition.

32. Don M. Wolfe, in his annotations of *CPW*, vol. 1, points out the connection between Milton's use of the word "strictnesse" here and the appearance of the adjective form in Sonnet 7: "It shall be still in strictest measure even" (line 12; *CPW*, 1:801n3).

33. Lewalski, *Life of John Milton*, 149; Hackenbracht, "Milton and the Parable of the Talents," 78. Unlike other commentators, Hackenbracht goes on to analyze Milton's second self-reference to the parable of the talents in *RCG* "as a continuation of" a "financial exchange metaphor" (80) that criticized the prelates "as deceitful investors" (79).

34. Sanchez, "From Polemic to Prophecy," 31–33.

35. See John F. Huntley, "The Images of Poet and Poetry in Milton's *The Reason of Church-Government*," in *Achievements of the Left Hand: Essays on the Prose of John Milton*, edited by Michael Lieb and John T. Shawcross (Amherst: University of Massachusetts Press, 1974), 83–120, at 109–15; Esterhammer, *Creating States*, 86–87; and Louis L. Martz, "Milton's Prophetic Voice," in *Of Poetry and Prose: New Essays on Milton and His World*, edited by P. G. Stanwood (Binghamton, N.Y.: Medieval and Renaissance Texts and Studies, 1995), 1–16.

36. Lewalski, *Life of John Milton*, 152.

37. See "The Second Helvetic Confession," fourth paragraph, http://www.ccel.org/creeds/helvetic.htm. See also the high view of preaching given in the Westminster Shorter Catechism, answer 89, https://www.opc.org/sc.html.

38. Lares states that in *RCG*, Milton "does not suggest that he is abandoning the ministry for poetry, as much as that he is turning poetry to account for the ministry." *Milton and the Preaching Arts*, 47.

39. The intensity of Milton's "burden" communicated here is only remotely approached in *An Apology Against a Pamphlet*, published in April 1642, some two or three months after *RCG*. In the opening paragraph of *An Apology*, we may note a less developed reference to the parable of the talents. Here, Milton writes that any success he might boast of should be "attribute[d] somewhat to guifts of God's imparting, which I boast not, but thankfully acknowledge, and feare also lest at my certaine account they be reckon'd to me many rather than few" (*CPW*, 1:869). The concerned tone of this statement may be seen more as sober self-examination, and does not match the emotional turmoil seen in *RCG*. At the same time, the basic rationale for Milton's fear of God remains rooted in the parable of the talents, and we may do well to interpret the words quoted above as simply a more restrained articulation of the unguarded self-disclosure of *RCG*.

40. Although he does not in much detail directly address the passages in *RCG* under discussion here, Stanley Fish's exploration of Milton's rather elastic use of the word "reason" in the tract is also applicable to our discussion. See "Reason in *The Reason of Church Government*," in Fish's *Self-Consuming Artifacts* (Pittsburgh: Duquesne University Press, 1994), 265–302.

41. Shawcross, *Self and the World*, considers throughout how Milton displays traits of a narcissistic personality.

42. Although some have argued for 1642 or 1644, most commentators contend that Sonnet 19 was written between 1651 and 1655. In an intriguing variation, Annabel Patterson, "That Old Man Eloquent," in *Literary Milton: Text, Pretext, Context*, edited by Diana Treviño Benet and Michael Lieb (Pittsburgh: Duquesne University Press, 1994), 22–44, suggests "that Milton wrote the sonnet in the early 1640s; but then resituated it, sometime in the late 1650s, in a sequence formed by hindsight" (35). Recently, Margaret Thickstun, in "Resisting Patience in Milton's Sonnet 19," *Milton Quarterly* 44, no. 3 (2010): 168–80, has denied "that Milton's speaker truly identifies with the unworthy servant" (173). I respond to Thickstun in David V. Urban, "Milton's Identification with the Unworthy Servant in Sonnet 19: A Response to Margaret Thickstun," *Connotations: A Journal for Critical Debate* 22, no. 2 (2012–13): 260–63.

43. Although I am stressing the autobiographical dimensions of Sonnet 19 here, I also agree with John T. Shawcross's observation that "we can recognize Milton within the sonnet, but we also should translate its substance—the 'I,' the contemporary problems for humankind, and the resolution of action and inaction—to our own individual world. We read the poem and are thereby read ourselves." Shawcross, *Rethinking Milton Studies: Time Present and Time Past* (Newark: University of Delaware Press, 2005), 67. In a particularly intriguing nonbiographical reading of Sonnet 19 as "a political poem," Hackenbracht, "Milton and the Parable of the Talents," argues that the sonnet "reflects not Milton's personal anguish at his blindness but the collective anguish of a nation caught in the 'work' that accompanies 'the birth of reformation,' as Milton described it in *The Reason of Church-Government* (I.795)" (83). See also Gary A. Stringer, "Milton's 'Thorn in the Flesh': Pauline Didacticism in *Sonnet XIX*," *Milton Studies* 10 (1977): 141–54, which distances Milton from the sonnet's speaker by arguing that "the 'I' in the poem voices a complaint that Milton the man would have regarded as absurd, for Milton the author clearly shows it to be so" (142).

44. Parker, in *Milton: A Biography*, demonstrates the consensus position when he writes, "'That one talent' must have seemed to him his long-felt, God-given capacity for composing a truly great poem—a capacity which, in the analogy of the parable, might have been taken from him for his failure to use it" (1:470). Angelica Duran, "The Blind Bard, According to John Milton and His Contemporaries," *Mosaic* 46, no. 3 (2013): 141–57, observes, "The *OED* 4.1 notes that the use of 'light' to indicate 'eyesight' precedes the early modern period" (155n2).

45. Haskin, *Milton's Burden of Interpretation*, 96. Haskin also suggests that, according to Milton's reading of parable of the talents, Milton "underst[ood] the talents both as the Word of God itself *and* as the natural abilities of those to whom the Word has been entrusted" (51). Gordon Teskey, *The Poetry of John Milton* (Cambridge, Mass.: Harvard University Press, 2015), in an excellent discussion of Sonnet 19, identifies the autobiographical speaker's "one talent" as Milton's "intellectual capacity, which is lodged useless in his mind because it can be active only when nourished by reading and expressed by writing, both of which require the eyes" (258). Teskey's point is helpful but again too limited, for it does not address the degree to which the speaker's spiritual anguish stems from his perceived inability to accomplish his long-felt calling as a Christian prophet-poet.

46. Michael Lieb, "Talents," in *A Milton Encyclopedia*, edited by William B. Hunter, vol. 8 (Lewisburg, Pa.: Bucknell University Press, 1980), 48–51, quoted at 49.

47. Roger L. Slakey, "Milton's Sonnet 'On His Blindness,'" *ELH* 27, no. 2 (1960): 122–30.

48. Calvin states that the unprofitable servant's perception of his lord ought not to be seen as the parable's endorsement of such a view of Christ, whom the lord represents: "This

hardness [see Matt. 25:24] is not part of the essence of the parable, and they are philosophising irreverently who here dispute how God acts towards his people severely and strictly. . . . Christ only means that there is no excuse for the slackness of those who both suppress God's gift and consume their age in idleness. From this we also gather that no form of life is more praiseworthy before God than that which yields usefulness to human society." *Harmony of the Gospels*, 2:289.

49. Here I concur with Dixon Fiske, "Milton in the Middle of Life: Sonnet XIX," *ELH* 41, no. 1 (1974): 37–49. Fiske writes, "the sonnet does not criticize the implications of the parable of the talents, but rather the speaker who sees the wrong implications" (45).

50. Fiske notes, but does not elaborate on, this allusion (46).

51. I thank John Leonard, ed., *John Milton: The Complete Poems* (New York: Penguin, 1998), 696n7, for observing this connection.

52. The similarity between Sonnet 19 and Herbert's "The Collar" comes to mind here. We recognize that for Herbert's speaker, the simple call "My child" is enough to quiet his discontented ranting and bring him to a state of humble worship. Milton's speaker requires a polemic of sorts to bring him to silent submission, and this contrast may attest to the degree to which he has convinced himself of God's cosmic injustice.

53. Russell M. Hillier, "The Patience to Prevent That Murmur: The Theodicy of John Milton's Nineteenth Sonnet," *Renascence* 59, no. 4 (2007): 247–73, at 260–69, argues persuasively that the sestet specifically refers to the redemptive work of Jesus.

54. *Milton's Sonnets*, edited by E. A. J. Honigmann (New York: St. Martin's Press, 1966), 176, note for Sonnet 19, lines 12–14.

55. Teskey emphasizes that Milton's blindness came about after, and indeed as a result of his frenetic activity in, writing his various political pamphlets, particularly *Pro Populo Anglicano Defensio* (1651), "the most famous work Milton ever published in his lifetime," which "cost him his eyesight, as his doctors had warned." *Poetry of John Milton*, 253.

56. Tobias Gregory, "Murmur and Reply: Rereading Milton's Sonnet 19," *Milton Studies* 50 (2011): 21–43, quoted at 34. Gregory is quoting my essay "Talented Mr. Milton," 12.

57. Gregory, 26. Gregory specifically says this in reference to Milton's use of the parable of the talents in the letter "To a Friend."

58. Gregory, 34.

59. Walter Bauer, *A Greek-English Lexicon of the New Testament and Other Early Christian Literature*, 2nd ed., edited by F. Wilbur Gingrich, William F. Arndt, and Frederick W. Danker (Chicago: University of Chicago Press, 1979), 104; cf. *Oxford English Dictionary Online*, s.v. "idle" (definition 4a), which, citing Matthew 20, also defines "idle" in this context as "unemployed."

60. Carol Barton, "'They Also Perform the Duties of a Servant Who Only Remain Erect on Their Feet in a Specified Place in Readiness to Receive Orders': The Dynamics of Stasis in Sonnet XIX ('When I Consider How My Light Is Spent')," *Milton Quarterly* 32, no. 4 (1998): 109–22, quoted at 109, 111, 115.

61. Angelica Duran notes that the sonnet's conclusion "defines God as part of" whatever community the speaker will obediently pursue, a message that "eschew[s] the long-standing belief of disability as an external sign of divine vengeance." "Blind Bard," 144.

62. Making no reference to the parable of the laborers, Teskey notes in *Poetry of John Milton* that Patience "cite[s] scripture against scripture," offering Christ's grace "against the harsh judgment of the master from the parable of the talents" (261)—and, I would add, against the speaker's misunderstanding of that parable. By the end of the sonnet, the speaker

is admonished "to listen to . . . the Word of God" (264). Teskey specifies the Psalms, but Milton's consequent willingness to listen to and meditate upon the broader word of God in the Bible prepared him for the greater vocation of writing the great scriptural epics of his final years, a matter explored in part 3, particularly chapter 9, of this study.

Chapter 2

1. The subject is discussed briefly in Dayton Haskin, *Milton's Burden of Interpretation* (Philadelphia: University of Pennsylvania Press, 1994), 169–70, and in John Guillory, "The Father's House: *Samson Agonistes* in Its Historical Moment," in *Re-membering Milton: Essays on the Texts and Traditions*, edited by Mary Nyquist and Margaret W. Ferguson (New York: Methuen, 1987), 148–76, at 158–59.

2. Carol Barton, "'In This Dark World and Wide': *Samson Agonistes* and the Meaning of Christian Heroism," *Early Modern Literary Studies* 5, no. 2 (1999): 3.5–11, offers a quite different application of Sonnet 19 to *Samson Agonistes*.

3. Critics who have in some significant way identified Samson with Milton include David Masson, *The Life of John Milton: Narrated in Connexion with the Political, Ecclesiastical, and Literary History of His Time*, 7 vols. (1859–81; reprint, New York: Peter Smith, 1946), 6:676–77; James Holly Hanford, "*Samson Agonistes* and Milton in Old Age," in *Studies in Shakespeare, Milton, and Donne*, edited by Members of the English Department of the University of Michigan (New York: Macmillan, 1925), 165–89, at 178–89, and, also by Hanford, *John Milton, Englishman* (New York: Crown, 1949), 213; A. S. P. Woodhouse, "*Samson Agonistes* and Milton's Experience," *Transactions of the Royal Society of Canada* 43 (1949): 157–75, at 170–71; Don Cameron Allen, *The Harmonious Vision: Studies in Milton's Poetry*, enl. ed. (Baltimore: Johns Hopkins University Press, 1970), 82; A. L. Rowse, *Milton the Puritan: Portrait of a Mind* (London: Macmillan, 1977), 255; Christopher Hill, *Milton and the English Revolution* (New York: Viking, 1977), 428–48; Mary Ann Radzinowicz, *Toward "Samson Agonistes": The Growth of Milton's Mind* (Princeton: Princeton University Press, 1978), 405–7; John Spencer Hill, *John Milton: Poet, Priest, and Prophet; A Study of Divine Vocation in Milton's Poetry and Prose* (London: Macmillan, 1979), 197–203; A. N. Wilson, *The Life of John Milton* (Oxford: Oxford University Press, 1983), 232–39; Gary D. Hamilton, "*The History of Britain* and Its Restoration Audience," in *Politics, Poetics, and Hermeneutics in Milton's Prose*, edited by David Loewenstein and James Grantham Turner (Cambridge: Cambridge University Press, 1990), 241–56, at 253; Michael Lieb, *Milton and the Culture of Violence* (Ithaca: Cornell University Press, 1994), 236; Blair Worden, "Milton, *Samson Agonistes*, and the Restoration," in *Culture and Society in the Stuart Restoration: Literature, Drama, History*, edited by Gerald MacLean (Cambridge: Cambridge University Press, 1995), 111–36; Barton, "'In This Dark World,'" 2–12; Thomas H. Luxon, *Single Imperfection: Milton, Marriage, and Friendship* (Pittsburgh: Duquesne University Press, 2005), 161–62; and Stephen M. Fallon, *Milton's Peculiar Grace: Self-Representation and Authority* (Ithaca: Cornell University Press, 2007), 237–39, 250–63. In *The Complicity of Imagination: The American Renaissance, Contests of Authority, and Seventeenth-Century English Culture* (Cambridge: Cambridge University Press, 1997), Robin Grey discusses Herman Melville's belief that Samson was "a provoked and perplexed Milton figure" (221).

4. Lieb, *Milton and the Culture of Violence*, 227; see also David Loewenstein, *Representing Revolution in Milton and His Contemporaries: Religion, Politics, and Polemics in Radical Puritanism* (Cambridge: Cambridge University Press, 2001), 375n3. *Samson's* thematic closeness

to Sonnet 19 and its likely partial composition at roughly the same time explains why I place my analysis of *Samson* directly after my analysis of the sonnet. Although I believe that *Samson* was probably composed over these two periods of time, I nonetheless count it as Milton's final poetic work, following the argument of Laura Lunger Knoppers, ed., *The 1671 Poems: "Paradise Regain'd" and "Samson Agonistes"* (Oxford: Oxford University Press, 2008). Knoppers argues that the fact that *Samson*, Milton's "Old Testament tragedy," was "placed after the New Testament epic suggests that this work was indeed Milton's final poetic reflection on freedom and servitude, obedience and failure, individual and nation, punishment endured and faith regained" (xcviii). Consequently, I believe that *Samson* should be understood as Milton's final resolution of his complex relationship with the parable of the talents and the parable of the laborers.

5. See, all by Michael Lieb, *The Sinews of Ulysses: Form and Convention in Milton's Works* (Pittsburgh: Duquesne University Press, 1989), 98–138; *Milton and the Culture of Violence*, 226–63; and "'Our Living Dread': The God of *Samson Agonistes*," in Lieb, *Theological Milton: Deity, Discourse, and Heresy in the Miltonic Canon* (Pittsburgh: Duquesne University Press, 2006), 184–209 (this essay first appeared, in slightly different form, in "The Miltonic Samson," edited by Albert C. Labriola and Michael Lieb, special issue, *Milton Studies* 33: 3–25). The section from *Milton and the Culture of Violence* is particularly valuable in demonstrating connections between *Samson Agonistes* and Milton's polemical prose. See David Loewenstein, *Milton and the Drama of History: Historical Vision, Iconoclasm, and the Literary Imagination* (Cambridge: Cambridge University Press, 1990), 126–51; and Loewenstein, "The Revenge of the Saint: Radical Religion and Politics in *Samson Agonistes*," in *Representing Revolution*, 269–91 (an earlier version of this essay appeared in Labriola and Lieb, "Miltonic Samson," 159–80). This essay is particularly valuable in demonstrating connections between *Samson Agonistes* and the writings of Milton's radical Puritan contemporaries. See also Janel Mueller, "The Figure and the Ground: Samson as Hero of London Nonconformity, 1662–1667," in *Milton and the Terms of Liberty*, edited by Graham Perry and Joad Raymond (Cambridge: D. S. Brewer, 2002), 137–62.

6. For a well-publicized and aggressive attack against those who hold a regenerationist interpretation of Milton's Samson, see John Carey, "A Work in Praise of Terrorism? September 11 and *Samson Agonistes*," *Times Literary Supplement*, September 6, 2002, 15–16, which specifically attacks Stanley Fish's *How Milton Works* (Cambridge, Mass.: Belknap Press of Harvard University Press, 2001) and distances God from Samson's destruction of the Philistines. Michael Lieb, "Returning the Gorgon Medusa's Gaze: Terror and Annihilation in Milton," in *Milton in the Age of Fish: Essays on Authorship, Text, and Terrorism*, edited by Michael Lieb and Albert C. Labriola (Pittsburgh: Duquesne University Press, 2006), 229–42, points out, however, that Carey's attack on Fish is misplaced in that Fish does not support the regenerationist position. Lieb whimsically suggests that Carey direct his criticism toward Lieb himself, who does believe that Milton condones Samson's violence. I would add that David Loewenstein might be another more appropriate target for Carey. For other incisive discussions of the challenges of reading *Samson Agonistes* in a post-9/11 context, see Feisal G. Mohamed, "Confronting Religious Violence: Milton's *Samson Agonistes*," *PMLA* 120, no. 2 (2005): 327–40 (which pays close attention to Carey's article); Mohamed, "Reading Samson in the New American Century," *Milton Studies* 46 (2007): 149–64; Mohamed, *Milton and the Post-Secular Present: Ethics, Politics, and Terrorism* (Stanford: Stanford University Press, 2011), 87–126; David Loewenstein, "*Samson Agonistes* and the Culture of Religious Terror," in Lieb and Labriola, *Milton in the Age of Fish*, 203–28; Stanley Fish, "'There Is Nothing He

Cannot Ask': Milton, Liberalism, and Terrorism," in Lieb and Labriola, *Milton in the Age of Fish*, 243–64; Tobias Gregory, "The Political Messages of *Samson Agonistes*," *SEL: Studies in English Literature, 1500–1900* 50, no. 1 (2010): 175–203; and John Leonard, *The Value of Milton* (Cambridge: Cambridge University Press, 2016), 127–48, which argues that "Samson's final act is willed and enabled by a God of Terror" (147). See also Loewenstein, "From Politics to Faith in the Great Poems?" in *Visionary Milton: Essays on Prophecy and Violence*, edited by Peter E. Medine, John T. Shawcross, and David V. Urban (Pittsburgh: Duquesne University Press, 2010), 269–85. For a critique of the practice of reading *Samson Agonistes* through a post-9/11 lens (or through the lens of current events in general), see Alan Rudrum, "Milton Scholarship and the *Agon* over *Samson Agonistes*," *Literature Compass* 1 (2004): 17C, 116, 2.

7. In spite of the Chorus's limitations, its views profit Samson as he develops the humility and patience necessary to process the Chorus's insights and to act in a manner that reveals the influence of the Chorus without being blindly obedient to it. Stanley Fish's comments encourage a balanced reception of the Chorus's words: "Early commentators on *Samson Agonistes*, recalling Milton's models, assumed too easily that the Chorus speaks for the author. We have perhaps erred in the opposite direction, for lately it has become the fashion to find fault with the Chorus' every word." *How Milton Works*, 406. John F. Huntley, "A Revaluation of the Chorus' Role in Milton's *Samson Agonistes*," *Modern Philology* 64 (1966): 132–45, marked a turning point in the movement toward the negative critical view of the Chorus. For a particularly negative view of the Chorus, see C. A. Patrides, "The Comic Dimension in Greek Tragedy and *Samson Agonistes*," *Milton Studies* 10 (1977): 3–21. For a comparatively recent defense of the Chorus, see John Steadman, "Efficient Causality and Catastrophe in *Samson Agonistes*," in "Riven Unities: Authority and Experience, Self and Other in Milton's Poetry," edited by Wendy Furman, Christopher Grose, and William Shullenberger, special issue, *Milton Studies* 28 (1992): 211–26.

8. Nancy Y. Hoffman, "Samson's Other Father: The Character of Manoa in *Samson Agonistes*," *Milton Studies* 2 (1970): 195–210, observes that in Manoa we recognize "a searching psychological study of the demands and limitations of parental love" (198); Allen, *Harmonious Vision*, notes that "Manoa unwittingly substitutes himself for God, and seeks to persuade his son to accept the plans of a loving father instead of awaiting those of a loving God" (85). For an insightful discussion of the complexity of Manoa's character, see Anthony Low, *The Blaze of Noon: A Reading of "Samson Agonistes"* (New York: Columbia University Press, 1974), 126–32.

9. Curiously enough, we might also see Manoa's statement as an allusion to the parable of the unmerciful servant, which tells of a king (representing God) who "forgave" his servant the enormous "debt" the servant owed him (Matt. 18:27).

10. Fredson Bowers, "*Samson Agonistes*: Justice and Reconciliation," in *The Dress of Wounds: Essays on Restoration and Eighteenth-Century Literature in Honor of Richmond Bond*, edited by Robert B. White Jr. (Lawrence: University of Kansas Libraries, 1978), 1–23, notes, "That sin, although it will be forgiven, must first be punished according to the law, and that no agent of God who sins in disobedience will ever be restored to the exact terms of his original mission is the heart of Milton's understanding, as it was Shakespeare's" (6).

11. Lieb, *Sinews of Ulysses*, 124.

12. Warren Chernaik, *Milton and the Burden of Freedom* (Cambridge: Cambridge University Press, 2017), 198.

13. That Samson's despairing attitude prevents both hope and genuine repentance is evident here. Bowers writes, "So long as this doctrine of despair holds, reconciliation is

impossible, for Samson will not have the understanding to perform his share of the reconciliation." "Justice and Reconciliation," 5. For a fine discussion of Samson's emergence from
despair, see Don Cameron Allen, "The Idea as Pattern: Despair and *Samson Agonistes*," in
Harmonious Vision, 71–94.

14. Blair Hoxby, "At the Public Mill of the Philistines: *Samson Agonistes* and the Problem
of Work After the Restoration," in *Altering Eyes: New Perspectives on "Samson Agonistes*,"
edited by Mark R. Kelley and Joseph Wittreich (Newark: University of Delaware Press,
2002), 220–52, wisely points out that "with its distinction between 'day labour' and 'man's
work' (on the one hand) and the broader notion of service that may be performed even by
those who only stand and wait (on the other), Milton's 'Sonnet 19' should alert us to the
possibility that Samson has too quickly leapt to the conclusion that the service he owes
Yahweh is to slave at the mill" (223).

15. *Milton's Sonnets*, edited by E. A. J. Honigmann (New York: St. Martin's Press, 1966),
176, note for Sonnet 19, lines 12–14.

16. For a thorough discussion of the significance of "patience" and the Chorus, see William
O. Harris, "Despair and 'Patience as the Truest Fortitude' in *Samson Agonistes*," *ELH* 30, no.
2 (1963): 107–20. Harris valuably highlights the emphasis on patience in suffering in Renaissance Christian humanism, specifically in Sir Phillip Sidney's *Arcadia* (ca. 1590) and Lodowick
Bryskett's *A Discourse of Civill Life* (1606) (279–81).

17. Judith H. Anderson, "Patience and Passion in Shakespeare and Milton," *Spenser Studies*
21 (2006): 205–20, quoted at 205.

18. See the section on *Paradise Regained* in chapter 3.

19. This is the position of John Carey, *Milton* (London: Evans Brothers, 1969), which
argues that "Milton uses [Samson] as a contrast" and "a barbaric foil" to the Son (138); see
also Joseph Wittreich, *Shifting Contexts: Reinterpreting "Samson Agonistes"* (Pittsburgh:
Duquesne University Press, 2002), 217; and, most extensively, Derek N. C. Wood, *"Exiled
From Light": Divine Law, Morality, and Violence in "Samson Agonistes"* (Toronto: Toronto
University Press, 2001), esp. 119–31.

20. Anderson, "Patience and Passion," 214.

21. Patrick Cullen, in *Infernal Triad: The Flesh, the World, and the Devil in Spenser and
Milton* (Princeton: Princeton University Press, 1974), writes, "Just as [Milton's] Christ, after
his two days of resistance, must proceed to a triumph on the pinnacle which foreshadows
His martyrdom, so Samson, having imitated Christ's resistance in the wilderness, must also
now imitate Christ's tragic martyrdom. . . . Samson's martyrdom at noon at once looks back
to Adam's fall and ahead to Christ's triumph over Adam at the cross" (234–35). See also
Anthony Low, "*Samson Agonistes* and the Irony of Alternatives," *PMLA* 84, no. 3 (1969):
514–19, at 519.

22. Russell M. Hillier, "Grotius's *Christus Patiens* and Milton's *Samson Agonistes*," *Explica-
tor* 65, no. 1 (2006): 9–13. Hillier quotes Milton on p. 9. See also Albert C. Labriola, "*Christus
Patience* and the Virtue of Patience in *Paradise Lost*, I–II," in *The Triumph of Patience:
Medieval and Renaissance Studies*, edited by Gerald J. Schiffhorst (Gainesville: University
Press of Florida, 1978), 138–46, at 138–39, which discusses Milton's outline of a never-written
tragedy focusing on Christ's sufferings, which he probably would have titled *Christus Patiens*.
Earlier typological readings of Samson in relation to Christ include, most prominently,
F. Michael Krouse, *Milton's Samson and the Christian Tradition* (Princeton: Princeton Uni-
versity Press, 1949), 79, 119–24; and (most convincingly) Cullen, *Infernal Triad*, 233–37; also
William G. Madsen, *From Shadowy Types to Truth: Studies in Milton's Symbolism* (New

Haven: Yale University Press, 1968), 187. See also John Coffey, who writes in "Pacifist, Quietist, or Patient Militant? John Milton and the Restoration," *Milton Studies* 42 (2002): 149–74, "One can read Samson as a type of Christ. Standing between the pillars of the temple with his arms outstretched, he recalls the Crucifixion, but also points forward to the vengeance and deliverance of the Second Coming" (170). Gregory, "Political Messages of *Samson Agonistes*," 192, points out similarities between Samson and *Paradise Regained's* Son.

23. Lieb, *Sinews of Ulysses*, accuses Dalila of employing "a consummate rhetoric of seduction" (126). For a particularly strong defense of Dalila's character, see Wood, *"Exiled from Light,"* 99–117. I discuss Samson's resistance of Dalila's sensual temptation in chapter 7.

24. Krouse, *Samson and the Christian Tradition*, 102.

25. Bowers, in "Justice and Reconciliation," writes, "As Adam and Eve must forgive each other before they can seek a reconciliation with God, so in forgiving Dalila Samson has finally healed the running sore of despair" (15). While I believe that Bowers is premature in saying that such healing occurs with finality in this scene, his observation is indeed valuable. Lieb, *Sinews of Ulysses*, offers a different position altogether, contending that Samson "refuses to forgive Dalila" and that "this refusal to forgive marks yet another step in Samson's rehabilitation" (126). Although I agree with Lieb that Samson is progressing by liberating himself "from the power of others" (126), I believe it a mistake to equate such liberation with a spirit of unforgiveness. Rather, Samson rejects Dalila's temptation even as he rises above outright vindictiveness. Lieb notes the importance of Samson's acknowledging in himself "a culpability that will not admit of excuse and a severity that will not allow of laxity" (126). Terry G. Sherwood, *The Self in Early Modern Literature: For the Common Good* (Pittsburgh: Duquesne University Press, 2007), observes that Samson's admission of guilt and his refusal "to blame God" protects him "against the temptation that earlier led to his failure" (313). See also Laurie P. Marrow, "The 'Meet and Happy Conversation': Dalila's Role in *Samson Agonistes*," *Milton Quarterly* 17, no. 2 (1983): 38–42, which argues that Samson's interaction with Dalila enables him to recognize and renounce his own sin.

26. Gregory, "Political Messages of *Samson*," 196; and Leonard, *Value of Milton*, 139–41.

27. Krouse, *Samson and the Christian Tradition*, 129.

28. Harris, "Despair and 'Patience,'" 118. Chernaik, in *Milton and the Burden of Freedom*, writes that here, "for virtually the first time in the poem," Samson "envisages a God who may at last be merciful to his fallible creatures" (200).

29. Allen, "Idea as Pattern," observes that "the conflict with Harapha . . . enable[s] [Samson] to subdue his apathy" (91). Loewenstein, *Milton and the Drama of History*, points out that Samson's interaction with the giant "specifically allies Samson with God's awesome power in history" (135).

30. Harris, "Despair and 'Patience,'" 118.

31. Harris commends the Chorus for the "proper balance" it brings to our perspective with these lines (119). "While the Chorus may be wrong in its understanding of patience," he continues, "its 'forecast' is ironically right. For the victory which Milton's Samson struggles for and has just begun to win is the one within—a victory over despair, whose antidote is patience, the higher attribute of fortitude, that cardinal virtue which Samson and his column had come to symbolize by Milton's age" (119–20).

32. Lieb, *Sinews of Ulysses*, 133. Lieb also affirms that the Chorus speaks better than it realizes (132). Similarly, Judith Anderson, commenting on lines 1292–96, writes, "The Chorus is still voting for patience, but it has clearly also registered Samson's increasingly assertive stance. Combining these possibilities or transcending their opposition is not an option the

Chorus envisions, however. At the same time, this is the very transcendence we have witnessed in *Paradise Regained*." "Patience and Passion," 214.

33. Irene Samuel, "*Samson Agonistes* as Tragedy," in *Calm of Mind: Tercentenary Essays on "Paradise Regained" and "Samson Agonistes" in Honor of John S. Diekhoff*, edited by Joseph Anthony Wittreich Jr. (Cleveland: Case Western Reserve University Press, 1971), 235–57, at 251.

34. See David V. Urban, "'Intimate Impulses,' 'Rousing Motions,' and the Written Law: Internal and External Scripture in *Samson Agonistes*," in *Uncircumscribed Mind: Reading Milton Deeply*, edited by Charles W. Durham and Kristin A. Pruitt (Selinsgrove, Pa.: Susquehanna University Press, 2008), 292–306 (revised as chapter 10 of this study).

35. *John Milton: Complete Poems and Major Prose*, edited by Merritt Y. Hughes (New York: Macmillan, 1957), 583, note at line 1346; *The Riverside Milton*, edited by Roy Flannagan (Boston: Houghton Mifflin, 1998), 835, gloss at line 1346.

36. Urban, "'Intimate Impulses,'" 299.

37. Lieb, *Sinews of Ulysses*, points out that Samson's ability to endure "the assaults of the enemy through an exercise of patience" proves that he is qualified to be "the true deliverer" (132–33). Samson's exercise of patience over the temptation to act with angry passion against those who mock him (as well as against Dalila earlier) finds a parallel in the Son in *Paradise Regained*, who chooses, in his responses to Satan's temptations, patience over passion in order to qualify himself to save humanity from sin.

38. Hill, *Poet, Priest, and Prophet*, 172; Albert R. Cirillo, "Time, Light, and the Phoenix: The Design of *Samson Agonistes*," in Wittreich, *Calm of Mind*, 219, 225. The notion that Samson is actually praying has come under scrutiny. In *How Milton Works*, Stanley Fish states that "the moment is radically indeterminate. 'As one who pray'd' says neither that he is or is not praying" (447). But to seriously entertain the notion that Samson is not praying here is to imply that Milton is not simply offering a variation on Samson's prayer in Judges 16:28 but that he denies the biblical account altogether; see Gregory, "Political Meanings of Samson," 177–79.

39. Lieb, *Theological Milton*, 200, 203.

40. Michael R. G. Spiller, "Directing the Audience in *Samson Agonistes*," in *Of Poetry and Politics: New Essays on Milton and His World*, edited by P. G. Stanwood (Binghamton, N.Y.: Medieval and Renaissance Texts and Studies, 1995), 121–29, at 126–27.

41. Sharon Achinstein, concluding her discussion of Samson in *Literature and Dissent in Milton's England* (Cambridge: Cambridge University Press, 2003), speaks to this notion of God's blessing through destruction of the enemy: "Violence, above all for Dissenters, offered certainty, the sure mark of God's care, the aftereffect by which divine agency and intention become visible" (144).

42. I am aware of how thoroughly my interpretation of Milton's Samson as a figure of dramatic resolution—as a self-referential character who embodies the two parables that remained in tension in Milton's early writings—clashes with late twentieth-century readings of Samson as unregenerate, and at the same time with those of the present century who have argued for Samson's "indeterminacy." Prominent advocates of Samson as unregenerate include Carey, *Milton*, 138–46, and Carey's more recent "Work in Praise of Terrorism"; Samuel, "*Samson Agonistes* as Tragedy," 235–58; and Joseph Wittreich, *Interpreting "Samson Agonistes"* (Princeton: Princeton University Press, 1986); see also Michael Bryson, *The Atheist Milton* (Farnham, Surrey: Ashgate, 2012), 135–62. Prominent advocates of Samson's "indeterminacy" include Fish, *How Milton Works*, 447; Wood, "*Exiled from Light*"; Wittreich,

Shifting Contexts; Wittreich, *Why Milton Matters: A New Preface to His Writings* (New York: Palgrave, 2006), 141–94; Peter C. Herman, *Destabilizing Milton: "Paradise Lost" and the Poetics of Incertitude* (New York: Palgrave Macmillan, 2005), 162–76; and Elizabeth Sauer, "Discontents with the Drama of Regeneration," in *The New Milton Criticism*, edited by Peter C. Herman and Elizabeth Sauer (Cambridge: Cambridge University Press, 2012), 120–36. Space limitations prevent a fuller response to these positions, but I thoroughly agree with Gregory, "Political Messages of *Samson*," that their conviction "that Milton wanted readers to dislike Samson, or at least wanted us not to be able to make up our minds" (176) runs counter to the evidence in *Samson*, Milton's other texts, and the writings of Milton's contemporaries. As Gregory concludes, "there can be little doubt that the poet's sympathies are with [Samson]" (194). And Sharon Achinstein, *Literature and Dissent*, asserts that "Milton's theological commitments" are not "clouded by indeterminacy" (144; see also previous note). For various connections between the violent heroism of *Samson Agonistes* and the violent imagery of Milton's prose writings, see Lieb, *Milton and the Culture of Violence*, 227–63. For thorough discussions of how Milton's portrayal of Samson coincides with those of his radical contemporaries, see Lowenstein, *Representing Revolution*, 269–91; and Mueller, "Figure and the Ground." See Gregory, "Political Messages of *Samson*," 176–93, for convincing refutations of three major arguments for an unregenerate or "indeterminate" Samson: that Milton modified his biblical sources to make his Samson less sympathetic (advocated by Carey); that many early modern biblical commentators viewed Samson negatively and that Milton follows this tradition (advocated by Wittreich); that the contrast between Milton's Samson and Milton's Son in *Paradise Regained* demonstrates that Milton wants his readers to embrace the Son and reject Samson (advocated by Wood). For a thorough refutation of Wittreich's thesis that many of Milton's contemporaries viewed Samson negatively, even satanically, see Everett Wade, "The Contemporary Context of Milton's Typology: Biblical Exegesis and Literature in the Seventeenth Century" (PhD diss., University of Memphis, 2015), 145–98. See also the following reviews of Wittreich's books, which demonstrate his misrepresentation of contemporary sources: Phillip J. Gallagher, "On Reading Joseph Wittreich: A Review Essay," *Milton Quarterly* 21, no. 3 (1987): 108–13; Anthony Low, review of *Interpreting "Samson Agonistes," Journal of English and Germanic Philology* 86, no. 3 (1987): 415–18; and David V. Urban, review of *The Uncertain World of "Samson Agonistes,"* by John T. Shawcross, *"Exiled from Light,"* by Derek N. C. Wood, *Shifting Contexts,* by Joseph Wittreich, and *Altering Eyes,* edited by Mark R. Kelley and Joseph Wittreich, *Religion and Literature* 36, no. 2 (2004): 119–28, at 123–26. In my review, I demonstrate, among other things, that three of the seventeenth-century commentators who Wittreich erroneously claims rejected Samson's heroism—John Trapp, John Diodati, and John Lightfoot—actually wrote that Samson was a type of Christ. See also David V. Urban, review of *Exiled from Light,* by Derek N. C. Wood, *Milton Quarterly* 37, no. 1 (2003): 43–46, which critiques Wood's argument that Milton's other writings demonstrate his lack of sympathy with Samson.

Chapter 3

1. Sharon Achinstein, *Literature and Dissent in Milton's England* (Cambridge: Cambridge University Press, 2003), 120. More recently, Warren Chernaik, *Milton and the Burden of Freedom* (Cambridge: Cambridge University Press, 2017), has called Abdiel "a model of conduct" and of "how one should behave, Milton suggests, in difficult conditions" (127).

2. James Holly Hanford, *John Milton, Englishman* (New York: Crown, 1949), 197.

3. Stephen M. Fallon, *Milton's Peculiar Grace: Self-Representation and Authority* (Ithaca: Cornell University Press, 2007), 181, 204; see also 168–72, 180–81. Other commentators who identify Abdiel with Milton include A. J. A. Waldock, *"Paradise Lost" and Its Critics* (Cambridge: Cambridge University Press, 1947; reprint, Gloucester, Mass.: Peter Smith, 1959), 71, 76; A. L. Rowse, *Milton the Puritan: Portrait of a Mind* (London: Macmillan, 1977), 226–27; Christopher Hill, *Milton and the English Revolution* (New York: Viking, 1977), 370; Michael Lieb, *The Poetics of the Holy: A Reading of "Paradise Lost"* (Chapel Hill: University of North Carolina Press, 1981), 381; Gary D. Hamilton, "*The History of Britain* and Its Restoration Audience," in *Politics, Poetics, and Hermeneutics in Milton's Prose*, edited by David Loewenstein and James Grantham Turner (Cambridge: Cambridge University Press, 1990), 241–56, at 253; Perez Zagorin, *Milton: Aristocrat and Rebel* (Rochester: University of Rochester Press, 1992), 126; and Paul A. Rahe, *Against Throne and Altar: Machiavelli and Political Theory Under the English Republic* (Cambridge: Cambridge University Press, 2008), 132.

4. Lieb, *Poetics of the Holy*, 381n118. Cf. Barbara K. Lewalski, "Public Milton," *Milton Quarterly* 50, no. 2 (2016): 71–74, "Satan's divine honors are an exaggerated version of the idolatry Milton long associated with the Stuart ideology of divine right kingship" (73).

5. Lewalski notes that "by portraying Satan as a self-styled grand rebel voicing Milton's own republican rhetoric from *The Tenure of Kings and Magistrates* against what he calls the tyranny of heaven, Milton presents readers with a poem-long challenge to make right distinctions: to understand with Abdiel that monarchy is proper to God as creator of all things, and with Adam [see *PL* 12.63–74] that it is unjust for any man to claim sovereign power over his equals." "Public Milton," 73. See Chernaik, *Milton and the Burden of Freedom*, 125–27, for a discussion of how Abdiel reflects the distinction in Milton's prose tracts between the royal God and earthly tyrants; see Achinstein, *Literature and Dissent*, 119–22, for a discussion of Abdiel, dissent, and dissent's consequent persecution.

6. Lieb, *Poetics of the Holy*, 290. See also Charles W. Durham, "'Suffering for Truth's Sake': The Conflict Between Abdiel and Satan in *Paradise Lost*," *CEA Critic* 68, no. 1 (2005–6): 60–66, which states that Abdiel embodies Milton's ideal, described in *Areopagitica*, of "'a true warfaring Christian'" whose virtue "is not a 'fugitive and cloistered virtue'" (63).

7. Stanley Fish, *Surprised by Sin: The Reader in "Paradise Lost"* (New York: Macmillan, 1967), 189. See also Stella P. Revard, *The War in Heaven: "Paradise Lost" and the Tradition of Satan's Rebellion* (Ithaca: Cornell University Press, 1980), which calls Abdiel "the humblest of angels" (241) and notes that most other early modern depictions of the war in heaven have the archangel Michael confront Satan (165). Margaret Olofson Thickstun, *Milton's "Paradise Lost": Moral Education* (New York: Palgrave Macmillan, 2007), notes "Abdiel's model humility" (60) and analyzes the psychological dynamics of peer pressure that affect the other angels, including the comparative ineffectiveness of a lowly angel's confronting an angel of Satan's stature (55–61).

8. Mason Tung, "The Abdiel Episode: A Contextual Reading," *Studies in Philology* 62, no. 4 (1965): 595–609, points out that Abdiel's standing firm against Satan contrasts with Eve's failure to stand against him, thus making the Abdiel episode central to the poem.

9. Significantly, Fallon, in *Milton's Peculiar Grace*, connects Milton's persona in *Defensio Secunda* with Abdiel, stating that "Milton's role foreshadows Abdiel's, as one who prevails in reason rather than in arms" (168). Gerald Richman, "A Third Choice: Adam, Eve, and Abdiel," *Early Modern Literary Studies* 9, no. 2 (2003): 6.1–5, argues that Abdiel's urging Satan to "hast'n to appease / Th' incensed Father, and th' incensed Son / While Pardon may be found

in time besought" (5.846–48) suggests that Milton believed that "if Eve had repented and Adam had refused to join her in sin, Eve would have found pardon" (4).

10. R. V. Young observes that Abdiel, in his "exemplary solitude" among the rebel angels, knows "the presence of God within," regardless of his geographical position. Young, "Milton and Solitude," *Ben Jonson Journal* 21, no. 1 (2014): 92–113, quoted at 105.

11. Making no direct reference to the parable of the laborers but paraphrasing Matthew 20:16 by way of Luke 13:30, Jane L. Riggs writes that Milton, in his depiction of Abdiel, "follow[s] God's penchant for the last being first (Lk. 13.30)." Riggs, "Sifted as Wheat: Abdiel, the Peter Pattern," *Kentucky Philological Review* 10 (1995): 33–38, quoted at 34.

12. Charles W. Durham, "'To Stand Approv'd in Sight of God': Abdiel, Obedience, and Hierarchy in *Paradise Lost*," *Milton Quarterly* 26, no. 1 (1992): 15–20, quoted at 18.

13. Fallon, *Milton's Peculiar Grace*, 238, 245. Other scholars who connect the Son with Milton include Hanford, *John Milton, Englishman*, 17, 201; Rowse, *Milton the Puritan*, 245–46; Ashraf H. A. Rushdy, *The Empty Garden: The Subject of the Late Milton* (Pittsburgh: University of Pittsburgh Press, 1992), 385–86; Roy Flannagan's edition of the poetry, *The Riverside Milton* (New York: Houghton Mifflin, 1998), 711; Barbara K. Lewalski, *The Life of John Milton: A Critical Biography* (Oxford: Blackwell, 2000), 511; John T. Shawcross, "'Unshak'n, Unseduc'd, Unterrifi'd': The Consistencies of John Milton's Thought," *Milton Studies* (Korea) 10 (2000): 317–35, at 317; Thomas N. Corns, "'With Unaltered Brow': Milton and the Son of God," *Milton Studies* 42 (2003): 106–21, at 108; and Achsah Guibbory, "Rethinking Millenarianism, Messianism, and Deliverance in *Paradise Regained*," *Milton Studies* 48 (2008): 135–59, at 138–41, 153–54.

14. See especially Derek N. C. Wood, *"Exiled from Light": Divine Law, Morality, and Violence in Milton's "Samson Agonistes"* (Toronto: University of Toronto Press, 2001), xxii, 120, 125, 191.

15. Commenting on 1.215–20, Joan Curbet Soler writes, "These are the aspirations of a potential conqueror and warrior, the kind of fantasies that would have been appropriate for a character in the ancient, aristocratic epic." Soler, "Towards a Miltonic Mariology: The Word and the Body of Mary in *Paradise Regain'd* (1671)," *Sederi* 22 (2012): 29–50, quoted at 43.

16. The gloss on "hardly" is from Flannagan, *Riverside Milton*, 730.

17. As many critics have noted, the language of the Son's statement—"And now by some strong motion I am led / Into this Wilderness" (1.290–91)—is echoed by Samson when he tells the Chorus, "I begin to feel / Some rousing motions in me" (1381–82), which propel him to accompany the Philistine Officer and perform at Dagon's temple, an echo that suggests that Samson's "motions" come authentically from God, just as the Son's do. (Cf. Luke 4:1: "And Jesus being full of the Holy Ghost returned from Jordan, and was led by the Spirit into the wilderness.") The degree to which the Son at this point understands the specific nature of his prophesied death is unclear, but as Albert C. Labriola says in "Christus Patiens: The Virtue of Patience in *Paradise Lost*, I–II," in *The Triumph of Patience: Medieval and Renaissance Studies*, edited by Gerald J. Schiffhorst (Gainesville: University Press of Florida, 1978), 138–46, the reader recognizes that "in *Paradise Regained*, Christ's exercise of patience in the wilderness is clearly preparatory to the supreme exercise later at the Passion and Death" (139). Emphasizing the Son's learned patience at this point in his narrative, Soler, "Towards a Miltonic Mariology," observes that "the Son learns to live in the 'not yet' (I.292) just as the mother has learnt to 'wait with patience' (II.102)" (47).

18. For an excellent discussion of the theme of Jesus's substitutionary atonement throughout Milton's writings, see Samuel Smith, "Milton's Theology of the Cross: Substitution and

Satisfaction in Christ's Atonement," *Christianity and Literature* 63, no. 1 (2013): 5–25. See also Russell M. Hillier, *Milton's Messiah: The Son of God in the Works of John Milton* (Oxford: Oxford University Press, 2011), 15–47. By contrast, Feisal G. Mohamed, "Milton Against Sacrifice," *Religion and Literature* 45, no. 1 (2013): 192–206, argues that Milton "downplay[s] the theological significance of Christ's death" and suggests "an absence of sacrifice in Milton's works" (193). For discussions of the crucifixion in *Paradise Regained*, see Charles A. Huttar, "The Passion of Christ in *Paradise Regained*," *English Language Notes* 19, no. 3 (1982): 236–60; Russell M. Hillier, "The Wreath, the Rock, and the Winepress: Passion Iconography in Milton's *Paradise Regain'd*," *Literature and Theology* 22, no. 4 (2008): 387–405; and Hillier, *Milton's Messiah*, 178–222.

19. For a discussion of how the Son's salvific sacrifice on the cross is predicated on, and the culmination of, his life of sinless obedience, see David V. Urban, "John Milton, Paradox, and the Atonement: Heresy, Orthodoxy, and the Son's Whole-Life Obedience," *Studies in Philology* 112, no. 4 (2015): 787–806. For an excellent discussion of the Son's overcoming Satan through his "conscientious obedience to God" (123), see David R. Schmitt, "Heroic Deeds of Conscience: Milton's Stand Against Religious Conformity in *Paradise Regained*," in "'Relation Stands': Essays on *Paradise Regained*," edited by John Rogers, special issue, *Huntington Library Quarterly* 76, no. 1 (2013): 105–35, at 119–26. Eric B. Song presents a false dichotomy in "Love Against Substitution: John Milton, Aphra Behn, and the Political Theology of Conjugal Narratives," *ELH* 80, no. 3 (2013): 681–714, when he writes that in *Paradise Regained*, "Jesus seems to achieve salvation not in death but in faithful obedience" (692).

20. Hill, *Milton and the English Revolution*, 416.

21. Emily Griffiths Jones, "Milton's Counter-Revision of Romantic Structure in *Paradise Regained*," in Rogers, "'Relation Stands,'" 59–81, quoted at 71. Jones quotes 1.156.

22. Note that 2.346 states that Satan's banquet includes shellfish, a violation of the Mosaic dietary law in Leviticus 11:12.

23. For analysis of the Son's virtuous self-government, see David V. Urban, "Liberty, License, and Virtuous Self-Government in John Milton's Writings," *Journal of Markets and Morality* 17, no. 1 (2014): 143–66, at 156–57.

24. Although most commentators on *Paradise Regained* focus on Job's relation to the Son with respect to patience (see especially Barbara Kiefer Lewalski, *Milton's Brief Epic: The Genre, Meaning, and Art of "Paradise Regained"* [Providence: Brown University Press, 1966]), Victoria Kahn, "Job's Complaint in *Paradise Regained*," *ELH* 76, no. 3 (2009): 625–60, argues that Job serves as a model "for the Son's distinctive rhetoric," particularly the Son's use of "quotation, irony, mimicry" and his "playing with the dual meaning of a single word or phrase" (626).

25. Gerald J. Schiffhorst, "Satan's False Heroism in *Paradise Lost* as a Perversion of Patience," *Christianity and Literature* 33, no. 2 (1984): 13–20, quoted at 13. See also Schiffhorst's introduction in *Triumph of Patience*, 1–31.

26. John Bunyan, *The Pilgrim's Progress* (New York: New Family Library, 1972), 32, 33. Achinstein, *Literature and Dissent*, notes Bunyan's appeal to patience at the conclusion of Bunyan's *Holy War*; she comments that Milton's Son, "like the many tempted by impatience during the Restoration, needs to repeat the lesson of fortitude, of resisting the temptation to hurry the work of the Lord" (136).

27. Laura Lunger Knoppers, "Satan and the Papacy in *Paradise Regained*," *Milton Studies* 42 (2002): 68–85, observes that Satan's taunts here, besides paraphrasing the Psalms, "also evoke the reviling of Christ upon the cross" in Matthew 27:40–42 (80).

28. Neil Forsyth, "Having Done All to Stand: Biblical and Classical Allusion in *Paradise Regained*," *Milton Studies* 21 (1985): 199–214, goes so far as to say, "It is Christ's ability to stand, rather than his verbal reply, on which the fall of Satan immediately follows" (201). Forsyth is right to emphasize the potency of the Son's standing—a phenomenon that, as Jameela Lares observes in *Milton and the Preaching Arts* (Pittsburgh: Duquesne University Press, 2001), 207, does not appear in Luke 4; Milton adds it to his narrative—but it is the combined effect of his standing and his words that brings about Satan's defeat. Consider Guibbory, who writes in "Rethinking Millenarianism," "In declaring, 'Tempt not the Lord thy God' . . . he may also be declaring himself 'the Lord thy God,' the Word speaking the Word. If he is asserting his divine as well as his human nature"—and I believe he is—"then his standing is a miraculous demonstration of a divine power within" (155). See also Judith Anderson's statement in n. 29 below. By contrast, John Leonard, *The Value of Milton* (Cambridge: Cambridge University Press, 2016), asserts that Jesus's words demonstrate the power of "the Son's *refusal* to play the divine trump" (121); the Son is "a single person who routs Satan in simple terms, as man" (122); I believe that Leonard is asserting a false dichotomy here. In a novel reading, Michael Bryson, "From Last Things to First: The Apophatic Vision of *Paradise Regain'd*," in *Visionary Milton: Essays on Prophecy and Violence*, edited by Peter E. Medine, John T. Shawcross, and David V. Urban (Pittsburgh: Duquesne University Press, 2010), 241–65, argues that when the Son says, "Tempt not the Lord thy God," he is telling Satan, "*do not tempt yourself*," for "*all* creatures, sharing in the divine as their origin, are also God" (261).

29. Marshall Grossman, "Poetry and Belief in *Paradise Regained, to Which Is Added, Samson Agonistes*," *Studies in Philology* 110, no. 2 (2013): 382–401, asserts that Jesus's temptation at the Temple pinnacle "looks forward to Jesus's own unspoken, but amply hinted at, future on the cross" (400). Judith H. Anderson, "Patience and Passion in Shakespeare and Milton," *Spenser Studies* 21 (2006): 205–20, observes that the Son's "invocation of 'the Lord thy God' at once grasps the potency of his own identity and accepts the suffering, the passive endurance, of his Passion" on the cross (213). Noam Reisner, "Spiritual Architectonics: Destroying and Rebuilding the Temple in *Paradise Regained*," *Milton Quarterly* 43, no. 3 (2009): 166–82, while acknowledging the temple's crucifixion imagery, goes on to affirm that "Milton's use of temple imagery in *Paradise Regained* finally emerges as a powerful trope for the very spirit of reform and instruction that so often animates his poetry" (167).

Chapter 4

1. *Milton's Sonnets*, edited by E. A. J. Honigmann (New York: St. Martin's Press, 1966), 107; A. N. Wilson, *The Life of John Milton* (Oxford: Oxford University Press, 1983), 118–19; Leo Miller, "John Milton's 'Lost' Sonnet to Mary Powell," *Milton Quarterly* 25, no. 3 (1991): 102–7; Leland Ryken, "'Lady That in the Prime of Earliest Youth': Milton's Sonnet 9 in Its Puritan Context," paper presented at the Conference on John Milton, Murfreesboro, Tennessee, October 24, 2003; Edward Jones, "'The Better Part with Mary and with Ruth': Sonnet 9 and Mrs. Isabel Webber," paper presented at the International Milton Congress, Pittsburgh, March 13, 2004.

2. William Riley Parker, *Milton: A Biography*, 2nd ed., edited by Gordon Campbell, 2 vols. (Oxford: Oxford University Press, 1996), 1:875; Nicholas W. Knight, "Milton's Sonnet IX: The Lady in 'Lady That in the Prime,'" *Publications of the Missouri Philological Association* 1 (1976): 14–23.

3. David Masson, *The Life of John Milton: Narrated in Connexion with the Political, Ecclesiastical, and Literary History of His Time*, 7 vols. (1859–81; reprint, New York: Peter Smith, 1946), 3:436.

4. *The Sonnets of John Milton*, edited by John S. Smart (Glasgow: Maclehose, Jackson, 1921), 51–52; Sara van den Berg, "Unruly Daughter, Virtuous Wife: The Double Subject and Double Occasion of Milton's Sonnet 9," in *To Repair the Ruins: Reading Milton*, edited by Mary C. Fenton and Louis Schwartz (Pittsburgh: Duquesne University Press, 2012), 231–51. Van den Berg first presented her argument for Mary Boyle Rich at her Newberry Library Milton Seminar, "Two Kings and a Lady: Milton and the Irish Protestants," Chicago, October 10, 1998.

5. In "Choosing the Better Part with Mary and with Ruth," in *Of Poetry and Politics: New Essays on Milton and His World*, edited by P. G. Stanwood (Binghamton, N.Y.: Medieval and Renaissance Texts and Studies, 1995), 153–69, Dayton Haskin remarks that "some will see Sonnet 9 . . . as carrying latent autobiographical implications with which one might reconstruct a narrative about an aspiring poet who seems to have been called 'the Lady' at Christ's College" (168). But Haskin neither significantly pursues this idea nor endorses it. In light of Milton's self-identification as "the Lady of Christ's College," his oft-noted similarities in thought and person to the Lady of *A Mask*, and his avowal of the virgins of the parable, I believe that the idea of Milton's addressing himself as a subtext of Sonnet 9 is entirely reasonable and valuable.

6. Milton's youthful nocturnal study habits—presumably by lamplight and thus recalling the wise virgins of the parable and the subject of Sonnet 9—were, according to John Aubrey, documented by his brother, Christopher. See Helen Darbishire, ed., *The Early Lives of John Milton* (London: Constable, 1932), 10.

7. John T. Shawcross, "The Temple of *Janus* and Milton Criticism in the New Millennium," *ANQ* 15, no. 4 (2002): 20–29, at 22–23.

8. Another connection between Milton and the parable of the virgins is noted in Charles A. Huttar, "Samson's Identity Crisis and Milton's," in *Imagination and the Spirit*, edited by Charles A. Huttar (Grand Rapids: Eerdmans, 1971), 101–57, at 150; Huttar observes that, in the opening line of Sonnet 19 ("When I consider how my light is spent"), "the poet" "fear[s]" that, like "the foolish virgins whose story is told in Matthew 25, his 'light is spent,' and their fate of being locked out at midnight from the bridal feast (out in 'this dark world and wide') looms before him." Huttar's connection is especially valuable in the context of the later Sonnet 19, where the discouraged speaker would be inclined to view himself very differently (i.e., as foolish) from the way he did in the earlier Sonnet 9, with his identification with the wise virgins.

9. Thomas Shepard, *The Parable of the Ten Virgins Opened and Applied* (1659), in *The Works of Thomas Shepard*, vol. 2 (Ligonier, Pa.: Solo Deo Gloria Publications, 1990), 16.

10. John Calvin, *A Harmony of the Gospels: Matthew, Mark, and Luke*, translated by T. H. L. Parker, edited by David W. Torrance and Thomas F. Torrance, 3 vols. (Grand Rapids: Eerdmans, 1979), 3:109; Matthew Poole, *A Commentary on the Holy Bible*, 3 vols. (1685; reprint, London: Banner of Truth, 1963), 3:118; John Trapp, *A Commentary on the New Testament*, 3rd ed., edited by W. Webster (1662; reprint, London: Richard D. Dickinson, 1877), 253.

11. For another example of the figure of the wise virgin's being specifically applied to a pious seventeenth-century woman, see the posthumously discovered and published spiritual narrative by Anne Venn (1627–1654), titled *A Wise Virgins Lamp Burning; Or, Gods sweet*

income of love to a gracious soul waiting for him (London, 1658). In his prefatory remarks, her stepfather and publisher, Thomas Weld, described Venn as one who kept "her Lamp burning" (A2). Weld expressed his hope that her writings would "convince some Christians of their slackness and awaken others" (A5). For recent scholarship on Venn, see Kate Narveson, *Bible Readers and Lay Writers in Early Modern England: Gender and Self-Definition in an Emergent Writing Culture* (Farnham, Surrey: Ashgate, 2012), 101–7, 121–28; Rachel Adock, "Anne Venn's *A Wise Virgins Lamp Burning* (1658) in the Household of Anne Dunch, Sister-in-Law to Richard Cromwell," *Notes and Queries* 57, no. 4 (2010): 501–3; and Rachel Adock, "'A Good Example to Women': The Biographer's Presence in Mid-Seventeenth-Century Women's Conversion Narratives," *Glass* 21 (Spring 2009): 11–19.

12. In a frequently quoted passage from his 1681 (?) (the date is uncertain) "Minutes of the Life of John Milton," John Aubrey writes, "he had light browne haire, his complexn exceeding faire . . . he was so faire yt they called him the Lady of Xts coll." Darbishire, *Early Lives of John Milton*, 3.

13. John T. Shawcross, *John Milton: The Self and the World* (Lexington: University Press of Kentucky, 1993), 40. In *The Life of John Milton: A Critical Biography* (Oxford: Blackwell, 2000), Barbara K. Lewalski comments, "it is not hard to imagine the taunts that fastened the nickname 'The Lady of Christ's' on a slender, refined, defiantly chaste, highly intellectual and artistically inclined adolescent" (31).

14. Stevie Davies, *Milton* (New York: St. Martin's Press, 1991), 70. I thank John P. Rumrich, *Milton Unbound: Controversy and Reinterpretation* (Cambridge: Cambridge University Press, 1996), 87, for this observation concerning Milton's comparison of himself to Electra.

15. Michael Lieb, *Milton and the Culture of Violence* (Ithaca: Cornell University Press, 1994), 85–86.

16. My discussion of the Sixth Prolusion is drawn largely from Lieb, *Milton and the Culture of Violence*, 86–99, which I recommend for a more detailed analysis of the prolusion in the context of Milton's sexual identity. For an analysis of Milton's manipulation of comedy for his own rhetorical purposes in the Sixth Prolusion, see Jessica Tvordi, "The Comic Personas of Milton's *Prolusion VI*: Negotiating Masculine Identity Through Self-Directed Humor," in *Laughter in the Middle Ages and Early Modern Times*, edited by Albrecht Classen (Berlin: Walter de Gruyter, 2010), 715–34. For an incisive but sexually overcharged discussion of the young Milton's developing gender identity, see John T. Shawcross, "Milton and Diodati: An Essay in Psychodynamic Meaning," in "'Eyes Fixt Fast': Current Perspectives in Milton Methodology," edited by Albert C. Labriola and Michael Lieb, special issue, *Milton Studies* 7 (1975): 127–63, rewritten as chapter 3 ("The Lady of Christ's") of Shawcross's biography *John Milton: The Self and the World*. In *Life of John Milton*, Lewalski offers an intelligent critique of Shawcross's emphasis on the allegedly homoerotic dynamic of the friendship between Milton and Diodati (who Shawcross claims was clearly homosexual). Lewalski writes, "These speculations seem to me to rest on a strained overreading of poems and letters exchanged between them," and asserts, "Had Milton recognized or acted upon a sexual attraction to men, he would not have idealized youthful virginity (his own and that of the Lady in *A Maske*), nor would he have routinely listed sodomy among the acts 'opposed to chastity' in *The Christian Doctrine* (*CPW* VI, 726–57). Milton's consistent habit is rather to justify his own impulses and experiences, sexual or otherwise—a disposition that prompted him to write defenses of chastity and arguments for polygamy and divorce" (557n66). Lewalski's argument echoes that of William Kerrigan in *The Sacred Complex: On the Psychogenesis of "Paradise Lost"* (Cambridge, Mass.: Harvard University Press, 1983), 49. See also John P. Rumrich, "The Erotic Milton,"

Texas Studies in Language and Literature 41, no. 2 (1999): 131. Although 1628 is the common dating of the Sixth Prolusion, John T. Shawcross, in *Rethinking Milton Studies: Time Present and Time Past* (Newark: University of Delaware Press, 2005), 86 and 182n1, and Gordon Campbell in "Milton and the Water Supply of Cambridge," *Southern African Journal of Medieval and Renaissance Studies* 15 (2006 for 2005): 121–26, have more recently suggested 1631 or 1632.

17. Lieb, *Milton and the Culture of Violence*, 87. For a detailed discussion of the practice of "salting" at Cambridge, see John K. Hale, "Milton Plays the Fool: The Christ's College Salting, 1628," *Classical and Modern Literature* 20, no. 3 (2000): 51–70.

18. Lewalski, *Life of John Milton*, 31.

19. Stephen Greenblatt, *Renaissance Self-Fashioning: From More to Shakespeare* (Chicago: University of Chicago Press, 1980), defines "male sexual anxieties" as "the fear of betrayal, the suspension and release of aggression, the intimations of complicity in one's own torment" (8); Andrew P. Williams, in his introduction to *The Image of Manhood in Early Modern Literature*, edited by Andrew P. Williams (Westport, Conn.: Greenwood Press, 1999), ix–xv, uses the terms "masculine anxiety" and "masculine anxiousness" to discuss similar phenomena (xiv).

20. In *John Milton, Englishman* (New York: Crown, 1949), James Holly Hanford comments that "the Lady is an ideal embodiment of the informed and fastidious innocence which had won him his academic nickname" (63), while in *Milton*, Davies, in a far more charged statement, asserts that "the Lady carries the full weight and value of Milton's eremitical repression and sublimation of his sexual desires" (71). In *The Sacred Complex*, Kerrigan, citing the aforementioned section of *An Apology for Smectymnuus*, states plainly, "Milton is also the Lady" (42); in "Gender Confusion in Milton and Everyone Else," *Hellas* 2, no. 2 (1991): 195–220, Kerrigan declares of the Lady, "she's Milton, of course, the first and unrevised Milton" (206). Katharine Eisaman Maus, *Inwardness and Theater in the English Renaissance* (Chicago: University of Chicago Press, 1995), discusses "the fact that Milton is imagining himself as *inhabiting* the Lady's body" (207). Margaret W. Ferguson, in her foreword to *Menacing Virgins: Representing Virginity in the Middle Ages and Renaissance*, edited by Kathleen Coyne Kelly and Marina Leslie (Newark: University of Delaware Press, 1999), 7–14, argues that the Protestant "search for 'signs' of election . . . clearly underlies Milton's creation of and identification with a virginal 'Lady' subjected to a symbolically excessive spiritual/physical test by Comus" (11). Stephen M. Fallon, *Milton's Peculiar Grace: Self-Representation and Authority* (Ithaca: Cornell University Press, 2007), says that the Lady's "celebration of chastity parallels Milton's self-construction as a poet" (63). Brendan Prawdzik, *Theatrical Milton: Politics and Poetics of the Staged Body* (Edinburgh: Edinburgh University Press, 2017), argues that "as a staged woman," the Lady "embodies the vulnerability of the divine poet [Milton] who would be public yet who also would be chaste" (54). For a well-developed discussion of Milton's identification with the Lady, see William Shullenberger, "Milton's Lady and Lady Milton: Chastity, Prophecy, and Gender in *A Maske Presented at Ludlow Castle*," in *Fault Lines and Controversies in the Study of Seventeenth-Century English Literature*, edited by Claude J. Summers and Ted-Larry Pebworth (Columbia: University of Missouri Press, 2002), 204–26; Shullenberger revised this essay as chapter 6 of *The Lady in the Labyrinth: Milton's "Comus" as Initiation* (Madison: Fairleigh Dickinson University Press, 2008), 203–25.

21. Lieb, *Milton and the Culture of Violence*, 99. A. S. P. Woodhouse makes a similar though somewhat less explicit statement in "*Comus, Lycidas, Epitaphium Damonis*," in Woodhouse's *The Heavenly Muse: A Preface to Milton*, edited by Hugh MacCallum (Toronto: University

of Toronto Press, 1972), 55–98: "Milton is indeed at the centre of *Comus* as he is at the centre of *Lycidas*. Remembering his sobriquet at Christ's College, we wonder whether there is not a hint of this in the name selected for the central character, the Lady" (59).

22. Warren Chernaik, *Milton and the Burden of Freedom* (Cambridge: Cambridge University Press, 2017), 65. Gordon Teskey, in *The Poetry of John Milton* (Cambridge, Mass.: Harvard University Press, 2015), considers the "theory" that Milton "distinguish[ed] systematically between *chastity* and *virginity*" to be "illusory" (163).

23. William Shullenberger, "Into the Woods: The Lady's Soliloquy in *Comus*," *Milton Quarterly* 35, no. 1 (2001): 33–43, quoted at 33.

24. *The Riverside Milton*, edited by Roy Flannagan (New York: Houghton Mifflin, 1998), 165n592.

25. Anna Nardo, *Milton's Sonnets and the Ideal Community* (Lincoln: University of Nebraska Press, 1979), 45.

26. For citations of the extensive scholarship affirming that Milton's Abdiel, the Son of *Paradise Regained*, and Samson are self-referential, see, respectively, chapter 3, notes 3 and 13, and chapter 2, note 3, above.

27. Miller, "John Milton's 'Lost' Sonnet," 103.

28. Miller, 105. In "Milton, Marriage, and a Woman's Right to Divorce," *SEL: Studies in English Literature, 1500–1900* 39, no. 1 (1999): 131–53, Matthew Biberman notes Sonnet 9's "carnal overtones": "If the bridegroom here is simply Jesus there is no reason for him to be 'passing' to bliss, since conventionally Christ is bliss itself. The word 'passes,' attached as it is to the bridegroom, thus prepares the reader to read 'thy' not as 'he has gained you thy entrance into heaven' but as 'he has come inside you,' a graphic pun that merits acknowledgement. Christ the bridegroom has 'entered' her being spiritually, and the mortal bridegroom has 'entered' her in coition" (134–35).

29. Miller, "John Milton's 'Lost' Sonnet," 105, 106.

30. Wilson, *Life of John Milton*, 118–19.

31. Lewalski, *Life of John Milton*, 156–57.

32. See, for example, Annabel Patterson, "'No Meer Amatorious Novel?'" in *Politics, Poetics, and Hermeneutics in Milton's Prose*, edited by David Loewenstein and James Grantham Turner (Cambridge: Cambridge University Press, 1990), 85–101, at 91–92; Sara van den Berg, "Women, Children, and the Rhetoric of Milton's Divorce Tracts," *Early Modern Literary Studies* 10, no. 1 (2004): 4.2; Stephen M. Fallon, "'The Spur of Self-Concernment': Milton in His Divorce Tracts," in *Milton Studies* 38 (2000): 220–42, at 224; and Fallon, *Milton's Peculiar Grace*, 111.

33. Wilson, *Life of John Milton*, 119.

34. Miller, "John Milton's 'Lost' Sonnet," 104.

35. Honigmann, *Milton's Sonnets*, 106.

36. A. S. P. Woodhouse and Douglas Bush, *A Variorum Commentary on the Poems of John Milton*, vol. 2, *The Minor English Poems*, part 3 (New York: Columbia University Press, 1972), 380. Woodhouse and Bush cite the *Oxford English Dictionary*, s.v. "prime," definition 1.8.

37. Honigmann, *Milton's Sonnets*, 107.

38. See John Halkett, *Milton and the Idea of Matrimony: A Study of the Divorce Tracts and "Paradise Lost"* (New Haven: Yale University Press, 1970), vii–97; and James Grantham Turner, *One Flesh: Paradisal Marriage and Sexual Relations in the Age of Milton* (Oxford: Clarendon Press, 1987), 73–95. The briefer discussion offered by Diane Kelsey McColley, *Milton's Eve* (Urbana: University of Illinois Press, 1983), 44–47, is also helpful. See also James

Turner Johnson, *A Society Ordained by God: English Puritan Marriage Doctrine in the First Half of the Seventeenth Century* (Nashville: Abingdon Press, 1970), which sees in Milton (amid serious discontinuity) more significant continuity with other Puritan beliefs about marriage and divorce. For an older statement asserting more continuity still, see William Haller and Malleville Haller, "The Puritan Art of Love," *Huntington Library Quarterly* 5, no. 2 (1942): 235–72.

39. Halkett, *Milton and the Idea of Matrimony*, 47.

40. Haskin, "Choosing the Better Part," 158.

41. See Katherine Ludwig Jansen, *The Making of the Magdalen: Preaching and Popular Devotion in the Later Middle Ages* (Princeton: Princeton University Press, 2000), 32–35.

42. Charles Wheatly, *Rational Illustration of the Book of Common Prayer of the Church of England* (London: H. G. Bohn, 1849), 66–67.

43. J. Frank Henderson, "The Disappearance of the Feast of Mary Magdalene from the Anglican Liturgy" (2004), 15, http://www.jfrankhenderson.com/pdf/disappearance_feast_marymagdalene.pdf (accessed June 7, 2018).

44. As just noted, many such commentators were not even convinced that Mary Magdalen was the woman of Luke 7:36–50, but they certainly rejected the notion that Mary the sister of Martha was that woman or that Luke 7:36–50 was describing the same episode that John 12:1–8, Matthew 26:6–13, and Mark 14:3–9 describe. See Calvin, *Harmony of the Gospels*, 2:85–88, 3:120–24; John Calvin, *The Gospel According to St. John 11–21 and The First Epistle of John*, translated by T. H. L. Parker (Grand Rapids: Eerdmans, 1961), 1–2, 24–27; Trapp, *Commentary on the New Testament*, 318; Poole, *Commentary on the Holy Bible*, 3:217; Giovanni Diodati, *Pious and Learned Annotations upon the Holy Bible* (London: Printed by T. B. for Nicholas Fussell, 1643), 48 (New Testament); H[enry] Hammond, *A Paraphrase and Annotations upon all the Books of the New Testament*, 2nd ed. (London, 1659), 214. A significant exception is John Lightfoot, *The Harmony Chronicle and Order of the New-Testament* (London, 1655), 28–29, 54.

45. See Calvin, *Harmony of the Gospels*, 3:120–23; Trapp, *Commentary on the New Testament*, 258; Poole, *Commentary on the Holy Bible*, 3:343; Diodati, *Pious and Learned Annotations*, 31, 76 (New Testament); Hammond, *Paraphrase and Annotations*, 214.

46. Calvin, *Harmony of the Gospels*, 3:122. Calvin's comments here find a curious parallel when the Father commends Abdiel for bearing "Universal reproach, far worse to bear / Than violence: for this was all care / To stand approv'd in the sight of God, though Worlds / Judg'd thee perverse" (*PL* 6.34–37).

47. Miller, "Milton's 'Lost' Sonnet," 106.

48. Haskin, "Choosing the Better Part," 167–68; Poole, *Commentary on the Holy Bible*, 3:510.

49. Poole, *Commentary on the Holy Bible*, 3:510, 511; Trapp, *Commentary on the New Testament*, 406, 407, 408. Edward Topsell, in *The Reward of Religion, Delivered in Sundrie Lectures upon the Booke of Ruth* (London, 1596), 152–71, writes approvingly of Naomi's loving parenting of Ruth in general and of her advice to Ruth concerning Boaz in particular.

50. *John Milton: Complete Poems and Major Prose*, edited by Merritt Y. Hughes (New York: Macmillan, 1957), 141, note at line 5; Flannagan, *Riverside Milton*, 87n2. Such a celebration is evident throughout Topsell, *Reward of Religion*; Richard Bernard, *Ruths Recompence: or, A Commentarie upon the Booke of Ruth* (London, 1628); Bartholomew Parsons, *Ruth and Boaz Blessed: or A Sacred Contract Honoured with a Solemne Benediction* (Oxford, 1633); and Thomas Fuller, *A Comment on Ruth* (London, 1654).

51. From an untitled prefatory poem by William Atterson in Parsons, *Ruth and Boaz Blessed*, 2.

52. John Carey, in his edition *John Milton: Complete Shorter Poems*, 2nd ed. (Harlow, UK: Longman, 1997), explicitly notes this allusion to Ruth's choice of Boaz (291, note at line 5).

53. Lewalski, *Life of John Milton*, 157.

54. Helpful discussions related to *Paradise Lost* and Eve's reciprocal "fitness" for Adam include McColley, *Milton's Eve*, 43–48; F[annie] Peczenik, "Fit Help: The Egalitarian Marriage in *Paradise Lost*," *Mosaic* 17, no. 1 (1984): 29–48; and Kristin A. Pruitt, *Gender and the Power of Relationship: "United as One Individual Soul" in "Paradise Lost"* (Pittsburgh: Duquesne University Press, 2003), 24–33 (all three argue in favor of the couple's essentially egalitarian relationship); and Mary Nyquist, "The Genesis of Gendered Subjectivity in the Divorce Tracts and in *Paradise Lost*," in *Re-membering Milton: Essays on the Texts and Traditions*, edited by Mary Nyquist and Margaret W. Ferguson (New York: Methuen, 1987), 99–127; and Desma Polydorou, "Gender and Spiritual Equality in Marriage: A Dialogic Reading of Rachel Speght and John Milton," *Milton Quarterly* 35, no. 1 (2001): 22–32 (both of which find such egalitarian descriptions overly optimistic).

55. Kerrigan, "Gender Confusion in Milton," 216. In *Specimens of the Table Talk of the Late Samuel Taylor Coleridge*, edited by Henry Nelson Coleridge, 2 vols. (London: John Murray, 1835), 2:240–41, Coleridge also affirms Milton's self-representation in both Adam and Eve. In her essay "'Consider First, That Great / Or Bright Infers Not Excellence': Mapping the Feminine in Mary Groom's Miltonic Cosmos," in "Riven Unities: Authority and Experience, Self and Other in Milton's Poetry," edited by Wendy Furman, Christopher Grose, and William Shullenberger, special issue, *Milton Studies* 28 (1992): 121–62, Wendy Furman lends this additional perspective: "On one level, [Milton's] portrait of Eve and Eden, and perhaps of the Son as well, grows out of a deep sense of loss—out of his anguished search for the ever longed-for and ever elusive feminine within" (158). Cf. John Rumrich, "Milton's God and the Matter of Chaos," *PMLA* 110, no. 5 (1995): 1035–46, which describes similar longings in "Milton's hermaphroditic deity," a deity who, at the core of the cosmos of *Paradise Lost*, "acquiesces in his own feminine otherness" and who "can only exercise sovereignty and creative power by virtue of her" (1044). Elsewhere, Rumrich asserts that "hermaphrodism is pervasive in *Paradise Lost*, and I take it to be the displaced effect of Milton's yearning for a Tiresias-like transcendence of limitations imposed by gender." Rumrich, "Milton's Poetics of Generation," *Texas Studies in Language and Literature* 38, no. 2 (1996): 191–208, quoted at 197.

56. Hanford makes such connections in *John Milton, Englishman*, 182–83. See also Edward Le Comte, *Milton and Sex* (New York: Columbia University Press, 1978), 117; and A. L. Rowse, *Milton the Puritan: Portrait of a Mind* (London: Macmillan, 1977), 236; cf. also Louis Schwartz, "'Spot of Child-Bed Taint': Seventeenth-Century Obstetrics in Milton's Sonnet 23 and *Paradise Lost* 8.462–78," *Milton Quarterly* 27, no. 3 (1993): 98–109; and B. J. Sokol, "Euripides' Alcestis and the 'Saint' of Milton's Reparative Twenty-Third Sonnet," *SEL: Studies in English Literature, 1500–1900* 33, no. 1 (1993): 131–47.

57. James W. Stone, "'Man's Effeminate S(lack)ness': Androgyny and the Divided Unity of Adam and Eve," *Milton Quarterly* 31, no. 2 (1997): 33–42, quoted at 36. See also Claudia M. Champagne, "Adam and His 'Other Self,'" *Milton Quarterly* 25, no. 2 (1991): 48–59; Champagne, within her own extensive discussion of Adam's narcissistic attraction to Eve, notes similar observations made by Arnold Stein, *Answerable Style: Essays on "Paradise Lost"*

(Minneapolis: University of Minnesota Press, 1953), 109; Stanley Fish, *Surprised by Sin: The Reader in "Paradise Lost"* (New York: Macmillan, 1967), 263; Kerrigan, *Sacred Complex*, 70; Shari A. Zimmerman, "Milton's *Paradise Lost*: Eve's Struggle for Identity," *American Imago* 38, no. 3 (1981): 247–67, at 250; and Wolfgang Rudat, "Milton's *Paradise Lost*: Augustinian Theology and Fantasy," *American Imago* 42, no. 3 (1985): 297–313, at 308. See also John C. Ulreich Jr., "Making Dreams Truths, and Fables Histories: Spenser and Milton on the Nature of Fiction," *Studies in Philology* 87, no. 3 (1990): 363–77, at 370–71. More recently, Roberta C. Martin, "'How Came I Thus?': Adam and Eve in the Mirror of the Other," *College Literature* 27, no. 2 (2000): 57–79, has argued that Adam's narcissism can be traced to Milton's narcissistic God.

58. Although Ephesians 5:28 declares, "He that loveth his wife loveth himself," the surrounding context for the "self" here is physical, as in Genesis 2. Paul writes, "So ought men to love their wives as their own bodies.... For no man ever yet hated his own flesh; but nourisheth and cherisheth it" (Eph. 5:28–29). Paul goes on to quote Genesis 2:24. There is no explicit mention of an intrinsic oneness of heart and soul. By contrast, David Oliver Davies, *Milton's Socratic Rationalization: The Conversations of Adam and Eve in "Paradise Lost"* (Lanham, Md.: Lexington Books, 2017), argues that Plato's *First Alcibiades* "informs Milton's optimal sense of a 'joyning to it self in conjugal fellowship a fit conversing soul' and of the domestic 'help meet' as 'another self'" (41). Davies quotes *DDD* at 2.251 and *Tetrachordon* at 2.600. Drawing on Aristotle's *Nicomachean Ethics*, Christopher Koester, "Solitude and Difference in Books 8 and 9 of *Paradise Lost*," *Milton Studies* 57 (2016): 155–84, suggests that "Milton's understanding of friendship is not based in likeness, but likeness-through-difference" (165).

59. John Trapp, *A Commentary on the Old and New Testaments*, vol. 1, edited by Hugh Martin (1662; reprint, London: Richard D. Dickinson, 1867), 13.

60. John Calvin, *Commentaries on the First Book of Moses Called Genesis*, vol. 1, translated by John King (Grand Rapids: Eerdmans, n.d.), 135.

61. Diodati, *Pious and Learned Annotations*, 5 (Old Testament).

62. Poole, *Commentary on the Holy Bible*, 1:8.

63. Julia M. Walker, *Medusa's Mirrors: Spenser, Shakespeare, Milton, and the Metamorphosis of the Female Self* (Newark: University of Delaware Press, 1998), 174. Stanley Fish, *How Milton Works* (Cambridge, Mass.: Belknap Press of Harvard University Press, 2001), well describes Milton's hermeneutical abuses, stating that in *DDD* Milton subjects scripture to "an interpretation so strenuous that even the word 'manipulation' is too mild to describe it" (236).

64. Note Halkett's comment in *Milton and the Idea of Matrimony* that such passages in *Paradise Lost* "grow out of the long tradition that [Adam and Eve's] marriage was the perfect pattern and archetype of all marriages" (116).

65. William Whately, *A Bride-Bush, or A Wedding Sermon* (1617) (Amsterdam: Theatrum Orbis Terrarum, 1975), A2.

66. Thatcher and Oxenbridge quoted in Edmund S. Morgan, *The Puritan Family: Religion and Domestic Relations in Seventeenth-Century New England*, rev. ed. (New York: Harper and Row, 1966), 52.

67. Daniel Rogers, *Matrimoniall Honour* (London, 1642), 202, 201.

68. J. I. Packer, *A Quest for Godliness: The Puritan Vision of the Christian Life* (Wheaton, Ill.: Crossway, 1994), 25.

69. Halkett, *Milton and the Idea of Matrimony*, 30.

70. Cheryl H. Fresch, "'Wither Thou Goest': *Paradise Lost* XII, 610–23 and the Book of Ruth," *Milton Studies* 32 (1995): 111–29, quoted at 124. Cf. Ruth 4:21–22; Matthew 1:5–6, 16; Luke 3:23, 31–32; and Flannagan, *Riverside Milton*, 709n188.

71. Fresch, "'Wither Thou Goest,'" 123. Fresch goes on to note, in the book of Ruth, "the association between the literal marriage of Ruth and Boaz and the mystic marriage with the redeemer." Adam and Eve's own marriage and soon-to-be renewed sexual union will also establish the line of the redeemer. Indeed, as Eric B. Song, "*Paradise Lost* and the Poetics of Delay: Virgil, Vida, Milton," *Milton Quarterly* 50, no. 3 (2016): 137–56, observes, "Adam and Eve's restored union looks ahead to the Son's work of Atonement" (147).

72. Ryken's contention, in "'Lady That in the Prime,'" that Sonnet 9 is a Puritan wedding poem is worth remembering here, as are Biberman's words regarding the sonnet's "carnal overtones," quoted in note 28 above.

Chapter 5

1. Alice-Lyle Scoufos, "The Mysteries in Milton's *Masque*," *Milton Studies* 6 (1974): 113–42, quoted at 120, 121.

2. John Foxe, *Christus Triumphans: Comodia Apocalyptica*, in *Two Latin Comedies by John Foxe the Martyrologist: "Titus et Gesippus," "Christus Triumphans,"* edited and translated by John Hazel Smith (Ithaca: Cornell University Press, 1973), 371.

3. Scoufos, "Mysteries in Milton's *Masque*," 122–23.

4. Catherine I. Cox, "The Garden Within: Milton's Ludlow Masque and the Tradition of Canticles," *Milton Studies* 31 (1994): 23–44, quoted at 24 (see also 39–40).

5. Cox, 28; Lauren Shohet, "Figuring Chastity: Milton's Ludlow Masque," in *Menacing Virgins: Representing Virginity in the Middle Ages and Renaissance*, edited by Kathleen Coyne Kelley and Marina Leslie (Newark: University of Delaware Press, 1999), 146–64, quoted at 147; Lucy Hutchinson, *Memoirs of the Life of Colonel Hutchinson*, edited by Julius Hutchinson, rev. ed. edited by C. H. Firth (London: George Routledge and Sons, 1906), 64.

6. Cox, "Garden Within," 29.

7. See also Scoufos, "Mysteries in Milton's *Masque*," 134; and Theresa M. DiPasquale, *Refiguring the Sacred Feminine: The Poems of John Donne, Aemilia Lanyer, and John Milton* (Pittsburgh: Duquesne University Press, 2008), 232–37. DiPasquale specifically argues that Milton emphasizes the Lady as a type "of the Church Militant, as Milton would portray her in *The Reason of Church Government*: a young virgin who, 'though she be well instructed, yet is . . . still under a more strait tuition' (YP 1:755)" (237).

8. William Shullenberger, "Into the Woods: The Lady's Soliloquy in *Comus*," *Milton Quarterly* 35, no. 1 (2001): 33–43, quoted at 33.

9. Cox, "Garden Within," 32.

10. Cox, 30, 31.

11. Cox, 32.

12. *The Riverside Milton*, edited by Roy Flannagan (Boston: Houghton Mifflin, 1998), 133n146.

13. J. Martin Evans, *The Miltonic Moment* (Lexington: University Press of Kentucky, 1998), 45.

14. William Shullenberger, *Lady in the Labyrinth: Milton's "Comus" as Initiation* (Madison: Fairleigh Dickinson University Press, 2008), 226.

15. In what I consider a highly problematic reading, Will Stockton, "The Seduction of Milton's Lady: Rape, Psychoanalysis, and the Erotics of Consumption in *Comus*," in *Sex Before Sex: Figuring the Act in Early Modern England*, edited by James M. Bromley and Will Stockton (Minneapolis: University of Minnesota Press, 2013), 233–61, which reads *A Mask* "as the Lady's rape fantasy" (234), sees "the threat of sexual assault" implied in these lines as an externalized "projection of the Lady's desire" (253).

16. DiPasquale, *Refiguring the Sacred Feminine*, 242.

17. Noticing the holistic connection between virtue and chastity, A. E. Dyson, "Virtue Unwavering: Milton's *Comus*," in *Milton: "Comus" and "Samson Agonistes"; A Casebook*, edited by Julian Lovelock (London: Macmillan, 1975), 106–33, says, "In *Comus* then, Chastity is more than an isolated virtue: it is symptomatic of spiritual wholeness and the life of grace" (108). Dyson adds that "the great 'debate'" in Milton's masque "is not between Chastity and incontinence, and still less between Virginity and Marriage, but between Reason and Passion as controlling factors in human conduct" (108–9).

18. Rosemund Tuve, *Images and Themes in Five Poems by Milton* (Cambridge, Mass.: Harvard University Press, 1957), 128.

19. Blaine Greteman, "'Perplex't Paths': Youth and Authority in Milton's *Mask*," *Renaissance Quarterly* 62, no. 2 (2009): 410–43, quoted at 432.

20. See John Leonard, "Saying 'No' to Freud: Milton's *A Mask* and Sexual Assault," *Milton Quarterly* 25, no. 4 (1991): 129–40, at 131–32. In his edition *John Milton: The Complete Poems* (London: Penguin, 1998), Leonard calls the Elder Brother "overconfident" and describes his views as those of "an idealistic eleven-year-old" (671, 672).

21. Most significant to *A Mask*'s immediate context is the rape of the fourteen-year-old serving maid Margery Evans, which took place in 1631. See Leah Sinanoglou Marcus, "The Milieu of Milton's *Comus*: Judicial Reform at Ludlow and the Problem of Sexual Assault," *Criticism* 25, no. 4 (1983): 293–327.

22. William Kerrigan, "The Politically Correct *Comus*: A Reply to John Leonard," *Milton Quarterly* 27, no. 4 (1993): 149–55, quoted at 152.

23. See Augustine, *The City of God*, translated by Marcus Dods (New York: Modern Library, 1950), 1.16 (pp. 21–22); and Aquinas, *In Quattuor Libros Sententiarum*, in *Opera Omnia I*, edited by Roberto Busa (Stuttgart: Frommann-Holzboog, 1980), 4.33.3.1.co, 601. Connie J. Saunders, *Rape and Ravishment in the Literature of Medieval England* (Cambridge: D. S. Brewer, 2001), 94, offers an English translation of this passage by Aquinas. Sarah Van der Laan, in "Circean Transformation and the Poetics of Milton's *Masque*," *Seventeenth Century* 31, no. 2 (2016): 139–60, writes that the Elder Brother "affirms with Augustine, Aquinas, and Sponde that his sister cannot be changed in essentials" apart from her free will (148–49). Nancy Weitz Miller, "Chastity, Rape, and Ideology in the Castlehaven Testimonies and Milton's Ludlow *Mask*," *Milton Studies* 32 (1995): 153–68, and Amy Greenstadt, *Rape and the Rise of the Author: Gendering Intention in Early Modern England* (Farnham, Surrey: Ashgate, 2009), 83–130, both offer extensive discussion of the matter of rape with reference to *Comus*.

24. Stephen Orgel, "The Case for Comus," *Representations* 81 (Winter 2003): 31–45, quoted at 36.

25. Observing the Lady's physical helplessness, coupled with her indefatigable spiritual and mental resolution, Stanley Fish remarks, "Friends, light, vision, hearing, direction—one by one they are taken from her, until in Comus' lair she is deprived even of her mobility and

is left with nothing at all. Yet, as it turns out, she is left with everything—*everything that matters*. That is what is meant when she says to Comus, 'Thou canst not touch the freedom of my mind'" (the emphasis is Fish's). Fish, *How Milton Works* (Cambridge, Mass.: Belknap Press of Harvard University Press, 2001), 152.

26. Louis Schwartz, *Milton and Maternal Mortality* (Cambridge: Cambridge University Press, 2009), 143. Although my discussion focuses on the logical force of Comus's argument, Barbara K. Lewalski, "Public Milton," *Milton Quarterly* 50, no. 2 (2016): 71–74, observes that Comus resembles "a smooth, sophisticated Cavalier libertine" who "echoes in richly sensuous language, mesmerizing in its very sounds and rhythms, countless Cavalier seduction poems on themes of *carpe diem* and *carpe florem*" (72).

27. See, for example, Psalm 14:1; Proverbs 1:7, 6:32, 7:7–12, 9:13–18, 12:15, 18:2, and 26:1–12; Isaiah 32:6; and Romans 1:21–25.

28. Georgia B. Christopher, "The Virginity of Faith: *Comus* as a Reformation Conceit," *ELH* 43, no. 4 (1976): 479–99, quoted at 490; Susan M. Felch, "The Intertextuality of *Comus* and Corinthians," *Milton Quarterly* 27, no. 2 (1993): 59–70, quoted at 60.

29. Fish, *How Milton Works*, 582n8.

30. Shullenberger, *Lady in the Labyrinth*, 167.

31. In Matthew 12:34–35, Jesus upbraids the Pharisees: "O generation of vipers, how can ye, being evil, speak good things? For out of the abundance of the heart the mouth speaketh. A good man out of the good treasure of the heart bringeth forth good things: and an evil man out of the evil treasure bringeth forth evil things."

32. For a similar reading of these lines, see Leonard, "Saying 'No' to Freud," 129–40; for opposing views, see Gale H. Carrithers Jr., "Milton's Ludlow Mask: From Chaos to Community," *ELH* 33, no. 1 (1966): 23–42, at 39; J. W. Flosdorf, "'Gums of Glutinous Heat': A Query," *Milton Quarterly* 7, no. 1 (1973): 4–5, at 5; Hugh M. Richmond, *The Christian Revolutionary: John Milton* (Berkeley: University of California Press, 1974), 72; William Kerrigan, *The Sacred Complex: On the Psychogenesis of "Paradise Lost"* (Cambridge, Mass.: Harvard University Press, 1983), 55; and Stockton, "Seduction of Milton's Lady," 253, which all strongly suggest that the Lady is sexually aroused by Comus and suppresses her arousal by rejecting him verbally. For a more sustained argument that the Lady is unintentionally aroused by Comus, see Debora Shuger, "'Gums of Glutinous Heat' and the Stream of Consciousness: The Theology of Milton's *Maske*," *Representations* 60 (Autumn 1997): 1–21. The same argument, with some modification, can be found in James W. Broaddus, "'Gums of Glutinous Heat' in Milton's *Mask* and Spenser's *Faerie Queene*," *Milton Quarterly* 37, no. 4 (2003): 205–14, at 207–11.

33. See John Leonard, "'Good Things': A Reply to William Kerrigan," *Milton Quarterly* 30, no. 3 (1996): 117–27, at 124–26, for a strong statement of this argument.

34. Maryanne Cale McGuire, *Milton's Puritan Masque* (Athens: University of Georgia Press, 1983), 142; Leonard, "'Good Things,'" 124. Leonard draws on Roland Mushat Frye, "The Teachings of Classical Puritanism on Conjugal Love," *Studies in the Renaissance* 2 (1955): 148–59, which draws on John Calvin's *Institutes of the Christian Religion*, bk. 4, chap. 12, sec. 28, "where Calvin distinguishes two kinds of virginity. The first kind is abstinence. The second is the chaste love of marriage." "Good Things,'" 124.

35. The biblical association between sexual immorality and idolatry can be seen, for example, in Isaiah 57:5, Ezekiel 16 and 23, Hosea 1–3, and Romans 1:18–27.

36. A. S. P. Woodhouse and Douglas Bush, *A Variorum Commentary on the Poems of John Milton*, vol. 2, *The Minor English Poems*, part 3 (New York: Columbia University Press, 1972),

946. Daniel 1.8, 11–13, 15, 17 reads as follows: "But Daniel purposed in his heart that he would not defile himself with the portion of the king's meat, nor with the wine which he drank. . . . Then said Daniel . . . let them give us pulse to eat, and water to drink. Then let our countenances be looked upon. . . . And . . . their countenances appeared fairer and fatter . . . than all the children which did eat the portion of the king's meat. . . . As for these four children, God gave them knowledge and . . . wisdom: and Daniel had understanding in all visions and dreams."

37. See Woodhouse and Bush, *A Variorum Commentary*, 946.

38. Commenting on these lines, Brendan Prawdzik, in *Theatrical Milton: Politics and Poetics of the Staged Body* (Edinburgh: Edinburgh University Press, 2017), writes, "Comus is attempting to substitute the inherent value of the Lady's embodied selfhood with a 'curr[e]nt' value, based on external beauty, determined by circulation" (66).

39. Richard Halpern, "Puritanism and Maenadism in *A Mask*," in *Rewriting the Renaissance: The Discourse of Sexual Difference in Early Modern Europe*, edited by Margaret W. Ferguson, Maureen Quilligan, and Nancy J. Vickers (Chicago: University of Chicago Press, 1986), 88–105, argues that *A Mask* "trace[s] the line that leads from virginity to married chastity" (88). Julie H. Kim, "The Lady's Unladylike Struggle: Redefining Patriarchal Boundaries in Milton's *Comus*," *Milton Studies* 35 (1997): 1–20, argues that Milton's patriarchal ideal of marital chastity in *A Mask* circumvents women's freedom of sexual choice. Melissa E. Sanchez, "'What Hath Night to Do with Sleep?': Biopolitics in Milton's *Mask*," in "Queer Milton," edited by Will Stockton and David Orvis, special issue, *Early Modern Culture* 10 (2014): 1–21, arguing from a queer studies perspective, states that "the idealization of chastity in *A Mask*, along with the philosophical and theological traditions from which it emerges, promotes heteronormativity insofar as it privileges certain sexual behaviors (those that are restrained, loving, monogamous, and procreative) over others (those that are uninhibited, anonymous, promiscuous, and nonprocreative)" (3). Sanchez has revised her essay as chapter 8 of *Queer Milton*, edited by David L. Orvis (London: Palgrave Macmillan, 2018).

40. I believe that the implicit discussion of marriage in the Lady's speech is sufficient to refute the short-sighted argument of Evans, *Miltonic Moment*, which contends that the Lady chooses to remain silent about monogamous marriage and that, for her, "Sexual abstinence, it now appears, is the only alternative to the promiscuous libertinism that Comus urges on her" (46). It is rather absurd to suggest that the Lady ought to engage in an eloquent discussion of why "true love waits" for the right marriage partner, and even more ridiculous to think that Comus would be persuaded by such an argument. In any event, the Lady's appeal for virginal chastity is entirely appropriate to her situation as an unmarried young woman. Equally myopic are the objections to the Lady's endorsement of chastity and virginity voiced in Kerrigan, *Sacred Complex*, 27–28; and Arthur Barker, *Milton and the Puritan Dilemma, 1641–1660* (Toronto: University of Toronto Press, 1942), 10–11, both of which Evans cites to buttress his arguments.

41. For a more complete rebuttal of such charges, see Leonard, "Saying 'No' to Freud," 129–40. In *The Value of Milton* (Cambridge: Cambridge University Press, 2016), his most recent discussion of *A Mask*, Leonard again champions the Lady and her prudent character, writing, "We need the Lady's temperance at the present time when Comus's philosophy has wrought so much damage in the world" (37).

42. That the Lady recognizes Comus's inability to understand "the sage / And serious doctrine of Virginity" is more than can be said for Barker, *Puritan Dilemma*, who, inexplicably championing Comus's openness to new ideas, contends, "What distinction is to be made

between these virtues [that she speaks of] and how they are to be related to temperance she deigns to tell neither Comus—who would perhaps not have understood but is easily convinced—nor us" (11). Comus is hardly "easily convinced," and a careful reading of her lines demonstrates that the Lady has done an adequate job of explaining her position.

43. David Gay, "'Rapt Spirits': 2 Corinthians 12.2–5 and the Language of Milton's Comus," *Milton Quarterly* 29, no. 3 (1995): 76–86, quoted at 77.

44. *John Milton: Complete Poems and Major Prose*, edited by Merritt Y. Hughes (New York: Macmillan, 1957), 108, note at line 785.

45. Orgel, "Case for Comus," states that although the Attendant Spirit views Comus's followers' condition "as misery," one could also argue that he enables them "to be what and where they want to be" (35). Timothy J. Burbery, *Milton the Dramatist* (Pittsburgh: Duquesne University Press, 2007), suggests that Milton may be trying "to convey the extent of Comus's depravity" by suggesting that he cannot recognize the change in his followers' appearance (54). For a discussion of liberty versus license in *A Mask*, see David V. Urban, "Liberty, License, and Virtuous Self-Government in John Milton's Writings," *Journal of Markets and Morality* 17, no. 1 (2014): 143–66, at 147–49.

46. For a discussion of this controversy, see Woodhouse and Bush, *Minor English Poems*, 955.

47. Shuger, "'Gums of Glutinous Heat,'" 9; DiPasquale, *Refiguring the Sacred Feminine*, 247. In a curious but textually unsubstantiated conjecture, Bryan Adams Hampton, in *Fleshly Tabernacles: Milton and the Incarnational Poetics of Revolutionary England* (Notre Dame: University of Notre Dame Press, 2012), postulates that the brothers destroy Comus's cup "perhaps at the very moment when the glass rim is upon the Lady's quivering lips," and suggests that the Lady "occupies a liminal space, poised between the extremes of a puissant potential that results in aligning herself to temperance, and an impotent surrender that results in yielding to intemperance" (178). Hampton offers no textual evidence to indicate that the Lady's lips were quivering or that her resistance was possibly wavering.

48. For a discussion of the various depictions of Sabrina in sixteenth- and seventeenth-century England and how shifts in historiography influence her depiction in *A Mask*, see Erin Murphy, "Sabrina and the Making of English History in *Poly-Olbion* and *A Maske Presented at Ludlow Castle*," *SEL: Studies in English Literature, 1500–1900* 51, no. 1 (2011): 87–110.

49. See Angus Fletcher, *Milton's Transcendental Masque: An Essay on Milton's "Comus"* (Ithaca: Cornell University Press, 1971), 240; Cox, "Garden Within," 36; Shullenberger, *Lady in the Labyrinth*, 92, 243–46; DiPasquale, *Refiguring the Sacred Feminine*, 253.

50. For a helpful discussion of the various interpretations of this phrase, see Michael Gillum, "Yet Once More, 'Gumms of Gluteous Heat,'" *Milton Quarterly* 44, no. 1 (2010): 47–51. Recently, Boyd Brogan, "The Masque and the Matrix: Alice Egerton, Richard Napier, and Suffocation of the Mother," *Milton Studies* 55 (2014): 3–52, esp. 27–29, has proposed that it refers to the discharge of the Lady's seed and menstrual blood that takes place upon Sabrina's release of the Lady, who has been suffering from "suffocation of the mother."

51. Cox, "Garden Within," 36.

52. Although both Kim, "Lady's Unladylike Struggle," 19, and Orgel, "Case for Comus," 41, challenge the rightness of *A Mask*'s celebration of this return, suggesting that the Lady's return to her father's house and its patriarchal family system undermines the notion of the Lady's freedom, Milton's text portrays her return as both blessed and joyful.

53. For a discussion of these matters with reference to Jesus's teachings in Mark 4, see David V. Urban, "Intentionality and Obscurity in Mark 4:11–12: Jesus' Parabolic Purposes," *Calvin Theological Journal* 49, no. 1 (2014): 112–32.

54. Scoufos, "Mysteries in Milton's *Masque*," 134. Cleanth Brooks and John Edward Hardy, *Poems of Mr. John Milton: The 1645 Edition with Essays in Analysis* (New York: Harcourt Brace, 1951), 232; James Holly Hanford, *John Milton, Poet and Humanist: Essays by James Holly Hanford* (Cleveland: Case Western Reserve University Press, 1966), 63; Kerrigan, *Sacred Complex*, 60–61; John Leonard, "Milton's Vow of Celibacy: A Reconsideration of the Evidence," in *Of Poetry and Politics: New Essays on Milton and His World*, edited by P. G. Stanwood (Binghamton, N.Y.: Medieval and Renaissance Texts and Studies, 1995), 187–201, at 195; Barbara K. Lewalski, *The Life of John Milton: A Critical Biography* (Oxford: Blackwell, 2000), 81; and Patrick Timmis, "Sanctifying Rites in Milton's *A Masque Presented at Ludlow Castle, 1634*," *Christianity and Literature* 68, no. 4 (forthcoming, 2019), also identify Milton's Cupid as Christ, and Milton's Psyche as the Lady and/or the individual believer and/or the church.

55. Leonard, "Milton's Vow of Celibacy," 195, 196.

56. Cox, "Garden Within," 39.

Chapter 6

1. Stephen M. Fallon, *Milton's Peculiar Grace: Self-Representation and Authority* (Ithaca: Cornell University Press, 2007), 206–8. Other critics who see Milton's self-representation in both Adam and Eve include Samuel Taylor Coleridge, *Specimens of the Table Talk of the Late Samuel Taylor Coleridge*, edited by Henry Nelson Coleridge, 2 vols. (London: John Murray, 1835), 2:240–41; Walter Raleigh, *Milton* (1900) (New York: Benjamin Blom, 1967), 147; James Holly Hanford, *John Milton, Englishman* (New York: Crown, 1949), 201; and William Kerrigan, "Gender Confusion in Milton and Everyone Else," *Hellas* 2 (1991): 195–220, at 216. Eve's similarity to Milton the poet is suggested by Diane McColley, "Eve and the Arts of Eden," in *Milton and the Idea of Woman*, edited by Julia M. Walker (Urbana: University of Illinois Press, 1988), 100–119, at 103; and Maggie Kilgour, "'Thy Perfect Image Viewing': Poetic Creation and Ovid's Narcissus in *Paradise Lost*," *Studies in Philology* 102, no. 3 (2005): 307–39, at 331–32.

2. See, for example, Coleridge, *Specimens of the Table Talk*, 2:240–41; Denis Saurat, *Milton: Man and Thinker* (New York: Dial Press, 1925), 217–19; A. J. A. Waldock, *"Paradise Lost" and Its Critics* (Cambridge: Cambridge University Press, 1947; reprint, Gloucester, Mass.: Peter Smith, 1959), 75; William G. Riggs, *The Christian Poet in "Paradise Lost"* (Berkeley: University of California Press, 1972), 15–45; William Kerrigan, *The Prophetic Milton* (Charlottesville: University Press of Virginia, 1974), 125–87; Neil Forsyth, *The Satanic Epic* (Princeton: Princeton University Press, 2003), 268–89; and Fallon, *Milton's Peculiar Grace*, 205–6.

3. Anne-Julia Zwierlein, "'Thyself in Me Thy Perfect Image Viewing': Mental Fixations, Narcissism, and Gendered Conceptions of Creative Autonomy in Early Modern Fiction and Poetics," in *Gender and Creation: Surveying Gendered Myths of Creativity, Authority, and Authorship*, edited by Anne-Julia Zwierlein (Heidelberg: Universitätsverlag Winter, 2010), 85–96, quoted at 91.

4. Edward Le Comte, *Milton and Sex* (New York: Columbia University Press, 1978), 69. In contrast to Le Comte's and my interpretations, Diana Treviño Benet, "The Fall of the Angels: Theology and Narrative," *Milton Quarterly* 50, no. 1 (2016): 1–13, asserts, "Satan does not summon sin. Without his awareness or participation, she appears spontaneously" (3).

5. Zwierlein, "'Thyself in Me,'" 91.

6. *The Riverside Milton*, edited by Roy Flannagan (Boston: Houghton Mifflin, 1998), 513n60.

7. I argue this point in David V. Urban, "Liberty, License, and Virtuous Self-Government in John Milton's Writings," *Journal of Markets and Morality* 17, no. 1 (2014): 143–66, at 156.

8. The timing of Satan's actual crossing over into sin is the subject of debate. See Andrew Escobedo, "Allegorical Agency and the Sins of Angels," *ELH* 75, no. 4 (2008): 787–818. Although it seems likely that Satan crosses over into actual sin in the course of his rebellious speech to his followers (5.772ff.) and his subsequent rejection of Abdiel's urging that he "Cease" his "impious rage" (5.845), my sense is that Sin's birth and rape take place after the events of book 5 and prior to the war in heaven in book 6.

9. Le Comte, *Milton and Sex*, 69.

10. John Mulryan, "Satan's Headache: The Perils and Pains of Giving Birth to a Bad Idea," *Milton Quarterly* 39, no. 1 (2005): 16–22, quoted at 16.

11. F. T. Prince, ed., *Paradise Lost, Books I and II* (Oxford: Oxford University Press, 1962), 165, note for 2.764. Neil Forsyth writes in *Satanic Epic* of "the disturbing parallels" between Sin and Eve (247), but Forsyth's cynicism should be mitigated by the contrasts between Sin and Eve offered by Diane Kelsey McColley, *Milton's Eve* (Urbana: University of Illinois Press, 1983), 84–85.

12. For an intriguing discussion of nakedness and dressing and their relation to paradise, the Fall, sexual sin, and redemption, see Edward C. Jacobs, "'These Troublesom Disguises Which Wee Wear': Dressing and Redressing in the Garden, Books 9–12," *Milton Quarterly* 51, no. 1 (2017): 38–43.

13. Thomas H. Blackburn, "'Uncloister'd Virtue': Adam and Eve in Milton's Paradise," *Milton Studies* 3 (1971): 119–37, intelligently discusses how Adam and Eve's "innocence" in Eden should not be equated with cloistered ignorance.

14. For a discussion of the rightness of God's boundaries and responsibilities among the gifts of Eden, see Margaret Olofson Thickstun, *Milton's "Paradise Lost": Moral Education* (New York: Palgrave Macmillan, 2007), 119–23.

15. That Eve cheerfully acknowledges Adam's superiority and at the same time demonstrates profound wisdom (and, for that matter, extreme complexity) speaks to Milton's complexity as an author. Barbara K. Lewalski, in "Milton on Women—Yet Once More," *Milton Studies* 6 (1974): 3–20, writes, "Milton of course accepted the categories of hierarchy and the natural inferiority of women, yet his reworking of the Adam and Eve myth has explored [the human condition] with remarkable incisiveness and profundity" (5). Mary Nyquist, in "The Genesis of Gendered Subjectivity in the Divorce Tracts and in *Paradise Lost*," in *Re-membering Milton: Essays on the Texts and Traditions*, edited by Mary Nyquist and Margaret W. Ferguson (New York: Methuen, 1987), 99–127, makes a valid point, however, when, comparing Milton's and John Calvin's interpretations of Genesis 2, she writes that "Milton's stridently masculinist, 'Hee for God only, shee for God in him' in *Paradise Lost* [4.299] obviously goes much further than Calvin in drawing out the masculinist implications" of the creation account of Adam and Eve (107). For a discussion of Milton's comparatively exalted depiction of Eve in *Paradise Lost*, see Diane McColley, "Milton and the Sexes," in *The Cambridge Companion to Milton*, 2nd ed., edited by Dennis Danielson (Cambridge: Cambridge University Press, 1999), 175–92, at 183–89. McColley's entire article provides valuable insight on this subject in Milton's works as a whole, as well as a helpful summary of critical perspectives. See also note 54 of chapter 4 in this book for other germane sources on this topic. Also worth pondering is Peter C. Herman, *Destabilizing Milton: "Paradise Lost" and the Poetics of Incertitude* (New York: Palgrave Macmillan, 2005), which states that despite "Adam's gestures of mutuality" in book 4, "Eve's rhetoric emphasizes inequality, subordina-

tion, and disparity" (135), a situation, Herman suggests, that leaves Eve vulnerable to the "empowerment" (138) her subsequent Satan-inspired dream will offer.

16. Lara Dodds, "'To Due Conversation Accessible': or, The Problem of Courtship in Milton's Divorce Tracts and *Paradise Lost*," *Texas Studies in Literature and Language* 56 (2014): 42–65, quoted at 60. Cf. Mandy Green, "The Virgin in the Garden: Milton's Ovidian Eve," *Modern Language Review* 100 (2005): 903–22, at 913–14. For a thorough survey of critical discussion of these lines through 1970, see Cheryl H. Fresch, *A Variorum Commentary on the Poems of John Milton*, vol. 5, part 4, *Paradise Lost*, book 4, edited by P. J. Klemp (Pittsburgh: Duquesne University Press, 2011), 243–49. Important post-1970 studies include Christine Froula, "When Eve Reads Milton," *Critical Inquiry* 10 (1983): 321–47, which argues that Eve is required here to "abandon not merely her image in the pool but her very self" (328); similarly, Julia M. Walker, *Medusa's Mirrors: Spenser, Shakespeare, Milton, and the Metamorphosis of the Female Self* (Newark: University of Delaware Press, 1998), critiques Milton's "patronizing" tone toward Eve (220), stating that "Eve never recognizes that image [in the lake] as herself" and arguing that "Eve's image on the surface of the lake is displaced in her creation story by the masculine body of Adam, the feminine identity being circumscribed by two male voices and two male hands, God's and Adam's" (168, 161). Froula's and Walker's skeptical readings can be contrasted with those of McColley, who argues in *Milton's Eve*, 74–85, that "Eve's narrow escape from narcissism is exigent and perilous, requiring her to lose herself in order to find herself while leaving her full freedom to fail" (75); Kristin A. Pruitt, who contends in *Gender and the Power of Relationship: "United as One Individual Soul" in "Paradise Lost"* (Pittsburgh: Duquesne University Press, 2003), that Eve, "like Adam, first discovers an independent identity and achieves a measure of self-knowledge, then comes to recognize the relationship of that self to another, and finally, apprehends the hierarchy of values on which the harmony of Paradise is based" (34–35); Maggie Kilgour, who writes in *Milton and the Metamorphosis of Ovid* (Oxford: Oxford University Press, 2012), "Unlike Narcissus, who entertains a choice only to evade it, or Homeric heroes whose actions are willed by Zeus, Eve faces and makes a real choice"—Kilgour adds, "Eve might have become a copy of Narcissus. Instead, like [Spenser's] Britomart, her narcissism is channeled into a higher form of love. Unlike Ovid's Narcissus, who turned from *corpus* to *umbra*, Eve is guided from her shadow to the body whose shadow, or image, she is. Properly instructed in self-knowledge, she follows a path that again recalls Plato's parable of the cave—now rescued from parody—as she is led from shadows to reality and to Adam" (208); and N. K. Sugimura, "Eve's Reflection and the Passion of Wonder in *Paradise Lost*," *Essays in Criticism* 64 (2014): 1–28, which draws on eighteenth-century editors and commentators on *Paradise Lost* to argue that "Eve's experience at the lake may be read as being less about narcissism . . . and more a subtle expression of the passion of wonder . . . a response to what we might call the prelapsarian sublime, or the awe-inspiring experience of innocence, beauty, and the divine in a yet unfallen world" (2). My own reading is sympathetic to McColley, Pruitt, and Kilgour, though I recognize the warning offered by A. Bartlett Giamatti, who argues in *The Earthly Paradise and the Renaissance Epic* (Princeton: Princeton University Press, 1966) that Milton makes "this overt suggestion of narcissism, not to lessen our immediate estimate of Eve so much as to provide a repository of doubt for larger exploitation" (316). I believe that Milton explicitly calls attention to Eve's *potential* for narcissism, but I do not think it appropriate to label Eve's behavior at the lake as narcissism, contra Beverly A. McCabe, "Eve: Victim, Villain, or Vehicle? The Forewarnings and Prefiguration of the Fall in *Paradise Lost*," *CLA Journal* 43 (1999): 73–88. Eric B. Song makes this important distinction in "*Paradise Lost*

and the Poetics of Delay: Virgil, Vida, Milton," *Milton Quarterly* 50, no. 3 (2016): 137–56: "Eve must be taught that her desire is vain, but she cannot be accused of having succumbed to *furor*" (144).

17. Walker, *Medusa's Mirrors*, 187.

18. Milton notes that Satan eyes the couple "with jealous leer maligne" (4.503), a phrase that prompts C. S. Lewis to famously call him "a mere peeping Tom leering and writhing in prurience as he overlooks the privacy of two lovers." Lewis, *A Preface to "Paradise Lost"* (Oxford: Oxford University Press, 1942), 97. Forsyth, *Satanic Epic*, notes here that while Adam and Eve are "imparadis't in one another's arms" (4.506), Satan experiences hell, "Where [is] neither joy nor love, but fierce desire" (4.509). Forsyth thus calls Satan "the archetypal voyeur," who has "an immediate motive for the temptation of Eve: sexual jealousy or frustration" (261).

19. Stanley Fish points out that Satan's words of indignation ("Knowledge forbidd'n?," etc.) in 4.515–17 form the verbal pattern on which both the dream temptation reported in book 5 and the actual temptation of Eve in book 9 are based. *Surprised by Sin: The Reader in "Paradise Lost"* (New York: Macmillan, 1967), 221–22.

20. Eve's lines have drawn considerable critical ire, including an early response from Mary Wollstonecraft, who writes in *A Vindication of the Rights of Woman* (Manchester: Northern Grove Publishing Project, n.d.) that they reflect "exactly the arguments that I have used to children" (30), and who suggests that Milton's portrayal of Eve "deprive[s] us [women] of souls, and insinuate[s] that we were beings only designed by sweet attractive grace, and docile blind obedience" (29). John Leonard, who denies that Milton is a misogynist, says in *Faithful Labourers: A Reception History of "Paradise Lost," 1667–1970*, 2 vols. (Oxford: Oxford University Press, 2013), that Wollstonecraft "faults Milton not for hating women but for loving them in the wrong way" (2:704).

21. Milton scholars have discussed Milton's celebration of sexual love at length. See especially Peter Lindenbaum, "Lovemaking in Milton's Paradise," *Milton Studies* 6 (1974): 277–306; and James Grantham Turner, *One Flesh: Paradisal Marriage and Sexual Relations in the Age of Milton* (Oxford: Clarendon Press, 1987). Milton's celebration of Adam and Eve's prelapsarian lovemaking places him at odds with the teachings of theologians before and during his lifetime. Barbara Kiefer Lewalski writes in "Innocence and Experience in Milton's Eden," in *New Essays on "Paradise Lost,"* edited by Thomas Kranidas (Berkeley: University of California Press, 1971), 86–117, "it was almost universally believed that Adam was expelled from the Garden before such intercourse took place" (98); and Turner writes that Milton's depiction "violates the universal consensus of the commentators, not to mention the law of biological probability, when he gives Adam and Eve a full but infertile sexual life in Paradise" (*One Flesh*, 37). More recently, both Kent R. Lehnhof, "'Nor Turned I Weene': *Paradise Lost* and Pre-Lapsarian Sexuality," *Milton Quarterly* 34, no. 3 (2000): 67–83, and Thomas H. Luxon, *Single Imperfection: Milton, Marriage, and Friendship* (Pittsburgh: Duquesne University Press, 2005), 123–49, have challenged the idea that Milton's Adam and Eve have sexual intercourse before the Fall, although Luxon appears to back away from his earlier view in "'How Human Life Began': Sexual Reproduction in Book 8 of *Paradise Lost*," in *Sex Before Sex: Figuring the Act in Early Modern England*, edited by James W. Bromley and Will Stockton (Minneapolis: University of Minnesota Press, 2013), 263–90, at 269.

22. See chapter 5, n. 54.

23. See chapter 5, n. 34, for discussion of the Puritan idea that marital chastity is tantamount to virginity.

24. Significantly, the narrator's admonition to Adam and Eve to "know to know no more" should not be seen as an across-the-board warning against the couple's gaining knowledge in general, or even knowledge of good and evil. See Blackburn, "'Uncloister'd Virtue,'" which says of the instruction they receive from Raphael before the Fall, "Unless one is willing to deny that knowledge may be acquired by a combination of direct admonition and concrete narrative example such as that which Raphael provides, and unless one refuses to accept as evidence of understanding the correct use of the words *good* and *evil* by Adam and Eve in their own speeches, it must be admitted that they already possess a 'knowledge of good and evil' before they violate the tree which bears that name. Informed and sophisticated rather than naïve or childlike, their innocence consists not of no acquaintance with evil but of no taint by it, of sinlessness rather than ignorance of sin" (124).

25. Le Comte, *Milton and Sex*, 78. Offering a complementary perspective on these lines, Katherine Cox writes, "Eve's fancy is an organ being played by Satan. . . . The forgery he applies to her imaginative 'organs' suggests the forge bellows used to power such instruments." Cox, "'How Cam'st Thou Speakable of Mute': Satanic Acoustics in *Paradise Lost*," *Milton Studies* 57 (2016): 233–60, at 236.

26. See William B. Hunter, "Eve's Demonic Dream," *ELH* 13, no. 4 (1946): 255–65, for a discussion of the seventeenth-century understanding of potential malevolent influence upon the "fancy" during sleep. For a discussion of seventeenth-century views regarding Satan's ability to "transfuse evil into sleeping men" (38), see Diana Treviño Benet, "Milton's Toad, or Satan's Dream," *Milton Studies* 45 (2006): 38–52.

27. Le Comte, *Milton and Sex*, 79.

28. Le Comte, 78. Erik Gray, in "Come Be My Love: The Song of Songs, *Paradise Lost*, and the Tradition of the Invitation Poem," *PMLA* 128, no. 2 (2013): 370–85, calls Satan's wooing a "perversion of the genre" of the invitation poem exemplified in the Song of Songs (380).

29. The idea that Eve could have exercised her reason while dreaming is problematic, to say the least. Hunter, in "Eve's Demonic Dream," notes that according to seventeenth-century writings on dreams, "the fancy or imagination" was "the only sense left active during sleep," and it was said to be "the immediate cause of dreams" (259). The dream state, then, put people into a uniquely vulnerable situation. Hunter adds, "The devil's operation upon the imagination or fantasy is intimately connected with the flow of blood, upon which he can work in order to sway indirectly the higher reason and will" (262). Consequently, Satan's attack on Eve's fancy is ultimately an attack on her reason and will. And although her inability to exercise reason while dreaming, and thus explicitly refuse to eat the forbidden fruit, is not a sin, Satan's assault on her fancy weakens her and makes it more difficult for her to exercise her reason properly when faced with the fullness of temptation in book 9.

30. Michael Lieb, *The Dialectics of Creation: Patterns of Birth and Regeneration in "Paradise Lost"* (Amherst: University of Massachusetts Press, 1970), 189. Rose Sneyd, in "The Proto-'Desynonymization' of 'Fancy' and 'Imagination' in *Paradise Lost*," *Milton Quarterly* 51, no. 2 (2017): 111–23, writes that "the father of lies appears to be working with sense impressions" as he manipulates "the visual appearance of the Tree of Knowledge." Sneyd affirms that "Milton's implication that the 'organs of . . . fancy' are aligned with sense images neatly coincides with Coleridge's suggestion that fancy is associated with sensual understanding, rather than reason" (117).

31. This matter has been disputed by various commentators. E. M. W. Tillyard, *Studies in Milton* (London: Chatto and Windus, 1951), argues that during her dream Eve does in fact

pass "from a state of innocence to sin" (12); and Millicent Bell, "The Fallacy of the Fall in *Paradise Lost*," *PMLA* 68, no. 4 (1953): 863–83, contends that Eve and Adam are fallen throughout *Paradise Lost*, exhibiting sinfulness from their initial appearances in the poem. Robert Wiznura, "Eve's Dream, Interpretation, and Shifting Paradigms: Books Four and Five of *Paradise Lost*," *Milton Studies* 49 (2009): 108–23, suggests that, because of the text's "uncertainty" (112), we cannot know whether Eve has fallen in her dream.

32. Significantly, Milton's text never actually says that Eve, in her dream, eats the prohibited fruit. Stanley Fish postulates that this "omission" exists because "Satan is unable to make Eve go through the motions of her disobedience, even in her fancy." *Surprised by Sin*, 222.

33. *Oxford English Dictionary Online*, s.v. "bold," definitions 2 and 1a; see definition 4a for its negative meaning.

34. A. B. Chambers, "Three Notes on Eve's Dream in *Paradise Lost*," *Philological Quarterly* 46, no. 2 (1967): 186–93, at 192. According to Herman, *Destabilizing Milton*, "Eve's dream reveals that one part of her chafes at her subordinate position, which is rooted in Adam's supposed intellectual superiority, and Satan knows this" (138). But Herman's intriguing assertion goes against Eve's explicit delight in her subordination to Adam in book 4. Instead, following what Milton's narrator explicitly states, I argue that Satan, working upon Eve's "Fancy," plants such "discontented thoughts" within her (4.802, 807).

35. As Wiznura puts it in "Eve's Dream," the dream "mitigates Eve's ignorance and forces her to contemplate horizons beyond those presented by Adam" (109).

36. I share the view, held by many Miltonists and summarized by Vincent P. Di Benedetto in "Scripture's Constraint and Adam's Self-Authoring Freedom: A Reading of the Fall in *Paradise Lost*," *Milton Quarterly* 25, no. 1 (1991): 1–14, "that Adam and Eve, though perfect in their unfallen state, are still free to err, misjudge, mischoose, or imagine evil at no cost to their perfection, so long as they do not consciously approve that sole act of disobedience which would bring sin and imperfection into their lives" (12n3). See Benet, "Milton's Toad," 50–51, for a list of scholars who hold this position. See also George Musacchio, *Milton's Adam and Eve: Fallible Perfection* (New York: Peter Lang, 1991), 69–89.

37. Hunter, "Eve's Demonic Dream," 261. For a recent analysis of Adam's problematic response, including his neglect of the power of fancy, see Wiznura, "Eve's Dream," 113–16.

38. Theresa M. DiPasquale, in *Refiguring the Sacred Feminine: The Poems of John Donne, Aemilia Lanyer, and John Milton* (Pittsburgh: Duquesne University Press, 2008), connecting Eve with the female figure of Wisdom in Proverbs 4 and 5, asserts that Milton "imagines" Eve as "a type of Wisdom" (256). I contend, however, that the aforementioned events in book 4 suggest that Milton portrays Eve's wisdom as largely derivative, contingent on her submission to God and to Adam, and relying on Adam's wise community to continue her growth in wisdom.

39. See Blackburn, "'Uncloister'd Virtue.'"

40. David Aers, "Interpreting Dreams: Reflections on Freud, Milton, and Chaucer," in *Reading Dreams: The Interpretation of Dreams from Chaucer to Shakespeare*, edited by Peter Brown (Oxford: Oxford University Press, 1999), 84–98, quoted at 91.

41. Walker, *Medusa's Mirrors*, 174.

42. Pruitt, *Gender and the Power*, attributes the self-contradiction in Adam's speech to "the effect of Eve's gender differences on Adam and his struggle to maintain a balance between reciprocity and hierarchy" (53). I believe that Pruitt downplays here the degree to which Adam's words stray from wise thinking.

43. The extent to which Adam's keeping of wisdom is inextricably entwined with his keeping of Eve is emphasized in Fredson Bowers, "Adam, Eve, and the Fall in *Paradise Lost*," *PMLA* 84, no. 2 (1969): 264–73. Regarding 8.562–66, Bowers observes, "By one of those verbal ambiguities which Milton used for profound effect, substitute Eve for Wisdom as the subject of the pronouns 'she' and 'her,' and one has the exact situation just before the Fall when Adam dismisses Eve when he needed her most by him, and she deserts him for Satan" (267). But DiPasquale, in *Refiguring the Sacred Feminine*, seems to miss the point of Raphael's rebuke and again overstates the degree of Eve's wisdom when she argues that "as long as Eve retains her likeness to divine Wisdom, Adam's reverence for her is fully in keeping with his obedience to God" (267). Bowers also suggests that Raphael's rebuke of Adam reflects Milton's own view (266), a claim denied by both Lindenbaum, "Lovemaking in Milton's Paradise," 295, and Pruitt, *Gender and the Power*, 54; both contend that Raphael, as an angel, doesn't rightly comprehend the human complexity of Adam's situation. Pruitt goes so far as to call Raphael's perspective "psychologically skewed" (170n18). By contrast, Thomas A. Copeland, "Raphael, the Angelic Virtue," *Milton Quarterly* 24, no. 4 (1990): 117–28, argues that Milton employs Raphael "to exemplify the nature of virtue" (117). For a developed defense of Raphael's reliability as a narrator, see Marc D. Cyr, "The Archangel Raphael: Narrative Authority in Milton's War in Heaven," *Journal of Narrative Technique* 17, no. 3 (1987): 309–16.

44. Marjorie Hope Nicolson, *John Milton: A Reader's Guide to His Poetry* (New York: Farrar, Straus and Giroux, 1963), 279. For an excellent discussion of Adam's process of choosing passion over "rational love" (2), see Di Benedetto, "Scripture's Constraint." Christopher Tilmouth, "Milton on Knowing Good from Evil," in *John Milton: Life, Writing, Reputation*, edited by Paul Hammond and Blair Worden (Oxford: Oxford University Press, 2010): 43–65, calls Adam "passion's slave" (53) here, but Tilmouth's word choice is not entirely accurate. The point is that Adam, having been thoroughly warned, *chooses* passion.

45. Bowers, "Adam, Eve, and the Fall," 267.

46. I differ on this point with Pruitt, who contends in *Gender and the Power*, 63–67, that Eve's logic in the separation scene equals or even surpasses Adam's. For a discussion of different scholarly positions on Eve's logic here, see Pruitt, 170–71. According to Deborah A. Interdonato, "'Render Me More Equal': Gender Inequality and the Fall in *Paradise Lost* 9," *Milton Quarterly* 29, no. 4 (1995): 95–106, Adam and Eve's conflict springs from how, apart from any "explicit direction from God" (99), they fall into gender inequality. At this point, they "cannot listen to each other in good faith . . . without imposing their own biases on the other" (103).

47. William G. Madsen, *From Shadowy Types to Truth: Studies in Milton's Symbolism* (New Haven: Yale University Press, 1968), 149.

48. Wiznura, "Eve's Dream," 109. For William G. Riggs, "The Temptation of Milton's Eve: 'Words, Impregn'd / With Reason,'" *Journal of English and Germanic Philology* 94, no. 3 (1995): 365–92, Eve's suggestion that she and Adam divide their labors involves a self-absorbed restatement of Adam's earlier celebration of their responsibility to work (see 4.623–29) and demonstrates a "defensive hostility" that "is a reassertion of self-love in a world now recognized as distinct and limiting" (380).

49. Diane Elizabeth Dreher, "Milton's Warning to Puritans in *Paradise Lost*: Another Look at the Separation Scene," *Christianity and Literature* 41, no. 1 (1991): 27–38, suggests that Eve's "excessive zeal" for efficiency is "Milton's warning to his contemporaries not to place labor in their vocation above other duties to God, themselves, and one another" (28).

50. Mary Jo Kietzman, "The Fall into Conversation with Eve: Discursive Difference in *Paradise Lost*," *Criticism* 39, no. 1 (1997): 55–88, quoted at 74. Contending that Adam's main mistake in his response to Eve's argument for efficiency is not so much his failure to exercise proper logic, but rather his failure to make clear to her "his own feelings" until "it is too late" (39), John Ulreich, "'Sufficient to Have Stood': Adam's Responsibility in Book IX," *Milton Quarterly* 5, no. 2 (1971): 38–42, states, "Had [Adam] said simply [immediately after Eve's suggestion that they separate]: 'Efficiency is beside the point, for we belong together; you are "flesh of my flesh" (VIII.495), and I can't get on without you,' the matter might have ended there" (39). Although I think Ulreich's statement does not sufficiently acknowledge the extent to which Eve's heart already has inclined away from Adam, I agree with him that Adam fails to lead emotionally as well as rationally.

51. Gordon Teskey, *The Poetry of John Milton* (Cambridge, Mass.: Harvard University Press, 2015), 440; Stanley Fish, *How Milton Works* (Cambridge, Mass.: Belknap Press of Harvard University Press, 2001), 544. At this point, Interdonato, "'Render Me More Equal,'" argues that Eve's "feelings of inferiority" and "ignorance of self" prevent her from hearing "the part of Adam's argument that emerges from heartfelt concern and wise caution" (101). There is truth in this claim, but Interdonato ignores the influence of Eve's Satan-induced dream on her behavior here.

52. McColley, *Milton's Eve*, 171, observes that Adam's insecurity here damages the rhetorical effectiveness of his sincerity.

53. Kietzman, "Fall into Conversation," 75.

54. These words display a wrongheaded application of the discussion of "double honour" in 1 Timothy 5:17. See David V. Urban, "An Allusion to 1 Timothy 5:17 in John Milton's *Paradise Lost* 9.332," *Notes and Queries* 63 (2016): 59.

55. Riggs, "Temptation of Milton's Eve," 382.

56. Teskey, *Poetry of John Milton*, 444.

57. Anthony Low, "The Parting in the Garden in *Paradise Lost*," *Philological Quarterly* 47, no. 1 (1968): 30–35, quoted at 35.

58. Low, 35.

59. Low, 35; Dennis Danielson, *Milton's Good God: A Study in Literary Theodicy* (Cambridge: Cambridge University Press, 1982), 127; Fish, *How Milton Works*, 533.

60. Low, "Parting in the Garden," 35. See also the similar argument of J. M. Evans, *Milton and the Genesis Tradition* (Oxford: Clarendon Press, 1968), 273. Stella P. Revard, "Eve and the Doctrine of Responsibility in *Paradise Lost*," *PMLA* 88, no. 1 (1973): 69–78, offers a similar but less forceful scenario when she writes that Adam should have "overcome his own feelings of rejection and voiced the loving plea which might have won his wife's consent. Thus he would have led her to choose wisely, not merely left her free to choose" (73). In a reading the language of which curiously suggests that Adam actually constrains Eve's free will in the opposite direction, Christopher Koester writes in "Solitude and Difference in Books 8 and 9 of *Paradise Lost*," *Milton Studies* 57 (2016): 155–84, that "Adam suddenly *insists* that she go" (171, emphasis added).

61. This dynamic explains why, as I put it in "The Falls of Satan, Eve, and Adam in Milton's *Paradise Lost*: A Study in Insincerity," *Christianity and Literature* 67, no. 1 (2017): 89–112, "Milton depicts Eve's departure as both unwise yet also sincere" (99).

62. See Lieb, *Dialectics of Creation*, 192–94.

63. John Bradshaw, *A Concordance to the Poetical Works of John Milton* (1894; reprint, Kennebunkport: Longwood Press, 1977), 332. Significantly, as Paul Hammond observes in

"Milton and the Poetry of the Fall," in Hammond and Worden, *Milton: Life, Writing, Reputation*, 67–89, crucial to Satan's rhetoric of seduction is "avoiding the careful analysis of key terms" (81). Satan makes such pronouncements, and the confused and flattered Eve appears to accept them even as Satan's assertive rhetoric prevents the necessary analysis of the terms he employs. As John Leonard comments in *Naming in Paradise: Milton and the Language of Adam and Eve* (Oxford: Clarendon Press, 1990), "Where Satan had been a master of rhetoric, Eve has become its slave" (209).

64. Leonard, *Naming in Paradise*, 202–3, discusses the rhetorical effectiveness of Satan's polytheistic language.

65. Bradshaw, *Concordance to the Poetical Works*, 5.

66. Riggs, "Temptation of Milton's Eve," 383.

67. Hammond, "Milton and the Poetry of the Fall," 80.

68. Hammond, 81. As I note in "Falls of Satan," Eve's speech "strikingly resembles Satan's in its content, syntax, and attitude toward God," and also makes clear Eve's self-justifying "choice to disobey God" and "demonstrates that her disobedience is a calculated decision" (99–100).

69. Hammond, "Milton and the Poetry of the Fall," 81. Hammond quotes Psalm 111:10 (Geneva Bible).

70. Lieb, *Dialectics of Creation*, 197.

71. C. S. Lewis, *A Preface to "Paradise Lost"* (Oxford: Oxford University Press, 1942), 122; Garrett A. Sullivan Jr., *Sleep, Romance, and Human Embodiment: Vitality from Spenser to Milton* (Cambridge: Cambridge University Press, 2012), 108. Recently, Seth Lobis, "Milton's Tended Garden and the Georgic Fall," *Milton Studies* 55 (2014): 89–111, has noted that Eve's satanic worship of the "Sovran" tree instead of God, the "sovran Planter" (4.691) she and Adam worshipped the day before, "turns the proper vertical order of creation upside down"; Lobis calls Eve's worship of the tree "an idolatrous parody of" Adam and Eve's "morning hymn" in book 5 (101).

72. Lewis, *Preface to "Paradise Lost,"* 122; Lieb, *Dialectics of Creation*, 196. See also Arnold Stein, *Answerable Style: Essays on "Paradise Lost"* (Minneapolis: University of Minnesota Press, 1953), 95.

73. In his *Preface to "Paradise Lost,"* Lewis writes, "I am not sure that critics always notice the precise sin which Eve is now committing, yet there is no mystery in it. Its name in English is murder" (121). And Russell M. Hillier writes of Eve's "'preposterous' self-love that leads to homicidal tendencies." Hillier, "The Good Communicated: Milton's Drama of the Fall and the Law of Charity," *Modern Language Review* 103, no. 1 (2008): 1–21, quoted at 21.

74. In "Choosing Death: Adam's Temptation to Martyrdom in *Paradise Lost,*" *Milton Studies* 46 (2007): 30–56, Margaret Justice Dean notes that "Adam becomes a false martyr," demonstrating an "idolatrous" commitment "to wrong causes (Eve, marriage, martyrdom itself)" (41). Commenting on Adam's agony in lines 911–13, as he is faced with the prospect of losing Eve, James Nohrnberg, in "The Religion of Adam and Eve in *Paradise Lost,*" *Religion and Literature* 45, no. 1 (2013): 160–79, writes, "Adam sees himself suffering an ongoing emotional trauma—virtually an affective stigmata, since his side-wound was typologically equated with Christ's" (167). Nohrnberg's observation may be connected with the position that Adam's decision to die with Eve is Christlike (see n. 76 below).

75. Fish, *Surprised by Sin*, 263.

76. David Quint, *Inside "Paradise Lost": Reading the Designs of Milton's Epic* (Princeton: Princeton University Press, 2014), 189; see also Waldock, *"Paradise Lost" and Its Critics*,

51–60, for a defense of Adam's Christlike decision to die because of his "true love" for Eve (52). John Peter, *A Critique of "Paradise Lost"* (New York: Columbia University Press, 1960), 130–32, follows Waldock's defense of Adam, even calling his decision to eat the fruit "a necessary and courageous sacrifice" (131); John S. Tanner, *Anxiety in Eden: A Kierkegaardian Reading of "Paradise Lost"* (Oxford: Oxford University Press, 1992), 115, expresses a view similar to Waldock's. Michael Bryson and Arpi Movsesian, *Love and Its Critics: From the Song of Songs to Shakespeare and Milton's Eden* (Cambridge: Open Book, 2017), lauds Adam's "courage" because "Adam chooses a human life, a life of love rather than an existence of obedience" (499), but this is a false dichotomy, flying in the face of Adam's repentant realization that "to obey is best, / And love with fear the only God" (12.561–62). I have discussed Adam's fall into theological and romantic self-deception in "Falls of Satan," 103–7.

77. Instead of seeing Adam's narcissism in 9.956–59, Christopher Koester writes that "though he claims that 'to lose thee would be to lose myself,' it is clear that Adam has already lost his sense of identity. His sense of self now appears entirely subsumed within Eve's." "Solitude and Difference," 177.

78. Lewis, *Preface to "Paradise Lost,"* 123.

79. Dennis Danielson, "Through the Telescope of Typology: What Adam Should Have Done," *Milton Quarterly* 23 (1989): 121–27; Leonard, *Naming in Paradise*, 217–19. Hillier also affirms this view in "Good Communicated," 19.

80. Anne Davidson Ferry, in *Milton's Epic Voice: The Narrator in "Paradise Lost"* (Cambridge, Mass.: Harvard University Press, 1963), observes that Adam's decision "to die with Eve, not for her" is grounded in the fact that "his fear is for his own loneliness without her, not for her plight" (60).

81. John Savoie, "'That Fallacious Fruit': Lapsarian Lovemaking in *Paradise Lost*," *Milton Quarterly* 45, no. 3 (2011): 161–71, analyzes at length Adam and Eve's fallen sexual expression.

82. See especially Daniel W. Doerksen, "'Let There Be Peace': Eve as Redemptive Peacemaker in *Paradise Lost*, Book X," *Milton Quarterly* 31, no. 4 (1997): 124–30, and the studies Doerksen cites. Thomas Festa, "Eve and the Ironic Theodicy of the New Milton Criticism," in *The New Milton Criticism*, edited by Peter C. Herman and Elizabeth Sauer (Cambridge: Cambridge University Press, 2012), 175–93, at 186, notes that various eighteenth-century commentators, most prominently Jonathan Richardson the elder, saw this scene "biographically," with Eve representing Mary Powell and Adam representing Milton.

83. Leah Whittington, in "Milton's Poetics of Supplication," *Milton Studies* 55 (2014): 113–45, demonstrates how Adam and Eve's repentant supplication and reconciliation in book 10 imitate the Son's words and actions on various levels.

84. 1 Corinthians 13:13, Saint Paul writes, "And now abideth faith, hope, charity, these three; but the greatest of these is charity." A. E. Dyson, "Virtue Unwavering: Milton's *Comus*," in *Milton: "Comus" and "Samson Agonistes"; A Casebook*, edited by Julian Lovelock (London: Macmillan, 1975), 106–33 quoted at 108.

85. Zwierlein, "'Thyself in Me,'" 92.

86. For the most recent extended study of the "paradise within" of 12.587, one that is germane to the concerns of this chapter, see Joshua R. Held, "Eve's 'Paradise Within' in *Paradise Lost*: A Stoic Mind, a Love Sonnet, and a Good Conscience," *Studies in Philology* 114, no. 1 (2017): 171–96.

Chapter 7

1. See Stephen M. Fallon, *Milton's Peculiar Grace: Self-Representation and Authority* (Ithaca: Cornell University Press, 2007), 237–63.

2. Cedric C. Brown notes in connection to this passage in *Paradise Regained* that Milton in the first *Defense* "reminded his readers that Solomon was lured into idolatry by his various wives." Brown, "Milton and the Idolatrous Consort," *Criticism* 35, no. 3 (1993): 419–39, quoted at 421.

3. See, for example, Gregory Bredbeck, "Milton's Ganymede: Negotiations of Homo-erotic Tradition in *Paradise Lost*," *PMLA* 106 (1991): 262–76; Philip Rollinson, "The Homo-erotic Aspect of Temptation in *Paradise Regained*," *English Language Notes* 32, no. 2 (1995): 31–35; Claude J. Summers, "The (Homo)sexual Temptation in Milton's *Paradise Regain'd*," *Journal of Homosexuality* 33, nos. 3–4 (1997): 45–69; John T. Shawcross, "Milton's *Paradise Regain'd* and the Second Temptation," *ANQ* 21, no. 2 (2008): 34–41; David V. Urban, "The Homosexual Temptation of the Son in Milton's *Paradise Regained*: A Reply to John T. Shawcross and Claude J. Summers, *Connotations: A Journal for Critical Debate* 21, nos. 2–3 (2011–12): 272–77.

4. Barbara Kiefer Lewalski, *Milton's Brief Epic: The Genre, Meaning, and Art of "Paradise Regained"* (Providence: Brown University Press, 1966), 224; Rollinson, "Homoerotic Aspect of Temptation," 32.

5. *Oxford English Dictionary Online*, s.v. "temperately," definition b. See Bryan Adams Hampton, *Fleshly Tabernacles: Milton and the Incarnational Poetics of Revolutionary England* (Notre Dame: University of Notre Dame Press, 2012), 206–23, for an extensive discussion of the Son's temperance in *Paradise Regained*. Earlier, Hampton notes that Milton connects temperance to virginity and chastity (177).

6. Eric B. Song, "'Unspeakable Desire to See, and Know': *Paradise Regained* and the Political Theology of Privacy," in "'Relation Stands': Essays on *Paradise Regained*," edited by John Rogers, special issue, *Huntington Library Quarterly* 76, no. 1 (2013): 137–60, quoted at 149.

7. My more conventional interpretation of "manlier objects" goes against that of Bred-beck, who argues in "Milton's Ganymede" that "these 'manlier objects' are figured homoerot-ically by the allusion to Ganymede and Hylas" (272). But Bredbeck quotes only 2.225–26a, ending at "constancy." The words that follow suggest that the "manlier objects" would elicit "honor, glory, and popular praise" (227), which the Son would forfeit were he to pursue homosexual gratification.

8. Theresa M. DiPasquale, *Refiguring the Sacred Feminine: The Poems of John Donne, Aemilia Lanyer, and John Milton* (Pittsburgh: Duquesne University Press, 2008), 307. For analysis of virtuous self-government in the Son of *Paradise Regained* and Samson's failure to exercise such self-government, see David V. Urban, "Liberty, License, and Virtuous Self-Government in John Milton's Writings," *Journal of Markets and Morality* 17, no. 1 (2014): 143–66, at 156–60.

9. David A. Harper, "'Perhaps More Than Enough': The Dangers of Mate-Idolatry in Milton's *Samson Agonistes*," *Milton Quarterly* 37, no. 3 (2003): 139–51, pursues a valuable theme in arguing that Samson's loss of favor with the God of Israel is brought about by his idolatry of Dalila.

10. Laura Lunger Knoppers, "'Sung and Proverb'd for a Fool': *Samson Agonistes* and Samson's Harlot," *Milton Studies* 26 (1990): 239–51, quoted at 243.

11. Fallon, *Milton's Peculiar Grace*, 258, 257. Along these same lines, see Helen Lynch, *Milton and the Politics of Public Speech* (Burlington, Vt.: Ashgate, 2015), 199–202.

12. Anna K. Nardo, "'Sung and Proverb'd for a Fool': Samson as Fool and Trickster," *Mosaic* 22, no. 1 (1989): 1–16, commenting on the larger Samson tradition, notes that "because [Samson] yields his secrets to importunate women, his enemies can render him impotent. In symbolic castrations, they cut off his hair and put out his eyes" (4). Drew Daniel, in *The Melancholy Assemblage: Affect and Epistemology in the English Renaissance* (New York: Fordham University Press, 2013), writes that "the sexual shaming implicit in Samson's capture, blinding, and shaving is both the occasion for the destruction of his masculinity and a priming condition or vector for his melancholy" (207). Christopher Kendrick, "Typological Impulses in *Samson Agonistes*," *University of Toronto Quarterly* 84, no. 2 (2015): 1–30, suggests that the Philistines' blinding of Samson carries with it their message that Samson "will look at our women no longer" (17).

13. See John T. Shawcross, *The Uncertain World of "Samson Agonistes"* (Cambridge: D. S. Brewer, 2001), 7–8.

14. For intriguing discussions of how Samson's rejection of Dalila shows that he is following the precepts of Milton's divorce tracts and consequently attaining spiritual regeneration, see Dayton Haskin, "Divorce as a Path to Union with God in *Samson Agonistes*," *ELH* 38 (1971): 358–76; and Ricki Heller, "Opposites of Wifehood: Eve and Dalila," *Milton Studies* 24 (1988): 187–202. Also connecting Samson and the divorce tracts is Catherine Gimelli Martin's essay "Dalila, Misogyny, and Milton's Christian Liberty of Divorce," in *Milton and Gender*, edited by Catherine Gimelli Martin (Cambridge: Cambridge University Press, 2004), 53–74, which, drawing considerable parallels between Milton and Samson, focuses on the appropriateness of Samson's divorce from Dalila, highlighting the fault of both characters and their mutual unfitness for marriage to each other. See also Elizabeth Sauer, "Pious Fraud: Extralegal Heroism in *Samson Agonistes*," *SEL: Studies in English Literature, 1500–1900* 53, no. 1 (2013): 179–96, which examines Samson and Dalila's exogamous relationship in relation to Milton's divorce tracts but also analyzes the couple's "complementarity" with relation to their respective "heroic self-sacrifices made in the name of *pietas*" (180).

15. Jackie DiSalvo, "'Spiritual Contagion': Male Psychology and the Culture of Idolatry in *Samson Agonistes*," in *Altering Eyes: New Perspectives on "Samson Agonistes*," edited by Mark R. Kelley and Joseph Wittreich (Newark: University of Delaware Press, 2002), 253–80, quoted at 256. Barbara K. Lewalski, "*Samson Agonistes* and the 'Tragedy' of the Apocalypse," *PMLA* 85 (1970): 1050–62, suggests that Dalila "foreshadows" "the Great Whore of Babylon, the epitome of all idolatry and sensuality, with whom the kings of the earth have committed fornication (idolatry)" (1059, 1058; see Rev. 17:3–7).

16. See Derek N. C. Wood, *"Exiled from Light": Divine Law, Morality, and Violence in Milton's "Samson Agonistes"* (Toronto: University of Toronto Press, 2001), 99–117, for a particularly strong defense of Dalila's character against Samson and various critics. See also William Empson, "A Defense of Dalila," *Sewanee Review* 68, no. 2 (1960): 240–55; and Joyce Colony, "An Argument for Milton's Dalila," *Yale Review* 66, no. 4 (1977): 562–75.

17. Gordon Teskey, *The Poetry of John Milton* (Cambridge, Mass.: Harvard University Press, 2015), 531; Susanne Woods, "Choice and Election in *Samson Agonistes*," in *Milton and the Grounds of Contention*, edited by Mark R. Kelley, Michael Lieb, and John T. Shawcross (Pittsburgh: Duquesne University Press, 2003), 174–87, quoted at 182.

18. Michael Lieb, *The Sinews of Ulysses: Form and Convention in Milton's Works* (Pittsburgh: Duquesne University Press, 1989), 126.

19. Fallon, *Milton's Peculiar Grace*, 257.

20. Edward K. Chambers, in his edition of *Samson Agonistes* (London: Blackie and Son, 1897), notes this at line 936.

21. Harper, "'Perhaps More Than Enough,'" 148; Paula Loscocco, "'Not Less Renown'd Than Jael': Heroic Chastity in *Samson Agonistes*," *Milton Studies* 40 (2001): 181–200, at 187, 181.

22. Lynch, *Politics of Public Speech*, 118.

23. John P. Rumrich, *Milton Unbound: Controversy and Reinterpretation* (Cambridge: Cambridge University Press, 1996), 90–93, discusses similarities between the Lady and Samson. Elsewhere, connecting Samson to the Lady, unfallen Adam and Eve, and the Son of *Paradise Regained*, Rumrich writes, "Milton's heroes resemble one another in that the temperance of the Nazarite—like that of the virgin, like that of unfallen humanity, like that of Jesus—depends on abstention." Rumrich, "Samson and the Excluded Middle," in Kelley and Wittreich, *Altering Eyes*, 307–32, at 319.

24. Thomas Kranidas, "Dalila's Role in *Samson Agonistes*," *SEL: Studies in English Literature, 1500–1900* 6, no. 1 (1966): 125–37, quoted at 135. But see Elizabeth Sauer, "Pious Fraud," 185–88, for a more complicated reading of Dalila's religious motivations for betraying Samson. Lynne A. Greenberg, "Dalila's 'Feminine Assaults': The Gendering and Engendering of Crime in *Samson Agonistes*," in Kelley and Wittreich, *Altering Eyes*, 192–219, argues that in betraying Samson, the "vulnerable" Dalia "lacks independent agency or freedom to choose." Rather, she is "required to act against her own interests for the sake of her survival" (211); but her speech at lines 850–70 also suggests that she is motivated by a desire for honor and glory (see esp. line 856) that anticipates her eventual gloating just before her departure from Samson.

25. Hampton, *Fleshly Tabernacles*, 190–91. Similarly, Loscocco, "'Not Less Renown'd Than Jael,'" describes Samson as "God's recovered spouse" (192).

26. Manoa's trustworthiness here is affirmed by Michael R. G. Spiller, "Directing the Audience in *Samson Agonistes*," in *Of Poetry and Politics: New Essays on Milton and His World*, edited by P. G. Stanwood (Binghamton, N.Y.: Medieval and Renaissance Texts and Studies, 1995), 121–29, at 123–25; Spiller argues that Milton uses Manoa here to direct his audience's understanding of Samson, his final act, and his legacy.

27. See Martin E. Mueller, "Pathos and Katharsis in *Samson Agonistes*," *ELH* 31 (1964): 156–74, at 162–68 (quotation at 157).

28. Judith H. Anderson, "Patience and Passion in Shakespeare and Milton," *Spenser Studies* 21 (2006): 205–20, at 207.

29. *The Riverside Milton*, edited by Roy Flannagan (Boston: Houghton Mifflin, 1998), 844n326.

Preface to Part 3

1. Barbara K. Lewalski, *The Life of John Milton: A Critical Biography* (Oxford: Blackwell, 2000), 37. My discussion in the first three paragraphs of this preface to part 3 are somewhat anticipated in Lewalski, "Milton: The Muses, the Prophets, the Spirit, and Prophetic Poetry," *Milton Studies* 54 (2013): 59–78, at 62–67.

2. Citations of "Elegy 6" are from *The Riverside Milton*, edited by Roy Flannagan (Boston: Houghton Mifflin, 1998).

3. Lewalski, "Milton: The Muses," 62–63, discusses Milton's use of Isaiah 6 in the nativity ode (December 1629).

4. John Milton, *The Doctrine and Discipline of Divorce* (1st ed.), in *The Divorce Tracts of John Milton: Texts and Contexts*, edited by Sara J. van den Berg and W. Scott Howard (Pittsburgh: Duquesne University Press, 2010) (hereafter *DDD*), 47.

5. See especially Stephen M. Fallon, "'The Spur of Self-Concernment': Milton in His Divorce Tracts," *Milton Studies* 38 (2000): 220–42, revised in *Milton's Peculiar Grace: Self-Representation and Authority* (Ithaca: Cornell University Press, 2007), 110–36.

6. See *DDD* (1st ed.), 50, 70; *DDD* (2nd ed.), in Van den Berg and Howard, *Divorce Tracts of John Milton*, 112, 115, 158; and *CPW*, 2:249, 253, 312.

7. See Fallon, *Milton's Peculiar Grace*, 110–20, for an extended discussion of Milton's self-exoneration in *DDD*.

Chapter 8

1. Dayton Haskin, *Milton's Burden of Interpretation* (Philadelphia: University of Pennsylvania Press, 1994), 51.

2. Matthew Poole, *A Commentary on the Holy Bible*, 3 vols. (1685; reprint, London: Banner of Truth, 1963), 3:66. John Calvin offers a somewhat different interpretation: "Many of the older writers understand 'new and old' as meaning the Law and the Gospel. But this seems forced to me. I take it more simply as the varied and manifold dispensation by which they [the 'doctors of the Church'] wisely and aptly accommodate the teaching to the grasp of each individual." Calvin, *Harmony of the Gospels: Matthew, Mark, and Luke*, translated by T. H. L. Parker, edited by David W. Torrance and Thomas F. Torrance, 3 vols. (Grand Rapids: Eerdmans, 1979), 2:84. Milton's own understanding of the parable, with his emphasis on the continued validity of the Mosaic teachings concerning divorce, clearly more closely resembles the interpretation of Poole and the "older writers" with whom Calvin disagrees.

3. Milton's translation in the second edition reads as follows: "Every Scribe instructed to the Kingdome of Heav'n, is like the Maister of a house which bringeth out of his treasury ['treasurie' in the first edition] things new and old." *CPW*, 2:221.

4. Haskin, *Milton's Burden of Interpretation*, 73.

5. Stephen De Courcelles, preface to James Arminius, *Examination of the Theses of Dr. Francis Gomarus Respecting Predestination*, translated by William Nichols, in *The Works of James Arminius: The London Edition*, edited by Carl Bangs, 3 vols. (1825–75; reprint, Grand Rapids: Baker, 1991), 3:522–25, quoted at 522.

6. William Cooper, preface to Jonathan Edwards, *The Distinguishing Marks of a Work of the Spirit of God*, in *The Great Awakening*, edited by C. C. Goen (New Haven: Yale University Press, 1972), 215–25, quoted at 224.

7. Douglas Trevor, *The Poetics of Melancholy in Early Modern England* (Cambridge: Cambridge University Press, 2004), 178.

8. *CPW*, 2:224n11. See also Edmund C. White, "'Uniform in Virtue': Discipline and Reform in Milton's *Doctrine and Discipline of Divorce* (1643 and 1644)," *Prose Studies* 36, no. 2 (2014): 97–116. White states that in the 1643 first edition of *DDD*, Milton positions himself and his advocacy of the doctrine and discipline of divorce against the "antithetical, undesirable extremes" of "the erroneous strictures of canon law," on one hand, and "the licentious mores of antinomian fanatics," on the other (104). It is worth noting that although he makes no use of the parable, John Calvin, in the prefatory address to King Francis that preceded the original 1536 version of his *Institutes of the Christian Religion*, claims that the Reformed Christianity he espouses is "not . . . some new gospel" but "that very gospel" of "Jesus Christ

and his disciples," now "restored to us by God's goodness" after having been "long unknown and buried" because of "man's impiety." See Calvin, *Institutes of the Christian Religion*, translated by Ford Lewis Battles, edited by John T. McNeil, 2 vols. (Philadelphia: Westminster Press, 1960), 1:16.

9. Haskin, *Milton's Burden of Interpretation*, 35.

10. Arthur Barker, *Milton and the Puritan Dilemma, 1641–1660* (Toronto: University of Toronto Press, 1942), 67.

11. R. Kenneth Kirby, "Milton's Biblical Hermeneutics in *The Doctrine and Discipline of Divorce*," *Milton Quarterly* 18, no. 4 (1984): 116–25, quoted at 118. More recently, Shari A. Zimmerman, "Disaffection, Dissimulation, and the Uncertain Ground of Silent Dismission: Juxtaposing John Milton and Elizabeth Carey," *ELH* 66, no. 3 (1999): 553–89, at 575–76 and 587, has discussed Milton's suspiciously novel use of the prophet Malachi's pronouncements against divorce (2:10–16) to justify an unhappy man's divorcing his wife.

12. See Sara J. van den Berg and W. Scott Howard, "Introduction: Milton's Divorce Tracts and the Temper of the Times," in *The Divorce Tracts of John Milton: Texts and Contexts*, edited by Sara J. van den Berg and W. Scott Howard (Pittsburgh: Duquesne University Press, 2010), 1–35, at 11–14, for discussion of Milton's personal, even mystical, reading of scripture in his divorce tracts. Amy R. McCready, in "Milton's Casuistry: The Case of *The Doctrine and Discipline of Divorce*," *Journal of Medieval and Renaissance Studies* 22, no. 3 (1992): 393–428, also challenges Barker's and Kirby's assertion that reason is paramount to Milton's hermeneutic in *DDD*. McCready argues that Milton interprets the Bible by "using a casuistical method" (393), employing "conscience" as his "guide for interpreting Scripture" (408).

13. Just before the quoted phrases, Milton claims to base his stated Pauline conception of "charity" on Ephesians 4:14–15. This passage reads, "that we henceforth be no more children, tossed to and fro, and carried about with every wind of doctrine, by the sleight of men, and cunning craftiness, whereby they lie in wait to deceive; but speaking the truth in love, may grow up into him in all things, which is the head, even Christ." We may legitimately question how Milton can reasonably base his allegedly Pauline hermeneutic on this passage. Milton's statement does, however, echo Augustine's *On Christian Doctrine*, 3.15.23, which asserts this principle: "what is read should be subjected to diligent scrutiny until an interpretation contributing to the reign of charity is produced" (D. W. Robertson's translation [New York: Macmillan, 1958], 93).

14. Stanley Fish, *How Milton Works* (Cambridge, Mass.: Belknap Press of Harvard University Press, 2001), 521.

15. In Van den Berg and Howard, *Divorce Tracts of John Milton*, see William Prynne, *Twelve Considerable Serious Questions* (1644), in Van den Berg and Howard, *Divorce Tracts of John Milton*, 394–95; Herbert Palmer, *The Glasse of Gods Providence* (1644), 398; and Daniel Fealty, *The Dippers Dipt* (1645), 450. For a discussion of how Milton defends divorce as a proper exercise of Christian liberty to combat licentiousness, see David V. Urban, "Liberty, License, and Virtuous Self-Government in John Milton's Writings," *Journal of Markets and Morality* 17, no. 1 (2014): 143–66, at 150–51. See also David Hawkes, "The Politics of Character in Milton's Divorce Tracts," *Journal of the History of Ideas* 62 (2001): 141–60, at 151–54.

16. Stephen M. Fallon, *Milton's Peculiar Grace: Self-Representation and Authority* (Ithaca: Cornell University Press, 2007), 116. See also Jennifer L. Nichols, "Milton's Claim for Self and Freedom in the Divorce Tracts," *Milton Studies* 49 (2009): 192–211, which argues that throughout his divorce tracts, Milton asserts that "one can control one's physical makeup

through righteous or unrighteous acts," a claim that Milton makes "out of an apparent need to see not just his soul but also his body as pure" (195).

17. Fish, *How Milton Works*, 236. Similarly, John Leonard, *The Value of Milton* (Cambridge: Cambridge University Press, 2016), agrees that in *DDD* "Milton wrenches scripture" (48). Cf. Christopher D'Addario, who writes in "Against Fescues and Ferulas: Personal Affront and the Path to Individual Liberty in Milton's Early Prose," in *The New Milton Criticism*, edited by Peter C. Herman and Elizabeth Sauer (Cambridge: Cambridge University Press, 2012), 139–55, that Milton's "heretical opinion on divorce," in which he "unabashedly reinterprets Christ's injunctions," is "justified with a radical theory of Scriptural exegesis" (147). Consider also Victoria Kahn, "'The Duty to Love': Passion and Obligation in Early Modern Political Theory," *Representations* 68 (Autumn 1999): 84–107, which suggests that "irremediable and resistless passion" largely motivates Milton's argument (92). I believe that Regina M. Schwartz, "Milton on the Bible," in *A Companion to Milton*, edited by Thomas N. Corns (Malden, Mass.: Blackwell, 2001), 37–54, correctly emphasizes the role of charity in Milton's hermeneutic in *DDD* but overstates the importance of reason in this hermeneutic. Schwartz summarizes Milton's position as follows: "In his charity, God has made available to human reason the justness and goodness—indeed the charity of his laws. . . . The Bible lay open to human reason; and, interpreted according to the principle of charity, God's justice and goodness also lay open to reason" (40). According to McCready, "Milton's Casuistry," readers of *DDD* can substitute "conscience" for Milton's uses of "charity" (415).

18. Peggy Samuels provides a compelling account of Milton's novel hermeneutic methodology of imitating Christ in *DDD*, asserting that Milton, moving away from the plain meaning of Christ's teaching against divorce, which proclaims him "an adulterer," pursues "the rewriting of Christ from the fragments of scripture available." Samuels, "Dueling Erasers: Milton and Scripture," *Studies in Philology* 96, no. 2 (1999): 180–203, quoted at 189, 192.

19. Calvin, *Institutes of the Christian Religion*; William Ames, *The Marrow of Sacred Divinity [Medulla Theologica]*, translated and edited by John Dykstra Eusden (Boston: Pilgrim, 1968); Johannes Wollebius, *Compendium Theologiae Christianae*, translated by John W. Beardslee III, in *Reformed Dogmatics*, edited by John W. Beardslee III (New York: Oxford University Press, 1965), 29–262; *Works of James Arminius* (as noted above, De Courcelles does cite the parable in his introduction, but Arminius himself makes no reference to Matt. 13:52). For discussions of Ames's and especially Wollebius's influences on *DDC*, see Maurice Kelley, "Milton's Debt to Wolleb's *Compendium Theologiae Christianae*," *PMLA* 50, no. 1 (1935): 156–65; Kelley, *This Great Argument: A Study of Milton's "De doctrina Christiana" as a Gloss upon "Paradise Lost"* (Princeton: Princeton University Press, 1941); and Kelley's introduction to annotations of vol. 6 of *CPW*, *Christian Doctrine*. More recently, see Jason A. Kerr and John K. Hale, "The Origins and Development of Milton's Theology in *De doctrina Christiana*, 1.17–18," *Milton Studies* 54 (2013): 181–206.

20. Basil Willey, *The Seventeenth-Century Background: Studies in the Thought of the Age in Relation to Poetry and Religion* (New York: Columbia University Press, 1950), 72.

21. The Westminster Larger Catechism, answer 4, states that "the Spirit of God bearing witness by and with the Scriptures in the heart of man, is alone able fully to persuade it that they are the very word of God," at https://www.opc.org/lc.html (accessed June 20, 2018). John Calvin states that scripture's "certainty" in the hearts of believers is attained "by the testimony of the Spirit." *Institutes of the Christian Religion*, 1:80 (bk. 1, chap. 7, sec. 4).

22. For discussions of Milton's use of the Bible in *DDC*, see George Newton Conklin, *Biblical Criticism and Heresy in Milton* (1949; reprint, New York: Octagon Books, 1972), 32–40; and Michael Lieb, *Theological Milton: Deity, Discourse, and Heresy in the Miltonic Canon* (Pittsburgh: Duquesne University Press, 2006), 15–50. For a recent discussion of parallels between Milton's divorce tracts and *DDC*, see Sharon Achinstein, "*De Doctrina Christiana*: Milton's Last Divorce Tract?" *Milton Quarterly* 51, no. 3 (2017): 153–62. My phrase "Spirit itself" (as opposed to "himself") is in keeping with the majority of Milton's pronoun references to the Spirit in his prose. (Cf. the Authorized Version's rendition of Rom. 8:16: "The Spirit itself beareth witness . . .")

23. Doubts about Milton's authorship of *DDC*—raised most fully by William B. Hunter, *Visitation Unimplor'd: Milton and the Authorship of "De Doctrina Christiana"* (Pittsburgh: Duquesne University Press, 1998)—have largely (but not entirely) disappeared from Milton studies since the publication of Gordon Campbell, Thomas N. Corns, John K. Hale, and Fiona J. Tweedie, *Milton and the Manuscript of "De Doctrina Christiana"* (Oxford: Oxford University Press, 2007). Nonetheless, it is worth noting that the similar manifestations of the parable of the householder in *DDD* and *DDC* reinforce the authenticity of *DDC* as a Miltonic text. Milton's authorship is all the more plausible in light of both works' similar emphasis on an enlightened spiritual interpretation of the biblical text alone—apart from the corrupt influence of church tradition—and a hermeneutic founded on and guided by the principle of charity. Alternatively, in light of the still valuable insights of Michael Lieb's "*De Doctrina Christiana* and the Question of Authorship," *Milton Studies* 41 (2002): 172–230, which discusses the problematic nature of ascribing complete authorship of *DDC* to any one individual, we might more cautiously assert that at least the parts of *DDC* that cite the parable of the householder are likely to be authentically Miltonic. Also significant to this discussion is John K. Hale and J. Donald Cullington, "*Universis Christi Ecclesiis*: Milton's Epistle for *De Doctrina Christiana*," *Milton Studies* 53 (2012): 3–15, at 12, which detects an allusion to the parable of the householder (not explicitly referenced in the text) in the introductory epistle of *DDC*, the portion of *DDC* that even Hunter concedes is probably Milton's (see *Visitation Unimplor'd*, 156). For recent challenges to the Miltonic authenticity of *DDC*, see Ernest Sullivan's review of Campbell et al., *Milton and the Manuscript, Review of English Studies* 60, no. 243 (2009): 153–54; Filippo Falcone, "More Challenges to Milton's Authorship of *De Doctrina Christiana*," *ACME* 63 (2010): 231–50; and Filippo Falcone, "*De Doctrina Christiana* and Milton: Elements of Continuity and Discontinuity," *Connotations: A Journal for Critical Debate* 27 (2018): 78–105.

Chapter 9

1. Dayton Haskin, *Milton's Burden of Interpretation* (Philadelphia: University of Pennsylvania Press, 1994), 138.

2. David Daiches, "The Opening of *Paradise Lost*," in *The Living Milton*, edited by Frank Kermode (London: Routledge and Kegan Paul, 1960), 55–69, at 61. More recently, Linda Tredennick, "Exteriority in Milton and Puritan Life Writing," *SEL: Studies in English Literature, 1500–1900* 51, no. 1 (2011): 159–79, calls Milton "a vatic poet, an identity that merges national and moral as well as aesthetic and religious components" (162).

3. For a discussion of the extent to which the reader shares in the scope of Milton's opening invocation, see Anne Davidson Ferry, *Milton's Epic Voice: The Narrator in "Paradise*

Lost" (Cambridge, Mass.: Harvard University Press, 1963), 22–24. See also John Spencer Hill, *John Milton: Poet, Priest, and Prophet; A Study of Divine Vocation in Milton's Poetry and Prose* (London: Macmillan, 1979), which observes that in *Paradise Lost* the "poet-prophet" Milton "turned his attention . . . from national to individual vocation and regeneration" (117).

4. See the preface to part 3 of this book.

5. John T. Shawcross, "Milton and the Visionary Mode: The Early Poems," in *Visionary Milton: Essays on Prophecy and Violence*, edited by Peter E. Medine, John T. Shawcross, and David V. Urban (Pittsburgh: Duquesne University Press, 2010), 3–22, emphasizes that line 26—"And justify the ways of God to men"—"echoes here for us as evidence that Milton believed in his truly being inspired by God" (4).

6. William Kerrigan, *The Prophetic Milton* (Charlottesville: University Press of Virginia, 1974), 126.

7. See Kerrigan, 126–27.

8. Kerrigan, 127.

9. Barbara K. Lewalski, "Milton: The Muses, the Prophets, the Spirit, and Prophetic Poetry," *Milton Studies* 54 (2013): 59–78, at 62–63, 67, recognizes that Milton's belief that purity precedes the poet's inspiration through the Spirit is already evident in the nativity ode and *The Reason of Church-Government*. See also the preface to part 3 of this book.

10. Kerrigan, *Prophetic Milton*, 128.

11. *The Riverside Milton*, edited by Roy Flannagan (Boston: Houghton Mifflin, 1998), 354n23.

12. In this sense, my interpretation goes beyond that of Golda Werman, who asserts in *Milton and Midrash* (Washington, D.C.: Catholic University of America Press, 1995) that Milton "based his doctrinal poem on the first three chapters of the Hebrew Bible and used both the methods and the materials of Midrash to compose a poetic commentary on the Genesis account of the Fall" (1). While I do not seek to dispute Werman's thesis that Milton employed "the methods and the materials of Midrash," I submit that what is going on in *Paradise Lost* is considerably more ambitious than that. In my view, Milton is employing the whole of scripture, by what he believes to be the inspiration of the Holy Spirit, to bring forth the Genesis account in the fullness of its meaning.

13. Andrew Marvell, "On *Paradise Lost*," in *John Milton: Complete Poems and Major Prose*, edited by Merritt Y. Hughes (New York: Macmillan, 1957), 209–10, lines 1–10.

14. Kerrigan, *Prophetic Milton*, 129.

15. Kerrigan, 129.

16. In his essay on *Paradise Lost* in the *Spectator*, January 5, 1712, Joseph Addison, noting the great "Caution" Milton exercised with any poetic additions "of his own Invention," writes that any such additions "bear so close an Analogy with what is delivered in Holy Writ, that it is capable of pleasing the most delicate Reader, without giving Offence to the most scrupulous." Addison, *Criticism on Milton's "Paradise Lost" from "The Spectator,"* edited by Edward Arber (London: Bloomsbury, 1869), 15–20, quoted at 19. I do not share Addison's confidence regarding the cautious nature of Milton's poetic inventions and assertions in *Paradise Lost*. Significantly, Addison is silent on the matter of Milton's claim of inspiration by the Holy Spirit. Some three centuries later, Matthew Stallard echoed Addison's view in his preface to *"Paradise Lost": The Biblically Annotated Edition* (Macon: Mercer University Press, 2011), vii–xxxvi: "At times, Milton makes *Paradise Lost* sound so much like the Bible that one is convinced he is hearing the words of the Bible" (xxiii).

17. Lewalski, "Milton: The Muses," 68–69, 67. Some three decades earlier, in *"Paradise Lost" and the Rhetoric of Literary Forms* (Princeton: Princeton University Press, 1985), Lewalski argued that that Milton "does not claim the extraordinary visions of a John of Patmos. Rather, he hopes for the mediated poetic vision of Dante" (33). Craig T. Fehrman takes a similar position in "Bible, Milton's Use of," in *The Milton Encyclopedia*, edited by Thomas N. Corns (New Haven: Yale University Press, 2012), when he writes that "the internal scripture of the Holy Spirit" (*CPW*, 6:587) of which Milton writes in *DDC* is Milton's "own interpretation of the Bible" (57).

18. Kari Boyd McBride and John C. Ulreich, "Answerable Styles: Biblical Poetics and Biblical Politics in the Poetry of Lanyer and Milton," *Journal of English and Germanic Philology* 100, no. 3 (2001): 333–54, quoted at 339.

19. Jason Rosenblatt, *Torah and Law in "Paradise Lost"* (Princeton: Princeton University Press, 1994), 146. See also Michael Lieb, *The Dialectics of Creation: Patterns of Birth and Regeneration in "Paradise Lost"* (Amherst: University of Massachusetts Press, 1970), 38–42, for discussion of Milton's inspired narrator and Moses.

20. Isabel MacCaffrey, "The Theme of *Paradise Lost*, Book III," in *New Essays on "Paradise Lost*," edited by Thomas Kranidas (Berkeley: University of California Press, 1971), 58–85, quoted at 58.

21. Rosenblatt, *Torah and Law*, 146.

22. See Maurice Kelley, *This Great Argument: A Study of Milton's "De Doctrina Christiana" as a Gloss upon "Paradise Lost"* (Princeton: Princeton University Press, 1941), 14–19, 80–84.

23. Consider also Joseph Addison's words in the *Spectator* of March 1, 1712, written more than a century before the discovery of *DDC*: "He [Milton] dares not give his Imagination its full Play, but chuses to confine himself to such Thoughts as are drawn from the Books of the most Orthodox Divines, and to such Expressions as may be met with in Scripture." Reprinted in Addison, *Criticism on Milton's "Paradise Lost*," 67–74, at 67–68. Stephanie Chidester offers a more skeptical perspective in "Milton's Unapproachable God," *Encyclia* 70 (1993): 39–45, writing, "It is blasphemous to make God in one's own image, and doing so is, in a sense, affecting God-head. Milton, for the most part, refrains from referring to God in human terms, but when he does, he has the excuse that he is being guided by the Holy Spirit, who is, in fact, dictating *Paradise Lost* to this mortal poet" (43).

24. Stevie Davies and William B. Hunter, "Milton's Urania: 'The Meaning, Not the Name I Call,'" *SEL: Studies in English Literature, 1500–1900* 28, no. 1 (1988): 95–111. For perspectives that see the muse of book 7 as distinct from the poem's earlier muses, see Amy Stackhouse, "Sleeping with the Muse: Milton and the Gender of Authorship," *Renaissance Papers* (1999): 137–45, at 144–45; and Lewalski, "Milton: The Muses," 71–73, 77–78.

25. Kerrigan, *Prophetic Milton*, 132–33. Referencing book 7's invocation, R. V. Young, in "Milton and Solitude," *Ben Jonson Journal* 21 (2014): 92–113, suggests that Milton, estranged from the established church and the royal court, was "aesthetically engrossed in his own world of divine inspiration," even as his blindness and social alienation drove him "deeper into spiritual isolation and self-sufficiency" (100).

26. For a discussion of books 11 and 12 as sacred history in light of the whole of scripture, see H. R. MacCallum, "Milton and Sacred History: Books XI and XII of *Paradise Lost*," in *Essays in English Literature from the Renaissance to the Victorian Age, Presented to A. S. P. Woodhouse*, edited by Millar MacLure and F. W. Watt (Toronto: University of Toronto Press, 1964), 149–68. For a discussion of books 11 and 12 as sermonic text, see Jameela Lares, *Milton and the Preaching Arts* (Pittsburgh: Duquesne University Press, 2001), 141–68.

27. Lewalski, "Milton: The Muses," 76.

28. Joseph Wittreich, "Lost Paradise Regained: The Twin Halves of Milton's Epic Vision," *University of Toronto Quarterly* 80, no. 3 (2011): 731–55, quoted at 747. Wittreich's afterword in *The New Milton Criticism*, edited by Peter C. Herman and Elizabeth Sauer (Cambridge: Cambridge University Press, 2012), 231–48, reaffirms this stance regarding both *Paradise Lost* and *Paradise Regained*, stating, "Both epics emerge as a new revelation, a scriptural·supplement" (236).

29. Allan H. Gilbert, "Temptation in *Paradise Regained*," *Journal of English and Germanic Philology* 15, no. 4 (1916): 599–611, quoted at 601–2, 606; Gilbert discusses Calvin at 601–3. Compare the quotations from Addison in nn. 16 and 23 of this chapter.

30. Elizabeth Marie Pope, "*Paradise Regained*": *The Tradition and the Poem* (New York: Russell and Russell, 1962), 2–5.

31. Michael Lieb, *Theological Milton: Deity, Discourse, and Heresy in the Miltonic Canon* (Pittsburgh: Duquesne University Press, 2006), 275.

32. My debt to Haskin, *Milton's Burden of Interpretation*, 131–39, is particularly great, and I commend these pages for a fuller discussion of Milton's Mary as a figure displaying Milton's larger interpretive principles. My discussion of the Son's interpretive "methodology," however, is largely independent of Haskin.

33. The Authorized Version of Luke 2:19 reads: "But Mary kept all these things [the events surrounding Jesus's birth] and pondered them in her heart." Luke 2:51b reads: "his mother kept all these sayings [which were spoken by Jesus during his childhood] in her heart." We may also note with interest that, in these verses, the New International Version, New Revised Standard Version, and English Standard Version all translate both *synetērei* and *dietērei* (which are both translated as "kept" in the Authorized Version) as "treasured" or "treasured up."

34. Milton biographers who explicitly connect this passage to Milton's own life include James Holly Hanford, *John Milton, Englishman* (New York: Crown, 1949), 17; A. L. Rowse, *Milton the Puritan: Portrait of a Mind* (London: Macmillan, 1977), 245–46; and Barbara K. Lewalski, *The Life of John Milton: A Critical Biography* (Oxford: Blackwell, 2000), 511.

35. Merritt Y. Hughes, "The Christ of *Paradise Regained* and the Renaissance Heroic Tradition," *Studies in Philology* 35, no. 2 (1938): 254–77, argues that Milton's focus on the Son in *Paradise Regained* is not theological but is rather a portrait of a supremely ethical man, one who essentially embodies the "Magnanimous Man" of Aristotle's *Nicomachean Ethics*. Barbara Kiefer Lewalski's *Milton's Brief Epic: The Genre, Meaning, and Art of "Paradise Regained"* (Providence: Brown University Press, 1966) includes a chapter titled "The Problem of Christ's Nature" (133–63), which essentially concludes that in *Paradise Regained*, "The incarnate Christ is the occasional recipient of special divine illumination activating the divine in himself, and may revert to the merely or nearly human on other occasions" (159). For the argument that the Son's deity in *Paradise Regained* is much more pronounced, see James H. Sims, *The Bible in Milton's Epics* (Gainesville: University Press of Florida, 1962), 192–200; and Stella P. Revard, "The Gospel of John and *Paradise Regained*: Jesus as 'True Light,'" in *Milton and Scriptural Tradition: The Bible into Poetry*, edited by James H. Sims and Leland Ryken (Columbia: University of Missouri Press, 1984), 142–59.

36. George H. McLoone, "Composing the Uneasy Station: Confession and Absence in *Paradise Regain'd*," *Milton Studies* 45 (2006): 53–81, quoted at 69.

37. In *Refiguring the Sacred Feminine: The Poems of John Donne, Aemilia Lanyer, and John Milton* (Pittsburgh: Duquesne University Press, 2008), Theresa M. DiPasquale notes that

although Mary herself, like Jesus, initially "still thinks of his role in largely political terms," the fact that her words "propel" him to reexamine the scriptures and rightly understand his vocation is what "nonetheless" makes her "an effective teacher" (298). More enthusiastically and, I believe, more appropriately, Joan Curbet Soler, "Towards a Miltonic Mariology: The Word and the Body of Mary in *Paradise Regain'd* (1671)," *Sederi* 22 (2012): 29–50, notes that with Mary's encouragement, the Son "moves from the word of the mother to the Word of God," and that Mary "leads the young Christ towards the Father, and by doing so helps him to acquire a full consciousness of his mission and purpose" (45).

38. Marjorie Hope Nicolson, *John Milton: A Reader's Guide to His Poetry* (New York: Farrar, Straus and Giroux, 1963), 332; Stanley Fish, "Milton and Interpretation," *Milton Studies* 56 (2015): 3–16, at 12. Fish makes his point at 1.280–82, which reads, "But as I rose out of the laving stream, / Heaven open'd her eternal doors, from whence / The Spirit descended on me like a Dove."

39. David Gay, "Astrology and Iconoclasm in Milton's *Paradise Regained*," *SEL: Studies in English Literature, 1500–1900* 41, no. 1 (2001): 175–90, notes that Satan seeks both "to provoke Jesus into producing a material sign of his messianic identity through the performance of a miracle" and "to deprive Jesus of the textual grounds of his identity through an exchange or substitution that supplants scripture by diverting Jesus' mission into demonic paradigms of power rather than grounding it in God's purpose" (176).

40. A. S. P. Woodhouse, "Theme and Pattern in *Paradise Regained*," *University of Toronto Quarterly* 25, no. 2 (1956): 167–82, quoted at 181. My agreement with Woodhouse here runs counter to John Leonard, *The Value of Milton* (Cambridge: Cambridge University Press, 2016), in which Leonard argues that Jesus's quoting of scripture "strikes Satan with amazement" because of Jesus's "*refusal* to play the divine trump. . . . [He] routs Satan in simple terms, as a man" (121, 122). I contend that the force of the Son's scriptural quotation is intensified immeasurably by the divinity of the speaker. For a thorough discussion of the Son's and Satan's respective uses of the Hebrew scriptures throughout their contest, see James H. Sims, "Jesus and Satan as Readers of Scripture in *Paradise Regained*," *Milton Studies* 32 (1995): 187–215. See also David Ainsworth, *Milton and the Spiritual Reader: Reading and Religion in Seventeenth-Century England* (New York: Routledge, 2008), 143–66, for a discussion of how Satan "pushes Jesus into clear and accurate spiritual interpretations" (145).

41. Haskin, *Milton's Burden of Interpretation*, 135–36.

42. Haskin, 136. Commenting on Mary's monologue in book 2, Joseph Mansky, in "Does Relation Stand? Textual and Social Relations in *Paradise Regain'd*," *Milton Studies* 56 (2015): 45–72, writes that "Mary overcomes this trial in the same way as Jesus does his: through comparative reading and thinking" (63).

43. David Gay, "'What He Meant I Mus'd': The Sayings of Mary in *Paradise Regained*," *English Studies in Canada* 18, no. 4 (1992): 383–402, argues that "Mary's sayings, by looking back upon biblical wisdom as well as forward to the revolutionary fulfillment of messianic prophecies, bring together the ideas of order and counter-order, concern and freedom, in a manner that typifies Milton's search for ultimate unity in these dichotomies" (387–88).

44. Haskin, *Milton's Burden of Interpretation*, 136–37. Haskin also points to John Spencer, *Kaina kai Palaia. Things New and Old, or, A store-house of similes, sentences, allegories . . . Collected and observed from the writings and sayings of the learned in all ages to this present. . . .* (London: Printed by W. Wilson and J. Streater for John Spencer, 1658).

45. Haskin, *Milton's Burden of Interpretation*, 138. The case for Milton's identification with Mary is furthered in DiPasquale, *Refiguring the Sacred Feminine*, which, approving of John

Shawcross's argument that *Paradise Regained* was composed throughout the 1640s and then revised after 1665, suggests that Milton's "mind, like Mary's heart, was 'a storehouse long of things / And sayings laid up' and only later brought forth" (297).

Chapter 10

1. For a thorough discussion of the Holy Spirit in *DDC*, see David Ainsworth, "Milton's Holy Spirit in *De Doctrina Christiana*," *Religion and Literature* 45, no. 2 (2013): 1–25.

2. Dayton Haskin, *Milton's Burden of Interpretation* (Philadelphia: University of Pennsylvania Press, 1994), 35.

3. Matthew Poole, *A Commentary on the Holy Bible*, 3 vols. (1685; reprint, London: Banner of Truth, 1963), 1:488–89.

4. Christopher Hill, *Milton and the English Revolution* (New York: Viking, 1977), 106 (see 104–6, 246–48, 447); see also David Loewenstein's more cautious assertions in *Representing Revolution in Milton and His Contemporaries: Religion, Politics, and Polemics in Radical Puritanism* (Cambridge: Cambridge University Press, 2001), 11–12, 244, 274–76, 279–91; Loewenstein also writes of Milton's similarities to radical Puritans. Brendan Prawdzik, in *Theatrical Milton: Politics and Poetics of the Staged Body* (Edinburgh: Edinburgh University Press, 2017), 173–84, cautions against connecting Milton's views too closely with the Quakers, though he agrees with Loewenstein that "Samson embodies attributes of early Quaker enthusiasm" (180).

5. William Yoo, "Presbyterian Church (USA)," in *Encyclopedia of Christianity in the United States*, vol. 5, edited by George Thomas Kurian and Mark A. Lamport (Lanham, Md.: Rowman and Littlefield, 2016), 1832–34, quoted at 1833.

6. See *The Riverside Milton*, edited by Roy Flannagan (Boston: Houghton Mifflin, 1998), 810, gloss on "dispence." Another germane use of "dispense" is found in the words of Thomas More's Vincent, who says, "god may dispence wher he will & whan he will, & may commannund [of his emissaries] . . . to do the contrary, . . . as sampson had by inspiracion of god, commaundment to kill him selfe, . . . pulling down the howse vppon his own hed at the fest of the phelisties." "A Dialogue of Comfort Against Tribulation" (1553), in *The Complete Works of St. Thomas More*, edited by Louis L. Martz and Frank Manley, 15 vols. (New Haven: Yale University Press, 1963–86), 12:140–41, quoted in Joseph Wittreich, *Shifting Contexts: Reinterpreting "Samson Agonistes"* (Pittsburgh: Duquesne University Press, 2002), 209. See also *Oxford English Dictionary Online*, s.v. "dispense," phrasal verbs: "to dispense with," especially entry 2: "To deal administratively with (a law or rule, ecclesiastical or civil) so as to relax or remit its penalty or obligation in a special case; to give special exemption or relief from." Examples listed include the following statement from Francis Bacon's *Elements of the Common Laws of England*, published in 1636: "Necessity dispenseth with the direct letter of a statute law."

7. For an altogether different interpretation of Milton's views on this matter, see Joan S. Bennett, *Reviving Liberty: Radical Christian Humanism in Milton's Great Poems* (Cambridge, Mass.: Harvard University Press, 1989), 129–32. Operating on the assumption that "Milton believed God's eternal laws to bind first of all God himself" (129), Bennett also holds a low opinion of the Chorus's perspective (120), a critical assumption of recent decades begun by John F. Huntley, "A Revaluation of the Chorus' Role in Milton's *Samson Agonistes*," *Modern Philology* 64, no. 2 (1966): 132–45, with which I generally do not concur. In any event, the meaning of "dispense" mitigates against Bennett's interpretation of God's relationship to his

laws. For a comparatively recent defense of the Chorus, see John Steadman, "Efficient Causality and Catastrophe in *Samson Agonistes*," in "Riven Unities: Authority and Experience, Self and Other in Milton's Poetry," edited by Wendy Furman, Christopher Grose, and William Shullenberger, special issue, *Milton Studies* 28 (1992): 211–26.

8. Significantly, Milton's Samson a bit later explicitly refers to Dalila as "A *Canaanite*" (380). Hughes's note to line 380 states, "The Philistines might be called Canaanites because they were the earliest conquerors of the land of Canaan" (561).

9. The notion that God prompted Samson to take the woman of Timna but not Dalila is supported by E. M. W. Tillyard, *Milton* (1930; reprint, London: Chatto and Windus, 1949), 338; and Arnold Stein, *Heroic Knowledge: An Interpretation of "Paradise Regained" and "Samson Agonistes"* (Minneapolis: University of Minnesota Press, 1957), 172. John T. Shawcross, in *The Uncertain World of "Samson Agonistes"* (Cambridge: D. S. Brewer, 2001), 7–8, attributes both marriages to Samson's "carnal desires," although he does not address Judges 14:4, which states that Samson's attraction "was of the LORD, that he sought an occasion against the Philistines." For Harold Skulsky, *Justice in the Dock: Milton's Experimental Tragedy* (Newark: University of Delaware Press, 1995), 56–57, Judges 14:4 "confirms" the view that Samson's first marriage was indeed divinely initiated. Tobias Gregory concurs; see his "Political Messages of *Samson Agonistes*," *SEL: Studies in English Literature, 1500–1900* 50, no. 1 (2010): 175–203, at 179–80. Stanley Fish, in *How Milton Works* (Cambridge, Mass.: Belknap Press of Harvard University Press, 2001), suggests indeterminacy when he asks whom we should believe concerning who *really* inspired Samson's taking of his wives. Fish notes that Samson sees, in hindsight, his first marriage as "of God" and his second as not; the Chorus sees "both [marriages] as manifestations of God's inscrutable will," while Manoa sees both marriages as "violation[s] of tribal law" (401). However, I believe that we can believe Samson's report and recognize that Fish unnecessarily confuses the matter by claiming that the Chorus in lines 300–321 is probably referring to either or both of Samson's marriages, when it seems clear enough that it is referring to his first. (See Flannagan, *Riverside Milton*, 811n90; compare also the similarity between lines 315–17 and Judg. 14:4.) Similarly, Warren Chernaik, *Milton and the Burden of Freedom* (Cambridge: Cambridge University Press, 2017), misreads the Chorus's words in lines 309–14 and 318, suggesting that the Chorus endorsed Samson's marriage to Dalila and that God's "'Heroic' champions have licence to override the strict prohibitions laid down in the Torah" (199). Chernaik fails to distinguish here between God's special promptings in the specific case of the woman of Timna and Samson's unwarranted presumption in the case of Dalila. Certainly, Samson does not have "licence" to "override" scriptural prohibitions.

10. Stein, *Heroic Knowledge*, 172.

11. Phillip J. Donnelly, *Milton's Scriptural Reasoning: Narrative and Protestant Toleration* (Cambridge: Cambridge University Press, 2009), 221. Donnelly goes on to write that the contrast between Samson's two marriages "implies that Samson could have distinguished between a divine command that overrides a given law and a presumption to divine warrant that masks mere license" (222).

12. An intriguing (albeit, I believe, incorrect) interpretation of the "divine impulsion" that Samson feels and that leads him to his respective marriages is given by Albert C. Labriola in "Divine Urgency as a Motive for Conduct in *Samson Agonistes*," *Philological Quarterly* 50, no. 1 (1971): 99–107. Labriola argues, using a portion of *DDC* for support, that in both instances God himself was in fact prompting Samson, but that these promptings were examples of "evil temptation, in which God 'presents occasions of sin' or 'blinds

the understanding' of the sinner" (100) (Labriola quotes *DDC* in *The Works of John Milton*, edited by Frank Patterson, 18 vols. [New York: Columbia University Press, 1931–38], 15:86–87). Labriola's argument places Milton's thought in *Samson Agonistes* more in line with the traditional Calvinist understanding of God's prompting of sinful action in wicked figures to accomplish his purpose. See John Calvin, *Institutes of the Christian Religion*, translated by Ford Lewis Battles, edited by John T. McNeil, 2 vols. (Philadelphia: Westminster Press, 1960), 1:18: "God so Uses the Works of the Ungodly, and so Bends Their Minds to Carry Out His Judgments, that He Remains Pure from Every Sin." But Labriola's argument does not address the Chorus's explicit statement that God's prompting Samson to marry the woman of Timna does in fact leave Samson "without taint / Of sin" (lines 312–13).

13. Hughes, *Complete Poems and Major Prose*, 583, note at line 1320.

14. Anthony Low's observations on this passage, in *The Blaze of Noon: A Reading of "Samson Agonistes"* (New York: Columbia University Press, 1974), are worthy of citation: "Although Samson now knows that he need not obey Mosaic law simply for its own sake, and recognizes how easily God can set it aside for some good cause, he also knows that he cannot dispense with the law himself, on his own judgment, and that no state has the authority to dispense him from it. He will not go to the temple because, unless he is inspired to the contrary, the law represents God's will in the matter, and God's will must come before man's" (200).

15. Hughes, *Complete Poems and Major Prose*, 584, note at line 1377.

16. Leonard Mustazza, "The Verbal Plot of *Samson Agonistes*," *Milton Studies* 23 (1987): 241–58, quoted at 254.

17. John M. Steadman, "'Faithful Champion': The Theological Basis of Milton's Hero of Faith," in *Milton: Modern Essays in Criticism*, edited by Arthur E. Barker (New York: Oxford University Press, 1965), 467–83, quoted at 480.

18. Robert Thomas Fallon, *Captain or Colonel: The Soldier in Milton's Life and Art* (Columbia: University of Missouri Press, 1985), 246.

19. See Matthew 4:1, Mark 1:12, and Luke 4:1. For a discussion positively comparing Samson's and the Son's leadings, see Don Cameron Allen, *The Harmonious Vision: Studies in Milton's Poetry* (Baltimore: Johns Hopkins University Press, 1954), 94. For a view that sees a significant difference between the Son's spiritual leadings and Samson's, see Wittreich, *Shifting Contexts*, 220.

20. As Skulsky observes in *Justice in the Dock*, these "motions" have "convinced" Samson that, in this particular situation, "the overriding purpose of the law [is] better served by going" to Dagon's temple "than by staying away" (66). Here I argue contra Kent Lehnhof, who asserts in "Arrested Spiritual Development in Milton's *Samson Agonistes*," *Renaissance Papers* (1999): 147–67, that, unlike the Son in *Paradise Regained*, Samson "lack[s]" a transformative "re-encounter with the Law" (156). Samson does indeed have such a re-encounter, but its violent results differ from the Son's nonviolence in his first earthly incarnation as Jesus. We should note, however, that in the second coming of Christ that Milton anticipated, Jesus's violence against his opponents transcends anything Samson accomplishes (see 2 Thess. 1:6–9, Rev. 19:19–21, and Milton's discussion in *DDC* of the returning and judging Christ's violence against his enemies [*CPW*, 6:613–19 and 6:621–30]).

21. Fish, *How Milton Works*, 419, 418.

22. Mary Ann Radzinowicz, *Toward "Samson Agonistes": The Growth of Milton's Mind* (Princeton: Princeton University Press, 1978), 345.

23. For a skeptical discussion of Samson's relationship to the law, see Wittreich, *Shifting Contexts*, 227–32. For a comparatively sympathetic discussion, see Shawcross, *Uncertain World*, 140–42.

24. The question of whether Samson's "rousing motions" are indeed a prompting of God's Spirit continues to be vigorously debated, and it is arguably the defining issue regarding whether Milton's Samson is read as ultimately regenerate or unregenerate. Additional studies that explicitly question these motions' divine origin include Irene Samuel, "Samson Agonistes as Tragedy," in *Calm of Mind: Tercentenary Essays on "Paradise Regained" and "Samson Agonistes" in Honor of John S. Diekhoff*, edited by Joseph Anthony Wittreich Jr. (Cleveland: Case Western Reserve University Press, 1971), 235–57, at 255; Derek N. C. Wood, *"Exiled From Light": Divine Law, Morality, and Violence in "Samson Agonistes"* (Toronto: University of Toronto Press, 2001), 129–39; Wittreich, *Shifting Contexts*, 230; and Abraham Stoll, "Milton Stages Cherbury: Revelation and Polytheism in *Samson Agonistes*," in *Altering Eyes: New Perspectives on "Samson Agonistes,"* edited by Mark R. Kelley and Joseph Wittreich (Newark: University of Delaware Press, 2002), 281–306. In recent decades, much of the most effective material defending the divine origin of Samson's final "motions" comes from authors who discuss forthrightly the unsettling degree of violence in Samson and his God. These include David Loewenstein, *Milton and the Drama of History: Historical Vision, Iconoclasm, and the Literary Imagination* (Cambridge: Cambridge University Press, 1990), 126–51; and Loewenstein, "The Revenge of the Saint: Radical Religion and Politics in *Samson Agonistes*," in "The Miltonic Samson," edited by Albert C. Labriola and Michael Lieb, special issue, *Milton Studies* 33 (1996): 159–80 (revised as chapter 9 in Loewenstein's *Representing Revolution*, 269–92); Skulsky, *Justice in the Dock*; Michael Lieb, "'Our Living Dread': The God of *Samson Agonistes*" in Labriola and Lieb, "Miltonic Samson," 3–25 (revised as chapter 6 in *Theological Milton: Deity, Discourse, and Heresy in the Miltonic Canon* [Pittsburgh: Duquesne University Press, 2006], 184–209). I cite *Theological Milton* in my references to Lieb's essay. Significantly, both Loewenstein and Lieb reaffirm their positions in their respective essays in *Milton in the Age of Fish: Essays on Authorship, Text, and Terrorism*, edited by Michael Lieb and Albert C. Labriola (Pittsburgh: Duquesne University Press, 2006)—see Loewenstein, "*Samson Agonistes* in the Age of Terror," 203–28; and Lieb, "Returning the Gorgon Medusa's Gaze: Terror and Annihilation in Milton," 229–42. Also affirming the divine origin of the "rousing motions" are Ashraf H. A. Rushdy, "According to Samson's Command: Some Contexts of Milton's Tragedy," *Milton Quarterly* 26 (1992): 69–80; Shawcross, *Uncertain World*, 132–33; Sharon Achinstein, *Literature and Dissent in Milton's England* (Cambridge: Cambridge University Press, 2003), 141; Donnelly, *Milton's Scriptural Reasoning*, 222; Gregory, "Political Messages of Samson," 175–79; and John Leonard's review of *The Atheist Milton*, by Michael Bryson, *Milton Quarterly* 47, no. 4 (2013): 235–41, at 239–40.

25. John Spencer Hill, *John Milton: Poet, Priest, and Prophet; A Study of Divine Vocation in Milton's Poetry and Prose* (London: Macmillan, 1979), 172.

26. Albert R. Cirillo, "Time, Light, and the Phoenix: The Design of *Samson Agonistes*," in Wittreich, *Calm of Mind*, 209–33, at 219, 225. The very notion that Samson is actually praying has come under scrutiny. In *How Milton Works*, Fish states that "the moment is radically indeterminate. 'As one who pray'd' says neither that he is nor that he is not praying" (447). But to seriously entertain the notion that Samson was not praying here implies that Milton is not simply offering a variation on Samson's prayer in Judges 16:28 but even a denial of the biblical account altogether; see Gregory, "Political Meanings of Samson," 177–79.

27. Lieb, *Theological Milton*, 201, 203.

28. For a perspective that argues that, because of Samson's final vengeful act of violence, the drama's "subject cannot be Samson restored to divine favor," see Samuel, "*Samson Agonistes* as Tragedy," 239. For fuller studies questioning the premise that *Samson Agonistes* shows Samson in a divinely regenerative role, see Wittreich, *Interpreting "Samson Agonistes"* and *Shifting Contexts*; and Wood, "*Exiled from Light*." As mentioned in note 24 above, aforementioned works by Lieb, Loewenstein, and Skulsky all present regenerative readings that directly address the disturbing degree of violence in Samson and his God. So too does John P. Rumrich, "Samson and the Excluded Middle," in Kelley and Wittreich, *Altering Eyes*, 307–32. A regenerative reading that addresses matters of violence more sympathetically is offered in Elizabeth Oldman, "Milton, Grotius, and the Law of War: A Reading of *Paradise Regained* and *Samson Agonistes*," *Studies in Philology* 104 (2007): 340–75.

29. Lieb, *Theological Milton*, 203, 202. Lieb cites Jeremiah 22:5 and 19:13, as well as Genesis 22:16 and Hebrews 6:13, both of which Milton cites in *DDC* at the beginning of his discussion of oath taking (*CPW*, 6:684).

30. Wittreich, *Interpreting "Samson Agonistes*," 111–12, and *Shifting Contexts*, 220–26.

31. Wittreich, *Shifting Contexts*, 224–25. Wittreich mistakenly cites Caiaphas's words in John 11:51 as appearing in John 11:52.

32. See the final endnote to chapter 2 above.

33. When I originally published my discoveries regarding "of my own accord" in John 10:18, Acts 12:10, and 2 Corinthians 8:16–17 (see David V. Urban, review of *The Uncertain World of "Samson Agonistes*," by John T. Shawcross; "*Exiled from Light*," by Derek N. C. Wood; *Shifting Contexts*, by Joseph Wittreich, and *Altering Eyes*, edited by Mark R. Kelley and Joseph Wittreich, *Religion and Literature* 36, no. 2 [2004]: 119–28, at 125–26), I did not realize that my findings had been discovered earlier (for John 10:18) by David Gay, in "John 10:18 and the Typology of *Samson Agonistes*," *English Language Notes* 27, no. 2 (1989): 49–52; and (for the other verses) by Anthony Low, in his review of *Interpreting "Samson Agonistes*," by Joseph Wittreich, *Journal of English and Germanic Philology* 86, no. 3 (1987): 415–18, at 418. I apologize to Professors Gay and Low for this oversight.

34. Skulsky, *Justice in the Dock*, 75, also directly links Samson's acting "of my own accord" with the God-sent "rousing motions" of line 1382.

35. Donnelly, *Milton's Scriptural Reasoning*, 223–24.

36. Achinstein, *Literature and Dissent*, 142, 143, 144.